Better Homes and Gardens.

the *ultimate* casseroles book

More than **400** heartwarming dishes—from dips to desserts

WILEY

John Wiley & Sons, Inc.

Meredith Corporation

Editor: Jan Miller

Contributing Editor: Lois White

Recipe Development and Testing: Better Homes and Gardens® Test Kitchen

John Wiley & Sons, Inc.

Publisher: Natalie Chapman

Associate Publisher: Jessica Goodman

Executive Editor: Anne Ficklen

Senior Editor: Linda Ingroia

Senior Production Editor: Jacqueline Beach

Production Director: Diana Cisek

Interior Design: Jill Budden

Layout: Holly Wittenberg

Manufacturing Manager: Tom Hyland

Our seal assures you that every recipe in *The Ultimate Casseroles Book* has been tested in the Better Homes and Gardens® Test Kitchen. This means that each recipe is practical and reliable and meets our high standards of taste appeal. We guarantee your satisfaction with this book for as long as you own it.

Pictured:
**Creamy Potato
Casserole,
page 399**

4

94

158

33

table of
contents

107

260

Pictured:
Lemony Tuna and Pasta,
page 150

Dig in to home-baked comfort!

Casseroles are a time-honored tradition of American cooking. When served to family and friends, these hot and bubbly gems have a unique power to satisfy and nurture, to spark good conversation, and to create special memories.

Inside you'll find delectable hot dishes, including breakfast and brunch bakes, party foods, easy everyday meals, lightened-up classics, dinner party dazzlers, and irresistible desserts. This unique collection of more than 400 kitchen-tested recipes includes every type of casserole you and your family crave—from timeless favorites, including the green bean casserole that ignited the casserole craze in the 1930s to contemporary dishes that introduce bold, new flavors and time-saving ingredients.

The enduring beauty of these dishes is that they're easy to prepare—many freeze well—and make great leftovers. In every chapter you'll find make-ahead directions and helpful hints to give you an edge in preparing each dish perfectly, wowing family and guests every time.

Make this the ultimate family-pleasing keepsake that you turn to for some of the most endearing hot dishes that warm the heart as well as the soul.

hot dish, hot

Making incredible casseroles becomes even more foolproof with the help of these timely tips. Check out some stunning oven-to-table bakeware; and learn the basics on prepping, freezing, and toting casseroles. Then get inspired to create your own hot dish using our never-fail formula.

tips

what a hot dish!

A casserole is both a baking dish and the bubbling hot food it contains. These vivid beauties let you show off homey fare in stunning oven-to-table bakeware. You'll find the dishes in superstores, kitchen specialty shops, or online.

going Dutch Tuck tantalizing ingredients inside an enameled covered cast-iron pot and relax as the flavors meld. Piping hot casseroles hold their heat well when served in these contemporary Dutch ovens. You'll find these vessels in a variety of colors.

multiple minis Small casseroles are just right for individual servings. Three favorites from the Le Creuset® Heritage Stoneware collection (clockwise from top left): Pate Terrine, 6½-inch Oval Gratin, and Classic Mini Round Cocotte. These are also ideal for hot appetizers and bubbly side dishes.

supersized Just imagine all the deliciousness you can pack into a 5-quart cast-iron casserole. Wide handles on easy-to-clean, enameled dishes like this one make it easy to slide your casserole in and out of the oven.

handled with care
When looking for 2-quart casseroles, you're likely to find a few understated but elegant dishes that are perfect for giving the food the glory of taking center stage at the dinner table. Handles make it easy to slide your casserole in and out of the oven.

ust for you
Bake a dainty dessert in oven-safe mugs. Shown is the Corningware® French White Pop-Ins 20-ounce mug.

fun and vibrant Excite dinner guests with contemporary shaped 2- and 3-quart stoneware casseroles, available in a range of colors. Wide, shallow dishes are must-haves for your kitchen collection, because they spread the heat evenly and gently while the casserole bakes, providing a golden roasted top for each serving.

tips for hot dishes

Cooperative, cook-friendly casseroles bend over backward to make magnificent meals. Follow our pointers for impressive results.

1. For perfect casseroles, use the size of baking dish that your recipe calls for.

2. If you do not have the correct size dish, think big and opt to use a dish with larger volume.

3. If you use a pan that is shallower than the one specified, reduce your baking time by 25 percent.

4. If you use a pan that is deeper than the one specified, increase the baking time by 25 percent.

5. To check casserole capacity, fill it with water one quart at a time.

6. Once you have determined the capacity of your casserole dish, mark it on the bottom with an indelible pen, so you won't have to repeat the process.

7. A cut above.

Stock up on pre-peeled and precut vegetables like carrots, onions, and broccoli florets. These time-shavers, available in the produce section or on the grocery store salad bar, make prep a snap.

8. Quick chick.

Call upon 4- to 6-ounce individually frozen chicken breasts to pare minutes from prep. These breasts will thaw in a bowl of cold water in less time than it takes to cook pasta or rice.

9. Slick prep.

When a recipe calls for greasing a casserole, dip a piece of waxed paper in shortening and wipe the dish with a light coating. Or use a light coating of nonstick cooking spray.

10. Count on veggies.

Don't fear frozen vegetables. Packages of smaller vegetables, like peas—or medleys of frozen diced vegetables—are nearly equal to fresh vegetables in quality and nutritional content. They do not need to be thawed before adding to casseroles.

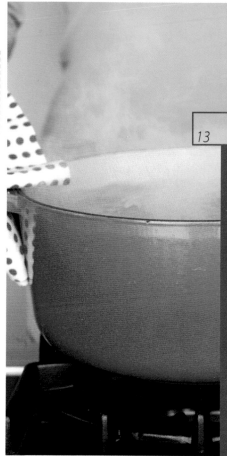

11. Pasta pointers.

Put the pasta pot on to boil as soon as you walk in the door. By the time you change into comfy clothes, the water will be ready for cooking pasta or rice. Use plenty of water, too. In general, count on about 3 quarts of water for 4 to 8 ounces of pasta.

12.

Easy and economical. With casseroles, luxury ingredients like shrimp or lobster go a long way, making them an affordable treat, even for feeding a crowd.

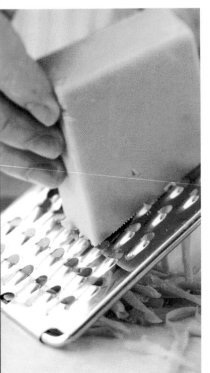

13.

Grate idea.
A sure way to pinch pennies is to grate your own cheese. Large blocks of casserole favorites like cheddar or Monterey Jack cost nearly a dollar less per pound, and pre-grated cheeses freeze beautifully.

14.

Love those leftovers. Why toss a half a bowl of corn, some leftover tomatoes, or a sliver of last night's ham when it can be tossed in to enrich and extend almost any casserole?

15.

Make it yours. Adjust recipes as you please. One of the most beautiful things about casseroles is that they're flexible. Does a cup of cheese sound like too much? Use half. Does the sauce seem too thick? Thin it with water or broth.

16. **How much is enough?** It's best to work with ratios when creating your own casseroles. For example, if you're planning a casserole that will serve 4 people, use 1 pound of meat, 1 to 2 cups of starch (pasta, rice, or polenta), 1 to 2 cups of vegetables, and 2 cups sauce.

17. **Top it off.** To jazz a casserole up with an au gratin topping, sprinkle the top of an almost baked casserole with grated cheese and bread crumbs moistened with a little melted butter. Bake the casserole, uncovered, for 10 minutes more to brown the topping.

18. **Break out the meatballs.** Frozen precooked meatballs will stand in for ground beef in a pinch. Just thaw, break them up with a fork, and then add to a casserole.

19. **Dry vs. fresh.** No need to splurge on fresh herbs for casserole making. Fresh herbs tend to lose their flavor in dishes that bake for longer periods of time, while dried herbs just make them better.

20. **Keep it golden.** If your casserole bakes golden on top before it's done in the center, cover the dish loosely with foil for the remaining baking time.

21. **Beef it up.** Purchase ground beef in bulk. Brown it, drain it, and then package it in one-pound parcels in freezer bags or containers. You'll appreciate having the beef ready to go, plus save about 20 percent on its purchase price.

22. Safe toting.

Keep your casserole piping hot as it travels. Choose a pan or dish with a tight-fitting lid. Or cover the casserole tightly with foil. Then wrap the tightly covered dish of hot food in layers of newspaper and kitchen towels and transport it in an insulated carrier. Fill gaps around the food container with crumpled newspaper or towels to prevent shifting or spills.

23. Testing doneness.

Take the temperature of the casserole to test doneness. For best flavor and food safety, a casserole needs to be heated to 160°F. When the casserole is bubbly around the edges, insert an instant-read thermometer at an angle in its center, being careful not to touch the sides or bottom of dish.

24. Let it stand.

Allowing a casserole to stand for several minutes after it comes out of the oven improves the texture and flavor. While standing, the food will firm up, allowing it to hold a cut edge. This is especially true with hot and cheesy dishes and layered casseroles.

potluck wish list

One of the easiest ways to explore a variety of casseroles is to host a seasonal potluck with family and friends. The key to a successful gathering starts when you begin planning a few weeks ahead.

- ☑ Compile a simple sign-up sheet for the types of dishes you need people to bring to make sure each menu item is covered. Encourage guests to make their own favorite hot dishes.

- ☑ Ask guests to attached identification tags to the pans or dishes they bring so you can return the items after the party.

- ☑ Set up a buffet so people can easily access the food from both sides. Place the plates at the front of the buffet line and flatware and napkins at the end. This way, guests won't be fumbling with too many things to hold while they are serving themselves. Be creative in laying out flatware. Ceramic planters, bread baskets, even cookie tins are delightful holders for knives, forks, and spoons.

good idea!

Use crisscrossed rubber bands to securely attach lids to pans and casseroles for transporting.

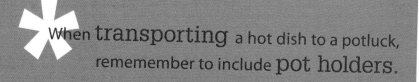

When **transporting** a hot dish to a potluck, rememember to include **pot holders**.

freeze with ease

Tossing together a casserole is usually easy enough that you might just want to double the batch and tuck one of the finished dishes into the freezer to enjoy later. Or simply freeze any leftovers. Here's what you need to know about freezing foods.

don't freeze

Some foods lose texture and quality when frozen. For best results, avoid freezing casseroles containing these ingredients:

Cottage cheese and ricotta cheese

Cool it. For quick cooling before freezing—a step that will keep bacteria from growing— divide finished foods into small portions in shallow freezer-safe containers. Arrange containers in a single layer in the freezer to allow cold air to circulate around the containers until frozen. Once completely frozen, it's OK to stack the containers.

Cooked egg whites and yolks

Thickeners such as cornstarch and flour

Stuffed chops or stuffed chicken breasts

Potatoes, which can darken and become mushy

contain it

*Baking Dishes: Use freezer-to-oven or freezer-to-microwave dishes and cover them tightly with plastic or freezer wrap or heavy-duty foil. Do not use foil to directly cover foods that contain acidic ingredients, such as tomatoes. Instead, first cover the food in plastic wrap, and then cover with foil. Remove plastic wrap before reheating.

*Freezer-Safe Containers: Look for an icon or phrase on the bottom of a container, which will indicate if it is designed for freezer use.

*Resealable Plastic Storage Bags and Plastic Wrap: Buy products specifically made for freezer use.

*Heavy-Duty Foil: Regular foil is not recommended for wrapping food for the freezer.

*Labels: Before storing, use a crayon or waterproof marking pen to label the food; include the date it was frozen.

Thaw and reheat. Thaw foods in the refrigerator, not at room temperature. Reheat food to 165°F. Soups and stews can be reheated to a safe temperature by bringing to a rolling boil in a covered saucepan.

super serve-alongs

Your casserole is the star of the table. Layered or mixed ingredients melded in the oven produce a virtual symphony of flavors, so simple is best for side dishes. Round out the meal with these quick and easy serve-alongs.

ranch deviled egg bites

Coat a small skillet with nonstick cooking spray; heat skillet over medium heat. Add 4 fresh jalapeño chile peppers to skillet; cook about 5 minutes or until lightly charred, turning occasionally. Let peppers stand until cool enough to handle. Using plastic or rubber gloves, halve peppers lengthwise. Remove seeds and membranes.

Cut 4 roma tomatoes in half; scoop out and discard pulp. Set tomatoes and peppers aside.

Peel and halve 8 hard-cooked eggs. Remove yolks and place in a medium bowl. Add 4 of the egg white halves to bowl; mash with a fork. Stir in ½ cup plain Greek yogurt, 2 tablespoons snipped fresh cilantro, ¼ cup thinly sliced scallions, one 1-ounce package ranch dry salad dressing mix, and 3 tablespoons olive oil. Spoon yolk mixture into jalapeño, tomato, and egg white halves. Cover and chill for up to 8 hours. If desired, garnish with cilantro leaves. Makes 14 (2-appetizer) servings.

bacon and tomato potato salad

Purchase 1 quart old-fashioned potato salad. Transfer to a serving bowl. In a small bowl toss together 4 slices crisp-cooked bacon, crumbled; ²/₃ cup halved grape tomatoes; and 2 tablespoons snipped fresh basil. Spoon mixture on top of potato salad. Makes 8 to 10 servings.

garlic-herb bread

Preheat oven to 375°F. In a small bowl stir together ½ cup butter, softened; 2 tablespoons snipped fresh Italian parsley; 3 cloves garlic, minced; ½ teaspoon salt; and pinch ground black pepper. Without cutting all the way through the bottom crust, slice one 14- to 18-ounce loaf baguette-style French or Italian bread into 1½-inch slices. Generously spread butter mixture between slices. Wrap baguette in heavy foil. Bake about 15 minutes or until heated through. Serve warm. Makes 10 to 12 slices.

With this ingenious master recipe, you can design endless combinations of tempting one-dish dinners. The never-fail formula allows you to easily swap ingredients while achieving a savory success every time.

make-it-mine casserole

prep: 30 minutes **bake:** 55 minutes
oven: 350°F **makes:** 6 servings **dish:** 2-quart

8	ounces packaged dried Pasta
1	pound Meat or two 6-ounce cans Tuna; or one 15-ounce can Beans, rinsed and drained
1	10.75-ounce can Condensed Soup
1½	cups Frozen Vegetable
1	cup Shredded Cheese (4 ounces)
¾	cup milk
¼	cup Goodie
1	teaspoon Seasoning
½	cup Topper (optional)

1 Preheat oven to 350°F. Grease a 2-quart casserole; set aside. Cook Pasta according to package directions; drain and return to pan.

2 In a large skillet cook Ground Meat until meat is brown. Drain fat; discard. (If using ham, tuna, or beans, skip this step.)

3 Add Meat, Condensed Soup, Frozen Vegetable, half of the Shredded Cheese, the milk, Goodie, and Seasoning to cooked Pasta; stir well to combine. Transfer Pasta mixture to the prepared casserole. Sprinkle with remaining Shredded Cheese.

4 Bake, covered, for 45 minutes. Uncover; if desired, sprinkle with Topper. Return to oven and bake for 10 to 15 minutes more or until heated through and Topper (if using) is lightly browned. Makes 6 servings.

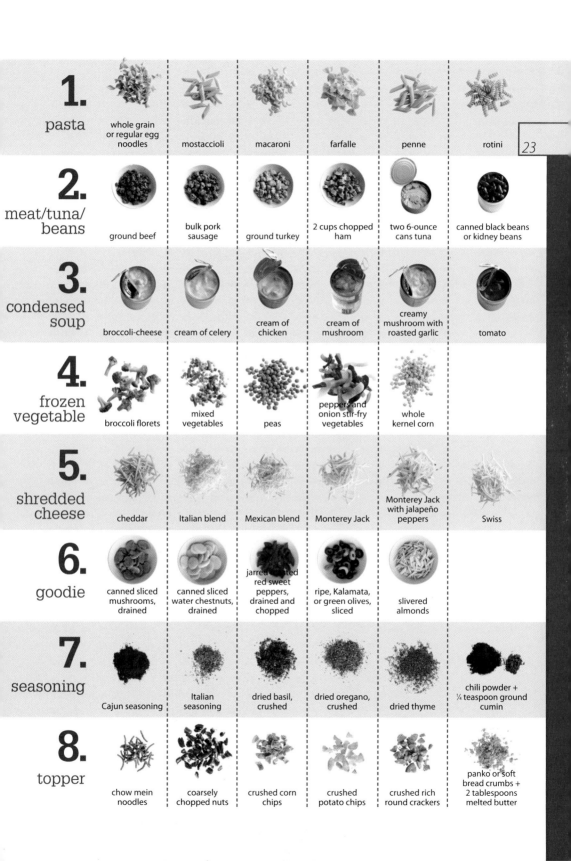

1. pasta
whole grain or regular egg noodles | mostaccioli | macaroni | farfalle | penne | rotini

2. meat/tuna/beans
ground beef | bulk pork sausage | ground turkey | 2 cups chopped ham | two 6-ounce cans tuna | canned black beans or kidney beans

3. condensed soup
broccoli-cheese | cream of celery | cream of chicken | cream of mushroom | creamy mushroom with roasted garlic | tomato

4. frozen vegetable
broccoli florets | mixed vegetables | peas | peppers and onion stir-fry vegetables | whole kernel corn

5. shredded cheese
cheddar | Italian blend | Mexican blend | Monterey Jack | Monterey Jack with jalapeño peppers | Swiss

6. goodie
canned sliced mushrooms, drained | canned sliced water chestnuts, drained | jarred roasted red sweet peppers, drained and chopped | ripe, Kalamata, or green olives, sliced | slivered almonds

7. seasoning
Cajun seasoning | Italian seasoning | dried basil, crushed | dried oregano, crushed | dried thyme | chili powder + ¼ teaspoon ground cumin

8. topper
chow mein noodles | coarsely chopped nuts | crushed corn chips | crushed potato chips | crushed rich round crackers | panko or soft bread crumbs + 2 tablespoons melted butter

casserole hall

2

Some of the tastiest time-honored classics popularized in the mid 1900s hold just as much distinction of bringing comfort to dinner tables, potluck suppers, and party buffets as the fresh, new flavor combos. From savory to sweet, you'll love these "greatest hits," including several you grew up with.

of
fame

A generous mound of mouthwatering meatballs crowns a spaghetti crust in a dish that's sure to make your family hungry for Italian. Bucatini, the signature pasta used here, looks like spaghetti, but is slightly thicker.

meatball pie

prep: 30 minutes bake: 1 hour stand: 15 minutes
oven: 350°F makes: 8 to 10 servings dish: 2-quart

3	eggs, lightly beaten
2/3	cup grated Parmesan cheese
8	ounces dried bucatini pasta or spaghetti
3	cups thinly sliced sweet onions (2 large)
2	tablespoons butter or margarine
1	cup ricotta cheese
2	tablespoons snipped fresh basil or 2 teaspoons dried basil, crushed
1/4	teaspoon ground black pepper
1	24- to 26-ounce jar purchased tomato and basil pasta sauce or marinara sauce
1 1/2	cups shredded mozzarella cheese (6 ounces)
1	pound frozen cooked Italian meatballs, thawed
	Small fresh basil leaves

1 Grease a 2-quart square baking dish. For pasta crust, in a small bowl stir together 2 of the eggs and the Parmesan.

2 In a large saucepan cook pasta according to package directions. Drain pasta; return to saucepan. Add egg mixture, tossing to coat. Press pasta mixture into bottom of prepared dish, building up sides slightly. Set aside.

3 Meanwhile, in a large skillet cook onions, covered, in hot butter over medium-low heat about 15 minutes or until onions are tender and lightly browned, stirring occasionally. Uncover; increase heat to medium. Cook about 5 minutes more or until onions are golden brown, stirring occasionally. Remove from heat.

4 Preheat oven to 350°F. In a small bowl stir together the remaining egg, the ricotta cheese, 2 tablespoons basil, and the pepper. Spread ricotta cheese mixture over pasta crust. Top with caramelized onions. Bake, uncovered, for 15 minutes. Spoon 3/4 cup of pasta sauce over layers in dish. Sprinkle with 1/2 cup of the mozzarella cheese.

5 Toss meatballs with 3/4 cup of the pasta sauce and 1/2 cup of the mozzarella cheese. Arrange meatball mixture over layers in pan, forming a mound. Top with 1/2 cup of the remaining pasta sauce (reserve the remaining pasta sauce and mozzarella cheese).

6 Tent casserole lightly with foil and bake for 45 to 50 minutes more or until heated through. Sprinkle with remaining mozzarella cheese. Let stand, uncovered, on a wire rack for 15 minutes. If desired, garnish with small basil leaves before serving. Heat and pass remaining pasta sauce.

nutrition facts per serving: 542 cal., 29 g total fat (15 g sat. fat), 157 mg chol., 1029 mg sodium, 41 g carb., 5 g dietary fiber, 29 g protein.

Offer this spicy bean medley topped with golden cornmeal dumplings for your next meatless meal. Most canned beans are packed in a thick, salty liquid, so it's a good idea to rinse them. Simply pour the beans into a colander and rinse well with cold running water.

three-bean tamale pie

prep: 30 minutes bake: 20 minutes oven: 400°F
makes: 8 servings dish: 3-quart

1 cup chopped green
   sweet pepper
   (1 medium)
1 cup chopped onion
   (1 medium)
3 cloves garlic, minced
1 tablespoon vegetable
   oil
1 15- to 16-ounce can
   kidney beans,
   rinsed, drained, and
   slightly mashed
1 15- to 16-ounce
   can pinto beans,
   rinsed, drained, and
   slightly mashed
1 15-ounce can black
   beans, rinsed,
   drained, and slightly
   mashed
1 11.5-ounce can
   (1⅓ cups)
   vegetable juice
1 4-ounce can diced
   green chile peppers,
   undrained
1¼ teaspoons chili
   powder
¾ teaspoon ground
   cumin
1 8.5-ounce package
   corn muffin mix
½ cup shredded cheddar
   cheese (2 ounces)
¼ cup snipped fresh
   cilantro or parsley
   Purchased salsa
   (optional)
   Sour cream (optional)

1 Grease a 3-quart rectangular baking dish; set aside. Preheat oven to 400°F.

2 In a large skillet cook sweet pepper, onion, and garlic in hot oil until tender. Stir in kidney beans, pinto beans, black beans, vegetable juice, chile peppers, chili powder, and cumin; heat through. Spoon bean mixture into prepared dish.

3 Prepare corn muffin mix according to package directions; add cheese and cilantro, stirring just until combined. Evenly spoon corn muffin mixture on bean mixture. Bake, uncovered, for 20 to 25 minutes or until golden. If desired, serve with salsa and/or sour cream.

nutrition facts per serving: 313 cal., 8 g total fat (3 g sat. fat), 8 mg chol., 994 mg sodium, 52 g carb., 12 g dietary fiber, 14 g protein.

Featured on the cover of one of our most recent casserole editions, this staff favorite is a family pleaser that's easy to tote to any gathering.

saucy bow tie pasta
casserole

prep: 35 minutes   bake: 35 minutes   stand: 5 minutes   oven: 350°F/400°F
makes: 8 servings   dish: 3-quart

3   cups dried bow tie, penne, or ziti pasta (8 ounces)
2   medium red onions, cut into thin wedges, or 5 medium leeks, sliced (about 2 cups)
2   cloves garlic, minced
1   tablespoon butter or margarine
1   24- to 26-ounce jar tomato pasta sauce
1   8-ounce can tomato sauce
1   10-ounce package frozen chopped spinach, thawed and well drained
1½ cups cubed lean cooked ham
2   medium tomatoes, seeded and chopped
⅓   cup grated Parmesan cheese (3 ounces)
2   cups shredded mozzarella or Muenster cheese (8 ounces)
    Grated Parmesan cheese (optional)
    Italian parsley sprigs (optional)

1 Preheat oven to 350°F. In a large pot cook pasta according to the package directions. Drain; rinse pasta with cold water. Drain again.

2 In the same pan cook onion and garlic, covered, in hot butter for 8 to 10 minutes or until onion is tender, stirring occasionally. Stir in the cooked pasta, pasta sauce, tomato sauce, spinach, ham, tomatoes, and ⅓ cup Parmesan cheese. Spoon mixture into an ungreased 3-quart rectangular baking dish.

3 Bake, covered, about 30 minutes or until heated through. Increase oven temperature to 400°F. Top with mozzarella cheese and, if desired, additional Parmesan cheese. Bake, uncovered, about 5 minutes more or until cheese is melted. Let stand for 5 minutes. If desired, garnish with parsley.

nutrition facts per serving: 291 cal., 11 g total fat (6 g sat. fat), 34 mg chol., 1046 mg sodium, 32 g carb., 5 g dietary fiber, 19 g protein.

In 1991, a reader of Better Homes and Gardens® *magazine submitted this homespun ground beef and noodle "hotdish" recipe, proclaiming that it was her favorite to take to church suppers. It was sensational then and still is today.*

eight-layer casserole

prep: 30 minutes bake: 55 minutes stand: 10 minutes oven: 350°F
makes: 8 servings dish: 2-quart

3 cups dried medium noodles (6 ounces)
1 pound ground beef
2 8-ounce cans tomato sauce
1 teaspoon dried basil, crushed
½ teaspoon sugar
½ teaspoon garlic powder
¼ teaspoon salt
¼ teaspoon ground black pepper
1 8-ounce carton sour cream
1 8-ounce package cream cheese, softened
½ cup milk
⅓ cup chopped onion (1 small)
1 10-ounce package frozen chopped spinach, cooked and well drained
1 cup shredded cheddar cheese (4 ounces)
   Chopped tomato (optional)
   Sliced scallion (optional)

1 Preheat oven to 350°F. Lightly grease a 2-quart casserole or square baking dish; set aside. Cook noodles according to package directions; drain and set aside.

2 Meanwhile, in a large skillet cook beef over medium heat until brown. Drain off fat. Stir in tomato sauce, basil, sugar, garlic powder, salt, and pepper into meat. Bring to boiling; reduce heat. Simmer, uncovered, for 5 minutes.

3 In a medium mixing bowl beat together sour cream and cream cheese with an electric mixer on medium speed until smooth. Stir in milk and onion.

4 In prepared casserole layer half of the noodles (about 2 cups), half of the meat mixture (about 1½ cups), half of the cream cheese mixture (about 1 cup), and all of the spinach. Top with the remaining meat mixture and noodles. Cover and chill the remaining cream cheese mixture until needed.

5 Bake, covered with lightly greased foil, about 45 minutes or until heated through. Spread with the remaining cream cheese mixture. Sprinkle with cheddar cheese. Bake, uncovered, about 10 minutes more or until cheese melts. Let stand for 10 minutes before serving. If desired, sprinkle tomato and scallion on top.

nutrition facts per serving: 448 cal., 30 g total fat (16 g sat. fat), 118 mg chol., 645 mg sodium, 24 g carb., 3 g dietary fiber, 22 g protein.

make-ahead directions: Prepare as above through Step 4. Cover with lightly greased foil; and chill for up to 24 hours. Bake in a 350°F oven for 60 to 70 minutes or until heated through. Spread with the remaining cream-cheese mixture. Sprinkle with the cheddar cheese. Bake, uncovered, about 10 minutes more or until cheese melts. Let stand for 10 minutes before serving.

Asparagus and tarragon flavor this contemporary version of scalloped potatoes. If you want a richer dish, substitute half-and-half for the milk.

potato and ham bake

prep: 25 minutes bake: 30 minutes stand: 5 minutes
oven: 400°F makes: 4 servings dish: 1½-quart

1	pound Yukon gold potatoes, sliced
1	8-ounce tub light cream cheese spread with chive and onion
¾	cup milk
¼	cup finely shredded Parmesan cheese
¼	teaspoon ground black pepper
1	tablespoon snipped fresh tarragon or ½ teaspoon dried tarragon, crushed
8	ounces cooked boneless ham, cut into bite-size slices
1	pound asparagus spears, trimmed and cut in 2- to 3-inch pieces*

1 Preheat oven to 400°F. In a medium saucepan cook potatoes, covered, in a small amount of lightly salted boiling water for 5 to 7 minutes or just until tender. Drain; transfer to bowl and set aside.

2 For sauce, in same saucepan combine cream cheese, milk, 2 tablespoons of the Parmesan cheese, and pepper. Heat and whisk until smooth and cheese melts. Remove from heat; stir in tarragon.

3 Layer half of the potatoes, ham, asparagus, and sauce in an ungreased 1½-quart baking dish. Repeat layers. Bake, covered, for 20 minutes. Sprinkle with the remaining Parmesan cheese. Bake, uncovered, for 10 to 12 minutes more or until heated through. Let stand for 5 minutes.

nutrition facts per serving: 346 cal., 16 g total fat (9 g sat. fat), 67 mg chol., 1162 mg sodium, 30 g carb., 5 g dietary fiber, 22 g protein.

*test kitchen tip: To trim asparagus spears, grasp a spear with one hand on the tapered end and one on the stem end. Bend until the stem breaks easily. The spear will naturally break to separate the tender spear from the tough stem.

Named after an Italian opera star, Luisa Tetrazzini, this dish features a creamy chicken, mushroom, and Parmesan sauce tossed with pasta, then baked. Halve or quarter larger mushrooms for 1- to 1½-inch pieces.

potluck chicken
tetrazzini

prep: 30 minutes bake: 15 minutes stand: 5 minutes
oven: 350°F makes: 10 servings dish: 3-quart

1 2- to 2½-pound purchased roasted chicken

8 ounces dried spaghetti or linguine, broken in half

12 ounces asparagus spears, trimmed and cut into 1-inch pieces

8 ounces small whole white mushrooms

3 medium red and/or yellow sweet peppers, seeded and cut into 1-inch pieces

2 tablespoons butter or margarine

¼ cup all-purpose flour

⅛ teaspoon ground black pepper

1 14-ounce can chicken broth

¾ cup milk

½ cup shredded Swiss cheese (2 ounces)

2 to 3 teaspoons finely shredded lemon zest

2 slices sourdough bread, cubed (about 1½ cups)

1 tablespoon olive oil

2 tablespoons snipped fresh parsley

1 Remove chicken from bones, discaarding skin and bones. Cut chicken into chunks to equal 3 cups. (Save the remaining chicken for another use.)

2 Cook pasta according to package directions. Add asparagus during the last minute of cooking; drain. Return pasta and asparagus to pan.

3 Meanwhile, preheat oven to 350°F. In a large skillet cook mushrooms and sweet peppers in hot butter over medium heat for 8 to 10 minutes or until mushrooms are tender, stirring occasionally. Stir in flour and black pepper until well combined. Add broth and milk all at once. Cook and stir until thickened and bubbly.

4 Add mushroom mixture, chicken, cheese, and half of the lemon zest to pasta and asparagus. Toss gently to coat. Spoon pasta mixture into an ungreased 3-quart rectangular baking dish.

5 In a medium bowl toss together bread cubes, olive oil, and the remaining lemon zest. Spread bread cube mixture over pasta mixture. Bake, uncovered, about 15 minutes or until heated through. Let stand for 5 minutes. Sprinkle with parsley before serving.

nutrition facts per serving: 282 cal., 10 g total fat (4 g sat. fat), 48 mg chol., 258 mg sodium, 28 g carb., 2 g dietary fiber, 20 g protein.

Here is one of the prettiest potpies you'll ever make, with decorative cutouts to show off the beautiful chicken and vegetable filling underneath. Using purchased piecrust makes it easy. Pictured on page 24.

quick chicken potpies

prep: 25 minutes bake: 20 minutes stand: 10 minutes
oven: 400°F makes: 6 servings dish: 10-ounce dishes

1   rolled refrigerated
    unbaked piecrust
    (½ of a 15-ounce
    package)
1   pound chicken breast
    strips for stir-frying
2   tablespoons butter or
    margarine
⅓   cup all-purpose flour
½   teaspoon snipped
    fresh thyme or
    oregano
¼   teaspoon ground
    black pepper
2½ cups reduced-sodium
    chicken broth
1½ cups packed
    julienned or
    coarsely shredded
    carrots
1½ cups frozen peas
    Milk (optional)
    Coarse salt (optional)

1 Preheat oven to 400°F. Let piecrust stand according to package directions. Meanwhile, cut up any large chicken pieces. In a large skillet melt butter over medium heat. Add chicken. Cook for 5 to 6 minutes or until chicken is light brown and no longer pink, stirring frequently. Stir in flour, thyme, and pepper. Add broth all at once. Stir in carrots. Cook and stir over medium heat until thickened and bubbly. Stir in peas; heat through. Cover and keep warm while preparing piecrust cutouts.

2 For topper, unroll piecrust on a lightly floured surface. Cut rounds from pastry to fit on top of six ungreased 10-ounce custard cups or individual casseroles (4 to 4½ inches), rerolling scraps, if necessary. Using 1- to 2-inch cutters, cut shapes from centers of each pastry round. Spoon chicken mixture into custard cups. Arrange piecrust rounds on top of casseroles. Brush shapes with milk (if using) and sprinkle with coarse salt (if using).

3 Place casseroles in a 15x10x1-inch baking pan. Bake, uncovered, about 20 minutes or until topper is golden brown and mixture is bubbly. Let stand for 10 minutes before serving.

nutrition facts per serving: 345 cal., 14 g total fat (6 g sat. fat), 57 mg chol., 516 mg sodium, 30 g carb., 3 g dietary fiber, 22 g protein.

This amazing egg dish is destined to become one of your favorite brunch dishes. While a few of the eggs are used in the egg-soaked bread mixture, the remaining eggs are added halfway through the baking time.

ham-asparagus egg
casserole

prep: 30 minutes chill: 2 hours bake: 50 minutes stand: 15 minutes
oven: 325°F makes: 6 to 8 servings dish: 3-quart

8 ounces asparagus spears, trimmed and cut into 2-inch pieces
5 cups French bread cubes
2 cups shredded Gruyère or white cheddar cheese (8 ounces)
½ cup chopped onion (1 medium)
¼ cup chopped chives or scallions
1½ cups finely chopped cooked ham (8 ounces)
10 eggs
1½ cups milk
Olive oil (optional)
Salt and cracked black pepper (optional)

1 Grease a 3-quart rectangular baking dish; set aside. In a medium saucepan cook asparagus in boiling salted water about 5 minutes or until bright green; drain.

2 Spread half of the bread cubes in prepared baking dish. Top evenly with cheese, onion, and chives. Add half of the cooked asparagus and half of the ham. Top with the remaining bread cubes.

3 In a medium bowl whisk together 4 of the eggs and the milk. Pour egg mixture evenly over layers in dish. Using the back of a spoon, gently press down on layers. Top with the remaining asparagus and the remaining ham. Cover and chill for 2 to 24 hours.

4 Preheat oven to 325°F. Bake, uncovered, for 30 minutes. Using the back of a wooden spoon, press 6 indentations in top of strata. Pour a whole egg into each indentation. Bake for 20 to 25 minutes more or until eggs are set and an instant-read thermometer inserted in the center of strata registers 170°F.

5 Let stand for 15 minutes before serving. If desired, drizzle lightly with oil and sprinkle with salt and pepper.

nutrition facts per serving: 454 cal., 26 g total fat (12 g sat. fat), 421 mg chol., 936 mg sodium, 22 g carb., 2 g dietary fiber, 34 g protein.

This flavorful baked bean medley, enhanced with bacon and a sweet molasses sauce, makes an excellent serve-along dish for barbecues or other casual fare.

five-bean bake

prep: 20 minutes bake: 1 hour oven: 375°F
makes: 12 to 16 servings dish: 3-quart

1 cup chopped onion (1 large)
6 slices bacon, cut up
1 clove garlic, minced
1 15.5- to 16-ounce can red kidney beans, rinsed and drained
1 15.25- to 16-ounce can lima beans, rinsed and drained
1 15- to 16-ounce can pork and beans in tomato sauce
1 15- to 16-ounce can garbanzo beans (chickpeas), rinsed and drained
1 15-ounce can butter beans, rinsed and drained
³/₄ cup ketchup
¹/₂ cup molasses
¹/₄ cup packed brown sugar
1 tablespoon yellow mustard
1 tablespoon Worcestershire sauce

1 Preheat oven to 375°F. In a large skillet cook onion, bacon, and garlic until bacon is crisp and onion is tender; drain.

2 In a large bowl combine onion mixture, beans, ketchup, molasses, brown sugar, mustard, and Worcestershire sauce. Transfer bean mixture to an ungreased 3-quart casserole.

3 Bake, covered, for 1 hour.

nutrition facts per serving: 245 cal., 3 g total fat (1 g sat. fat), 5 mg chol., 882 mg sodium, 47 g carb., 9 g dietary fiber, 10 g protein.

Medium-starch potatoes such as Yukon gold and Finnish Yellow contain more moisture than high-starch potatoes such as russets. They're a good choice for gratins and casseroles because they retain their shape after cooking.

cheesy garlic-potato gratin

prep: 25 minutes bake: 1 hour 30 minutes stand: 10 minutes oven: 350°F
makes: 6 servings dish: 2-quart

4   medium Yukon gold
    or other yellow-
    fleshed potatoes
    (1½ pounds), thinly
    sliced (about 5 cups)
⅓   cup sliced scallions (3)
    or thinly sliced leek
4   cloves garlic, minced
1   teaspoon salt
¼   teaspoon ground
    black pepper
1½ cups shredded Swiss,
    Gruyère, provolone,
    or Jarslberg cheese
    (6 ounces)
1   cup whipping cream

1 Preheat oven to 350°F. Grease a 2-quart square baking dish. Layer half of the sliced potatoes and half of the scallions in prepared dish. Sprinkle with half of the garlic, salt, and pepper. Sprinkle with half of the cheese. Repeat layers. Pour whipping cream over top.

2 Bake, covered, 1 hour and 10 minutes. Bake, uncovered, for 20 to 30 minutes more or until potatoes are tender when pierced with a fork and top is golden brown. Let stand for 10 minutes before serving.

nutrition facts per serving: 354 cal., 24 g total fat (15 g sat. fat), 85 mg chol., 474 mg sodium, 23 g carb., 3 g dietary fiber, 12 g protein.

cheesy garlic–sweet potato gratin: Prepare as above, except substitute sweet potatoes for half of the Yukon gold potatoes.

This layered beauty stacks up with fresh vegetables, baby greens, aromatic herbs, three kinds of Italian cheeses, and a rich, hearty tomato-basil sauce. It's ideal for a special-occasion dinner.

mile-high lasagna pie

prep: 50 minutes bake: 1 hour stand: 15 minutes oven: 375°F
makes: 10 servings dish: 9-inch Springform pan

14 dried whole wheat or whole grain lasagna noodles
2 tablespoons olive oil
1½ cups finely chopped carrots (3 medium)
2 cups finely chopped zucchini (1 medium)
4 cloves garlic, minced
3 cups sliced fresh button mushrooms (8 ounces)
2 6-ounce packages fresh baby spinach
2 tablespoons snipped fresh basil
1 egg, beaten
1 15-ounce container ricotta cheese
⅓ cup finely shredded Parmesan cheese
½ teaspoon salt
¼ teaspoon ground black pepper
1 26-ounce jar tomato-and-basil pasta sauce (2½ cups)
2 cups shredded Italian fontina or mozzarella cheese (8 ounces)
Rosemary sprigs (optional)

1 Preheat oven to 375°F. In a large saucepan cook noodles according to package directions. Drain noodles; rinse with cold water. Drain well; set aside.

2 Meanwhile, in a large skillet heat 1 tablespoon of the olive oil over medium-high heat. Add carrots, zucchini, and half of the garlic. Cook and stir about 5 minutes or until crisp-tender. Transfer vegetables to a bowl. Add the remaining oil to the same skillet and heat over medium-high heat. Add mushrooms and remaining garlic. Cook and stir about 5 minutes or until tender. Gradually add spinach. Cook and stir until spinach is wilted, 1 to 2 minutes. Remove from skillet with a slotted spoon; stir in basil.

3 In a small bowl, stir together egg, ricotta cheese, Parmesan cheese, salt, and pepper.

4 To assemble pie, in the bottom of a 9×3-inch springform pan spread ½ cup of the pasta sauce. Arrange 3 to 4 of the cooked noodles over the sauce, trimming and overlapping as necessary to cover sauce with one layer. Top with half of the spinach-mushroom mixture. Spoon half of the ricotta cheese mixture over spinach mixture. Top with another layer of noodles. Spread with half of the remaining pasta sauce. Top with all of the zucchini-carrot mixture. Sprinkle with half the fontina cheese. Top with another layer of noodles. Layer with the remaining spinach-mushroom mixture and the remaining ricotta cheese mixture. Top with another layer of noodles and remaining sauce (may have extra noodles). Gently press down pie with the back of a spatula.

5 Place springform pan on a foil-lined baking sheet. Bake about 1 hour or until heated through, topping with the remaining fontina cheese for the last 15 minutes of baking. Cover and let stand on a wire rack for 15 minutes before serving. Carefully remove sides of pan and cut lasagna into wedges. If desired, garnish with rosemary.

nutrition facts per serving: 463 cal., 23 g total fat (12 g sat. fat), 82 mg chol., 965 mg sodium, 38 g carb., 8 g dietary fiber, 28 g protein.

40

If you love smoked salmon, you will adore this exceptional pasta dish in which the salmon is flaky in texture and fragrant with smoke.

smoky salmon casserole

prep: 30 minutes bake: 25 minutes stand: 10 minutes
oven: 350°F makes: 6 servings dish: 2-quart

8	ounces dried bow tie or penne pasta (3½ cups)
1	cup chopped red sweet pepper
½	cup chopped scallions (4)
2	tablespoons butter
2	tablespoons all-purpose flour
¼	teaspoon ground black pepper
2½	cups fat-free milk
1½	cups smoked shredded Gouda cheese (6 ounces)
½	teaspoon finely shredded lemon zest
1	tablespoon lemon juice
1	14-ounce can quartered artichoke hearts, drained
1	4-ounce piece smoked salmon, flaked and skin and bones removed
1	cup soft bread crumbs or panko (Japanese-style bread crumbs)
¼	cup pine nuts Freshly ground black pepper

1 Preheat oven to 350°F. Cook pasta according to package directions. Drain and set aside.

2 In a large skillet cook sweet pepper and scallions in hot butter over medium heat about 3 minutes or until tender. Stir in flour and ¼ teaspoon pepper. Gradually stir in milk. Cook and stir until slightly thickened and bubbly. Gradually add cheese, stirring until melted. Stir in lemon zest and lemon juice (mixture may appear curdled).

3 In a large bowl combine cooked pasta, cheese mixture, artichoke hearts, and smoked salmon. Transfer mixture to an ungreased 2-quart baking dish.

4 Sprinkle casserole with bread crumbs, pine nuts, and freshly ground black pepper. Bake, uncovered, for 25 to 30 minutes or until mixture is heated through and crumbs are golden. Let stand for 10 minutes before serving.

nutrition facts per serving: 470 cal., 19 g total fat (10 g sat. fat), 74 mg chol., 780 mg sodium, 45 g carb., 4 g dietary fiber, 30 g protein.

make-ahead directions: Prepare as directed through Step 3. Cover and chill for 2 to 24 hours. To serve, sprinkle casserole with bread crumbs, pine nuts, and freshly ground pepper. Bake, uncovered, in a 350°F oven for 45 to 50 minutes or until mixture is heated through and crumbs are golden. Let stand for 10 minutes before serving.

Jumbo shells, filled with an irresistibly rich cheese and shell sauce, are a match made in heaven. Baking them in a flavorful vodka sauce and topping with brick cheese adds even more flavor and richness.

cheesy shell-stuffed
shells

prep: 40 minutes bake: 45 minutes stand: 10 minutes
oven: 350°F makes: 6 servings dish: 3-quart

24   dried jumbo macaroni shells

2   cups dried tiny shell macaroni (8 ounces)

2   cups shredded Gruyère cheese (8 ounces)

2   cups shredded sharp cheddar cheese (8 ounces)

¾   cup half-and-half or light cream

⅛   teaspoon ground white or black pepper

1   24-ounce jar vodka sauce or your favorite tomato pasta sauce

1   cup shredded brick cheese or mozzarella cheese (4 ounces)

Fresh basil leaves (optional)

1 Preheat oven to 350°F. Cook jumbo shells according to package directions. Using a large slotted spoon, transfer shells to a colander. Rinse with cold water; drain well and set aside. In same pan cook tiny shells according to package directions. Drain.

2 Meanwhile, in a large saucepan combine Gruyère cheese, cheddar cheese, half-and-half, and pepper. Heat over medium-low heat until cheese is melted and smooth, stirring frequently. Stir in tiny shells.

3 Spread about ½ cup of the pasta sauce in the bottom of a 3-quart rectangular baking dish. Spoon cheese-shell mixture into drained jumbo shells; place stuffed shells in prepared baking dish. Top with the remaining pasta sauce.

4 Bake, covered, for 30 minutes. Uncover and sprinkle with brick cheese. Bake, uncovered, about 15 minutes more or until heated through. Let stand 10 minutes before serving. Top with fresh basil.

nutrition facts per serving: 858 cal., 42 g total fat (25 g sat. fat), 128 mg chol., 1035 mg sodium, 79 g carb., 3 g dietary fiber, 40 g protein.

Creamy chicken and vegetables tucked under flaky pastry—it's the perfect dish for warming your heart and soul. It's also very simple to make when you pick up a rotisserie chicken to provide the base for the filling.

deep-dish chicken potpie

prep: 50 minutes bake: 35 minutes stand: 20 minutes
oven: 400°F makes: 9 servings dish: 3-quart

3	tablespoons butter or margarine
1½	cups chopped leeks or onions
1½	cups sliced fresh mushrooms
1¼	cups sliced celery
1	cup chopped red sweet pepper (1 large)
½	cup all-purpose flour
1½	teaspoons poultry seasoning
¼	teaspoon salt
¼	teaspoon ground black pepper
2¼	cups chicken broth
1½	cups half-and-half, light cream, or milk
3¾	cups chopped cooked chicken (about 1¼ pounds)
1½	cups frozen peas and carrots or frozen peas
1	recipe Lattice Pastry Strips
1	egg, lightly beaten

1 Preheat oven to 400°F. In a large saucepan melt butter over medium heat. Add leeks, mushrooms, celery, and sweet pepper. Cook for 5 to 8 minutes or until vegetables are tender. Stir in flour, poultry seasoning, salt, and black pepper. Add chicken broth and half-and-half all at once. Cook and stir until thickened and bubbly. Stir in chicken and peas. Pour mixture into an ungreased 3-quart rectangular baking dish.

2 Place some of the Lattice Pastry Strips over chicken mixture 1 inch apart. Give dish a quarter turn and arrange the remaining strips perpendicular to the first batch of strips on filling. Brush pastry strips with egg.

3 Bake, uncovered, for 35 to 40 minutes or until pastry is golden. Let stand for 20 minutes before serving.

nutrition facts per serving: 520 cal., 30 g total fat (11 g sat. fat), 101 mg chol., 644 mg sodium, 38 g carb., 3 g dietary fiber, 22 g protein.

lattice pastry strips: In a large bowl stir together 2¼ cups all-purpose flour and ¾ teaspoon salt. Using a pastry blender, cut in ⅔ cup shortening until pieces are pea-size. Sprinkle 1 tablespoon cold water over part of the mixture; gently toss with a fork. Push moistened dough to side of bowl. Repeat, using 1 tablespoon cold water at a time, until all of the flour mixture is moistened (7 to 9 tablespoons cold water total). Form dough into a ball. On a lightly floured surface, roll out pastry and cut into 1-inch-wide strips.

Using fines herbes makes this a flavorful side for chicken or fish. Fines herbes is a blend of chervil, chives, parsley, and tarragon. Crush the herbs in the palm of your hand to release the aromatic oils and boost their flavor.

herbed root vegetable
cobbler

prep: 45 minutes   bake: 1 hour 12 minutes   stand: 20 minutes
oven: 400°F   makes: 12 side-dish servings   dish: 3-quart

1   pound Yukon gold potatoes, cut into 1-inch pieces
1   pound rutabaga, peeled and cut into 1-inch pieces
4   medium carrots, cut into 1-inch pieces
2   medium parsnips, peeled and cut into 1-inch pieces
1   small red onion, cut into thin wedges
2   cloves garlic, minced
1   cup chicken broth
1½ teaspoons dried fines herbes, herbes de Provence, or Italian seasoning, crushed
½   teaspoon salt
¼   teaspoon ground black pepper
1   4- to 5.2-ounce container semisoft cheese with garlic and herbs
1   recipe Herbed Parmesan Dumplings

1 Preheat oven to 400°F. In an ungreased 3-quart baking dish combine potatoes, rutabaga, carrots, parsnips, onion, and garlic.

2 In a small bowl combine broth, fines herbes, salt, and pepper. Pour over vegetables, stirring to coat. Bake, covered, about 1 hour or until vegetables are nearly tender. Carefully uncover vegetables;* stir in semisoft cheese.

3 Drop Herbed Parmesan Dumplings into 12 mounds on top of hot vegetables. Bake, uncovered, for 12 to 15 minutes more or until a toothpick inserted in centers of dumplings comes out clean. Let stand for 20 minutes before serving.

nutrition facts per serving: 233 cal., 12 g total fat (7 g sat. fat), 53 mg chol., 499 mg sodium, 28 g carb., 3 g dietary fiber, 6 g protein.

herbed parmesan dumplings: In a medium bowl stir together 1½ cups all-purpose flour; 2 teaspoons baking powder; 1½ teaspoons dried fines herbes, herbes de Provence, or Italian seasoning, crushed; and ½ teaspoon salt. Using a pastry blender, cut in 6 tablespoons butter until mixture resembles coarse crumbs. Stir in ¼ cup finely shredded Parmesan cheese (1 ounce). In a small bowl combine 2 lightly beaten eggs and ⅓ cup milk. Add all at once to flour mixture, stirring just until moistened.

*test kitchen tip: Be sure to uncover the vegetables so the steam escapes away from you.

The mixture of green beans and cream of mushroom soup topped with French-fried onions has been a treasured serve-along at family gatherings for decades. It's very simple and goes great with a holiday menu featuring ham or turkey.

home-style green bean bake

prep: 15 minutes   bake: 45 minutes   oven: 350°F
makes: 6 servings   dish: 1½-quart

1   10.75-ounce can condensed cream of mushroom or cream of celery soup

½   cup shredded cheddar or American cheese (2 ounces)

1   2-ounce jar sliced pimientos, drained (optional)

3   14.5-ounce cans French-cut green beans or cut green beans, drained, or 6 cups frozen French-cut green beans or cut green beans, thawed and drained

1   2.8-ounce can french-fried onions

1 Preheat oven to 350°F. In a large bowl stir together soup, cheese, and, if desired, pimiento. Stir in green beans. Transfer bean mixture to an ungreased 1½-quart casserole.

2 Bake, uncovered, for 40 minutes. Remove from oven and stir; sprinkle with french-fried onions. Bake about 5 minutes more or until heated through.

nutrition facts per serving: 194 cal., 12 g total fat (3 g sat. fat), 12 mg chol., 1180 mg sodium, 16 g carb., 2 g dietary fiber, 6 g protein.

calico bean bake: Prepare as directed, except substitute one 14.5-ounce can cut wax beans for 1 can of green beans.

Give this childhood comfort food grown-up appeal with Dijon mustard and roasted red sweet pepper. For a nostalgic touch, top the casserole with whole potato chips.

tuna noodle casserole

prep: 30 minutes bake: 25 minutes stand: 5 minutes oven: 375°F
makes: 4 to 6 servings dish: 1½-quart

3   cups dried wide
      noodles (about
      5 ounces)
1   cup chopped sweet
      red pepper
      (1 medium)
1   cup chopped celery
      (2 stalks)
¼   cup chopped onion
¼   cup butter or
      margarine
¼   cup all-purpose flour
1   to 2 tablespoons
      Dijon mustard
½   teaspoon salt
¼   teaspoon ground
      black pepper
2¼ cups milk
1   12-ounce can chunk
      white tuna (water-
      pack), drained and
      broken into chunks;
      two 5-ounce pouches
      chunk light tuna in
      water, drained; or
      two 6-ounce cans
      skinless, boneless
      salmon, drained
½   cup panko (Japanese-
      style bread crumbs)
      or soft bread crumbs
¼   cup freshly grated
      Parmesan cheese
1   tablespoon snipped
      fresh parsley
1   tablespoon butter,
      melted

1 Preheat oven to 375°F. Lightly grease a 1½-quart casserole; set aside. In a large saucepan cook noodles according to package directions. Drain; return noodles to pan.

2 Meanwhile, for sauce, in a medium saucepan cook sweet pepper, celery, and onion in ¼ cup hot butter over medium heat for 8 to 10 minutes or until tender. Stir in flour, mustard, salt and black pepper. Add milk all at once; cook and stir until slightly thickened and bubbly.

3 Gently fold sauce and tuna into cooked noodles. Transfer noodle mixture to prepared casserole. In a small bowl combine bread crumbs, cheese, parsley, and melted butter. Sprinkle the crumb mixture over the noodle mixture.

4 Bake, uncovered, for 25 to 30 minutes or until heated through. Let stand for 5 minutes before serving.

nutrition facts per serving: 495 cal., 23 g total fat (12 g sat. fat), 115 mg chol., 1040 mg sodium, 42 g carb., 3 g dietary fiber, 33 g protein.

cheesy tuna noodle casserole: Prepare as above, except add 1 cup cheddar cheese cubes (4 ounces) with the tuna.

This all-American classic vegetable side is full of flavor—earthy mushroom soup, creamy cheese, and buttery bread crumb topping make it so!

broccoli-cauliflower bake

prep: 25 minutes bake: 20 minutes oven: 375°F
makes: 8 servings dish: 1½-quart

4 cups broccoli florets*
3 cups cauliflower florets*
½ cup chopped onion (1 medium)
1 tablespoon butter or margarine
1 10.75-ounce can condensed cream of mushroom or cream of chicken soup
3 ounces American cheese, cubed, or process Swiss cheese, torn
¼ cup milk
½ teaspoon dried basil, thyme, or marjoram, crushed
¾ cup soft bread crumbs (1 slice bread)**
1 tablespoon butter, melted

1 Preheat oven to 375°F. In a large covered saucepan cook broccoli and cauliflower in a small amount of lightly salted boiling water for 6 to 8 minutes or until vegetables are crisp-tender. Drain well.

2 In the same saucepan cook onion in 1 tablespoon hot butter over medium heat until tender, stirring occasionally. Stir in soup, cheese, milk, and basil. Cook and stir over medium-low heat until cheese is melted. Stir in cooked broccoli and cauliflower. Transfer vegetable mixture to an ungreased 1½-quart casserole. Toss together bread crumbs and the 1 tablespoon melted butter; sprinkle over vegetable mixture.

3 Bake, uncovered, about 20 minutes or until heated through.

nutrition facts per serving: 137 cal., 9 g total fat (5 g sat. fat), 20 mg chol., 497 mg sodium, 11 g carb., 3 g dietary fiber, 5 g protein.

*test kitchen tip: You can substitute 8 cups frozen broccoli and cauliflower, thawed, for the fresh broccoli and cauliflower florets. Prepare as above except omit Step 1 and bake about 35 minutes or until heated through.

**test kitchen tip: Use a blender or food processor to make fluffy soft bread crumbs. One slice yields ¾ cup crumbs.

When fresh corn is available, try a sweeter variety in this chile-spiked dish. To check for freshness, feel the kernels through the husks and select ears with kernels in tightly packed rows and moist, pale yellow silk peeking out of the top.

corn-off-the-cob pudding

prep: 30 minutes chill: 2 hours bake: 45 minutes stand: 10 minutes
oven: 350°F makes: 12 servings dish: 2-quart

3 ears of corn or
   1½ cups frozen
   whole kernel corn,
   thawed
1 cup finely chopped
   onion (1 large)
1 tablespoon olive oil
12 ounces crusty country
   Italian bread, cut
   into 1-inch cubes
   (6 cups)
2 to 3 fresh jalapeño
   chile peppers,
   seeded and finely
   chopped
2 cups fat-free milk
1 cup refrigerated or
   frozen egg product,
   thawed, or 4 eggs,
   lightly beaten

1 Lightly grease a 2-quart square baking dish; set aside. If using fresh corn, remove husks and silks from ears of corn. Using a sharp knife, cut corn kernels off cobs. In a large skillet cook onion in hot oil over medium heat for 3 to 4 minutes or until tender, stirring occasionally. Stir in fresh or thawed corn. Cook and stir for 2 minutes more. Cool slightly.

2 In a large bowl combine corn mixture, bread cubes, and jalapeño peppers. In a medium bowl combine milk and egg. Pour milk mixture over bread mixture; stir gently to coat. Transfer mixture to the prepared baking dish. Cover and chill for 2 to 24 hours.

3 Preheat oven to 350°F. Bake, uncovered, about 45 minutes or until center is set and top is lightly browned. Let stand for 10 minutes before serving.

nutrition facts per serving: 136 cal., 2 g total fat (0 g sat. fat), 1 mg chol., 225 mg sodium, 22 g carb., 2 g dietary fiber, 7 g protein.

*test kitchen tip: Because hot chile peppers, such as poblanos and Anaheims, contain volatile oils that can burn skin and eyes, wear kitchen gloves when working with the peppers and avoid direct contact as much as possible. When bare hands touch chile peppers, wash them well with soap and water.

This elegant lasagna gets its pesto flavor from basil, garlic, pine nuts, and cheese. Serve it with a dry red wine and a loaf of crusty bread.

creamy artichoke lasagna bake

prep: 50 minutes bake: 35 minutes stand: 15 minutes oven: 350°F
makes: 12 servings dish: 3-quart

9 dried lasagna noodles
3 tablespoons olive oil
2 9-ounce packages frozen artichoke hearts, thawed and halved lengthwise
½ cup pine nuts
4 cloves garlic, minced
1 15-ounce carton ricotta cheese
1 cup finely shredded Parmesan cheese (4 ounces)
1 cup snipped fresh basil
1 egg
¾ teaspoon salt
1 cup chicken or vegetable broth
¼ cup all-purpose flour
2 cups half-and-half or light cream
1 cup shredded mozzarella cheese (4 ounces)

1 Preheat oven to 350°F. Cook lasagna noodles according to package directions; drain. Rinse with cold water; drain again. Place lasagna noodles in a single layer on a sheet of foil; set aside.

2 In a large saucepan heat 2 tablespoons of the oil over medium heat. Add artichokes, pine nuts, and half of the garlic. Cook for 2 to 3 minutes or until artichokes are tender, stirring frequently. Transfer to a large bowl. Stir in ricotta cheese, ½ cup of the Parmesan cheese, ½ cup of the basil, the egg, and salt.

3 For sauce, in a small bowl combine broth and flour. In the same saucepan heat the remaining 1 tablespoon oil over medium heat. Add the remaining garlic; cook and stir until garlic is tender. Stir in flour mixture and half-and-half. Cook and stir until mixture is thickened and bubbly. Remove from heat. Stir in the remaining ½ cup basil.

4 In a small bowl combine mozzarella cheese and the remaining ½ cup Parmesan cheese.

5 Spread about 1 cup of the sauce evenly in an ungreased 3-quart rectangular baking dish. Arrange three of the cooked lasagna noodles over the sauce in dish. Spread with one-third of the artichoke mixture and one-third of the remaining sauce. Sprinkle with ½ cup of the mozzarella mixture. Repeat layers two more times, starting with noodles and ending with mozzarella mixture.

6 Bake, uncovered, for 35 to 40 minutes or until edges are bubbly and top is lightly browned. Let stand for 15 minutes before serving.

nutrition facts per serving: 350 cal., 21 g total fat (10 g sat. fat), 64 mg chol., 470 mg sodium, 25 g carb., 3 g dietary fiber, 16 g protein.

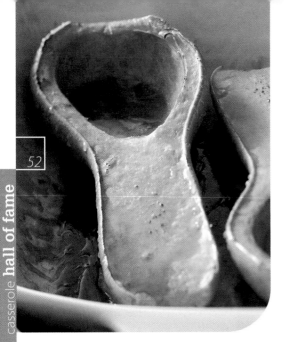

The buttery maple syrup glaze in this side dish is certain to make converts to the brilliant butternut, one of early autumn's most flavorful squashes.

butternut squash with

maple and bourbon

prep: 10 minutes   bake: 1 hour 15 minutes   oven: 350°F
makes: 4 servings   dish: 3-quart

1   1½ - to 2-pound butternut squash, halved lengthwise and seeded
¼   cup pure maple syrup
¼   cup butter
2   tablespoons bourbon, apple juice, or apple cider
½   teaspoon salt

1 Preheat oven to 350°F. Place squash halves, cut sides up, in an ungreased 3-quart rectangular baking dish.

2 In a small saucepan combine maple syrup, butter, and bourbon. Cook over medium-low heat until butter melts. Remove from heat; pour over the cut sides of the squash. Sprinkle with salt. Cover and bake for 30 minutes. Bake, uncovered, about 45 minutes more or until squash is tender, basting occasionally.

nutrition facts per serving: 234 cal., 12 g total fat (7 g sat. fat), 31 mg chol., 380 mg sodium, 30 g carb., 3 g dietary fiber, 2 g protein.

shortcut squash with maple and bourbon: Place two 12-ounce packages fresh cubed butternut squash in a 2-quart baking dish. Prepare maple syrup mixture as directed; pour over squash. Sprinkle with salt. Bake, covered, for 35 minutes. Uncover and bake about 25 minutes more or until squash is tender and begins to brown.

When you're looking for an any-occasion side dish that you know will please a crowd, turn to this easy recipe. It's a keeper!

best-ever potluck potatoes

prep: 10 minutes   bake: 1 hour 15 minutes   stand: 5 minutes   oven: 350°F
makes: 12 servings   dish: 2-quart

1   32-ounce package
    frozen loose-pack
    diced hash brown
    potatoes, thawed
    (7½ cups)
1   10.75-ounce can
    reduced-fat and
    reduced-sodium
    condensed cream of
    chicken soup
1   8-ounce carton sour
    cream
2   tablespoons butter or
    margarine, melted
1   cup shredded
    cheddar cheese
    (4 ounces)
¼   cup sliced scallions (2)
¼   cup milk
½   teaspoon garlic salt
¼   teaspoon ground
    black pepper

1 Preheat oven to 350°F. In a large bowl stir together the potatoes, soup, sour cream, and butter. Stir in ½ cup of the cheddar cheese, 3 tablespoons of the scallions, the milk, garlic salt, and pepper. Transfer mixture to an ungreased 2-quart rectangular baking dish.

2 Bake, covered, about 1¼ hours or until potatoes are tender. Sprinkle with the remaining ½ cup cheddar cheese. Let stand for 5 minutes. Sprinkle with the remaining scallion.

nutrition facts per serving: 173 cal., 10 g total fat (6 g sat. fat), 26 mg chol., 241 mg sodium, 17 g carb., 1 g dietary fiber, 5 g protein.

Having dinner guests over? Replace your regular mashed potatoes with a distinctive side that comes with an interesting mix of cheeses, garlic, and fresh herbs. A crumb topper adds a nice finish.

tuscan cheese-potato bake

prep: 30 minutes **bake:** 20 minutes **oven:** 400°F
makes: 8 to 10 servings **dish:** 2-quart

2 pounds red potatoes
¼ cup butter
3 or 4 cloves garlic, minced
1½ teaspoons snipped fresh thyme or ½ teaspoon dried thyme, crushed
1 cup buttermilk
½ teaspoon salt
¼ teaspoon ground black pepper
1 cup shredded fontina cheese (4 ounces)
1 cup finely shredded Parmesan cheese (4 ounces)
⅓ cup crumbled blue cheese
½ cup panko (Japanese-style bread crumbs)
¼ teaspoon dried Italian seasoning, crushed
1 tablespoon olive oil
Snipped fresh parsley (optional)

1 Preheat oven to 400°F. Lightly grease a 2-quart square baking dish; set aside. Scrub potatoes; cut into 1-inch pieces. In a large saucepan cook potatoes in enough lightly salted boiling water to cover 12 to 15 minutes or until tender; drain.

2 In a 12-inch skillet melt butter over medium heat. Add garlic and thyme; cook and stir for 1 minute. Add potatoes; coarsely mash with a potato masher. Stir in buttermilk, salt, and pepper. Fold in fontina cheese, half of the Parmesan cheese, and the blue cheese. Evenly spread in prepared baking dish.

3 In a small bowl combine the remaining Parmesan cheese, panko, Italian seasoning, and olive oil; toss with a fork to combine. Evenly sprinkle over potato mixture in dish. Bake, uncovered, about 20 minutes or until bubbly and top is golden. Sprinkle with snipped parsley.

nutrition facts per serving: 304 cal., 18 g total fat (10 g sat. fat), 47 mg chol., 653 mg sodium, 23 g carb., 2 g dietary fiber, 14 g protein.

In this classic comfort dish, potatoes are baked in a creamy milk-based sauce with leeks providing a subtle, sweet undertone. It's a perfect dish for a large gathering.

scalloped new
potatoes and leeks

prep: 30 minutes bake: 30 minutes stand: 10 minutes oven: 325°F
makes: 12 servings dish: 2-quart

Nonstick cooking
  spray
2½ pounds tiny new
  potatoes, sliced
2 tablespoons butter or
  margarine
1½ cups chopped leeks
3 cloves garlic, minced
⅓ cup all-purpose flour
1½ teaspoons dried
  thyme, crushed
½ teaspoon salt
¼ teaspoon ground
  black pepper
3 cups milk
1½ cups shredded
  Gruyère or Swiss
  cheese (6 ounces)

1 Preheat oven to 325°F. Coat a 2-quart oval or rectangular baking dish with cooking spray; set aside. In a large covered saucepan cook potatoes in salted boiling water for 5 minutes. Drain and set aside in a bowl.

2 Meanwhile, in a large saucepan melt butter over medium heat. Add leeks and garlic; cook about 5 minutes or just until tender. Stir in flour, thyme, salt, and pepper. Stir in milk all at once. Cook and stir over medium heat until thickened and bubbly. Add 1 cup of the cheese, stirring until melted.

3 Pour sauce over potatoes. Stir gently until coated. Spoon potato mixture into prepared baking dish. Set baking dish on a baking sheet.

4 Sprinkle with the remaining ½ cup cheese. Bake, uncovered, for 30 to 35 minutes or until edges are bubbly and cheese on top is golden brown. Let stand for 10 minutes before serving.

nutrition facts per serving: 193 cal., 8 g total fat (5 g sat. fat), 26 mg chol., 191 mg sodium, 23 g carb., 2 g dietary fiber, 9 g protein.

make-ahead directions: Prepare mixture as directed, except after sprinkling with cheese, cover dish with foil and chill for up to 24 hours. Place baking dish on a baking sheet. Bake, covered, in a 325°F oven for 25 minutes. Remove foil and bake about 35 minutes more or until bubbly and heated through. Let stand for 10 minutes before serving.

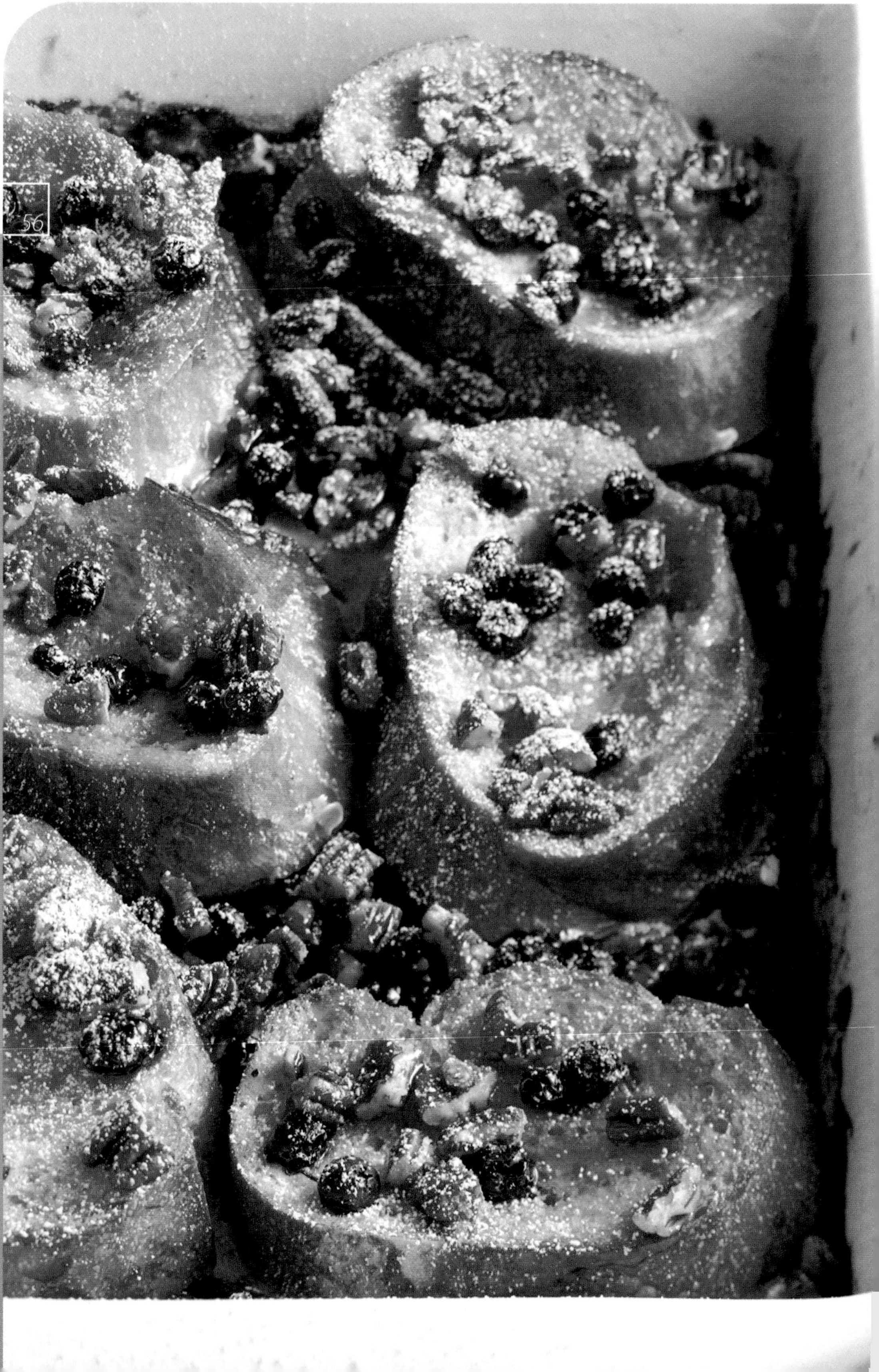

Topped with fresh blueberry syrup, this spin on a timeless breakfast favorite doesn't get any better. Bacon or sausage links make an excellent accompaniment.

baked blueberry-pecan french toast

prep: 30 minutes   chill: 8 hours   bake: 35 minutes   stand: 10 minutes
oven: 350°F   makes: 6 to 8 servings   dish: 3-quart

Butter
12 ounces Italian bread, cut into 6 to 8 slices (each about 1 inch thick)
5 eggs, beaten
2½ cups milk, half-and-half, or light cream
⅔ cup packed brown sugar
1 teaspoon vanilla
½ teaspoon ground nutmeg
2 cups fresh blueberries
1 cup coarsely chopped pecans
¼ cup packed brown sugar
¼ cup butter, melted
Powdered sugar
1 cup fresh blueberries
½ cup maple syrup
1 tablespoon lemon juice

1 Butter a 3-quart rectangular baking dish. Arrange bread slices in dish, overlapping if necessary.

2 In a large bowl combine eggs, milk, ⅔ cup brown sugar, vanilla, and nutmeg. Slowly pour egg mixture evenly over bread. Press lightly with a rubber spatula or the back of a large spoon to moisten bread. Cover and chill for 8 to 24 hours.

3 Preheat oven to 350°F. Evenly sprinkle 2 cups blueberries and pecans over bread mixture. In a small bowl stir together ¼ cup brown sugar and ¼ cup melted butter. Drizzle butter mixture over pecans.

4 Bake, uncovered, for 35 to 40 minutes or until a knife inserted near the center comes out clean. Let stand for 10 minutes before serving. Sprinkle with powdered sugar.

5 Meanwhile, for blueberry syrup*, in a small saucepan combine 1 cup blueberries and maple syrup; cook and stir over medium heat about 3 minutes or until blueberries have burst. Pour syrup through a sieve into a heatproof pitcher, pressing juice out of blueberries. Stir in lemon juice.*

nutrition facts per serving: 716 cal., 31 g total fat (10 g sat. fat), 210 mg chol., 516 mg sodium, 97 g carb., 5 g dietary fiber, 15 g protein.

*test kitchen tip: The blueberry syrup may be made up to 1 day ahead. Cover and refrigerate; reheat before serving.

Bakery-fresh doughnuts make this cobbler ultra easy. Use a mixture of sweet and tart apples for a well-rounded apple flavor. For the tart apples, look for Northern Spy, Rhode Island Greening, or Granny Smith. Sweet apples include Cortland and McIntosh.

doughnut-apple cobbler

prep: 45 minutes   bake: 45 minutes   oven: 375°F
makes: 12 servings   dish: 3-quart

4	medium Northern Spy or Granny Smith apples
2	medium Rhode Island Greening or Granny Smith apples
2	medium Cortland apples
2	medium McIntosh apples
1	large lemon
½	cup sugar
⅓	cup all-purpose flour
8	cinnamon-sugar-coated apple cider or other cake doughnuts
5	tablespoons butter, melted

1 Preheat oven to 375°F. Peel, core, and cut apples into wedges; halve wedges crosswise so the pieces are smaller than 2 inches. Juice the lemon, retaining as much pulp as possible; toss juice and pulp with apples. Sprinkle with sugar and flour; toss until apples are coated. Arrange apples in a 3-quart rectangular baking dish.

2 Top apples with doughnuts and drizzle with melted butter. Bake about 45 minutes or until filling is bubbly, covering with foil if necessary to prevent overbrowning. Serve warm.

nutrition facts per serving: 322 cal., 12 g total fat (5 g sat. fat), 13 mg chol., 216 mg sodium, 56 g carb., 5 g dietary fiber, 3 g protein.

Originally from a 1944 Better Homes and Gardens® magazine, this homey dessert is still winning people over. The batter separates while baking, creating a tender cake on top and a rich fudgy sauce on the bottom.

brownie pudding cake

prep: 20 minutes bake: 40 minutes cool: 45 minutes oven: 350°F
makes: 6 to 8 servings dish: 2-quart

1   cup all-purpose flour
¾   cup granulated sugar
2   tablespoons unsweetened cocoa powder
2   teaspoons baking powder
¼   teaspoon salt
½   cup milk
2   tablespoons vegetable oil
1   teaspoon vanilla
½   cup chopped walnuts
¾   cup packed brown sugar
¼   cup unsweetened cocoa powder
1½   cups boiling water
     Vanilla ice cream (optional)

1 Preheat oven to 350°F. Grease a 2-quart square baking dish; set aside. In a medium bowl stir together the flour, granulated sugar, 2 tablespoons cocoa powder, the baking powder, and salt. Stir in milk, oil, and vanilla. Stir in walnuts.

2 Pour batter into prepared dish. In a small bowl stir together brown sugar and ¼ cup cocoa powder. Stir in the boiling water. Slowly pour brown sugar mixture over batter.

3 Bake, uncovered, for 40 minutes. Cool in pan on a wire rack for 45 to 60 minutes. Serve warm. Spoon cake into dessert bowls; spoon sauce from dish over cake. If desired, serve with vanilla ice cream.

nutrition facts per serving: 406 cal., 12 g total fat (2 g sat. fat), 2 mg chol., 237 mg sodium, 74 g carb., 3 g dietary fiber, 5 g protein.

hearty

meat

dis

Succulent beef, lamb, pork, and a variety of sausages make up our tasty lineup of mouthwatering meals. Choose from casual everyday fare for busy weeknights—starring pork chops, meatballs, and hamburger—to more sophisticated dishes, such as individual sausage pies, for entertaining.

3

hes

Precooked roast cuts the prep time for this timeless classic while adding rich flavor and fork-tender qualities. On top? A horseradish–sour cream sauce adds a lively bite.

beef **stroganoff** casserole

prep: 35 minutes   bake: 30 minutes   oven: 350°F
makes: 6 servings   dish: 3-quart

4 cups dried campanelle or penne pasta (12 ounces)
1 17-ounce package refrigerated cooked beef roast au jus
2 large portobello mushrooms
1 medium sweet onion, cut into thin wedges
2 cloves garlic, minced
2 tablespoons butter or margarine
3 tablespoons all-purpose flour
2 tablespoons tomato paste
1 14-ounce can beef broth
1 tablespoon Worcestershire sauce
1 teaspoon smoked paprika or Spanish paprika
¼ teaspoon salt
¼ teaspoon ground black pepper
   Snipped fresh Italian parsley (optional)
½ cup sour cream
1 tablespoon prepared horseradish
1 teaspoon snipped fresh dill or ¼ teaspoon dried dillweed

1 Preheat oven to 350°F. Cook pasta according to package directions; drain. Return pasta to hot saucepan; cover and keep warm. Place roast on a cutting board; reserve juices. Using 2 forks, pull meat apart into bite-sized pieces; set aside.

2 Remove stems and gills from mushrooms; coarsely chop. (You should have about 4 cups.) In a 12-inch skillet cook mushrooms, onion, and garlic in hot butter over medium heat for 4 to 5 minutes or until tender. Stir in flour and tomato paste. Add reserved meat juices, beef broth, Worcestershire sauce, paprika, salt, and pepper. Cook and stir until thickened and bubbly. Remove from heat.

3 Add pasta and beef to mushroom mixture in skillet; stir to combine. Transfer meat mixture to an ungreased 3-quart casserole or rectangular baking dish. Bake, covered, about 30 minutes or until heated through. If desired, sprinkle with parsley. Meanwhile, in a small bowl combine sour cream, horseradish, and dill. Spoon some of the mixture over each serving.

nutrition facts per serving: 450 cal., 14 g total fat (7 g sat. fat), 61 mg chol., 57 g carb., 4 g dietary fiber, 26 g protein.

NOT BAD!!

This potluck staple—layers of meat, noodles, and cheese—will disappear fast. Even fussy eaters (most notably kids) will gobble up its cheesy goodness.

hamburger-cheese
hot dish

prep: 30 minutes bake: 45 minutes oven: 350°F
makes: 6 servings dish: 2-quart

8 ounces dried medium noodles (4 cups)
12 ounces lean ground beef
½ cup chopped onion (1 medium)
1 15-ounce can tomato sauce
1 teaspoon sugar
¼ teaspoon salt
¼ teaspoon garlic powder
¼ teaspoon ground black pepper
1 cup cream-style cottage cheese
½ of an 8-ounce package cream cheese, softened
⅓ cup sliced scallions (3)
¼ cup sour cream
¼ cup chopped green sweet pepper
¼ cup grated or shredded Parmesan cheese

1 Preheat oven to 350°F. Cook noodles according to package directions; drain and set aside.

2 Meanwhile, in a large skillet cook ground beef and onion over medium heat until meat is brown and onion is tender. Drain off fat. Stir in tomato sauce, sugar, salt, garlic powder, and black pepper. Remove from heat.

3 In a medium bowl combine cottage cheese, cream cheese, scallions, sour cream, and sweet pepper.

4 Spread half of the noodles in an ungreased 2-quart rectangular baking dish. Top with half of the meat mixture. Top with the cottage cheese mixture. Top with the remaining noodles and meat mixture. Sprinkle with Parmesan cheese.

5 Bake, covered, for 30 minutes. Uncover. Bake about 15 minutes more or until heated through.

nutrition facts per serving: 351 cal., 17 g total fat (9 g sat. fat), 92 mg chol., 700 mg sodium, 26 g carb., 2 g dietary fiber, 22 g protein.

hearty **meat dishes**

Try a new twist on Sunday's roast beef dinner, a comfort-food classic, with this savory pie. Here, a precooked roast is cut up, while its juices form the basis for a tasty gravy. Carrots, parsnips, and peas are added to lend color and flavor.

deep-dish
steak and vegetable pie

prep: 40 minutes bake: 25 minutes stand: 10 minutes
oven: 400°F makes: 8 servings dish: 10-inch pie plate

½   of a 15-ounce package
     rolled refrigerated
     unbaked piecrust
     (1 crust)
¾   cup beef broth
1   teaspoon dried
     marjoram, crushed
2   cloves garlic, minced
¼   teaspoon salt
¼   teaspoon ground
     black pepper
2   medium parsnips
     (about 10 ounces),
     peeled and cut into
     ½-inch pieces
⅔   cup thinly sliced
     carrots (2 small)
½   cup chopped onion
     (1 medium)
2   17-ounce packages
     refrigerated cooked
     beef roast au jus
1   cup half-and-half or
     light cream
¼   cup all-purpose flour
¾   cup frozen peas

1 Let refrigerated piecrust stand at room temperature according to package directions.

2 In a large saucepan combine beef broth, marjoram, garlic, salt, and pepper; bring to boiling. Stir in parsnips, carrots, and onion; reduce heat. Simmer, covered, for 10 minutes.

3 Remove meat from package, reserving juices. Cut meat into ¾-inch pieces. In a small bowl combine half-and-half and flour; gradually stir into vegetable mixture. Cook and stir until thickened and bubbly. Stir in meat, meat juices, and peas; heat through. Remove from heat; cover and keep warm.

4 Preheat oven to 400°F. On a lightly floured surface, roll piecrust into a circle 2 inches larger than the diameter of the top of a 10-inch deep-dish pie plate or a 2-quart casserole. Transfer meat mixture to the ungreased pie plate. Center pastry on top of meat mixture. Trim pastry 1 inch beyond edge of pie plate. Turn pastry under and flute to edge of pie plate. Cut small slits in top of pastry to allow steam to escape.

5 Bake, uncovered, for 25 to 30 minutes or until crust is golden. Let stand for 15 minutes before serving.

nutrition facts per serving: 387 cal., 19 g total fat (10 g sat. fat), 81 mg chol., 719 mg sodium, 30 g carb., 3 g dietary fiber, 26 g protein.

Definitely not your ordinary meat loaf, these little gems boast a melty mozzarella and prosciutto filling. If you can't find prosciutto, use ham instead.

individual **sicilian** meat loaves

prep: 20 minutes   bake: 20 minutes   oven: 400°F
makes: 4 servings   dish: 3-quart

1   egg, lightly beaten
1   14-ounce jar garlic
    and onion pasta
    sauce (1¾ cups)
¼   cup seasoned fine dry
    bread crumbs
¼   teaspoon salt
¼   teaspoon ground
    black pepper
12 ounces ground beef
2   ounces mozzarella
    cheese*
4   thin slices prosciutto
    or cooked ham
    (about 2 ounces)
1   9-ounce package
    refrigerated plain or
    spinach fettuccine
    Finely shredded
    Parmesan cheese
    (optional)

1 Preheat oven to 400°F. In a medium bowl combine egg, ¼ cup of the pasta sauce, the bread crumbs, salt, and pepper. Add ground beef; mix well.

2 Cut mozzarella cheese into four logs each measuring approximately 2¼×¾×½ inches. Wrap a slice of prosciutto around each cheese log. Shape one-fourth of the ground beef mixture around each cheese log to form a loaf. Flatten each meat loaf to 1½ inches thick and place in an ungreased 3-quart rectangular baking dish.

3 Bake loaves, uncovered, about 20 minutes or until done (160°F).**

4 Meanwhile, prepare fettuccine according to package directions; drain. In a small saucepan heat the remaining pasta sauce over medium heat until bubbly.

5 Arrange meat loaves over hot cooked pasta. Spoon sauce over and, if desired, sprinkle with Parmesan cheese.

nutrition facts per serving: 618 cal., 29 g total fat (11 g sat. fat), 171 mg chol., 1150 mg sodium, 55 g carb., 3 g dietary fiber, 31 g protein.

*test kitchen tip: You can substitute two sticks of mozzarella (string) cheese, cut in half crosswise.

**test kitchen tip: The internal color of a meat loaf is not a reliable doneness indicator. A beef loaf cooked to 160°F is safe, regardless of color. To measure the doneness of a meat loaf, insert an instant-read thermometer into the center of the meat loaf.

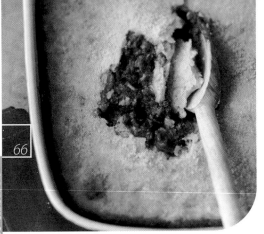

hearty **meat dishes**

Mashed potatoes are the surprise ingredient in the crust of this pizzalike dish. Feel free to experiment with different olives and cheeses for more flavor variety.

double-crust
pizza casserole

prep: 25 minutes bake: 25 minutes stand: 5 minutes oven: 425°F
makes: 12 servings dish: 3-quart

3	cups all-purpose flour
3	cups instant mashed potatoes
2	cups milk
1/3	cup olive oil
1	pound lean ground beef
12	ounces bulk Italian sausage
1	cup coarsely chopped onion (1 large)
1	8-ounce can tomato sauce
1	6-ounce can Italian-style tomato paste
1	2.25-ounce can sliced pitted black olives, drained (optional)
1/2	of a 1.25- to 1.5-ounce package sloppy joe seasoning mix (about 2 tablespoons)
1	cup shredded mozzarella cheese (4 ounces)
1	tablespoon yellow cornmeal

1 Preheat oven to 425°F. In a large bowl combine flour, dry potatoes, milk, and oil; set aside. (Dough will stiffen slightly as it stands.)

2 For filling, in a large skillet cook ground beef, sausage, and onion over medium heat until meat is brown and onion is tender. Drain off fat. Stir in tomato sauce, tomato paste, olives (if using), and seasoning mix.

3 Using floured fingers, press half of the dough onto the bottom and about 1½ inches up the sides of an ungreased 3-quart rectangular baking dish. Spread filling over crust; sprinkle with cheese.

4 Place the remaining dough on a lightly floured sheet of waxed paper. Sprinkle dough lightly with flour; top with another sheet of waxed paper. Roll dough into a 15×11-inch rectangle; remove top paper. Invert dough onto filling; remove paper. Trim edges as necessary. Turn under edges of top crust and seal to bottom crust. Sprinkle with cornmeal.

5 Bake, uncovered, for 25 to 30 minutes or until filling is heated through and crust is golden. Let stand for 5 minutes before serving.

nutrition facts per serving: 390 cal., 25 g total fat (12 g sat. fat), 25 mg chol., 1012 mg sodium, 28 g carb., 6 g dietary fiber, 14 g protein.

Break through the top crust of this inviting pie—made easy with crescent rolls—and you'll be rewarded with the rich aroma of tomatoes, beef, and cheese.

italian crescent casserole

prep: 25 minutes bake: 20 minutes oven: 375°F
makes: 12 servings dish: 3-quart

2   pounds lean ground beef
½   cup chopped onion (1 medium)
2   cups bottled spaghetti sauce or tomato pasta sauce
3   cups shredded mozzarella or Monterey Jack cheese (12 ounces)
1   8-ounce carton sour cream
1   8-ounce package refrigerated crescent rolls (8)
2   tablespoons butter or margarine, melted
½   cup grated Parmesan cheese

1 Preheat oven to 375°F. In a 12-inch skillet cook ground beef and onion until meat is cooked through. Drain off fat. Stir spaghetti sauce into meat mixture and heat through. Spread meat mixture in an ungreased 3-quart rectangular baking dish.

2 Meanwhile, in a medium bowl combine mozzarella cheese and sour cream; spoon over meat mixture.

3 Unroll crescent rolls, but do not separate into triangles. On a lightly floured surface, press dough edges together and roll out slightly to fit baking dish. Place dough over the cheese–sour cream layer. Brush with melted butter and sprinkle with Parmesan cheese. Bake, uncovered, for 20 to 25 minutes or until top is deep golden brown.

nutrition facts per serving: 360 cal., 23 g total fat (11 g sat. fat), 81 mg chol., 593 mg sodium, 14 g carb., 0 g dietary fiber, 25 g protein.

Pork sausage and spices from the Mexican-style stewed tomatoes give this casserole its punch of flavor. For more heat, use shredded Monterey Jack cheese with jalapeños instead of cheddar.

mexican rice and black bean casserole

prep: 20 minutes bake: 40 minutes stand: 5 minutes oven: 350°F
makes: 8 servings dish: 3-quart

1 pound bulk pork sausage
2 14.5-ounce cans Mexican-style stewed tomatoes, undrained
2 cups cooked white rice*
1 15-ounce can black beans, rinsed and drained
3/4 cup coarsely chopped green sweet pepper (1 medium)
1/2 cup shredded cheddar cheese (2 ounces)
Sour cream (optional)

1 Preheat oven to 350°F. In a 12-inch skillet cook sausage over medium heat until brown. Drain off fat. Stir in tomatoes, cooked rice, black beans, and sweet pepper. Transfer mixture to an ungreased 3-quart rectangular baking dish.

2 Bake, covered, for 40 to 45 minutes or until heated through. Sprinkle with cheese. Let stand for 5 minutes before serving. If desired, serve with sour cream.

nutrition facts per serving: 343 cal., 19 g total fat (8 g sat. fat), 40 mg chol., 811 mg sodium, 27 g carb., 3 g dietary fiber, 14 g protein.

*test kitchen tip: To prepare 2 cups cooked rice, in a medium saucepan combine 1 1/3 cups water and 2/3 cup uncooked long grain white rice. Bring to boiling; reduce heat. Simmer, covered, for 15 to 18 minutes or until rice is tender.

Classic Reuben sandwich fixings—sauerkraut, Swiss cheese, and corned beef—are layered with seasonings and croutons in this tasty casserole.

reuben sandwich casserole

prep: 20 minutes bake: 35 minutes oven: 375°F
makes: 10 servings dish: 3-quart

1 32-ounce jar sauerkraut, rinsed and drained
½ cup chopped onion (1 medium)
4 teaspoons dried parsley flakes, crushed
2 teaspoons caraway seeds
4 cups shredded Swiss cheese (1 pound)
1⅓ cups bottled Thousand Island salad dressing
12 ounces thinly sliced cooked corned beef, coarsely chopped
6 slices rye bread, cut into ½-inch cubes
¼ cup butter or margarine, melted

1 Preheat oven to 375°F. In a large bowl combine sauerkraut, onion, parsley, and caraway seeds. Spread sauerkraut mixture evenly into an ungreased 3-quart rectangular baking dish.

2 Top with half of the cheese, half of the salad dressing, and the corned beef. Top with the remaining salad dressing and the remaining cheese.

3 In a large bowl toss bread cubes with melted butter to coat. Sprinkle bread cubes over casserole.

4 Bake, uncovered, about 35 minutes or until heated through and bread cubes are browned.

nutrition facts per serving: 477 cal., 36 g total fat (14 g sat. fat), 96 mg chol., 3097 mg sodium, 18 g carb., 8 g dietary fiber, 21 g protein.

hearty **meat dishes**

Shepherd's pie is a classic mashed potato–topped casserole from England. Here, instant potato flakes and a can of soup make it all go together more quickly than ever.

easy **shepherd's** pie

prep: 30 minutes bake: 25 minutes oven: 425°F
makes: 8 servings dish: 3-quart

2 pounds ground beef or ground lamb
¼ cup all-purpose flour
1 envelope (½ of a 2-ounce package) onion soup mix
1 10.75-ounce can condensed cream of mushroom soup
1 8-ounce carton sour cream
¾ cup water
1 tablespoon ketchup
1½ cups water
¼ cup butter or margarine
½ teaspoon salt
2 cups instant mashed potato flakes
½ cup milk
2 eggs, lightly beaten
1 cup all-purpose flour
2 teaspoons baking powder

1 Preheat oven to 425°F. In an extra-large skillet cook ground beef over medium heat until brown. Dain off fat. Stir ¼ cup flour and dry onion soup mix into meat. Stir in cream of mushroom soup, sour cream, the ¾ cup water, and the ketchup. Cook until heated through, stirring occasionally.

2 Meanwhile, in a medium saucepan combine the 1½ cups water, butter, and salt. Bring to boiling; remove from heat. Add dry potato flakes and milk, stirring until combined. Stir in eggs, 1 cup flour, and baking powder.

3 Spoon meat mixture into an ungreased 3-quart rectangular baking dish; spoon potato mixture in mounds on top.

4 Bake, uncovered, about 25 minutes or until tops of potatoes are golden.

nutrition facts per serving: 465 cal., 24 g total fat (11 g sat. fat), 143 mg chol., 911 mg sodium, 32 g carb., 1 g dietary fiber, 24 g protein.

A medley of vegetables—onion, carrot, tomatoes, and spinach—two kinds of meat, and four kinds of cheese star in this hearty dish.

meat and four-cheese lasagna

prep: 1 hour 15 minutes bake: 55 minutes stand: 15 minutes oven: 350°F
makes: 9 servings dish: 3-quart

9 dried lasagna noodles
  Nonstick cooking spray
8 ounces lean ground beef or ground pork
8 ounces bulk pork sausage
1 cup chopped onion
½ cup finely chopped carrot (1 medium)
6 cloves garlic, minced
1 28-ounce can crushed tomatoes in puree
½ of a 6-ounce can tomato paste (⅓ cup)
2 teaspoons packed brown sugar
2 teaspoons dried oregano, crushed
1 bay leaf
¼ cup snipped fresh basil
1 egg
1 cup light ricotta cheese
1 cup low-fat cottage cheese
¾ cup grated Parmesan or Romano cheese
⅛ teaspoon ground black pepper
½ of a 10-ounce package frozen chopped spinach, thawed and well drained
2¾ cups shredded mozzarella cheese

1 Preheat oven to 350°F. Cook lasagna noodles according to package directions, except omit any oil or salt; drain. Rinse with cold water; drain again. Place noodles in a single layer on a sheet of foil; set aside. Lightly coat a 3-quart rectangular baking dish with cooking spray; set aside.

2 For meat sauce, in a 4- to 5-quart Dutch oven cook and stir beef, sausage, onion, carrot, and garlic over medium-high heat until meat is browned. Drain off fat. Stir in tomatoes in puree, tomato paste, brown sugar, oregano, and bay leaf. Bring to boiling; reduce heat. Cover and simmer for 15 minutes, stirring occasionally. Remove from heat; stir in basil. Remove bay leaf; discard. Set sauce aside.

3 For filling, in a medium bowl combine egg, ricotta cheese, cottage cheese, ½ cup of the Parmesan cheese, and pepper. Stir in spinach.

4 To assemble, spread ½ cup of the sauce evenly in the bottom of prepared baking dish. Arrange 3 lasagna noodles in the dish. Spread with half of the filling. Top with 1 cup of the mozzarella cheese. Top with half of the remaining sauce, spreading to evenly cover cheese. Top with 3 more noodles, remaining filling, and 1 cup mozzarella. Top with remaining noodles and sauce.

5 Bake, covered, for 40 minutes. Uncover; sprinkle with the remaining mozzarella cheese and remaining Parmesan cheese. Bake, uncovered, for 15 to 20 minutes more or until heated through. Let stand for 15 minutes before serving.

nutrition facts per serving: 472 cal., 24 g total fat (11 g sat. fat), 102 mg chol., 974 mg sodium, 32 g carb., 4 g dietary fiber, 30 g protein.

An essential ingredient for this richly sauced dish is mafalda (mah-FAHL-dah), narrow, curly-edged noodles that resemble lasagna noodles. Can't find it? Penne, rigatoni, or rotini all serve as good substitutes.

italian-style
meatballs and pasta

prep: 25 minutes bake: 25 minutes oven: 350°F
makes: 4 servings dish: 1½-quart

1½ cups dried mafalda
      pasta* (about
      4 ounces)
  1 14.5-ounce can
      Italian-style
      stewed tomatoes,
      undrained
  1 8-ounce can tomato
      sauce
  ¼ cup dry red wine
  2 tablespoons onion
      soup mix
  1 tablespoon snipped
      fresh oregano or
      ½ teaspoon dried
      oregano, crushed
      Pinch ground black
      pepper
  ½ of a 16-ounce package
      frozen cooked
      Italian-style
      meatballs
  ½ cup shredded
      mozzarella cheese
      (2 ounces)

1 Preheat oven to 350°F. Cook pasta according to package directions; drain. Meanwhile, in a large saucepan combine tomatoes, tomato sauce, wine, soup mix, oregano, and pepper. Stir in meatballs. Bring to boiling over medium heat. Stir in cooked pasta.

2 Transfer mixture to an ungreased 1½-quart casserole. Bake, covered, about 20 minutes or until heated through. Sprinkle with cheese. Bake, uncovered, about 5 minutes more or until cheese is melted.

nutrition facts per serving: 389 cal., 16 g total fat (7 g sat. fat), 45 mg chol., 1308 mg sodium, 39 g carb., 4 g dietary fiber, 18 g protein.

∗test kitchen tip: If you purchase the longer mafalda pasta, break into 1- to 1½-inch pieces before measuring.

These plump cabbage rolls are nestled on a bed of sauerkraut. Not fond of sauerkraut? Just omit the kraut layer in the bottom of the dish. You can also use ground pork, sausage, or ground lamb in place of the beef.

stuffed cabbage rolls

prep: 50 minutes bake: 40 minutes oven: 350°F
makes: 4 (2-roll) servings dish: 2-quart

8   medium to large cabbage leaves
12   ounces lean ground beef
½   cup chopped onion (1 medium)
1   cup cooked white rice
1   egg, lightly beaten
2   tablespoons snipped fresh parsley
¼   teaspoon salt
1   14-ounce jar sauerkraut, rinsed and well drained
1   8-ounce can tomato sauce
2   tablespoons water
2   tablespoons packed brown sugar
2   teaspoons lemon juice
  Pinch ground allspice or ground cloves

1 Preheat oven to 350°F. Lightly grease a 2-quart rectangular or square baking dish; set aside. Trim veins from cabbage leaves. Immerse leaves, four at a time, into boiling water. Cook for 2 to 3 minutes or just until leaves are limp. Carefully remove leaves with tongs or a slotted spoon; drain well.

2 Meanwhile, for filling, in a large skillet cook ground beef and onion over medium-high heat until meat is brown. Drain off fat. In a medium bowl combine cooked beef mixture, rice, egg, parsley, and salt.

3 Spread sauerkraut over the bottom of the prepared dish.

4 Place about ⅓ cup of the filling in the center of each cabbage leaf; fold in sides. Starting at an unfolded edge, carefully roll up each leaf, making sure folded sides stay tucked in the roll. Arrange cabbage rolls on sauerkraut in baking dish.

5 For sauce, in a small bowl stir together tomato sauce, the water, brown sugar, lemon juice, and allspice; pour sauce over cabbage rolls.

6 Bake, covered, about 40 minutes or until heated through.

nutrition facts per serving: 285 cal., 10 g total fat (4 g sat. fat), 107 mg chol., 1242 mg sodium, 29 g carb., 6 g dietary fiber, 19 g protein.

Even the name of this recipe sounds fun. This is a classic casserole that keeps coming back—all ages love it.

cheeseburger-and-fries
casserole

prep: 15 minutes   bake: 45 minutes   oven: 350°F
makes: 8 to 10 servings   dish: 3-quart

2   pounds lean ground
    beef
1   10.75-ounce can
    condensed golden
    mushroom soup
1   10.75-ounce can
    condensed cheddar
    cheese soup
1   20-ounce package
    frozen french-fried
    crinkle-cut potatoes
    Toppings (chopped
    pickles, chopped
    tomato, ketchup,
    and/or mustard;
    optional)

1 Preheat oven to 350°F. In an extra-large skillet cook ground beef over medium-high heat until cooked through, breaking up meat as it cooks; drain off fat. Transfer meat to an ungreased 3-quart rectangular baking dish. Repeat with remaining ground beef.

2 In a medium bowl combine mushroom and cheese soups; spread over beef. Top with potatoes.

3 Bake, uncovered, for 45 to 55 minutes or until potatoes are golden. If desired, serve with toppings.

nutrition facts per serving: 348 cal., 18 g total fat (6 g sat. fat), 78 mg chol., 654 mg sodium, 24 g carb., 2 g dietary fiber, 24 g protein.

Use a glass pie plate for this family-pleasing casserole so you can keep an eye on the crust to make sure it browns properly.

chili beef pie with biscuit crust

prep: 25 minutes bake: 30 minutes stand: 10 minutes oven: 375°F
makes: 8 servings dish: 9-inch pie plate

1 pound lean ground beef
1 cup chopped onion (1 medium)
½ cup coarsely chopped green sweet pepper (1 small)
1 15-ounce can chili beans in chili gravy, undrained
1 8-ounce can tomato sauce
1 6-ounce can tomato paste
1 tablespoon chili powder
½ teaspoon ground cumin
½ teaspoon bottled hot pepper sauce
1 12-ounce package refrigerated honey butter flaky biscuits (10)
1 8-ounce carton sour cream
2 tablespoons all-purpose flour
2 cups corn chips, coarsely crushed
1 cup shredded cheddar cheese (4 ounces)
Chopped scallions

1 Preheat oven to 375°F. In a large skillet cook ground meat, onion, and sweet pepper over medium heat until meat is brown and onion is tender. Drain off fat. Stir in beans, tomato sauce, tomato paste, chili powder, cumin, and hot pepper sauce. Bring to boiling; reduce heat. Simmer, uncovered, for 5 minutes, stirring frequently.

2 Meanwhile, lightly grease a 9- or 10-inch deep-dish pie plate. For crust, unwrap and separate biscuits. Press biscuits onto the bottom and up the side of the prepared pie plate, extending biscuits about ½ inch above edge. Spoon meat mixture into crust. In a small bowl, combine sour cream and flour; spread over meat mixture. Sprinkle with chips and cheese.

3 Place pie plate on a baking sheet. Bake, uncovered, about 30 minutes or until mixture is heated through and crust is golden. Let stand for 10 minutes before serving. Sprinkle with scallions.

nutrition facts per serving: 501 cal., 27 g total fat (10 g sat. fat), 66 mg chol., 1010 mg sodium, 42 g carb., 5 g dietary fiber, 23 g protein.

Often, making individual portions of an entree is a slow, tedious process. But these personal, potato-filled meat loaves assemble quickly—thanks to ready-to-go ingredients.

meat and potato loaves

prep: 25 minutes bake: 35 minutes oven: 350°F
makes: 4 servings dish: 3-quart

1   egg, beaten
⅓   cup fine dry bread crumbs
¼   cup finely chopped onion
¼   cup beef broth
¼   teaspoon salt
¼   teaspoon ground black pepper
1   pound ground beef
1¼ cups loose-pack frozen shredded hash brown potatoes, thawed
1   cup shredded Mexican cheese blend (4 ounces)
¾   cup purchased chunky salsa

1 Preheat oven to 350°F. In a large bowl combine egg, bread crumbs, onion, broth, salt, and pepper. Add ground beef; mix well. Divide into four portions.

2 In a medium bowl combine potatoes, ½ cup of the cheese, and ¼ cup of the salsa.

3 On a sheet of foil, pat each portion of meat mixture into a 5-inch square. Place one-fourth of the potato mixture down the center of each square, leaving a 1-inch border on each side. Shape meat mixture around potato mixture, pressing to seal. Place loaves, seam sides down, in an ungreased 3-quart rectangular baking dish.

4 Bake, uncovered, about 30 minutes or until done (160°F).* Top with the remaining ½ cup salsa and the remaining ½ cup cheese. Bake for 5 minutes more.

nutrition facts per serving: 612 cal., 45 g total fat (19 g sat. fat), 166 mg chol., 863 mg sodium, 23 g carb., 2 g dietary fiber, 27 g protein.

*test kitchen tip: The internal color of a meat loaf is not a reliable doneness indicator. A beef loaf cooked to 160°F is safe, regardless of color. To measure the doneness of a meat loaf, insert an instant-read thermometer into the center of the meat loaf.

Spoon into this colorful casserole for a full-fledged fiesta baked beneath a tender crust of corn bread. The Fresh Tomato Toss topper makes this pretty enough for a dinner party. Pictured on page 60.

mexicali hamburger casserole

prep: 30 minutes bake: 30 minutes stand: 5 minutes oven: 350°F
makes: 6 servings dish: 2-quart

1½ pounds lean ground beef
1   15-ounce can Mexican-style diced tomatoes, undrained
1   cup frozen whole kernel corn, thawed
½   cup finely shredded Mexican cheese blend
½   cup all-purpose flour
½   cup yellow cornmeal
1   tablespoon sugar
1¼ teaspoons baking powder
½   teaspoon salt
1   egg, beaten
⅔   cup milk
2   tablespoons vegetable oil
2   tablespoons finely shredded Mexican cheese blend
    Fresh Tomato Toss

1 Preheat oven to 350°F. In a 12-inch skillet cook ground beef over medium heat until brown. Drain off fat. Stir in tomatoes and corn; heat through. Transfer to a greased 2-quart baking dish. Sprinkle with ½ cup cheese.

2 For corn bread topping, in a medium bowl combine flour, cornmeal, sugar, baking powder, and salt. Stir in egg, milk, and oil. Evenly spread on beef mixture. Sprinkle with 2 tablespoons cheese. Bake, uncovered, about 30 minutes or until topping is set. Let stand for 5 minutes. Serve topped with Fresh Tomato Toss.

nutrition facts per serving: 506 cal., 27 g total fat (10 g sat. fat), 125 mg chol., 603 mg sodium, 38 g carb., 2 g dietary fiber, 30 g protein.

fresh tomato toss: In a small bowl stir together 1 cup red grape tomatoes, halved; ¼ cup coarsely chopped fresh cilantro; ⅓ cup green olives, halved; and, if desired, ½ cup frozen whole kernel corn, thawed.

Assemble these pizzas in a fun, kid-pleasing way. Place the pizza toppings and pasta mixture in individual casseroles. Shape crusts over the top and bake. Then invert to serve.

pizza in a bowl

prep: 30 minutes bake: 25 minutes stand: 5 minutes oven: 375°F
makes: 6 servings dish: 10-ounce dishes

Nonstick cooking
  spray
2 cups dried rotini
  pasta (6 ounces)
½ of a 3.5-ounce
  package thinly
  sliced pepperoni
1 pound lean ground
  beef
½ cup finely chopped
  onion (1 medium)
1 26-ounce jar tomato
  pasta sauce
2 cups shredded
  mozzarella cheese
  (8 ounces)
1 13.8-ounce can
  refrigerated pizza
  crust
  Grated Parmesan
  cheese (optional)

1 Preheat oven to 375°F. Coat six 10- to 12-ounce individual casseroles with cooking spray; set aside. Cook pasta according to package directions; drain. Meanwhile, cut pepperoni slices into quarters.

2 In a large skillet cook ground beef and onion over medium heat until meat is brown and onion is tender, using a wooden spoon to break up meat as it cooks. Drain off fat. Stir pasta sauce, mozzarella cheese, cooked rotini, and pepperoni into meat mixture in skillet; heat through.

3 Divide pasta mixture evenly among prepared casseroles. Unroll pizza crust and cut into 6 equal pieces. Place one piece over the top of each casserole. Tuck corners of dough inside the edge of the dishes to make rounded tops. Bake for 25 to 30 minutes or until pizza dough is golden brown. Let stand for 5 minutes. Carefully invert each casserole to serve. If desired, sprinkle with grated Parmesan.

nutrition facts per serving: 632 cal., 30 g total fat (12 g sat. fat), 83 mg chol., 1050 mg sodium, 57 g carb., 4 g dietary fiber, 34 g protein.

A mild poblano chile pepper provides a hint of heat in this modern dish. When buying, look for peppers that are firm and dark green.

roast beef tamale casserole

prep: 30 minutes bake: 25 minutes stand: 5 minutes oven: 350°F
makes: 4 to 6 servings dish: 2-quart

1   17-ounce package refrigerated cooked beef roast au jus
1   medium fresh poblano or Anaheim chile pepper, seeded and sliced*
½   cup chopped onion (1 medium)
2   tablespoons butter
2   tablespoons all-purpose flour
1   15-ounce can pinto beans, rinsed and drained
1½ cups 1-inch pieces zucchini and/or yellow summer squash
1   cup grape tomatoes, halved if desired
¾   of a 16-ounce tube refrigerated cooked polenta, cut into ½-inch slices
1   cup shredded Monterey Jack cheese with jalapeño chile peppers (4 ounces)
½   cup sour cream
1   tablespoon snipped fresh cilantro
    Lime wedges

1 Preheat oven to 350°F. Lightly grease a 2-quart square baking dish; set aside. Heat meat with juices according to package directions. Pour juices into a glass measuring cup; add enough water to equal 1 cup. Using two forks, coarsely shred meat.

2 In large skillet cook poblano pepper and onion in hot butter over medium heat until tender. Stir in flour. Gradually stir in the 1 cup meat juices. Cook and stir until thickened and bubbly. Stir in shredded meat, beans, squash, and tomatoes. Transfer mixture to the prepared baking dish. Arrange polenta slices around edges.

3 Bake, uncovered, for 20 minutes. Sprinkle with cheese. Bake, uncovered, for 5 to 10 minutes more or until cheese is melted. Let stand for 5 minutes before serving.

4 Meanwhile, in a small bowl combine sour cream and cilantro. Serve casserole with sour cream mixture and lime wedges.

nutrition facts per serving: 578 cal., 31 g total fat (18 g sat. fat), 125 mg chol., 1155 mg sodium, 40 g carb., 8 g dietary fiber, 41 g protein.

∗test kitchen tip: Because hot chile peppers, such as poblanos and Anaheims, contain volatile oils that can burn skin and eyes, wear kitchen gloves when working with the peppers and avoid direct contact as much as possible. When bare hands touch chile peppers, wash them well with soap and water.

Like things a little spicier? Just add a can of green chile peppers or substitute Monterey Jack cheese with jalapeño chile peppers for the cheddar cheese.

guadalupe beef pie

prep: 30 minutes bake: 30 minutes oven: 375°F
makes: 8 to 10 servings dish: 3-quart

2¼ cups packaged
      biscuit mix
½   cup cold water
1   pound ground beef
1   8-ounce carton sour
      cream
1   cup shredded
      cheddar cheese
      (4 ounces)
⅔   cup mayonnaise
2   tablespoons chopped
      onion
2   medium tomatoes,
      thinly sliced
¾   cup chopped green
      sweet pepper
      (1 medium)
      Pimiento-stuffed
      green olives, halved
      (optional)

1 Preheat oven to 375°F. Grease a 3-quart rectangular baking dish; set aside. For crust, in a medium bowl combine biscuit mix and the cold water, stirring with a fork until biscuit mix is moistened and a soft dough has formed. Press mixture onto the bottom and ½ inch up the sides of the prepared baking dish. Bake, uncovered, about 12 minutes or until lightly browned.

2 Meanwhile, in a large skillet cook ground beef over medium heat until brown. Drain off fat. In a medium bowl combine sour cream, cheese, mayonnaise, and onion.

3 Sprinkle cooked meat over baked crust. Layer tomatoes over meat and sprinkle with sweet pepper. Spread sour cream mixture over ingredients in dish.

4 Bake, uncovered, about 30 minutes or until bubbly around the edges. If desired, top with olives.

nutrition facts per serving: 516 cal., 43 g total fat (15 g sat. fat), 75 mg chol., 653 mg sodium, 26 g carb., 1 g dietary fiber, 17 g protein.

Eggplant, ground beef, sweet pepper, and Italian cheese blend join forces in this delicious dinner-in-a-dish.

eggplant and beef
casserole

prep: 50 minutes   bake: 30 minutes   stand: 10 minutes
oven: 350°F   makes: 8 servings   dish: 3-quart

³/₄   cup milk
1   egg, beaten
³/₄   cup all-purpose flour
¹/₂   teaspoon salt
¹/₄   teaspoon ground
      black pepper
1   1¹/₂-pound eggplant,
      peeled and cut into
      ¹/₂-inch slices
3   tablespoons
      vegetable oil
1   pound lean ground
      beef
1   cup chopped green
      sweet pepper
      (1 large)
³/₄   cup chopped onion
      (1 medium)
1   15-ounce can tomato
      sauce
1   8-ounce can tomato
      sauce
1¹/₂   teaspoons dried
      Italian seasoning,
      crushed
2   cups shredded Italian
      cheese blend
      (8 ounces)

1 Grease a 3-quart rectangular baking dish; set aside. In a small bowl combine milk and egg. In a shallow dish combine flour, salt, and pepper.

2 Dip eggplant slices into egg mixture; coat with flour mixture. In a 12-inch skillet heat oil over medium heat. Add several of the eggplant slices; cook about 4 minutes or until golden brown, turning once. Repeat with the remaining eggplant slices, adding more oil if necessary. Drain on paper towels.

3 Preheat oven to 350°F. In a large skillet cook ground beef, sweet pepper, and onion until meat is cooked through, using a wooden spoon to break up meat as it cooks; drain off fat. Stir tomato sauce and Italian seasoning into meat mixture.

4 Layer half of the eggplant slices in the prepared baking dish, cutting slices to fit. Spread with half of the meat mixture; sprinkle with half of the cheese. Repeat layers.

5 Bake, covered, for 20 minutes. Uncover and bake for 10 to 15 minutes more or until heated through. Let stand for 10 minutes before serving.

nutrition facts per serving: 340 cal., 19 g total fat (7 g sat. fat), 84 mg chol., 796 mg sodium, 23 g carb., 4 g dietary fiber, 22 g protein.

A layer of hearty corn bread crowns this comfort-food classic. The cornmeal mixture uses buttermilk for liquid and baking soda for leavening, a combination that creates a light, airy crumb.

hot tamale pie

prep: 30 minutes bake: 20 minutes oven: 425°F
makes: 6 to 8 servings dish: 2-quart

1½ pounds lean ground beef
1 cup chopped onion (1 large)
1 10.75-ounce can condensed tomato soup
1 8-ounce can tomato sauce
¾ cup frozen whole kernel corn
½ cup chopped pitted black olives
2 tablespoons chili powder
½ teaspoon ground black pepper
¾ cup yellow cornmeal
½ cup all-purpose flour
1 teaspoon baking powder
½ teaspoon baking soda
½ teaspoon salt
1 egg
1 cup buttermilk or sour milk*
2 tablespoons vegetable oil
½ cup shredded cheddar cheese (2 ounces; optional)

1 Preheat oven to 425°F. In a large skillet cook ground beef and onion over medium heat until meat is brown and onion is tender. Drain off fat. Stir in soup, tomato sauce, corn, olives, chili powder, and pepper. Bring just to boiling. Transfer to an ungreased 2-quart square baking dish; set aside.

2 In a medium bowl combine cornmeal, flour, baking powder, baking soda, and salt. In a small bowl whisk together egg, buttermilk, and oil. Add to cornmeal mixture; stir just until batter is smooth. Fold in cheese, if using. Spread over meat mixture in baking dish.

3 Bake, uncovered, for 20 to 25 minutes or until golden.

nutrition facts per serving: 534 cal., 30 g total fat (10 g sat. fat), 119 mg chol., 1138 mg sodium, 40 g carb., 4 g dietary fiber, 27 g protein.

*test kitchen tip: To make 1 cup sour milk, place 1 tablespoon lemon juice or vinegar in a glass measuring cup. Add enough milk to make 1 cup total liquid; stir. Let mixture stand for 5 minutes before using.

Garam masala, an Indian spice blend found in Asian markets, gives this meat and vegetable combo a distinctly sweet and spicy flavor. Another time use curry powder to flavor this dish.

ground lamb, spinach, and cauliflower bake

prep: 25 minutes bake: 20 minutes oven: 350°F
makes: 4 to 6 servings dish: 2-quart

1 pound lean ground lamb or ground beef
1 cup chopped onion (1 large)
½ of a 2-pound head cauliflower, cut into small florets (3 cups)
1 tablespoon garam masala*
½ teaspoon salt
1 10-ounce package frozen chopped spinach, thawed and well drained
1 8-ounce package cream cheese, cut up
   Chopped peanuts (optional)
   Pita bread wedges or naan bread

1 Preheat oven to 350°F. In a large skillet cook ground lamb and onion until meat is browned and onion is tender. Drain off fat. Return meat mixture to skillet; add cauliflower. Cook and stir for 1 minute. Stir in garam masala and salt. Add spinach and cream cheese. Heat and stir just until cream cheese is melted. Spoon into an ungreased 2-quart square baking dish.

2 Bake, covered, for 20 to 25 minutes or until bubbly. If desired, sprinkle with peanuts. Serve with pita bread or naan.

nutrition facts per serving: 746 cal., 48 g total fat (23 g sat. fat), 147 mg chol., 944 mg sodium, 47 g carb., 6 g dietary fiber, 33 g protein.

*test kitchen tip: Garam masala is excellent for flavoring many dishes. Sprinkle some over a squash before roasting or a bowl of pumpkin soup before serving, or onto corn on the cob that has been brushed with oil or butter.

A stuffing mixture creates a bottom layer and topper for this tasty dish. It's a great way to use your summer crop of zucchini.

zucchini-sausage
casserole

prep: 25 minutes   bake: 30 minutes   oven: 350°F
makes: 8 to 10 servings   dish: 3-quart

1   pound bulk pork
    sausage
4   medium zucchini
1   10.75-ounce can
    condensed cream of
    chicken soup
1   8-ounce carton sour
    cream
4   cups chicken-flavor
    stuffing mix
¹⁄₃ cup butter, melted

1 Preheat oven to 350°F. Lightly grease a 3-quart baking dish; set aside. In a 12-inch skillet cook sausage over medium heat until brown. Drain off fat.

2 Meanwhile, halve zucchini lengthwise; cut crosswise into ¼-inch pieces. Add zucchini to sausage in skillet. In a small bowl combine soup and sour cream; stir into sausage mixture. In a large bowl combine stuffing mix and melted butter.

3 Spoon half of the stuffing mixture into the prepared baking dish. Spread sausage mixture over stuffing in dish. Spoon the remaining stuffing mixture evenly over sausage mixture. Bake, covered, about 30 minutes or until heated through.

nutrition facts per serving: 487 cal., 34 g total fat (16 g sat. fat), 70 mg chol., 1128 mg sodium, 28 g carb., 2 g dietary fiber, 14 g protein.

Also known as corn grits, polenta pairs well with sausage. Instant polenta makes this dish even easier to put together.

polenta and sausage pies

prep: 30 minutes   bake: 25 minutes   oven: 350°F
makes: 6 servings   dish: 8-ounce dishes

1	pound hot Italian sausage (casings removed if present)
1½	cups chopped red sweet peppers (2 medium)
1½	cups chopped green sweet peppers (2 medium)
½	cup chopped onion (1 medium)
1	clove garlic, thinly sliced
½	teaspoon dried Italian seasoning, crushed
1	14.5-ounce can stewed tomatoes, drained
¼	teaspoon salt
⅛	teaspoon ground black pepper
2	tablespoons instant polenta
4	cups water
1½	teaspoons salt
1⅓	cups instant polenta
½	cup grated Parmesan cheese (2 ounces)

1 Preheat oven to 350°F. Grease six 8- to 10-ounce ramekins; set aside. For filling, heat a large skillet over medium-high heat. Add sausage; cook about 5 minutes or until brown, using a wooden spoon to break up meat as it cooks. Drain off fat.

2 Add sweet peppers, onion, garlic, and Italian seasoning to sausage in skillet. Reduce heat to medium; cook for 5 minutes more. Stir in tomatoes, ¼ teaspoon salt, and black pepper. Cook for 3 minutes more. Remove skillet from heat. Stir in the 2 tablespoons instant polenta.

3 For polenta mixture, in a medium saucepan bring the water and the 1½ teaspoons salt to boiling. Add the 1⅓ cups instant polenta to boiling water in a thin stream, stirring constantly. Reduce heat to medium; cook and stir polenta about 3 minutes or until medium-soft. Remove from heat. Stir in ⅓ cup of the Parmesan cheese.

4 Divide filling among prepared ramekins. Top filling in each ramekin with about ½ cup of the polenta mixture. Sprinkle with the remaining Parmesan cheese.

5 Bake, uncovered, for 25 minutes or until heated through.

nutrition facts per serving: 345 cal., 13 g total fat (6 g sat. fat), 40 mg chol., 1330 mg sodium, 41 g carb., 3 g dietary fiber, 16 g protein.

make-ahead directions: Prepare casseroles as directed through Step 4. Cover with plastic wrap; overwrap with foil. Freeze for up to 1 month. Thaw casseroles in refrigerator overnight. Bake in 350°F oven about 25 minutes; broil for 1 to 2 minutes. (Or prepare as directed through Step 4. Cover with plastic wrap; store in refrigerator for up to 24 hours. Microwave on 100 percent power [high] about 2 minutes or until hot in center, turning once halfway through cooking, or bake as directed in Step 5.)

Red chili paste and five-spice powder work together to add a sassy kick to this one-dish meal. Five-spice powder, available in most markets, contains cinnamon, cloves, fennel seeds, star anise, and Szechwan peppercorns. Chili paste, found in Asian markets, is made from fermented fava beans, hot red chiles, and garlic.

hot-spiced pork and rice

prep: 45 minutes bake: 1 hour stand: 10 minutes
oven: 375°F makes: 6 servings dish: 3-quart

2 to 2¼ pounds
  boneless pork
  shoulder roast
3 tablespoons
  vegetable oil
2 cups thinly sliced
  carrots (4 medium)
1 cup yellow sweet
  pepper strips
  (1 medium)
1 8-ounce can sliced
  water chestnuts,
  drained
1 cup chopped onion
  (1 large)
1 cup long grain
  white rice
1 14-ounce can
  reduced-sodium
  chicken broth
½ cup water
¼ cup soy sauce
2 tablespoons molasses
2 tablespoons light
  corn syrup
1 to 2 teaspoons red
  chili paste
1 teaspoon five-spice
  powder
⅓ cup sliced
  scallions (3)

1 Preheat oven to 375°F. Trim fat from meat. Cut meat into ¾-inch pieces. In an extra-large skillet heat 2 tablespoons of the oil over medium-high heat. Cook meat, half at a time, in hot oil until brown. Transfer meat to an ungreased 3-quart rectangular baking dish. Stir in carrots, sweet pepper, and water chestnuts.

2 Add the remaining 1 tablespoon oil to skillet. Add onion; cook just until tender. Add rice; cook and stir for 1 minute. Stir in broth, water, soy sauce, molasses, corn syrup, chili paste, and five-spice powder. Cook and stir just until mixture comes to boiling. Carefully add to meat mixture; stir to combine. Cover dish with foil.

3 Bake about 1 hour or until meat and rice are tender. Let stand, covered, for 10 minutes before serving. Stir gently. Sprinkle with scallions.

nutrition facts per serving: 439 cal., 14 g total fat (3 g sat. fat), 91 mg chol., 980 mg sodium, 47 g carb., 3 g dietary fiber, 34 g protein.

A bed of diced potatoes and onions develops a delectable flavor when topped with smoked pork chops and a cheese-flavored soup sauce. This is perfect for nights when you're looking for a quick-to-assemble oven meal.

pork chops with
scalloped potatoes

prep: 20 minutes bake: 40 minutes oven: 350°F
makes: 4 servings dish: 3-quart

1   10.75-ounce can
    condensed cream of
    celery soup
1   cup milk
1/3 cup sliced
    scallions (3)
4   slices American
    cheese (4 ounces),
    torn
1   20-ounce package
    refrigerated diced
    potatoes with
    onions
4   cooked smoked pork
    chops (1½ to
    2 pounds total)
1/8 teaspoon ground
    black pepper
2   tablespoons snipped
    fresh chives

1 Preheat oven to 350°F. In a medium saucepan combine cream of celery soup, milk, and scallions. Heat through over medium heat. Stir in cheese; cook and stir until cheese is melted. Remove from heat.

2 Arrange potatoes in a single layer in an ungreased 3-quart rectangular baking dish. Place pork chops on top of potatoes. Sprinkle chops with pepper. Pour soup mixture evenly over chops and potatoes.

3 Bake, covered, about 40 minutes or until heated through. Sprinkle with chives just before serving.

nutrition facts per serving: 541 cal., 23 g total fat (11 g sat. fat), 123 mg chol., 3226 mg sodium, 39 g carb., 4 g dietary fiber, 43 g protein.

Old-fashioned ham loaves glistening with a rich mahogany-colored glaze make a memorable meal. The flavors are a pleasant mix of sweet, salty and smoky. Adding ground pork to the mix makes the loaves extra moist.

ham balls in
barbecue sauce

prep: 20 minutes   bake: 45 minutes   oven: 350°F
makes: 6 servings   dish: 3-quart

2 eggs, lightly beaten
1½ cups soft bread
   crumbs (2 slices)
½ cup finely chopped
   onion (1 small)
2 tablespoons milk
1 teaspoon dry mustard
¼ teaspoon ground
   black pepper
12 ounces ground
   cooked ham
12 ounces ground pork
   or ground beef
¾ cup packed brown
   sugar
½ cup ketchup
2 tablespoons vinegar
1 teaspoon dry mustard

1 Preheat oven to 350°F. Lightly grease a 3-quart rectangular baking dish; set aside. In a large bowl combine eggs, bread crumbs, onion, milk, 1 teaspoon dry mustard, and pepper. Add ground ham and ground pork; mix well. Shape into 12 balls, using about ⅓ cup of the ham mixture for each ball. Place ham balls in prepared dish.

2 In a small bowl combine brown sugar, ketchup, vinegar, and 1 teaspoon dry mustard. Stir until brown sugar is dissolved. Pour over meatballs.

3 Bake, uncovered, about 45 minutes or until done (160°F).*

nutrition facts per serving: 428 cal., 19 g total fat (7 g sat. fat), 144 mg chol., 1107 mg sodium, 42 g carb., 1 g dietary fiber, 23 g protein.

*test kitchen tip: The internal color of a meatball is not a reliable doneness indicator. A beef or pork meatball cooked to 160°F is safe, regardless of color. To measure the doneness of a meatball, insert an instant-read thermometer into the center of the meatball.

Here, the good old-fashioned pork chop and rice bake gets an update with a new style of cream of mushroom soup—one that's been infused with roasted garlic.

pork chop and rice bake

prep: 25 minutes   bake: 35 minutes   stand: 10 minutes
oven: 375°F   makes: 4 servings   dish: 3-quart

4   bone-in pork rib
    chops, cut ½ inch
    thick (about
    2 pounds total)
1   tablespoon
    vegetable oil
    Ground black pepper
1   small onion,
    thinly sliced and
    separated into rings
1   10.75-ounce can
    condensed cream
    of mushroom with
    roasted garlic soup
¾   cup water
½   cup dry white wine
¾   cup uncooked long
    grain rice
1   4-ounce can (drained
    weight) sliced
    mushrooms,
    drained
1   teaspoon
    Worcestershire
    sauce
¼   teaspoon dried
    thyme, crushed
2   tablespoons snipped
    fresh parsley

1 Preheat oven to 375°F. In a 12-inch skillet cook chops in hot oil until browned, turning to brown all sides. Remove chops from skillet, reserving drippings. Season chops with pepper.

2 In the same skillet cook onion in reserved drippings until tender. In a large bowl combine soup, the water, and wine; stir in rice, mushrooms, Worcestershire sauce, and thyme. Spoon into an ungreased 3-quart rectangular baking dish. Top with browned pork chops and cooked onion.

3 Bake, covered, for 35 to 40 minutes or until rice is done and chops are tender and juices run clear (160°F). Let stand, covered, for 10 minutes before serving. Sprinkle with parsley.

nutrition facts per serving: 602 cal., 22 g total fat (7 g sat. fat), 124 mg chol., 735 mg sodium, 36 g carb., 2 g dietary fiber, 55 g protein.

hearty **meat dishes**

Unlike the traditional cassoulet that simmers for hours, this easier version bakes unattended in the oven for 40 minutes. For a touch of freshness, top with snipped fresh herbs just before serving.

pork and turkey cassoulet

prep: 20 minutes   bake: 40 minutes   oven: 325°F
makes: 5 servings   dish: Dutch oven

Nonstick cooking
  spray
12 ounces lean boneless
  pork, cut into
  ½-inch cubes
1 teaspoon
  vegetable oil
1 cup chopped onion
  (1 large)
1 cup chopped carrots
  (2 medium)
3 cloves garlic, minced
2 15-ounce cans white
  kidney beans
  (cannellini), rinsed
  and drained
4 roma tomatoes,
  chopped
⅔ cup reduced-sodium
  chicken broth
⅔ cup water
2 ounces smoked
  turkey or pork
  sausage, halved
  lengthwise and cut
  into ¼-inch slices
1 teaspoon dried
  thyme, crushed
¼ teaspoon dried
  rosemary, crushed
¼ teaspoon ground
  black pepper
2 tablespoons snipped
  fresh thyme or
  Italian parsley

1 Preheat oven to 325°F. Lightly coat an unheated Dutch oven with nonstick cooking spray. Preheat over medium-high heat. Add pork to Dutch oven; cook and stir until pork is browned. Remove pork from Dutch oven. Reduce heat. Carefully add oil to hot Dutch oven. Add onion, carrots, and garlic; cook until onion is tender. Stir pork, beans, tomatoes, broth, the water, sausage, thyme, rosemary, and pepper into Dutch oven.

2 Bake, covered, for 40 to 45 minutes or until pork and carrots are tender. To serve, spoon into individual casseroles or bowls; sprinkle each serving with thyme.

nutrition facts per serving: 263 cal., 6 g total fat (2 g sat. fat), 48 mg chol., 500 mg sodium, 33 g carb., 10 g dietary fiber, 28 g protein.

This recipe draws upon a classic vintner's trick in which grapes are cooked alongside sausages and coaxed to a jammy deliciousness.

sizzling sausage
and grapes

prep: 30 minutes bake: 50 minutes oven: 350°F
makes: 4 servings dish: 3-quart

1½ pounds seedless red
      grapes, removed
      from stems
1   16-ounce tube
      refrigerated cooked
      polenta, cut into
      ½-inch cubes
1   small red onion, cut
      into thin wedges
1   to 2 tablespoons
      olive oil
1   teaspoon snipped
      fresh rosemary
6   sweet and/or spicy
      Italian sausage
      links (about
      1½ pounds)
1   to 2 tablespoons
      balsamic vinegar

1 Preheat oven to 350°F. In an ungreased 3-quart rectangular baking dish combine grapes, polenta, onion, oil, and rosemary. Toss to coat.

2 Using a fork, prick each sausage in several places. Add sausages to mixture in baking dish, nestling them into the grape mixture.

3 Bake, uncovered, for 50 to 60 minutes or until sausages are cooked through and grapes are slightly shriveled. Drizzle with balsamic vinegar; toss to coat.

nutrition facts per serving: 478 cal., 20 g total fat (8 g sat. fat), 58 mg chol., 1156 mg sodium, 46 g carb., 2 g dietary fiber, 31 g protein.

hearty **meat dishes**

Covering this dish while baking helps the pasta to steam and cook through. It's especially important when using no-boil noodles, which are uncooked before they go into the oven.

smoked sausage lasagna

prep: 25 minutes bake: 50 minutes stand: 20 minutes
oven: 350°F makes: 6 servings dish: 2-quart

Nonstick cooking
  spray
2 cups purchased
  tomato pasta sauce
  (such as tomato-
  basil or roasted
  garlic and onion)
½ cup pitted black
  olives, halved
6 no-boil lasagna
  noodles
½ of a 15-ounce carton
  ricotta cheese
6 ounces smoked or
  regular provolone
  cheese, shredded
  (1½ cups)
¼ cup finely shredded
  Parmesan cheese
8 ounces cooked Italian
  sausage links,
  halved lengthwise
  and sliced*
½ cup chopped bottled
  roasted red sweet
  peppers

1 Preheat oven to 350°F. Lightly coat a 2-quart square baking dish with cooking spray; set aside. In a medium bowl stir together pasta sauce and olives. Spoon ⅓ cup of the sauce mixture into prepared dish. Top with two of the lasagna noodles. In a small bowl stir together ricotta cheese and 1 cup of the provolone cheese. Spoon half of the cheese mixture over the noodles in baking dish. Sprinkle with 2 tablespoons of the Parmesan cheese. Top with half of the sausage and half of the roasted red sweet peppers. Spoon half of the remaining sauce mixture over the sausage layer.

2 Top with two more noodles, the remaining ricotta mixture, the remaining sausage, and the remaining roasted peppers. Top with the remaining two noodles and the remaining sauce mixture. Sprinkle with the remaining ½ cup provolone cheese and the remaining 2 tablespoons Parmesan cheese.

3 Bake, covered, for 50 minutes. Let stand, covered, on a wire rack for 20 minutes before serving.

nutrition facts per serving: 406 cal., 25 g total fat (12 g sat. fat), 62 mg chol., 1150 mg sodium, 21 g carb., 2 g dietary fiber, 23 g protein.

make-ahead directions: Prepare as directed through Step 2. Cover baking dish with plastic wrap. Chill for 2 to 24 hours. Remove plastic wrap and cover with foil. Bake in a 350°F oven for 1¼ hours. Let stand, covered, on a wire rack for 20 minutes before serving.

*test kitchen tip: For another flavorful version, try cooked chicken-apple sausage.

Feel free to get creative with the sausage you choose for this casserole. Any cooked sausage—such as turkey kielbasa, smoked bratwurst, or andouille—will bake beautifully under the casserole's corn bread blanket.

corn bread–topped
sausage bake

prep: 25 minutes bake: 20 minutes oven: 425°F
makes: 6 servings dish: 2-quart

1   8.5-ounce package
      corn muffin mix
1   medium carrot,
      chopped (½ cup)
¼   cup chopped onion
¼   cup chopped green
      sweet pepper
¼   cup chopped celery
2   tablespoons
      vegetable oil
1   11.5-ounce can
      condensed bean
      with bacon soup
¾   cup milk
2   teaspoons yellow
      mustard
1   pound cooked
      smoked Polish
      sausage, sliced
      Shredded cheddar
      cheese (optional)

1 Preheat oven to 425°F. For corn bread, prepare muffin mix according to package directions (do not bake).

2 In a medium saucepan cook carrot, onion, sweet pepper, and celery in hot oil over medium heat until tender. Stir in bean with bacon soup, milk, and mustard; stir in sausage. Cook and stir until bubbly. Transfer mixture to an ungreased 2-quart rectangular baking dish. Pour corn bread batter over hot sausage mixture, spreading evenly.

3 Bake, uncovered, for 20 to 25 minutes or until a toothpick inserted in corn bread comes out clean. If desired, sprinkle each serving with cheese.

nutrition facts per serving: 562 cal., 34 g total fat (11 g sat. fat), 94 mg chol., 1566 mg sodium, 43 g carb., 6 g dietary fiber, 20 g protein.

poultry

plea

4

Economical and versatile, poultry takes beautifully to a wide range of casseroles. Savor pasta-and-sauce dishes, a hearty potpie, sausage medleys, rice bakes, and more.

sers

This old-fashioned pasta, chicken, and veggie dish is perfect for a Sunday dinner. Invite family and friends over to rekindle the tradition.

chicken supreme casserole

prep: 25 minutes bake: 30 minutes stand: 10 minutes oven: 350°F
makes: 6 to 8 servings dish: 3-quart

8   ounces dried rotini pasta
1   16-ounce package frozen stir-fry vegetables (broccoli, carrots, onions, red peppers, celery, water chestnuts, and mushrooms)
2   10.75-ounce cans condensed cream of chicken soup
2   cups milk
¼   cup mayonnaise or salad dressing
¼   teaspoon ground black pepper
2   cups chopped cooked chicken (about 10 ounces)
2   cups cubed French bread (about 3 slices, cut into ½-inch cubes)
2   tablespoons butter or margarine, melted
¼   teaspoon garlic powder
    Ground black pepper

1 Preheat oven to 350°F. Cook pasta according to package directions, except add the stir-fry vegetables for the last 5 minutes of cooking; drain well.

2 Meanwhile, in a large bowl stir together cream of chicken soup, milk, mayonnaise, and pepper. Stir in cooked pasta mixture and chicken.

3 Spoon into an ungreased 3-quart rectangular baking dish. In a medium bowl toss bread cubes with melted butter and garlic powder; sprinkle over pasta mixture.

4 Bake, uncovered, for 30 to 35 minutes or until heated through and bread cubes are golden brown. Let stand for 10 minutes before serving. Sprinkle with pepper.

nutrition facts per serving: 584 cal., 25 g total fat (8 g sat. fat), 71 mg chol., 1123 mg sodium, 60 g carb., 4 g dietary fiber, 28 g protein.

Baking makes classic sweet-and-sour chicken easier to make—and more totable. For a family-size version, serve this with hot cooked rice.

sweet-and-sour
baked chicken

prep: 25 minutes bake: 30 minutes oven: 350°F
makes: 8 servings dish: 3-quart

8 skinless, boneless chicken breast halves (about 2½ pounds)
Salt and ground black pepper
2 tablespoons vegetable oil
1 20-ounce can pineapple chunks (juice pack), undrained
1 cup jellied cranberry sauce
¼ cup cornstarch
¼ cup packed brown sugar
¼ cup rice vinegar* or cider vinegar
¼ cup frozen orange juice concentrate, thawed
¼ cup dry sherry, chicken broth, or water
¼ cup soy sauce
½ teaspoon ground ginger
2 medium green sweet peppers, cut into bite-size strips

1 Preheat oven to 350°F. Sprinkle chicken lightly with salt and black pepper. In a large skillet heat oil over medium-high heat. Add chicken; cook about 4 minutes or until brown, turning once. (If necessary, brown chicken in batches.) Transfer chicken to an ungreased 3-quart rectangular baking dish. Drain pineapple, reserving ⅔ cup juice. Spoon pineapple chunks over chicken.

2 For sauce, in a medium saucepan whisk together the reserved ⅔ cup pineapple juice, cranberry sauce, cornstarch, brown sugar, vinegar, orange juice concentrate, sherry, soy sauce, and ginger. Cook and stir over medium heat until thickened and bubbly. Pour over chicken and pineapple in dish.

3 Bake, covered, for 25 minutes. Add sweet peppers, stirring gently to coat with sauce. Bake, uncovered, about 5 minutes more or until chicken is no longer pink (170°F).

nutrition facts per serving: 354 cal., 5 g total fat (1 g sat. fat), 82 mg chol., 669 mg sodium, 37 g carb., 2 g dietary fiber, 34 g protein.

*test kitchen tip: Rice vinegar, made from fermented rice, tastes a bit milder and less acidic than cider vinegar.

A thick, puffy, crunchy topping makes this dish a delightful blend of crisp and comforting. Puff pastry, found in the grocery store freezer section, makes a super-fast and stunning topping for potpies.

chicken potpie in puff pastry

prep: 30 minutes bake: 20 minutes oven: 425°F
makes: 4 servings dish: 8-ounce dishes

1 **Thaw puff pastry according to package directions.**

2 **Preheat oven to 425°F. In a large skillet melt butter over medium-high heat. Add chicken, sweet pepper (if using), and shallots. Cook for 4 to 5 minutes or until chicken is no longer pink, stirring frequently. Stir in flour, salt, tarragon, and black pepper. Add milk all at once. Cook and stir until thickened and bubbly. Stir in wine. Stir in peas and/or corn; heat through. Keep mixture warm while preparing pastry.**

3 **For pastry, unfold puff pastry sheet. On a lightly floured surface, roll pastry sheet into an 11-inch square. Cut into four equal squares. Transfer the hot chicken mixture to four 8-ounce individual casseroles. Place a pastry square on top of each casserole. Cut slits in the pastry for steam to escape.**

4 **Bake, uncovered, about 20 minutes or until crust is puffed and golden brown.**

- 1 sheet frozen puff pastry (½ of a 17.25-ounce package)
- 2 tablespoons butter
- 12 ounces skinless, boneless chicken breast halves, cut into bite-size pieces
- ¼ cup chopped red sweet pepper (optional)
- 2 medium shallots, thinly sliced
- 2 tablespoons all-purpose flour
- ¾ teaspoon salt
- ½ teaspoon dried tarragon, crushed
- ¼ teaspoon ground black pepper
- 1¼ cups milk
- ⅓ cup dry white wine or chicken broth
- ½ cup frozen peas and/or corn

nutrition facts per serving: 490 cal., 29 g total fat (3 g sat. fat), 50 mg chol., 790 mg sodium, 31 g carb., 1 g dietary fiber, 23 g protein.

Chipotle chile peppers are smoked jalapeño peppers. If you can't find canned chipotle chiles, reconstitute two dried chipotles in very hot water until softened. Drain chiles and remove stems and seeds before chopping.

chipotle-chicken
casserole

prep: 25 minutes bake: 20 minutes oven: 375°F
makes: 4 servings dish: 2-quart

Nonstick cooking spray
2 cups frozen or fresh whole kernel corn
3 cups frozen diced hash brown potatoes
1 14.5-ounce can diced tomatoes with basil, oregano, and garlic, undrained
2 tablespoons chopped canned chipotle chile peppers in adobo sauce
½ teaspoon chili powder
½ teaspoon ground cumin
½ teaspoon dried oregano, crushed
¼ teaspoon salt
1 tablespoon olive oil
4 skinless, boneless chicken breast halves (about 1¼ pounds)
¼ teaspoon salt
¼ teaspoon chili powder
¼ teaspoon ground cumin
¾ cup shredded Colby and Monterey Jack cheese (3 ounces)

1 Preheat oven to 375°F. Coat a 2-quart rectangular baking dish with cooking spray; set aside. Coat a large nonstick skillet with cooking spray; heat skillet over medium-high heat. Add corn; cook about 5 minutes or until corn starts to brown, stirring occasionally. Add potatoes; cook for 5 to 8 minutes or until potatoes start to brown, stirring frequently. Stir in tomatoes, chipotle peppers, ½ teaspoon chili powder, ½ teaspoon cumin, oregano, and ¼ teaspoon salt. Transfer mixture to the prepared baking dish.

2 Wipe skillet clean. Add oil to skillet; heat over medium-high heat. Sprinkle chicken with ¼ teaspoon salt, ¼ teaspoon chili powder, and ¼ teaspoon cumin. Cook chicken in hot oil until brown on both sides. Place chicken on top of potato mixture.

3 Bake, uncovered, for 20 to 25 minutes or until chicken is no longer pink (170°F) and mixture is heated through. Sprinkle with cheese.

nutrition facts per serving: 519 cal., 14 g total fat (6 g sat. fat), 101 mg chol., 1134 mg sodium, 56 g carb., 5 g dietary fiber, 45 g protein.

This is it—a chicken and noodle dish that's so simple and so good, you can't help but fix it time and time again. Even kids will love this!

garlic-parmesan chicken and noodles

oven: 450°F   prep: 30 minutes   bake: 5 minutes
makes: 4 servings   dish: 16-ounce dishes

6   ounces extra-wide
    egg noodles
1   2- to 2¼-pound
    purchased roasted
    chicken
1   cup frozen peas
4   cloves garlic, minced
1¾ cups whole milk or
    light cream
½   slice white or wheat
    bread
¾   cup shredded
    Parmesan cheese
2   tablespoons butter,
    melted
    Snipped fresh thyme
    (optional)

1 Preheat oven to 450°F. In Dutch oven bring 6 cups salted water to boiling; add noodles. Cook for 10 minutes or until tender. Drain.

2 Meanwhile, remove chicken from bones. Discard skin and bones; shred chicken. In a medium saucepan combine chicken, peas, garlic, and milk; heat through. Cover and keep warm.

3 In blender or food processor blend or process bread into coarse crumbs. Transfer to small bowl. Add ¼ cup of the Parmesan cheese and melted butter.

4 Stir noodles and the remaining Parmesan into hot chicken mixture. Heat and stir until bubbly. Divide among four 16-ounce casserole dishes. Top each with some of the bread crumb mixture. Bake about 5 minutes or until top begins to brown. Top with fresh thyme.

nutrition facts per serving: 701 cal., 37 g total fat (16 g sat. fat), 222 mg chol., 1388 mg sodium, 45 g carb., 3 g dietary fiber, 50 g protein.

Adding sweet pepper and spinach to the filling boosts the nutrition in this Tex-Mex layered meal-in-a-dish.

chicken taco casserole

prep: 25 minutes bake: 30 minutes stand: 5 minutes oven: 350°F
makes: 6 servings dish: 2-quart

Nonstick cooking
  spray
12 ounces chicken
  breast strips for
  stir-frying
2 cloves garlic, minced
1 teaspoon chili
  powder
2 teaspoons canola oil
1 medium onion,
  halved and thinly
  sliced
¾ cup chopped red or
  green sweet pepper
  (1 medium)
1 10-ounce package
  frozen chopped
  spinach, thawed
  and squeezed dry
1½ cups purchased salsa
4 6-inch corn tortillas,
  coarsely torn
3 ounces reduced-fat
  Monterey Jack
  cheese, shredded
  (¾ cup)
½ cup cherry tomatoes,
  quartered or
  chopped (optional)
½ of an avocado,
  pitted, peeled, and
  chopped (optional)
  Corn chips, baked
  tortilla chips, or
  broken taco shells
  (optional)

1 Preheat oven to 350°F. Coat an unheated large nonstick skillet with cooking spray. Preheat skillet over medium-high heat. In a medium bowl toss together chicken, garlic, and chili powder. Add to hot skillet. Cook for 4 to 6 minutes or until chicken is no longer pink, stirring frequently. Remove chicken from skillet; set aside.

2 Add canola oil to skillet. Add onion and sweet pepper. Cook over medium heat about 5 minutes or until tender, stirring occasionally. Stir in spinach.

3 Coat a 2-quart square baking dish with cooking spray. Spread about ½ cup of the salsa in the baking dish. Top with half of the tortilla pieces, half of the chicken mixture, and half of the vegetable mixture. Pour half of the remaining salsa over the vegetables and top with half of the cheese. Repeat layers once, except do not top with the remaining cheese.

4 Bake, covered, for 30 to 35 minutes or until heated through. Sprinkle with the remaining cheese. Let stand for 5 minutes before serving. If desired, garnish with cherry tomatoes, chopped avocado, and/or corn chips.

nutrition facts per serving: 196 cal., 6 g total fat (2 g sat. fat), 43 mg chol., 544 mg sodium, 15 g carb., 4 g dietary fiber, 20 g protein.

Chicken breast and chopped broccoli combine with a tangy soup-based cream sauce and tender noodles in this potluck-style dish.

creamy chicken-broccoli bake

prep: 30 minutes bake: 55 minutes oven: 350°F
makes: 12 servings dish: 3-quart

Nonstick cooking
  spray
10 ounces dried medium
  noodles
1½ pounds skinless,
  boneless chicken
  breasts, cut into
  bite-size pieces
3 cups sliced fresh
  mushrooms
1 cup sliced
  scallions (8)
½ cup chopped red
  sweet pepper
  (1 medium)
2 10.75-ounce cans
  condensed cream
  of broccoli soup
2 8-ounce cartons sour
  cream
⅓ cup chicken broth
2 teaspoons dry
  mustard
¼ teaspoon ground
  black pepper
1 16-ounce package
  frozen chopped
  broccoli, thawed
  and drained
½ cup fine dry bread
  crumbs
2 tablespoons butter or
  margarine, melted

1 Preheat oven to 350°F. Coat a 3-quart rectangular baking dish with nonstick cooking spray; set aside.

2 Cook noodles according to package directions; drain. Rinse with cold water; drain again.

3 Meanwhile, coat an unheated large skillet with nonstick cooking spray. Preheat over medium heat. Add chicken to hot skillet. Cook and stir about 3 minutes or until chicken is no longer pink. Transfer chicken to a large bowl.

4 Add mushrooms, scallions, and sweet pepper to skillet. Cook and stir until vegetables are tender. (If necessary, add 1 tablespoon vegetable oil to skillet.)

5 Transfer vegetables to bowl with chicken. Stir in cream of broccoli soup, sour cream, broth, mustard, and black pepper. Gently stir in cooked noodles and broccoli.

6 Spoon chicken mixture into prepared dish. In a small bowl combine bread crumbs and melted butter; sprinkle over chicken mixture. Bake, covered, for 30 minutes. Uncover and bake about 25 minutes more or until heated through.

nutrition facts per serving: 336 cal., 15 g total fat (8 g sat. fat), 79 mg chol., 515 mg sodium, 29 g carb., 3 g dietary fiber, 21 g protein.

This classic favorite—flavored with mushrooms, Parmesan cheese, and sliced almonds—comes together quickly, thanks to the convenience of deli roasted chicken.

chicken tetrazzini

prep: 30 minutes   bake: 15 minutes   oven: 350°F
makes: 6 servings   dish: 2-quart

8 ounces packaged dried spaghetti or linguine

2 cups sliced fresh mushrooms

½ cup sliced scallions (4)

2 tablespoons butter or margarine

¼ cup all-purpose flour

⅛ teaspoon ground black pepper

⅛ teaspoon ground nutmeg

1¼ cups chicken broth

1¼ cups half-and-half, light cream, or milk

2 cups chopped purchased roasted chicken (without skin), chopped cooked chicken, or chopped cooked turkey

2 tablespoons dry sherry or milk

¼ cup grated Parmesan cheese

¼ cup sliced almonds, toasted*

2 tablespoons snipped fresh parsley (optional)

1 Preheat oven to 350°F. Cook spaghetti according to package directions; drain.

2 Meanwhile, in a large saucepan cook mushrooms and scallions in hot butter over medium heat until tender. Stir in flour, pepper, and nutmeg. Add broth and half-and-half all at once. Cook and stir until thickened and bubbly. Stir in chicken, sherry, and half of the Parmesan cheese. Add cooked spaghetti; stir gently to coat.

3 Transfer pasta mixture to an ungreased 2-quart rectangular baking dish. Sprinkle with the remaining Parmesan cheese and the almonds. Bake, uncovered, about 15 minutes or until heated through. If desired, sprinkle with parsley before serving.

nutrition facts per serving: 421 cal., 21 g total fat (9 g sat. fat), 82 mg chol., 630 mg sodium, 38 g carb., 2 g dietary fiber, 21 g protein.

✳test kitchen tip: To toast almonds, spread them in a shallow pan. Bake in a 350°F oven for 5 to 10 minutes or until lightly toasted, shaking the pan once or twice.

chicken and vegetable tetrazzini: Prepare as directed, except add 8 ounces fresh asparagus, trimmed and cut into 1-inch pieces, or 1½ cups small fresh broccoli florets to the pasta water during the last minute of cooking.

This one-dish meal is perfect for a busy weeknight, thanks to the convenience of purchased rotisserie chicken and a super-easy sauce made by combining milk and soft cheese with garlic and herbs.

herbed chicken and orzo

prep: 25 minutes bake: 30 minutes stand: 5 minutes oven: 350°F
makes: 6 servings dish: 3-quart

8   ounces dried orzo
1½   cups green beans,
      trimmed and cut
      into 1-inch pieces
      (8 ounces)
1   2- to 2¼-pound
      purchased roasted
      chicken
2   5.2-ounce containers
      semisoft cheese
      with garlic and
      herbs
½   cup milk
1½   cups shredded
      carrots (3 medium)

1 Preheat oven to 350°F. Grease a 3-quart rectangular baking dish; set aside.

2 Cook pasta according to package directions, adding green beans for the last 3 minutes of cooking; drain. Meanwhile, cut chicken into six pieces.

3 In a large bowl whisk together cheese and milk until combined. Add cooked pasta mixture; stir gently to coat. Stir in carrots. Transfer mixture to the prepared baking dish. Top with chicken.

4 Bake, covered, for 30 to 40 minutes or until heated through. Let stand for 5 minutes before serving.

nutrition facts per serving: 566 cal., 32 g total fat (16 g sat. fat), 147 mg chol., 685 mg sodium, 37 g carb., 3 g dietary fiber, 31 g protein.

This tasty combination of chicken, ham, and Gruyère cheese is rolled up and fried, then baked in a creamy mushroom sauce. It's a beautifully elegant dish that's easy to make and sure to impress.

chicken **cordon bleu**

prep: 30 minutes bake: 40 minutes oven: 350°F
makes: 6 servings dish: 3-quart

2 6-ounce packages uncooked long grain and wild rice mix
3 ounces Gruyère cheese (3×1½× 1-inch block)
6 very thin slices Black Forest or country ham
6 large skinless, boneless chicken breast halves
½ teaspoon salt
¼ teaspoon ground black pepper
⅓ cup all-purpose flour
2 eggs
2 tablespoons water
1½ cups panko (Japanese-style bread crumbs) or soft bread crumbs
¼ cup vegetable oil
2 tablespoons butter
2 cups sliced fresh mushrooms
¼ cup sliced scallions (2)
2 cloves garlic, minced
2 tablespoons all-purpose flour
2 cups half-and-half, light cream, or whole milk
½ cup shredded Gruyère cheese (2 ounces)

1 Preheat oven to 350°F. Prepare rice mixes according to package directions. Evenly spread rice mixes in a 3-quart rectangular baking dish; keep warm.

2 Cut cheese into six 3×½×½-inch logs. Wrap a slice of ham around each log. In the thickest side of each chicken breast half, cut a horizontal slit to, but not through, the other side. Stuff ham-wrapped Gruyère into slit of chicken. Secure with wooden toothpicks. Sprinkle chicken with salt and pepper.

3 In a shallow dish place ⅓ cup flour. In a second dish lightly beat eggs and water. In a third shallow dish place panko. Coat chicken with flour. Dip in egg mixture; coat with panko.

4 In a 12-inch skillet cook half of the coated stuffed chicken in hot oil about 4 minutes or until golden, turning to brown all sides. Remove chicken from skillet. Repeat with the remaining oil and chicken. Remove toothpicks. Place chicken on top of rice.

5 Meanwhile, for sauce, in a medium saucepan melt butter over medium heat. Add mushrooms, scallions, and garlic and cook until tender. Stir in 2 tablespoons flour. Gradually stir in half-and-half. Cook and stir until thickened and bubbly. Stir shredded cheese into sauce until cheese melts. Spoon sauce over chicken. Cover dish with foil.

6 Bake for 40 to 45 minutes or until chicken is no longer pink (170°F).

nutrition facts per serving: 836 cal., 35 g total fat (15 g sat. fat), 243 mg chol., 1518 mg sodium, 66 g carb., 3 g dietary fiber, 63 g protein.

It's a fiesta of flavor in every bite when jumbo shell macaroni combines with chicken and spicy Mexican ingredients in this sure-to-please casserole.

chicken **enchilada** pasta

prep: 40 minutes bake: 35 minutes Cook: 10 minutes oven: 350°F
makes: 8 to 10 servings dish: 3-quart

1   12-ounce package dried jumbo macaroni shells
3   cups chopped green and/or red sweet peppers (3 large)
1½ cups chopped red onions (3 medium)
1   fresh jalapeño chile pepper, seeded and chopped*
¼ teaspoon salt
2   tablespoons vegetable oil
2   cups chopped cooked chicken
1   16-ounce can refried beans
½ of a 1.25-ounce envelope taco seasoning mix (3 tablespoons)
2   10-ounce cans enchilada sauce
1   8-ounce package shredded Mexican cheese blend
1   cup sliced scallions (8)
2   cups nacho cheese–flavored tortilla chips, crushed (2 ounces)
   Sour cream and/or avocado dip

1 Preheat oven to 350°F. Cook pasta according to package directions; drain. Rinse; drain and set aside.

2 In a large skillet cook sweet peppers, onions, chile pepper, and salt in hot oil over medium heat about 5 minutes or until tender. Stir in chicken, beans, taco seasoning mix, and ½ cup of the enchilada sauce. Cook and stir for 5 minutes. Stir in ½ cup each of the cheese and scallions.

3 Divide filling among shells. Spread 1 cup of the remaining enchilada sauce in 3-quart rectangular baking dish. Arrange shells atop sauce. Drizzle with the remaining enchilada sauce.

4 Bake, covered, for 30 minutes. Uncover; sprinkle with the remaining cheese. Bake for 5 minutes more or until cheese is melted. Sprinkle with chips and the remaining scallions. Serve with sour cream and/or avocado dip.

nutrition facts per serving: 520 cal., 20 g total fat (8 g sat. fat), 56 mg chol., 1338 mg sodium, 60 g carb., 6 g dietary fiber, 27 g protein.

*test kitchen tip: See tip on handling chile peppers, page 80.

Flag this recipe as a crowd-pleasing choice for potlucks and casual parties.

creamy chicken
enchiladas

prep: 55 minutes bake: 40 minutes stand: 5 minutes oven: 350°F
makes: 12 servings dish: 3-quart

1 pound skinless, boneless chicken breasts
1 10-ounce package frozen chopped spinach, thawed and well drained
½ cup thinly sliced scallions
2 8-ounce cartons light sour cream
½ cup plain yogurt
¼ cup all-purpose flour
½ teaspoon salt
½ teaspoon ground cumin
1 cup milk
2 4-ounce cans diced green chile peppers, drained
12 7-inch flour tortillas
⅔ cup shredded Monterey Jack or cheddar cheese
Fresh cilantro sprigs (optional)
Salsa and/or thinly sliced scallions (optional)

1 In a large saucepan place chicken in enough water to cover. Bring to boiling; reduce heat. Cover and simmer for 12 to 14 minutes or until chicken is no longer pink (170°F). Drain well. When cool enough to handle, use a fork to shred chicken into bite-size pieces.

2 In a large bowl combine shredded chicken, spinach, and the ½ cup scallions. For sauce, stir together sour cream, yogurt, flour, salt, and cumin. Stir in milk and chile peppers. Divide sauce in half.

3 Preheat oven to 350°F. For filling, combine one portion of the sauce and the chicken-spinach mixture; divide mixture into 12 portions. Place one portion of the filling near one end of a tortilla; roll up into a spiral. Place filled tortilla, seam side down, in an ungreased 3-quart rectangular baking dish. Repeat with the remaining tortillas and the remaining filling.

4 Spoon the remaining sauce over tortillas. Bake, uncovered, about 40 minutes or until heated through. Remove from oven; sprinkle with cheese. Let stand for 5 minutes before serving. If desired, garnish with cilantro sprigs and serve with salsa and/or additional scallions.

nutrition facts per serving: 247 cal., 9 g total fat (4 g sat. fat), 44 mg chol., 395 mg sodium, 23 g carb., 1 g dietary fiber, 18 g protein.

110

At a loss for what to take to the next bring-a-dish gathering? You can't go wrong with a chicken-and-stuffing concoction. Tote this one—and watch it disappear!

buffet chicken scallop

prep: 25 minutes bake: 25 minutes stand: 10 minutes oven: 350°F
makes: 12 servings dish: 3-quart

1 cup chopped onion (1 large)
³/₄ cup chopped green sweet pepper (1 medium)
2 tablespoons butter or margarine
3 cups herb-seasoned stuffing mix
1 cup chicken broth
3 eggs, lightly beaten
1 10.75-ounce can condensed cream of celery soup
4 cups chopped cooked chicken or turkey (about 1¼ pounds)
1½ cups cooked rice*
1 10.75-ounce can condensed cream of chicken soup
½ cup sour cream
¼ cup milk

1 Preheat oven to 350°F. In a large skillet cook onion and sweet pepper in hot butter over medium heat until tender.

2 In large bowl combine stuffing mix and chicken broth; stir in eggs and cream of celery soup. Stir in onion mixture, chicken, and rice. Spread in a lightly greased 3-quart rectangular baking dish.

3 Bake, uncovered, for 25 to 30 minutes or until an instant-read thermometer inserted in the center registers 160°F. Let stand for 10 minutes.

4 Meanwhile, for sauce, in a small saucepan combine cream of chicken soup, sour cream, and milk; heat and stir until smooth and heated through. Serve sauce with baked chicken mixture.

nutrition facts per serving: 286 cal., 12 g total fat (5 g sat. fat), 106 mg chol., 758 mg sodium, 23 g carb., 2 g dietary fiber, 19 g protein.

*test kitchen tip: For 1½ cups cooked rice, in a medium saucepan combine 1 cup water and ½ cup uncooked long grain rice. Bring to boiling; reduce heat. Simmer, covered, for 15 to 18 minutes or until rice is tender.

Individual lasagna rolls make this dish both fun and easy to eat—no messy cutting. Just add crusty Italian bread or breadsticks and you have a meal.

chicken lasagna rolls with chive-cream sauce

prep: 40 minutes bake: 35 minutes oven: 350°F
makes: 6 servings dish: 3-quart

6   dried lasagna noodles
1   8-ounce package
       reduced-fat cream
       cheese (Neufchâtel),
       softened
½   cup milk
¼   cup grated Romano
       or Parmesan cheese
1   tablespoon snipped
       fresh chives
1½ cups chopped cooked
       chicken
½   of a 10-ounce package
       frozen chopped
       broccoli, thawed
       and drained (1 cup)
½   cup bottled roasted
       sweet red peppers,
       drained and sliced
⅛   teaspoon ground
       black pepper
1   cup marinara pasta
       sauce

1 Preheat oven to 350°F. Cook lasagna noodles according to package directions. Drain noodles, rinsing with cold water. Cut each noodle in half crosswise; set aside.

2 For white sauce, in a medium mixing bowl beat cream cheese with an electric mixer on medium speed for 30 seconds. Slowly add milk, beating until smooth. Stir in Romano cheese and chives.

3 For filling, in a medium bowl stir together ½ cup of the white sauce, the chicken, broccoli, roasted sweet red peppers, and black pepper. Place about ¼ cup of the filling at an end of each cooked noodle and roll. Arrange rolls, seam sides down, in an ungreased 3-quart rectangular baking dish.

4 Spoon the marinara sauce over the rolls. Spoon the remaining white sauce over marinara sauce. Cover with foil. Bake for 35 to 40 minutes or until heated through.

nutrition facts per serving: 288 cal., 13 g total fat (7 g sat. fat), 65 mg chol., 412 mg sodium, 22 g carb., 2 g dietary fiber, 19 g protein.

chicken pasta casserole

prep: 30 minutes bake: 35 minutes oven: 350°F
makes: 5 or 6 servings dish: 2-quart

8   ounces dried bow-tie
     pasta
2   tablespoons olive oil
6   cloves garlic, minced
1   pound skinless,
     boneless chicken
     breast halves, cut
     into 1-inch pieces
1   teaspoon dried basil,
     crushed
½   teaspoon salt
¼   teaspoon ground
     black pepper
1   medium onion,
     chopped
½   cup chopped red
     sweet pepper
     (1 small)
1   cup frozen cut
     asparagus
1   8-ounce tub cream
     cheese spread with
     chive and onion
¾   cup half-and-half,
     light cream, or milk
½   cup panko (Japanese-
     style bread crumbs)
     or soft bread
     crumbs
¼   cup sliced almonds
1   tablespoon butter,
     melted

1 Preheat oven to 350°F. Cook pasta according to package directions; drain. Return pasta to pan.

2 Meanwhile, in a large skillet heat oil; add garlic and cook for 30 seconds. Season chicken with basil, salt, and pepper. Add chicken to the skillet; cook about 3 minutes or until no pink remains. Remove from skillet. Add onion and sweet pepper to skillet; cook until tender. Stir in cooked chicken and asparagus. Remove from heat and set aside.

3 Stir cheese into pasta until melted. Stir in chicken mixture and half-and-half. Transfer to a 2-quart rectangular baking dish. In a small bowl combine bread crumbs, almonds, and butter; sprinkle over casserole.

4 Bake, uncovered, about 35 minutes or until heated through.

nutrition facts per serving: 615 cal., 31 g total fat (16 g sat. fat), 116 mg chol., 531 mg sodium, 48 g carb., 4 g dietary fiber, 33 g protein.

Meaty chicken thighs, rice-shape orzo pasta, lemon, and kalamata olives make a delectable combination.

kalamata-lemon chicken

prep: 10 minutes bake: 35 minutes oven: 400°F
makes: 4 servings dish: 2-quart

1 tablespoon olive oil
1 to 1¼ pounds skinless, boneless chicken thighs
1 14-ounce can chicken broth
⅔ cup dried orzo
½ cup drained pitted kalamata olives
½ of a lemon, cut into wedges or chunks
1 tablespoon lemon juice
1 teaspoon dried Greek seasoning or dried oregano, crushed
¼ teaspoon salt
¼ teaspoon ground black pepper
Hot chicken broth (optional)
Fresh snipped oregano (optional)

1 Preheat oven to 400°F. In a 4-quart Dutch oven heat oil over medium-high heat. Add chicken; cook about 5 minutes or until brown, turning once. Stir in broth, orzo, olives, lemon wedges, lemon juice, Greek seasoning, salt, and pepper. Transfer mixture to a 2-quart rectangular baking dish.

2 Bake, covered, about 35 minutes or until chicken is tender and no longer pink (180°F). If desired, serve in shallow bowls with hot chicken broth and top with fresh oregano.

nutrition facts per serving: 304 cal., 10 g total fat (2 g sat. fat), 95 mg chol., 830 mg sodium, 25 g carb., 2 g dietary fiber, 27 g protein.

This hearty dish calls for fresh oregano. You may substitute
2 tablespoons of dried oregano leaves. Because the oils in dried
herbs are more concentrated, you need less.

chicken, spinach, and rice casserole

prep: 15 minutes bake: 1 hour 15 minutes oven: 375°F
makes: 6 servings dish: 3-quart

Nonstick cooking
   spray
1 10-ounce package
   frozen chopped
   spinach, thawed
   and well drained
½ of an 8-ounce tub
   cream cheese
   spread with chives
   and onion
1 10.75-ounce can
   condensed cream of
   chicken soup
1 cup milk
¼ cup snipped fresh
   oregano
¼ cup grated Parmesan
   cheese
2 cloves garlic, minced
¼ teaspoon crushed red
   pepper
1 cup long grain rice
6 small bone-in chicken
   breast halves,
   skinned
Salt and ground black
   pepper

1 Preheat oven to 375°F. Lightly coat a 3-quart rectangular baking dish with cooking spray. In a medium bowl combine spinach and cream cheese; spread in bottom of prepared dish.

2 In a medium mixing bowl combine soup, milk, 3 tablespoons of the oregano, 3 tablespoons of the cheese, the garlic, and crushed red pepper; reserve ½ cup of mixture. Stir rice into the remaining soup mixture and spoon over the spinach. Place chicken, bone sides down, in dish. Sprinkle chicken with salt and pepper. Spoon reserved soup mixture over chicken.

3 Bake, covered, for 1¼ hours or until rice is tender and chicken is no longer pink. Sprinkle with the remaining oregano and the remaining cheese before serving.

nutrition facts per serving: 470 cal., 13 g total fat (6 g sat. fat), 137 mg chol., 743 mg sodium, 33 g carb., 2 g dietary fiber, 51 g protein.

This warm and homey potpie-style dish takes a clever shortcut with the help of refrigerated breadsticks that form the topping.

chicken with **breadstick twists**

prep: 20 minutes bake: 18 minutes oven: 400°F
makes: 4 servings dish: 16-ounce dishes

¹/₂ cup all-purpose flour
¹/₂ teaspoon ground sage
¹/₄ teaspoon salt
¹/₄ teaspoon ground black pepper
12 ounces skinless, boneless chicken breast halves
2 tablespoons vegetable oil
2 cups frozen mixed vegetables
1 14-ounce can reduced-sodium chicken broth
¹/₂ cup milk
1 11-ounce package refrigerated breadsticks (12)
¹/₂ cup shredded Mexican cheese blend (2 ounces)

1 Preheat oven to 400°F. In a large resealable plastic bag combine flour, sage, salt, and pepper. Cut chicken into bite-size pieces. Add chicken to bag; seal bag and shake to coat.

2 In a large skillet heat oil over medium-high heat. Add chicken to hot oil; sprinkle any remaining flour mixture over chicken. Cook chicken for 2 minutes (chicken will not be completely cooked), stirring to brown evenly. Place vegetables in a sieve or colander. Run cold water over vegetables to thaw. Add vegetables, broth, and milk to chicken in skillet. Bring to boiling, stirring once. Open package of breadsticks and separate into 12 pieces.

3 Divide chicken mixture among four 16-ounce au gratin dishes or individual casseroles. Arrange three breadsticks across the top of each dish. Sprinkle with cheese. Bake about 18 minutes or until breadstick twists are browned and the filling is bubbly.

nutrition facts per serving: 544 cal., 17 g total fat (7 g sat. fat), 64 mg chol., 1138 mg sodium, 61 g carb., 4 g dietary fiber, 35 g protein.

This simple yet sophisticated main dish is a unique combo of rice-like orzo pasta, chicken, veggies, and a mustard-caper sauce. Pine nuts sprinkled on top add another flavorful bite.

mediterranean-style chicken

prep: 30 minutes bake: 35 minutes oven: 350°F
makes: 6 to 8 servings dish: 3-quart

8 ounces dried orzo (1 cup)

1 2- to 2¼-pound purchased roasted chicken

2 tablespoons butter or margarine

2 tablespoons all-purpose flour

1 14-ounce can chicken broth

2 tablespoons capers, drained

2 tablespoons snipped fresh dill

1 tablespoon Dijon-style mustard

1 teaspoon finely shredded lemon zest

1 tablespoon lemon juice

½ teaspoon salt

¼ teaspoon ground black pepper

2 cups baby pattypan squash, halved, or 1 medium yellow summer squash, halved lengthwise and sliced (1¼ cups)

1 medium red sweet pepper, cut into bite-size strips (1 cup)

½ of a small red onion, thinly sliced

¼ cup pine nuts, toasted*
Fresh dill

1 Preheat oven to 350°F. Cook orzo according to package directions; drain. Meanwhile, remove chicken from bones, discarding skin and bones. Using two forks, coarsely shred chicken.

2 In a medium saucepan melt butter over medium heat. Stir in flour. Gradually stir in broth. Cook and stir until mixture is thickened and bubbly. Stir in capers, 2 tablespoons dill, mustard, lemon zest, lemon juice, salt, and pepper.

3 Stir shredded chicken, squash, sweet pepper, onion, and pasta into pan; combine well. Transfer mixture to an ungreased 3-quart baking dish.

4 Bake, covered, about 35 minutes or until heated through. Sprinkle with pine nuts and garnish with additional fresh dill.

nutrition facts per serving: 598 cal., 33 g total fat (11 g sat. fat), 178 mg chol., 1724 mg sodium, 37 g carb., 3 g dietary fiber, 42 g protein.

*test kitchen tip: To toast pine nuts, spread them in a shallow pan. Bake in a 350°F oven for 5 to 10 minutes or until lightly toasted, shaking the pan once or twice.

When a recipe calls for cooked or leftover chicken and you don't have any, buy a rotisserie bird at your local supermarket and remove the meat from the bones. Freeze extra chicken for future use.

hot and cheesy
chicken casserole

prep: 25 minutes   bake: 40 minutes   oven: 350°F
makes: 8 to 10 servings   dish: 3-quart

3   cups chopped cooked chicken
1   14-ounce package frozen broccoli florets
2   cups cooked white rice*
1½   cups frozen peas
1   10.75-ounce can condensed cream of chicken soup
1   10.75-ounce can condensed nacho cheese soup
1   10-ounce can diced tomatoes and green chile peppers, undrained
½   cup milk
½   teaspoon crushed red pepper (optional)
½   cup shredded cheddar cheese (2 ounces)
½   cup shredded mozzarella cheese (2 ounces)
1   cup crushed rich round crackers

1 Preheat oven to 350°F. Place chicken in the bottom of an ungreased 3-quart rectangular baking dish. In a large bowl combine broccoli, cooked rice, and peas. Spread mixture over chicken.

2 In a medium bowl combine chicken soup, cheese soup, tomatoes, milk, and crushed red peppers (if using). Stir in ¼ cup of the cheddar cheese and ¼ cup of the mozzarella cheese. Pour soup mixture over broccoli mixture. Sprinkle with crackers, the remaining ¼ cup cheddar cheese, and the remaining ¼ cup mozzarella cheese.

3 Bake, uncovered, for 40 to 50 minutes or until heated through.

nutrition facts per serving: 354 cal., 15 g total fat (6 g sat. fat), 65 mg chol., 886 mg sodium, 29 g carb., 4 g dietary fiber, 26 g protein.

*test kitchen tip: To prepare 2 cups cooked rice, in a medium saucepan combine 1⅓ cups water and ⅔ cup uncooked long grain white rice. Bring to boiling; reduce heat. Simmer, covered, for 15 to 18 minutes or until rice is tender.

The robust tomato sauce tastes just as good when tossed with spaghetti as it does in this classic baked pasta.

turkey manicotti

prep: 30 minutes   cook: 30 minutes   bake: 25 minutes   stand: 10 minutes
oven: 350°F   makes: 6 servings   dish: 3-quart

12	dried manicotti shells*
½	cup chopped onion (1 medium)
4	cloves garlic, minced
2	tablespoons olive oil
2	14.5-ounce cans fire-roasted diced tomatoes, undrained
⅓	cup dry red wine
2	tablespoons tomato paste
2	cups chopped cooked turkey (12 ounces)
1	cup shredded mozzarella cheese (4 ounces)
½	of a 15-ounce carton ricotta cheese (¾ cup)
½	of an 8-ounce tub cream cheese spread with chive and onion
¼	cup grated Parmesan cheese
1	teaspoon dried basil, crushed
½	teaspoon dried oregano, crushed
¼	teaspoon salt
¼	teaspoon ground black pepper

1 Cook manicotti according to package directions; drain. Rinse with cold water; drain again. Meanwhile, for sauce, in a medium saucepan cook onion and garlic in hot oil over medium-high heat until onion is tender. Stir in tomatoes, wine, and tomato paste. Bring to boiling; reduce heat. Cover and simmer for 30 minutes.

2 Preheat oven to 350°F. For filling, in a large bowl combine turkey, ½ cup of the mozzarella cheese, the ricotta, cream cheese spread, Parmesan cheese, basil, oregano, salt, and pepper. Using a small spoon, carefully fill each manicotti shell with about ¼ cup filling. Arrange filled shells in a 3-quart rectangular baking dish. Pour sauce over shells. Sprinkle with the remaining ½ cup mozzarella cheese. Cover dish with foil.

3 Bake for 25 to 30 minutes or until heated through. Let stand, covered, for 10 minutes before serving.

nutrition facts per serving: 503 cal., 22 g total fat (11 g sat. fat), 83 mg chol., 777 mg sodium, 42 g carb., 2 g dietary fiber, 30 g protein.

*test kitchen tip: Cook a few extra manicotti shells to allow for any that break.

Take lasagna to Cajun country with the addition of spicy andouille sausage.

andouille-chicken
lasagna

prep: 45 minutes bake: 1 hour stand: 15 minutes
oven: 350°F makes: 12 servings dish: 3-quart

16 dried lasagna noodles
1 pound cooked andouille sausage or smoked pork sausage, quartered lengthwise and sliced
1 pound skinless, boneless chicken breast halves, cut into ¾-inch pieces
2 to 3 teaspoons Cajun seasoning
1 teaspoon dried sage, crushed
½ cup chopped onion (1 medium)
½ cup chopped celery (1 stalk)
½ cup chopped red and/or green sweet pepper
6 cloves garlic, minced
2 10-ounce containers refrigerated Alfredo pasta sauce
½ cup grated Parmesan cheese
  Nonstick cooking spray
1½ cups shredded mozzarella cheese (6 ounces)

1 Preheat oven to 350°F. Cook lasagna noodles according to package directions. Drain noodles; rinse with cold water. Drain well.

2 Meanwhile, in a large bowl combine sausage, chicken, Cajun seasoning, and sage. In a large skillet cook and stir chicken mixture about 8 minutes or until chicken is no longer pink. Using a slotted spoon, remove chicken mixture from skillet, reserving drippings in skillet. In the same skillet cook onion, celery, sweet pepper, and garlic in reserved drippings until vegetables are tender. Return chicken mixture to skillet; stir in half of the Alfredo sauce and the Parmesan cheese.

3 Lightly coat a 3-quart rectangular baking dish with cooking spray. Place one-fourth of the noodles in the bottom of the dish, cutting as necessary to fit. Spread with one-third of the chicken-vegetable mixture. Sprinkle with one-third of the mozzarella cheese. Repeat layers twice; top with the remaining noodles. Carefully spread the remaining Alfredo sauce over the top.

4 Bake, covered, about 1 hour or until heated through. Let stand for 15 to 20 minutes before serving.

nutrition facts per serving: 507 cal., 31 g total fat (7 g sat. fat), 83 mg chol., 938 mg sodium, 27 g carb., 1 g dietary fiber, 29 g protein.

Refrigerated pasta sauce trades places with soup as a rich, no-fuss base for this homey dish, while leftover cubed chicken—roasted or fried—keeps the whole dish simple.

chicken alfredo and rice casserole

prep: 25 minutes bake: 50 minutes oven: 350°F
makes: 4 servings dish: 1½-quart

1 10-ounce container
  refrigerated light
  Alfredo pasta sauce
½ cup milk
2½ cups cooked white
  rice or wild rice
2 cups cubed cooked
  chicken
1 cup frozen peas
⅓ cup chopped bottled
  roasted red sweet
  peppers
¼ cup slivered almonds,
  toasted (optional)
1 tablespoon snipped
  fresh basil or
  ½ teaspoon dried
  basil, crushed
1 cup soft bread
  crumbs
1 tablespoon butter,
  melted

1 Preheat oven to 350°F. In large bowl combine pasta sauce and milk. Stir in rice, chicken, peas, sweet peppers, almonds (if using), and basil. Transfer to an ungreased 1½-quart baking dish.

2 Bake, covered, for 30 minutes. Uncover and stir. Combine bread crumbs and melted butter; sprinkle over top. Bake, uncovered, for 20 to 25 minutes more or until heated through and crumbs are golden brown. Let stand for 5 minutes before serving.

nutrition facts per serving: 456 cal., 16 g total fat (8 g sat. fat), 97 mg chol., 672 mg sodium, 45 g carb., 3 g dietary fiber, 32 g protein.

Tender chicken, a ricotta-and-rice stuffing, and a roasted red pepper sauce create an outstanding dish.

wild rice–stuffed
chicken with red pepper sauce

123

prep: 35 minutes   bake: 30 minutes   oven: 350°F
makes: 6 servings   dish: 3-quart

1 cup hot cooked
   wild rice
1 cup ricotta cheese
1/3 cup finely shredded
   Parmesan cheese
12 cloves garlic, minced
1 teaspoon snipped
   fresh rosemary or
   1/2 teaspoon dried
   rosemary, crushed
1/2 teaspoon snipped
   fresh parsley
   (optional)
   Salt and ground black
   pepper
6 skinless, boneless
   chicken breast
   halves (about
   2 pounds)
2 tablespoons butter
1 recipe Red Pepper
   Sauce

1 Preheat oven to 350°F. In a medium bowl stir together wild rice, ricotta cheese, Parmesan cheese, garlic, rosemary, and parsley. Season to taste with salt and pepper; set aside.

2 Place each chicken breast half, boned side down, between two pieces of plastic wrap. Using the flat side of a meat mallet and working from the center out, pound each half lightly into a rectangle about 1/8 inch thick. Remove plastic wrap. Spoon about 1/3 cup of the stuffing into the center of each chicken breast piece. Fold in bottom and sides; roll up each piece into a spiral, pressing edges to seal. Secure with wooden toothpicks.

3 In a medium skillet melt butter over medium heat. Add chicken, half at a time; cook until browned, turning to brown evenly. Transfer chicken to an ungreased 3-quart rectangular baking dish. Set the skillet aside for sauce.

4 Bake chicken, uncovered, for 30 to 35 minutes or until chicken is no longer pink. Remove toothpicks.

5 To serve, cut each chicken roll into slices. Spoon Red Pepper Sauce over chicken.

nutrition facts per serving: 483 cal., 27 g total fat (16 g sat. fat), 177 mg chol., 488 mg sodium, 14 g carb., 2 g dietary fiber, 44 g protein.

red pepper sauce: In the reserved skillet combine 1/4 cup chicken broth and 2 tablespoons dry white wine or chicken broth. Cook over medium heat about 2 minutes or until reduced by half, stirring to loosen browned bits. Stir in 2 tablespoons chopped scallion, 1 tablespoon minced shallot or scallion, 1 1/2 teaspoons snipped fresh parsley, and 1 clove garlic, minced. Cook for 1 minute. Stir in 1 cup whipping cream. Bring to boiling; reduce heat to medium. Cook for 3 to 4 minutes or until slightly thickened, stirring occasionally. Stir in one 12-ounce jar roasted red sweet peppers, drained and cut into strips, and 4 teaspoons snipped fresh chives.

Frozen spinach holds a lot of liquid. To make sure that it is adequately drained, use the heel of your hand to firmly press spinach against the side of a colander until all liquid is released.

florentine chicken
pasta bake

prep: 30 minutes   bake: 30 minutes   oven: 350°F
makes: 6 to 8 servings   dish: 3-quart

3½   cups dried bow tie or
     rotini pasta
     (8 ounces)
½   cup chopped onion
     (1 small)
2   tablespoons butter
2   eggs
1¼   cups milk
1   teaspoon dried Italian
     seasoning, crushed
½   teaspoon salt
¼   teaspoon ground
     black pepper
¼   to ½ teaspoon
     crushed red pepper
     (optional)
2   cups chopped cooked
     chicken
2   cups shredded
     Monterey Jack
     cheese (8 ounces)
1   14-ounce can
     artichoke hearts,
     drained and
     quartered
1   10-ounce package
     frozen chopped
     spinach, thawed
     and well drained
½   cup oil-packed dried
     tomatoes, drained
     and chopped
¼   cup grated Parmesan
     cheese
½   cup soft bread crumbs
½   teaspoon paprika

1 Preheat oven to 350°F. Cook pasta according to package directions. Drain. Meanwhile, in a medium skillet cook onion in 1 tablespoon of the butter over medium heat about 5 minutes or until tender. Remove from heat.

2 In very large bowl whisk together eggs, milk, Italian seasoning, salt, black pepper, and crushed red pepper. Stir in cooked pasta, cooked onion mixture, chicken, Monterey Jack cheese, artichoke hearts, spinach, tomatoes, half of the Parmesan cheese. Transfer mixture to a 3-quart rectangular baking dish.

3 Bake, covered, for 20 minutes. Meanwhile, in a small saucepan melt the remaining butter; remove from heat. Stir in the remaining Parmesan cheese, bread crumbs, and paprika. Sprinkle crumb mixture over pasta. Bake, uncovered, about 10 minutes more or until heated through.

nutrition facts per serving: 531 cal., 24 g total fat (13 g sat. fat), 163 mg chol., 897 mg sodium, 41 g carb., 5 g dietary fiber, 36 g protein.

A corn bread topping rises to any occasion, especially when spooned on top of individual chili casseroles.

turkey chili corn bread casseroles

prep: 35 minutes   bake: 25 minutes   oven: 375°F
makes: 8 servings   dish: 16-ounce dishes

1 tablespoon vegetable oil
1½ pounds ground turkey
2 cups coarsely chopped onions (2 large)
2½ tablespoons chili powder
6 cloves garlic, minced
1 28-ounce can crushed tomatoes, undrained
1 10-ounce package frozen corn
1 15.5-ounce can black beans, rinsed and drained
1 cup yellow cornmeal
1 cup all-purpose flour
2 tablespoons sugar
2 teaspoons baking powder
1 teaspoon coarse salt
¼ teaspoon baking soda
1 cup buttermilk
2 eggs
6 tablespoons butter, melted and cooled
½ cup chopped scallions (green part only)

1 Preheat oven to 375°F. Lightly grease eight 16-ounce ramekins or individual casseroles.

2 In a 5-quart Dutch oven heat oil over medium-high heat. Add turkey; cook until brown, using a wooden spoon to break up meat as it cooks. Using a wooden spoon, transfer cooked turkey to a medium bowl, reserving drippings. Add onions to reserved drippings in Dutch oven; cook and stir about 2 minutes or until softened. Add chili powder and garlic; cook and stir for 1 minute more. Add cooked turkey, tomatoes, and corn; simmer for 10 minutes, stirring occasionally. Remove from heat. Stir in beans. Season to taste with salt and pepper.

3 In a medium bowl combine cornmeal, flour, sugar, baking powder, the 1 teaspoon coarse salt, and the baking soda. In a small bowl whisk together buttermilk, eggs, and butter; stir in scallions. Add buttermilk mixture to cornmeal mixture, stirring just until combined.

4 Spoon about 1 cup of the turkey mixture into each prepared ramekin. Divide cornmeal mixture among ramekins, spreading evenly over tops. Place ramekins on a baking sheet. Place baking sheet in middle of the oven. Bake, uncovered, about 25 minutes or until corn bread is golden brown and turkey mixture is bubbling.

nutrition facts per serving: 570 cal., 24 g total fat (9 g sat. fat), 160 mg chol., 855 mg sodium, 62 g carb., 7 g dietary fiber, 30 g protein.

This creamy casserole is a delicious way to use up leftovers from a roasted turkey or chicken as well as leftover cooked white or wild rice.

artichoke-turkey
casserole

prep: 20 minutes bake: 40 minutes stand: 10 minutes
oven: 350°F makes: 6 servings dish: 2-quart

1 tablespoon butter or margarine

½ cup chopped carrot (1 medium)

½ cup chopped red sweet pepper (1 small)

¼ cup sliced scallions (2)

1 10.75-ounce can condensed cream of chicken soup

1 8- to 9-ounce package frozen artichoke hearts, thawed and cut up

1½ cups chopped cooked turkey or chicken (about 8 ounces)

1 cup cooked white or wild rice

⅔ cup milk

½ cup shredded mozzarella cheese (2 ounces)

2 slices bacon, crisp-cooked, drained, and crumbled

½ teaspoon dried thyme, crushed

3 tablespoons grated Parmesan cheese

1 Preheat oven to 350°F. In a large skillet melt butter over medium heat. Add carrot, sweet pepper, and scallions. Cook until carrot is crisp-tender. Remove skillet from heat. Stir in soup, artichoke hearts, turkey, rice, milk, mozzarella cheese, bacon, and thyme. Transfer to an ungreased 2-quart rectangular baking dish. Sprinkle with Parmesan cheese.

2 Bake, covered, for 20 minutes. Bake, uncovered, about 20 minutes more or until bubbly. Let stand for 10 minutes before serving.

nutrition facts per serving: 248 cal., 11 g total fat (5 g sat. fat), 47 mg chol., 611 mg sodium, 18 g carb., 3 g dietary fiber, 18 g protein.

make-ahead directions: Prepare casserole as directed, but do not bake. Cover casserole with plastic wrap. Refrigerate for up 24 hours. To serve, remove and discard plastic wrap. Cover casserole with foil. Bake, covered, in a 350°F oven for 30 minutes. Uncover and bake about 20 minutes more or until bubbly. Let stand for 10 minutes before serving.

Two cheeses, a packaged rice mix, and cream of chicken soup transform leftover roasted turkey into a rich oven meal.

turkey–wild rice bake

prep: 35 minutes bake: 15 minutes oven: 350°F
makes: 6 servings dish: 3-quart

1   6-ounce package
    long grain and
    wild rice mix
1   tablespoon butter or
    margarine
1   large onion, chopped
3   cloves garlic, minced
1   10.75-ounce can
    condensed cream of
    chicken soup
1   cup milk
1½ teaspoons dried basil,
    crushed
2   cups shredded Swiss
    cheese (8 ounces)
3   cups chopped cooked
    turkey (about
    1 pound)
1   4-ounce jar (drained
    weight) sliced
    mushrooms,
    drained
½   cup shredded
    Parmesan cheese
    (2 ounces)
⅓   cup sliced almonds,
    toasted*

1 Preheat oven to 350°F. Prepare long grain and wild rice mix according to package directions, except discard the seasoning packet.

2 In a 12-inch skillet melt butter over medium heat. Add onion and garlic. Cook until onion is tender. Stir in cream of chicken soup, milk, and basil; heat through. Slowly add Swiss cheese, stirring until cheese is melted. Stir in cooked long grain and wild rice, turkey, and mushrooms. Transfer to an ungreased 3-quart rectangular baking dish.

3 Sprinkle with Parmesan cheese. Bake, uncovered, for 15 to 20 minutes or until heated through. Sprinkle with almonds.

nutrition facts per serving: 700 cal., 36 g total fat (19 g sat. fat), 132 mg chol., 1400 mg sodium, 37 g carb., 4 g dietary fiber, 56 g protein.

*test kitchen tip: To toast almonds, spread them in a shallow pan. Bake in a 350°F oven for 5 to 10 minutes or until lightly toasted, shaking the pan once or twice.

Wild rice is actually a grass, not a true rice. The long, narrow black-brown grains have an intriguing nutty flavor and wonderful chewy texture. Using a box blend of wild and long grain rice helps speed up cooking time.

chicken and wild rice
casserole

prep: 30 minutes   bake: 35 minutes   oven: 350°F
makes: 4 servings   dish: 2-quart

1   6-ounce package long grain and wild rice mix
½   cup chopped onion (1 medium)
½   cup chopped celery (1 stalk)
2   tablespoons butter
1   10.5- or 10.75-ounce can condensed chicken with white and wild rice soup or cream of chicken soup
½   cup sour cream
⅓   cup dry white wine or chicken broth
2   tablespoons snipped fresh basil or ½ teaspoon dried basil, crushed
2   cups shredded cooked chicken or turkey
⅓   cup finely shredded Parmesan cheese

1 Prepare rice mix according to package directions.

2 Meanwhile, preheat oven to 350°F. In a large skillet cook onion and celery in hot butter over medium heat until tender. Stir in soup, sour cream, wine, and basil. Stir in cooked rice and chicken.

3 Transfer mixture to an ungreased 2-quart baking dish. Sprinkle with Parmesan cheese. Bake, uncovered, about 35 minutes or until heated through.

nutrition facts per serving: 479 cal., 20 g total fat (10 g sat. fat), 101 mg chol., 1559 mg sodium, 42 g carb., 2 g dietary fiber, 30 g protein.

Not only is this comforting entrée full of flavor, it's extremely adaptable. Another time, substitute spinach for broccoli or chicken for turkey.

turkey-broccoli casserole

prep: 25 minutes **bake:** 25 minutes **oven:** 350°F
makes: 8 servings **dish:** 3-quart

- 2   10-ounce packages frozen chopped broccoli or chopped spinach
- 2   10.75-ounce cans reduced-fat and reduced-sodium condensed cream of celery soup
- 2   cups water
- ¼   cup butter or margarine
- 6   cups herb-seasoned stuffing mix
- 4   cups chopped cooked turkey or chicken (about 1¼ pounds)
- ⅔   cup milk
- 2   tablespoons grated Parmesan cheese

1 Preheat oven to 350°F. In a Dutch oven or large saucepan combine broccoli, half of the cream of celery soup, the water, and butter. Bring to boiling. Cover and simmer for 5 minutes.

2 Add the stuffing mix to mixture in saucepan; stir to moisten. Spread mixture in an ungreased 3-quart rectangular baking dish; top with turkey. Stir milk into the remaining soup; pour over turkey. Sprinkle with cheese.

3 Bake, uncovered, about 25 minutes or until heated through.

nutrition facts per serving: 375 cal., 12 g total fat (5 g sat. fat), 65 mg chol., 1065 mg sodium, 44 g carb., 5 g dietary fiber, 23 g protein.

Reminiscent of the classic Irish potato dish called colcannon, this version leans toward the lighter side by skipping the traditional cream, butter, and often-used bacon.

turkey sausage casserole

prep: 35 minutes bake: 35 minutes stand: 10 minutes oven: 375°F
makes: 6 servings dish: 2½-quart

1	pound ground turkey
1	pound bulk turkey sausage
3	tablespoons butter
2	tablespoons olive oil
1	cup chopped celery (2 stalks)
½	cup chopped onion (1 medium)
2	tablespoons all-purpose flour
1½	teaspoons herbes de Provence
¼	teaspoon ground black pepper
1	14-ounce can chicken broth
1	5-ounce can evaporated milk
3	cups finely shredded cabbage
⅓	cup sliced scallions (3)
3	cups refrigerated packaged mashed potatoes
1	shallot, cut in thin wedges (optional)
1	tablespoon olive oil (optional)

1 Preheat oven to 375°F. Grease a 2½- to 3-quart oval or rectangular baking dish; set aside.

2 In a 12-inch skillet cook ground turkey and turkey sausage over medium heat until brown, using a wooden spoon to break up meat as it cooks. Remove meat from skillet. In the same skillet combine 1 tablespoon of the butter and 2 tablespoons of the oil; heat over medium heat until butter is melted. Add celery and onion; cook until vegetables are tender. Stir in flour, herbes de Provence, and ⅛ teaspoon of the pepper. Add broth and evaporated milk. Cook and stir until bubbly. Stir in cooked turkey and turkey sausage. Transfer mixture to prepared dish.

3 Meanwhile, in a large skillet heat the remaining 2 tablespoons butter. Add cabbage, scallions, and the remaining ⅛ teaspoon pepper; cook just until cabbage is tender. Add mashed potatoes; heat through. Spoon potato mixture over turkey mixture; spread evenly to cover the turkey mixture.

4 Bake, uncovered, for 35 to 40 minutes or until edges are bubbly. Let stand for 10 minutes before serving. If desired, cook shallot in hot oil over medium heat about 5 minutes or until golden brown. Top casserole with shallots.

nutrition facts per serving: 492 cal., 29 g total fat (12 g sat. fat), 133 mg chol., 1451 mg sodium, 28 g carb., 4 g dietary fiber, 30 g protein.

Here's everything you love about turkey dinner in one easy dish, and you don't have to wait for a holiday to enjoy it. Cranberry sauce is the perfect accompaniment.

turkey and stuffing
bake

prep: 20 minutes cook: 20 minutes bake: 35 minutes stand: 5 minutes
oven: 350°F makes: 8 servings dish: 3-quart

1	cup water
1	cup chopped red sweet pepper (1 large)
½	cup chopped onion (1 medium)
½	cup uncooked long grain rice
1	8-ounce package herb-seasoned stuffing mix
2	cups water
4	cups diced cooked turkey or chicken (about 1¼ pounds)
3	eggs, lightly beaten
1	10.75-ounce can condensed cream of chicken soup
½	cup sour cream
¼	cup milk
2	teaspoons dry sherry (optional)

1 In a medium saucepan bring the 1 cup water to boiling. Stir in sweet pepper, onion, and rice. Reduce heat to low. Cover and simmer about 20 minutes or until rice and vegetables are tender and water is absorbed.

2 Preheat oven to 350°F. In a large bowl combine stuffing mix and the 2 cups water. Stir in turkey, eggs, and half of the soup. Stir in cooked rice mixture. Spread in a greased 3-quart rectangular baking dish.

3 Bake, uncovered, for 35 to 40 minutes or until heated through.

4 Meanwhile, for sauce, in a small saucepan combine the remaining soup, the sour cream, and milk. Cook over low heat until heated through. If desired, stir in sherry.

5 Let casserole stand for 5 minutes before serving. Cut into squares to serve. Spoon sauce over squares.

nutrition facts per serving: 383 cal., 12 g total fat (4 g sat. fat), 142 mg chol., 765 mg sodium, 38 g carb., 3 g dietary fiber, 29 g protein.

If your family enjoys nachos with all the fixings, you'll love this no-fuss casserole.

nacho turkey casserole

prep: 20 minutes   bake: 30 minutes   oven: 350°F
makes: 8 servings   dish: 3-quart

5   cups lightly crushed tortilla chips
4   cups cubed cooked turkey or chicken (about 1¼ pounds)
2   16-ounce jars salsa
1   10-ounce package frozen whole kernel corn
½   cup sour cream
2   tablespoons all-purpose flour
1   cup shredded Monterey Jack cheese with jalapeño chile peppers or mozzarella cheese (4 ounces)
1   fresh jalapeño chile pepper, thinly sliced* (optional)

1 Preheat oven to 350°F. Place 3 cups of the tortilla chips in a greased 3-quart rectangular baking dish. In a large bowl combine turkey, salsa, corn, sour cream, and flour; spoon over tortilla chips.

2 Bake, uncovered, for 25 minutes. Sprinkle with the remaining 2 cups tortilla chips and the cheese. Bake for 5 to 10 minutes more or until heated through. If desired, garnish with fresh jalapeño pepper.

nutrition facts per serving: 444 cal., 17 g total fat (7 g sat. fat), 74 mg chol., 1127 mg sodium, 46 g carb., 4 g dietary fiber, 29 g protein.

*test kitchen tip: Because chile peppers contain oils that can burn your skin and eyes, avoid direct contact with them as much as possible. When working with chile peppers, wear plastic or rubber gloves. If your bare hands do touch the peppers, wash your hands and nails well with soap and water.

Roll lasagna noodles around a cheesy spinach filling and then top them with a ground turkey and tomato sauce.

turkey-spinach
lasagna rolls

prep: 25 minutes bake: 40 minutes stand: 5 minutes oven: 375°F
makes: 8 servings dish: 2-quart

8	dried lasagna noodles
8	ounces ground turkey
2	cups meatless tomato pasta sauce
1	egg, lightly beaten
1	15-ounce carton ricotta cheese
1	10-ounce package frozen chopped spinach, thawed and well drained
1¼	cups shredded mozzarella cheese (5 ounces)
¾	cup grated Parmesan cheese

1 Cook lasagna noodles according to package directions; drain and set aside.

2 Meanwhile, for sauce, in a large skillet cook ground turkey over medium-high heat until no longer pink; drain. Stir in pasta sauce; set aside.

3 For filling, in a medium bowl stir together egg, ricotta cheese, spinach, 1 cup of the mozzarella cheese, and the Parmesan cheese.

4 Preheat oven to 375°F. Place ¾ cup of the sauce in the bottom of an ungreased 2-quart rectangular baking dish. To assemble rolls, spread about ½ cup of the filling over each lasagna noodle. Roll up noodles, starting from a short end. Place lasagna rolls, seam sides down, on top of the sauce. Pour the remaining sauce over lasagna rolls.

5 Bake, covered, about 40 minutes or until rolls are heated through. Remove foil; sprinkle with the remaining ¼ cup mozzarella cheese. Let stand for 5 minutes before serving.

nutrition facts per serving: 376 cal., 18 g total fat (9 g sat. fat), 93 mg chol., 604 mg sodium, 30 g carb., 3 g dietary fiber, 24 g protein.

make-ahead directions: Prepare rolls as directed through Step 4. Cover dish with plastic wrap, then foil, and refrigerate for up to 24 hours. To serve, remove and discard plastic wrap. Bake, covered with foil, in a 375°F oven about 45 minutes or until rolls are heated through. Remove foil; sprinkle with the remaining ¼ cup mozzarella cheese. Let stand for 5 minutes before serving.

5

succulent

Enjoy the taste of the sea in recipes that demonstrate delectable ways to enhance fish, as well as shrimp, lobster, and crab. Casseroles are an easy way to stretch expensive seafood by combining it with other ingredients, such as pasta and rice.

fish

sea

&
food

Bay scallops are small, about the size of a marble. Larger sea scallops may be used in this dish, but they should be cut into smaller pieces.

mediterranean
scallop casserole

prep: 30 minutes bake: 20 minutes oven: 350°F
makes: 4 servings dish: 2-quart

1	pound fresh or frozen bay scallops
½	cup dried orzo
3	cups coarsely chopped peeled (if desired) eggplant (12 ounces)
½	cup chopped onion (1 medium)
½	cup chopped red sweet pepper (1 small)
4	cloves garlic, minced
1	tablespoon olive oil
1	14.5-ounce can diced tomatoes, drained
1	8-ounce can tomato sauce
2	teaspoons dried basil, crushed
¼	teaspoon salt
¼	teaspoon ground black pepper
½	cup fine dry bread crumbs
¼	cup grated Parmesan cheese
2	tablespoons butter, melted
	Fresh marjoram sprigs (optional)

1 Thaw scallops, if frozen. Preheat oven to 350°F. Lightly grease a 2-quart casserole; set aside. Cook orzo according to package directions; drain.

2 Meanwhile, in a large nonstick skillet cook eggplant, onion, sweet pepper, and garlic in hot oil over medium heat for 4 to 5 minutes or until onion is tender. Stir in cooked pasta, tomatoes, tomato sauce, basil, salt, and black pepper. Bring to boiling. Transfer pasta mixture to the prepared casserole.

3 Rinse scallops; pat dry with paper towels. Place scallops on top of pasta mixture. In a small bowl combine bread crumbs and cheese; stir in melted butter. Sprinkle over scallops.

4 Bake, uncovered, for 20 to 25 minutes or until scallops are opaque. If desired, garnish with marjoram.

nutrition facts per serving: 407 cal., 13 g total fat (5 g sat. fat), 58 mg chol., 1241 mg sodium, 44 g carb., 5 g dietary fiber, 28 g protein.

Six cheeses, a splash of sherry, and smoked salmon give this grown-up lasagna its distinctive flavor.

smoked salmon lasagna

prep: 50 minutes bake: 50 minutes stand: 15 minutes
oven: 375°F makes: 12 servings dish: 3-quart

12	dried lasagna noodles
⅓	cup butter or margarine
⅓	cup all-purpose flour
4	cups milk
½	teaspoon salt
½	teaspoon ground black pepper
¼	cup finely shredded Parmesan cheese (1 ounce)
¼	cup shredded Swiss cheese (1 ounce)
2	tablespoons dry sherry
1½	cups finely shredded Pecorino Romano cheese (6 ounces)
1	cup shredded mozzarella cheese (4 ounces)
1	cup shredded provolone cheese (4 ounces)
½	cup shredded cheddar cheese (2 ounces)
3	large roma tomatoes, peeled, seeded, chopped, and drained
1	4-ounce jar (drained weight) sliced mushrooms, drained
8	ounces smoked salmon, flaked, skin and bones removed

1 Preheat oven to 375°F. Lightly grease a 3-quart rectangular baking dish; set aside. Cook noodles according to package directions; drain. Rinse with cold water; drain again.

2 Meanwhile, for sauce, in a medium saucepan heat butter over low heat. Add flour; cook and stir for 4 minutes (be careful not to let flour brown). Gradually whisk in milk, salt, and pepper. Cook and stir until slightly thickened and bubbly. Reduce heat; stir in Parmesan cheese, Swiss cheese, and sherry. Cook and stir until cheeses are melted.

3 In a medium bowl combine Pecorino Romano cheese, mozzarella cheese, provolone cheese, and cheddar cheese.

4 To assemble, sprinkle one-fourth of the cheese mixture over the bottom of the prepared baking dish. Layer with one-third of the noodles, one-third of the sauce, half of the tomatoes, half of the mushrooms, half of the salmon, and another one-fourth of the cheese mixture. Repeat layering noodles, sauce, tomatoes, mushrooms, salmon, and cheese mixture. Top with the remaining noodles, sauce, and cheese mixture.

5 Bake, uncovered, for 50 to 55 minutes or until edges are bubbly and top is lightly browned. Let stand for 15 minutes before serving.

nutrition facts per serving: 352 cal., 17 g total fat (10 g sat. fat), 52 mg chol., 751 mg sodium, 28 g carb., 1 g dietary fiber, 22 g protein.

Choose the type of canned tuna according to your flavor preference. Tuna packed in olive oil is rich. Light tuna packed in water is an all-around, economical favorite.

tuna with cheese biscuits

prep: 20 minutes **bake:** 30 minutes **oven:** 425°F
makes: 4 to 6 servings **dish:** 1½-quart

½ cup chopped onion
(1 medium)
½ cup chopped green
sweet pepper
(1 small)
3 tablespoons butter
1 10.75-ounce can
condensed cream of
chicken soup
1 cup milk
1 9-ounce can tuna,
drained and flaked
2 teaspoons lemon juice
1 7.75-ounce package
cheese-garlic
or three-cheese
complete biscuit mix
Snipped scallions
or fresh chives
(optional)

1 Preheat oven to 425°F. In a large saucepan cook onion and sweet pepper in hot butter over medium heat until tender. Stir in soup and milk. Cook and stir until bubbly. Stir in tuna and lemon juice.

2 Transfer mixture to an ungreased 1½-quart casserole. Bake, uncovered, for 15 minutes.

3 Meanwhile, prepare biscuit mix according to package directions, except do not bake. Drop batter into 10 to 12 mounds on top of hot tuna mixture. Bake, uncovered, for 15 to 20 minutes more or until biscuits are golden and a toothpick inserted in centers of biscuits comes out clean. If desired, sprinkle with scallions.

nutrition facts per serving: 564 cal., 31 g total fat (12 g sat. fat), 46 mg chol., 1470 mg sodium, 45 g carb., 1 g dietary fiber, 26 g protein.

To keep prep time to a minimum, purchase cooked shrimp from your supermarket's seafood counter or deli section.

shrimp, cheese, and wild rice bake

prep: 25 minutes bake: 40 minutes stand: 10 minutes
oven: 375°F makes: 6 servings dish: 3-quart

1 6-ounce package
   long grain and
   wild rice mix
1 cup chopped green
   sweet pepper
   (1 large)
1 cup chopped celery
   (2 stalks)
1 cup chopped onion
   (1 large)
¼ cup butter or
   margarine
1 10.75-ounce can
   condensed cream of
   mushroom soup
1 cup shredded
   cheddar cheese
   (4 ounces)
1 cup shredded Swiss
   cheese (4 ounces)
1 to 1½ pounds
   cooked, peeled, and
   deveined shrimp
¼ teaspoon ground
   black pepper
2 lemons, very thinly
   sliced

1 Preheat oven to 375°F. Prepare rice mix according to package directions. Meanwhile, in a medium saucepan cook and stir sweet pepper, celery, and onion in hot butter about 5 minutes or just until tender.

2 In a very large bowl combine cooked rice, cooked vegetable mixture, cream of mushroom soup, cheddar cheese, and Swiss cheese. Stir in cooked shrimp.

3 Spoon mixture into an ungreased 3-quart rectangular baking dish. Sprinkle with half of the black pepper. Arrange lemon slices over shrimp mixture. Sprinkle with the remaining black pepper.

4 Bake, covered, about 40 minutes or until heated through. Let stand for 10 minutes before serving.

nutrition facts per serving: 488 cal., 26 g total fat (14 g sat. fat), 207 mg chol., 1313 mg sodium, 33 g carb., 2 g dietary fiber, 31 g protein.

A tiny bottle of truffle oil—usually sold for about ten dollars—lasts a long time and is a great way to add the luxurious flavor of truffles affordably. Use truffle oil very sparingly as a liberal pour can very easily overwhelm a dish like this one.

lobster macaroni and cheese

prep: 35 minutes bake: 30 minutes stand: 10 minutes
oven: 350°F makes: 6 to 8 servings dish: 3-quart

12	ounces dried mini bow tie or mini penne pasta
6	slices apple wood–smoked bacon
3	cups sliced fresh cremini mushrooms (8 ounces)
2	medium leeks, sliced (²/₃ cup)
8	ounces cooked lobster meat,* chopped
8	ounces process Gruyère cheese, cut up
1½	cups half-and-half or light cream
1	cup crumbled blue cheese (4 ounces)
1	tablespoon truffle-flavor oil
⅛	teaspoon cayenne pepper
1½	cups coarse soft bread crumbs (2 slices)
1	tablespoon butter or margarine, melted

1 Preheat oven to 350°F. Grease a 3-quart rectangular baking dish; set aside. Cook pasta according to package directions; drain. Return to pan.

2 Meanwhile, in a large skillet cook bacon over medium heat until crisp. Drain bacon on paper towels, reserving 2 tablespoons drippings in skillet. Crumble bacon. Add mushrooms and leeks to the reserved drippings; cook about 5 minutes or until tender.

3 Stir crumbled bacon, mushroom mixture, lobster meat, Gruyère cheese, half-and-half, blue cheese, truffle oil, and cayenne into cooked pasta. Transfer mixture to the prepared baking dish.

4 Bake, covered, for 20 minutes. Stir gently. In a small bowl combine bread crumbs and melted butter; sprinkle over pasta mixture. Bake, uncovered, for 10 to 15 minutes more or until mixture is heated through and crumbs are lightly browned. Let stand for 10 minutes before serving.

nutrition facts per serving: 693 cal., 36 g total fat (19 g sat. fat), 115 mg chol., 996 mg sodium, 56 g carb., 3 g dietary fiber, 34 g protein.

*test kitchen tip: For 8 ounces cooked lobster meat, start with two 8-ounce fresh or frozen lobster tails. Thaw lobster, if frozen. Preheat broiler. Butterfly the lobster tails by cutting through the center of the hard top shells and meat. Spread the tail halves apart. Place lobster tails, meat sides up, on the unheated rack of a broiler pan. Broil 4 inches from the heat for 12 to 14 minutes or until lobster meat is opaque. Remove meat from shells.

Imported from Denmark, creamy Havarti is a mild buttery cheese with an extra-smooth texture and wonderfully enhanced with the bold flavor of dill. It pairs well with smoked salmon.

salmon-dill penne and cheese

prep: 25 minutes **bake:** 30 minutes **oven:** 350°F
makes: 8 servings **dish:** 3-quart

3 cups dried multigrain penne pasta (about 12 ounces)
1¼ cups whole milk
1 pound Havarti cheese with dill, shredded (4 cups)
1 tablespoon all-purpose flour
2 teaspoons finely shredded lemon zest
¼ teaspoon salt
8 ounces smoked salmon, flaked, skin and bones removed
1 cup crushed crisp rye crackers (8)

1 Preheat oven to 350°F. Cook pasta according to package directions for minimum cooking time. Drain and return to pan. Stir in milk. In a medium bowl toss cheese with flour, lemon zest, and salt; stir into pasta mixture. Stir in salmon. Transfer to an ungreased 3-quart rectangular baking dish.

2 Cover and bake for 25 minutes; uncover. Gently stir and sprinkle with crushed crackers. Bake, uncovered, for 5 to 10 minutes more or until heated through.

nutrition facts per serving: 791 cal., 51 g total fat (10 g sat. fat), 160 mg chol., 1181 mg sodium, 43 g carb., 4 g dietary fiber, 43 g protein.

If lobster is not available, try this recipe with another kind of seafood, such as shrimp, scallops, or cod. Remember, the recipe calls for cooked seafood, so precook whatever type you choose to use.

lobster manicotti
with chive cream sauce

prep: 45 minutes **bake:** 30 minutes **oven:** 350°F
makes: 6 servings **dish:** 3-quart

12 dried manicotti
1 tablespoon butter or margarine
1 tablespoon all-purpose flour
1¼ cups milk
1 8-ounce tub cream cheese with chives and onion
¼ cup grated Romano or Parmesan cheese
12 ounces chopped cooked lobster or chunk-style imitation lobster (about 2⅔ cups)
1 10-ounce package frozen chopped broccoli, thawed and well drained
½ of a 7-ounce jar roasted red sweet peppers, drained and chopped, or one 4-ounce jar diced pimientos, drained
¼ teaspoon ground black pepper
Paprika

1 Cook manicotti shells according to package directions; drain and set aside.

2 Meanwhile, for cheese sauce, in a medium saucepan melt butter over medium heat. Add flour and stir until combined. Add 1 cup of the milk all at once. Cook and stir over medium heat until mixture is thickened and bubbly. Reduce heat to low. Gradually add cream cheese, stirring until smooth. Stir in Romano cheese.

3 Preheat oven to 350°F. For filling, in a medium bowl combine ¾ cup of the cheese sauce, the lobster, broccoli, roasted sweet peppers, and black pepper. Using a small spoon, carefully fill each manicotti shell with about ⅓ cup of the filling. Arrange the filled shells in an ungreased 3-quart rectangular baking dish or 6 individual casseroles. Stir the remaining ¼ cup milk into the remaining sauce. Pour sauce over the shells. Sprinkle with paprika.

4 Cover dish (or dishes) with foil. Bake for 30 to 40 minutes or until heated through.

nutrition facts per serving: 386 cal., 17 g total fat (11 g sat. fat), 90 mg chol., 471 mg sodium, 34 g carb., 2 g dietary fiber, 21 g protein.

In Italian, orzo *means "barley," but it's actually a tiny, rice-shaped pasta, slightly smaller than a pine nut. In this case, it makes a great stand-in for rice.*

greek orzo shrimp
casserole

prep: 30 minutes bake: 45 minutes stand: 10 minutes
oven: 350°F makes: 8 servings dish: 3-quart

12 ounces dried orzo
1 pound fresh or frozen peeled and deveined medium shrimp
1 tablespoon olive oil
2 medium green and/or red sweet peppers, seeded and cut into bite-size strips
1 8-ounce package sliced fresh mushrooms
⅓ cup chopped onion (1 small)
1 clove garlic, minced
2 cups shredded Italian cheese blend (8 ounces)
4 ounces feta or kasseri cheese, crumbled
½ cup chopped pitted kalamata olives
1 26-ounce jar marinara sauce

1 Cook orzo according to package directions; drain. Set aside. Thaw shrimp, if frozen. Rinse shrimp; pat dry with paper towels. Preheat oven to 350°F.

2 In a 12-inch skillet heat oil over medium heat. Add sweet peppers, mushrooms, onion, and garlic; cook until peppers and onion are tender. Add shrimp; cook about 3 minutes or until shrimp are opaque.

3 In a very large bowl combine cooked orzo, shrimp mixture, 1½ cups of the Italian-style cheese, the feta cheese, and olives. Add marinara sauce and stir until well coated. Transfer mixture to an ungreased 3-quart rectangular baking dish.

4 Bake, covered, about 45 minutes or until heated through. Sprinkle with the remaining ½ cup Italian-style cheese. Let stand for 10 minutes before serving.

nutrition facts per serving: 428 cal., 17 g total fat (7 g sat. fat), 97 mg chol., 878 mg sodium, 44 g carb., 4 g dietary fiber, 26 g protein.

Turn an everyday tuna-noodle casserole into a kid-friendly meal by sprinkling a handful of fish-shape crackers on top.

tuna and green bean bake

prep: 35 minutes   bake: 25 minutes   oven: 350°F
makes: 6 servings   dish: 2-quart

4 ounces packaged dried medium noodles

10 ounces fresh green beans, trimmed and cut into 2-inch pieces, or one 10-ounce package frozen cut green beans

1 cup sliced fresh mushrooms

³/₄ cup chopped red or green sweet pepper (1 medium)

½ cup chopped onion (1 medium)

½ cup sliced celery (1 stalk)

½ cup water

2 cloves garlic, minced

1 10.75-ounce can reduced-sodium and reduced-fat condensed cream of mushroom soup

½ cup fat-free milk

½ cup cubed or shredded reduced-fat American or process Swiss cheese (2 ounces)

2 4.5-ounce cans very low sodium chunk white tuna in spring water, drained and flaked

Fish-shape crackers (optional)

1 Preheat oven to 350°F. Cook noodles according to package directions; drain and set aside.

2 In a large saucepan combine green beans, mushrooms, sweet pepper, onion, celery, the water, and garlic. Bring to boiling; reduce heat. Simmer, covered, about 5 minutes or until vegetables are tender.

3 Stir cream of mushroom soup and milk into vegetable mixture. Cook and stir until heated through. Remove from heat. Add cheese, stirring until melted. Stir in cooked noodles and tuna.

4 Spoon mixture into an ungreased 2-quart casserole. Bake, uncovered, for 25 to 30 minutes or until tuna mixture is bubbly. If desired, top with fish-shape crackers.

nutrition facts per serving: 228 cal., 6 g total fat (2 g sat. fat), 49 mg chol., 403 mg sodium, 27 g carb., 3 g dietary fiber, 18 g protein.

An intriguing mix of curry, apples, and tomatoes tops halibut, a firm white, mild fish. Couscous is a North African staple, used here as a bed for the fish.

curried halibut and couscous casserole

prep: 25 minutes bake: 20 minutes oven: 450°F
makes: 6 servings dish: 3-quart

1½ pounds fresh or frozen halibut steaks or cod fillets

1 tablespoon butter or margarine

1½ cups thinly sliced onion

1 to 2 teaspoons curry powder

1 large apple, cored and cut into thin wedges

1 cup chopped roma tomatoes

¼ teaspoon salt

⅛ teaspoon ground black pepper

1 10-ounce package couscous

2½ cups chicken broth
Salt and ground black pepper
Chutney (optional)

1 Thaw fish, if frozen. Rinse fish; pat dry with paper towels. If necessary, cut fish into six serving-size pieces. Set aside. Preheat oven to 450°F.

2 In a large skillet melt butter over medium heat. Add onion; cook about 5 minutes or until tender. Stir in curry powder. Remove from heat. Stir in apple, tomatoes, the ¼ teaspoon salt, and ⅛ teaspoon pepper.

3 In an ungreased 3-quart rectangular baking dish combine uncooked couscous and broth. Arrange fish on top in a single layer. Sprinkle with additional salt and pepper. Top with onion-apple mixture.

4 Bake, covered, for 20 to 25 minutes or until fish flakes easily when tested with a fork. If desired, serve with chutney.

nutrition facts per serving: 358 cal., 5 g total fat (1 g sat. fat), 42 mg chol., 612 mg sodium, 45 g carb., 4 g dietary fiber, 31 g protein.

This seafaring dish, complete with mashed potatoes, will remind you of shepherd's pie.

all-in-one salmon dinner

prep: 20 minutes bake: 25 minutes oven: 350°F
makes: 4 servings dish: 16-ounce dishes

1	pound fresh or frozen skinless salmon fillets, cut into four serving-size portions
1	20-ounce package refrigerated mashed potatoes
⅓	cup purchased basil pesto
¼	cup plain yogurt
½	teaspoon salt
½	teaspoon ground black pepper
2	tablespoons butter
2	tablespoons all-purpose flour
1	14-ounce can chicken broth
3	cups frozen sweet soybeans (edamame) or peas, thawed
½	cup snipped fresh basil
1	cup grape tomatoes or small cherry tomatoes
	Fresh basil

1 Thaw fish, if frozen. Preheat oven to 350°F. Rinse fish; pat dry with paper towels. In a medium bowl stir together mashed potatoes, pesto, yogurt, ¼ teaspoon of the salt, and ¼ teaspoon of the pepper. Set aside.

2 In a large skillet melt butter over medium-low heat. Stir in flour. Whisk in chicken broth. Bring to boiling and stir in edamame and ½ cup basil. Cook and stir for 3 minutes. Stir in tomatoes.

3 Divide mixture among four ungreased 16-ounce individual casseroles or au gratin dishes. Place fish on top of bean-tomato mixture. Sprinkle fish with the remaining ¼ teaspoon salt and the remaining ¼ teaspoon pepper. Divide the potato mixture among the casseroles, spooning into a mound on one side of the fish.

4 Bake, uncovered, about 25 minutes or just until fish begins to flake easily when tested with a fork. Garnish with fresh basil.

nutrition facts per serving: 718 cal., 40 g total fat (10 g sat. fat), 86 mg chol., 1216 mg sodium, 41 g carb., 8 g dietary fiber, 46 g protein.

Using shortcut ingredients—cheese blend, prepared salsa, and canned salmon and chile peppers—makes this surprisingly easily.

creamy cheesy
salmon enchiladas

prep: 25 minutes **bake:** 35 minutes **oven:** 375°F
makes: 6 servings **dish:** 3-quart

2 cups shredded
    Mexican cheese
    blend (8 ounces)
1 16-ounce jar salsa
1 3-ounce package
    cream cheese,
    softened
1 4-ounce can diced
    green chile peppers,
    drained
2 14.75-ounce cans
    salmon, drained,
    flaked, and skin and
    bones removed
6 10- to 12-inch flour
    tortillas

1 Preheat oven to 375°F. For filling, in a large bowl combine 1 cup of the Mexican cheese, 2 tablespoons of the salsa, the cream cheese, and chile peppers. Gently stir in salmon.

2 Spoon about ¾ cup of the filling across each tortilla slightly below center. Fold in ends and roll up tortilla. Arrange tortillas, seam sides down, in an ungreased 3-quart rectangular baking dish. Top with the remaining salsa and the remaining 1 cup Mexican cheese.

3 Bake, covered, for 25 minutes. Bake, uncovered, about 10 minutes more or until heated through.

nutrition facts per serving: 546 cal., 28 g total fat (12 g sat. fat), 126 mg chol., 1824 mg sodium, 30 g carb., 2 g dietary fiber, 41 g protein.

Say it with salmon. And peas. In a flavor-packed broth tucked beneath a golden brown piecrust, it's seriously sensational.

salmon potpie

prep: 45 minutes   bake: 30 minutes   stand: 20 minutes
oven: 400°F   makes: 6 servings   dish: 10-ounce dishes

1   15-ounce package
    (2-crust) rolled
    refrigerated
    piecrust
2   tablespoons butter
1   cup chopped onion
    (1 medium) or leeks
1   cup sliced celery
    (2 stalks)
1   cup chopped red,
    green, or yellow
    sweet peppers
    (2 small)
¼   cup all-purpose flour
¾   teaspoon dried thyme
¼   teaspoon salt
¼   to ½ teaspoon
    cayenne pepper
1   cup chicken broth or
    vegetable broth
¾   cup milk
1   12.5-ounce can
    skinless, boneless
    salmon, drained and
    flaked, or 12 ounces
    smoked salmon,
    flaked
1   cup frozen peas
¼   cup snipped fresh
    parsley (optional)
1   egg, beaten
    Fresh thyme sprigs
    (optional)

1 Preheat oven to 400°F. Let piecrust stand at room temperature according to package directions.

2 In a large saucepan melt butter over medium heat. Add onion, celery, and sweet peppers; cook for 4 to 5 minutes or until vegetables are tender. Stir in the flour, thyme, salt, and cayenne. Add broth and milk all at once. Cook and stir until thickened and bubbly. Stir in salmon, frozen peas, and parsley (if using).

3 Divide salmon mixture among six individual baking dishes, such as 10- to 14-ounce au gratin dishes or ramekins. Unroll piecrusts onto a lightly floured surface. Roll each piecrust into a 13-inch circle. Using a fluted cutter, cut six circles or ovals 1 inch larger than the top of the dishes.

4 Place piecrusts over hot salmon mixture in each dish. Brush piecrust with egg.

5 Bake for 20 to 25 minutes or until crusts are golden brown. Let stand for 10 minutes before serving. If desired, garnish with fresh thyme sprigs.

nutrition facts per serving: 483 cal., 26 g total fat (14 g sat. fat), 141 mg chol., 704 mg sodium, 37 g carb., 3 g dietary fiber, 25 g protein.

Crawfish, sometimes called crayfish, is a Louisiana specialty with a sweet rich flavor. Here it stars with fettuccine for a distinctive dinner. Another time, substitute shrimp for the crawfish.

crawfish fettuccine

prep: 25 minutes   bake: 20 minutes   oven: 350°F
makes: 8 servings   dish: 3-quart

1   pound fresh or frozen peeled, cooked crawfish tails
1   pound dried fettuccine, broken
1   cup coarsely chopped green sweet pepper
¾   cup chopped onion (1 large)
4   cloves garlic, minced
¼   cup butter or margarine
3   tablespoons all-purpose flour
¼   to ½ teaspoon cayenne pepper
¼   teaspoon salt
2   cups half-and-half, light cream, or milk
1½ cups shredded American cheese (6 ounces)
2   tablespoons snipped fresh parsley
⅓   cup grated Parmesan cheese

1 Thaw crawfish, if frozen. Preheat oven to 350°F. In a Dutch oven cook fettuccine according to package directions. Drain; return to Dutch oven.

2 Meanwhile, for sauce, in a large saucepan cook sweet pepper, onion, and garlic in hot butter about 5 minutes or until tender. Stir in flour, cayenne, and salt. Add half-and-half all at once. Cook and stir over medium heat until thickened and bubbly. Add cheese, stirring until melted. Remove from heat; stir in crawfish and parsley.

3 Pour crawfish mixture over fettuccine, tossing gently to coat. Spoon mixture into an ungreased 3-quart rectangular baking dish. Sprinkle with Parmesan cheese. Bake, covered, for 20 to 25 minutes or until heated through.

nutrition facts per serving: 506 cal., 22 g total fat (13 g sat. fat), 123 mg chol., 574 mg sodium, 51 g carb., 2 g dietary fiber, 25 g protein.

The definitive "cupboard casserole" gets fresh with dashes of lemon and dill, rich olive oil–packed tuna, and the crunch of coarsely chopped celery. Top with lemon slices and capers and it's ready for company.

lemony tuna and pasta

prep: 30 minutes **bake:** 20 minutes **stand:** 5 minutes
oven: 375°F **makes:** 4 to 6 servings **dish:** 1½-quart

2   cups dried rigatoni
    or penne pasta
    (6 ounces)
1   cup coarsely chopped
    celery (2 stalks)
¼   cup chopped onion
2   cloves garlic, minced
¼   cup olive oil
¼   cup all-purpose flour
2   tablespoons Dijon
    mustard
1   tablespoon snipped
    fresh dill or
    1 teaspoon dried dill
1   teaspoon finely
    shredded lemon
    zest
¼   teaspoon ground
    black pepper
2   cups reduced-sodium
    chicken broth
2   6-ounce cans chunk
    tuna (packed in
    olive oil), drained
½   cup finely crushed
    herb-seasoned
    croutons
2   tablespoons butter,
    melted
1   small lemon, thinly
    sliced
1   tablespoon capers,
    drained (optional)
    Fresh dill sprigs
    (optional)

1 Preheat oven to 375°F. Grease a 1½-quart baking dish; set aside. Cook pasta according to package directions; drain.

2 Meanwhile, in a medium saucepan cook celery, onion, and garlic in hot oil over medium heat until tender. Stir in flour, mustard, 1 tablespoon dill, lemon zest, and pepper. Gradually stir in broth. Cook and stir until thickened and bubbly. Stir in cooked pasta and tuna.

3 Transfer mixture to the prepared baking dish. In small bowl stir together croutons and melted butter. Sprinkle over tuna mixture.

4 Bake, covered, for 15 minutes. Top with lemon slices. Bake, uncovered, about 5 minutes more or until heated through. Let stand for 5 minutes before serving. If desired, garnish with capers and dill sprigs.

nutrition facts per serving: 565 cal., 27 g total fat (7 g sat. fat), 30 mg chol., 868 mg sodium, 47 g carb., 4 g dietary fiber, 32 g protein.

Get to know fontina, one of Italy's great cheeses. Its mild, buttery, and slightly nutty taste makes it the perfect cheese for most any use.

crab, spinach, and pasta with fontina

prep: 25 minutes bake: 30 minutes stand: 10 minutes
oven: 375°F makes: 6 servings dish: 2-quart

2 cups dried bow tie pasta (8 ounces)
1 26-ounce jar tomato pasta sauce
2 6-ounce cans crabmeat, drained, flaked, and cartilage removed
1 10-ounce package frozen chopped spinach, thawed and well drained
1½ cups shredded fontina cheese (6 ounces)

1 Preheat oven to 375°F. Lightly grease a 2-quart square baking dish; set aside. Cook pasta according to package directions; drain.

2 Meanwhile, in a large bowl combine pasta sauce, crabmeat, spinach, and ¾ cup of the cheese. Add cooked pasta; toss gently to combine. Transfer mixture to prepared baking dish. Sprinkle with the remaining ¾ cup cheese.

3 Bake, uncovered, for 30 to 35 minutes or until mixture is bubbly around edges and cheese is lightly browned. Let stand for 10 minutes before serving.

nutrition facts per serving: 359 cal., 11 g total fat (6 g sat. fat), 105 mg chol., 912 mg sodium, 39 g carb., 4 g dietary fiber, 26 g protein.

Layer shrimp and crabmeat in a creamy mushroom sauce with noodles and two cheeses in this delicately flavored lasagna.

seafood lasagna

prep: 40 minutes bake: 45 minutes stand: 10 minutes
oven: 350°F makes: 12 servings dish: 3-quart

12 ounces fresh or frozen cooked, peeled, and deveined shrimp, halved lengthwise
8 dried lasagna noodles
2 tablespoons butter or margarine
1 cup chopped onion (1 large)
1 3-ounce package cream cheese, softened and cut up
1 12-ounce carton cream-style cottage cheese
1 egg, lightly beaten
2 teaspoons dried basil, crushed
¼ teaspoon salt
⅛ teaspoon ground black pepper
2 10.75-ounce cans condensed cream of mushroom soup
⅓ cup milk
1 6.5-ounce can crabmeat, drained, flaked, and cartilage removed
¼ cup finely shredded Parmesan cheese (1 ounce)

1 Thaw shrimp, if frozen. Rinse shrimp; pat dry with paper towels. Cook lasagna noodles according to package directions; drain well and set aside.

2 Preheat oven to 350°F. Arrange four of the noodles in the bottom of a greased 3-quart rectangular baking dish.

3 In a medium skillet melt butter over medium heat. Add onion; cook until tender. Remove from heat. Add cream cheese and stir until melted. Stir in cottage cheese, egg, basil, salt, and pepper. Spread half of the cheese mixture over the noodles.

4 In a large bowl combine soup and milk; stir in shrimp and crabmeat. Spread half of the shrimp mixture over cheese layer. Repeat noodle, cheese, and shrimp layers. Sprinkle with Parmesan cheese.

5 Bake, uncovered, about 45 minutes or until hot and bubbly. Let stand for 10 to 15 minutes before serving.

nutrition facts per serving: 243 cal., 11 g total fat (5 g sat. fat), 112 mg chol., 720 mg sodium, 18 g carb., 1 g dietary fiber, 17 g protein.

Many cooks will fondly remember this dish—it's quintessential ladies' luncheon fare. More saucy and delicate than a typical casserole, it's best served with crusty bread.

crab-mushroom bake

prep: 20 minutes **bake:** 25 minutes **oven:** 350°F
makes: 4 servings **dish:** 9-inch pie plate

½ cup finely chopped celery (1 stalk)

1 tablespoon butter

1 10.75-ounce can condensed cream of shrimp soup

¾ cup soft bread crumbs (1 slice)

1 4-ounce can (drained weight) sliced mushrooms, drained

⅓ cup milk

2 tablespoons dry sherry

1 6-ounce can crabmeat, drained, flaked, and cartilage removed

⅓ cup finely shredded Parmesan cheese
Lemon wedges (optional)

1 Preheat oven to 350°F. In a medium saucepan cook celery in hot butter over medium heat until tender. Stir in soup, ½ cup of the bread crumbs, the mushrooms, milk, and sherry. Bring just to boiling, stirring constantly. Stir in crabmeat. Transfer mixture to an ungreased 9-inch pie plate.

2 In a small bowl combine the remaining ¼ cup bread crumbs and cheese. Sprinkle over crab mixture.

3 Bake, uncovered, about 25 minutes or until mixture is heated through and top is golden. If desired, serve with lemon wedges.

nutrition facts per serving: 276 cal., 10 g total fat (6 g sat. fat), 83 mg chol., 1260 mg sodium, 26 g carb., 2 g dietary fiber, 17 g protein.

meatless

won

6

Tried-and-true pantry staples, including rice, grains, and beans, are remarkably versatile in casseroles. Use the inspiring recipes here to create marvelous meatless meals that will win rave reviews from everyone at the table, including the meat lovers.

ders

Cheesy and rich-tasting, this vegetarian casserole will please the calorie watchers on your guest list. To spice it up even more, use a chunky chili-tomato sauce.

black bean lasagna

prep: 45 minutes **bake:** 35 minutes **stand:** 10 minutes
oven: 350°F **makes:** 8 servings **dish:** 3-quart

9 dried lasagna noodles
1 egg, lightly beaten
1½ cups shredded Monterey Jack cheese (6 ounces)
1 12-ounce carton cream-style cottage cheese
1 8-ounce package cream cheese, softened and cut up
2 15-ounce cans black beans, rinsed and drained
1 cup chopped onion (1 large)
¾ cup chopped green sweet pepper (1 medium)
2 cloves garlic, minced
1 tablespoon vegetable oil
1 15-ounce can Italian-style tomato sauce
4 teaspoons dried cilantro, crushed
1 teaspoon ground cumin
Coarsely chopped tomato
Snipped fresh cilantro (optional)

1 Preheat oven to 350°F. Lightly grease a 3-quart rectangular baking dish; set aside. Cook lasagna noodles according to package directions; drain. Rinse with cold water; drain again. Place noodles in a single layer on a sheet of foil; set aside.

2 Meanwhile, in a medium bowl combine egg, 1 cup of the Monterey Jack cheese, the cottage cheese, and cream cheese; set aside.

3 In a small bowl mash one can of the beans with a potato masher. In a large skillet cook onion, sweet pepper, and garlic in hot oil over medium-high heat until tender. Stir in mashed beans, the remaining can of whole beans, tomato sauce, dried cilantro, and cumin; heat through.

4 Arrange three of the cooked lasagna noodles in the bottom of prepared baking dish. Top with one-third of the bean mixture and half of the cheese mixture. Repeat layers. Top with the remaining noodles and bean mixture.

5 Bake, covered, for 35 to 40 minutes or until heated through. Sprinkle with the remaining ½ cup Monterey Jack cheese. Let stand for 10 minutes before serving. Sprinkle with tomato and, if desired, fresh cilantro.

nutrition facts per serving: 456 cal., 22 g total fat (12 g sat. fat), 83 mg chol., 857 mg sodium, 46 g carb., 8 g dietary fiber, 25 g protein.

The combination of green chiles and Monterey Jack cheese with jalapeños gives this egg and asparagus bake a nice kick.

chiles and cheese
individual casseroles

prep: 25 minutes **chill:** 2 to 24 hours **bake:** 40 minutes **stand:** 10 minutes
oven: 350°F **makes:** 4 servings **dish:** 12-ounce dishes

2 4-ounce cans whole green chile peppers, drained
1 cup 1-inch pieces fresh asparagus or frozen cut asparagus, thawed
1 small red onion, quartered and thinly sliced
1 tablespoon butter
1 cup shredded Monterey Jack cheese with jalapeño chile peppers or Monterey Jack cheese (4 ounces)
1 tablespoon all-purpose flour
4 eggs, lightly beaten
1¼ cups half-and-half, light cream, or milk
¼ teaspoon salt
¼ teaspoon ground black pepper
½ cup chopped tomato (1 medium)

1 Lightly grease four 12- to 16-ounce au gratin dishes; set aside. Pat chile peppers with paper towels to remove excess liquid. Make a slit along one side of each pepper and lay flat. Discard any seeds. Pat again with paper towels. Arrange chile peppers in a single layer in the bottoms of the prepared au gratin dishes, cutting as necessary to fit.

2 In a medium skillet cook asparagus and onion in hot butter over medium heat about 5 minutes or just until tender. Divide asparagus mixture among au gratin dishes. In a small bowl combine cheese and flour; toss gently to coat. Divide cheese among dishes.

3 In a medium bowl combine eggs, half-and-half, salt, and black pepper. Divide evenly among dishes. Cover and chill for 2 to 24 hours.

4 Preheat oven to 350°F. Place au gratin dishes in a 15×10×1-inch baking pan. Bake, uncovered, for 40 to 45 minutes or until mixture is set. Let stand for 10 minutes before serving. Sprinkle with tomato.

nutrition facts per serving: 342 cal., 26 g total fat (14 g sat. fat), 272 mg chol., 578 mg sodium, 11 g carb., 1 g dietary fiber, 18 g protein.

You won't even miss the corned beef in this meatless casserole that tastes just like a Reuben sandwich. Pictured on page 154.

cabbage-swiss
bread pudding

prep: 25 minutes bake: 35 minutes stand: 10 minutes
oven: 300°F/375°F makes: 6 to 8 servings dish: 2-quart

6	cups cubed light rye bread
2	tablespoons olive oil
4	cups coarsely chopped red and/or green cabbage
½	cup chopped onion (1 medium)
2	tablespoons balsamic vinegar
4	cloves garlic, minced
2	teaspoons caraway seeds
8	eggs, lightly beaten
1½	cups milk
1½	cups shredded Swiss cheese (6 ounces)
½	teaspoon salt
¼	teaspoon ground black pepper
	Thousand Island salad dressing (optional)

1 Preheat oven to 300°F. Grease a 2-quart rectangular baking dish; set aside. Spread bread cubes in a 15×10×1-inch baking pan. Bake, uncovered, about 10 minutes or until lightly toasted, stirring once. Cool in pan on wire rack. Increase oven temperature to 375°F.

2 In a large skillet heat oil over medium heat. Add cabbage and onion; cook about 10 minutes or until cabbage is crisp-tender, stirring occasionally. Stir in balsamic vinegar, garlic, and caraway seeds; cook for 1 minute more. Remove from heat.

3 In a large bowl combine eggs, milk, 1 cup of the cheese, the salt, and pepper. Stir in the bread cubes and cabbage mixture. Transfer to prepared baking dish.

4 Bake, uncovered, for 30 minutes. Top with the remaining ½ cup cheese. Bake, uncovered, about 5 minutes more or until a knife inserted near the center comes out clean. Let stand for 10 minutes before serving. If desired, serve with Thousand Island salad dressing.

nutrition facts per serving: 389 cal., 22 g total fat (9 g sat. fat), 313 mg chol., 600 mg sodium, 28 g carb., 3 g dietary fiber, 22 g protein.

Rich, creamy, and packed with spicy curry flavor, the sauce in this dish features natural peanut butter, a more healthful form of peanut butter that doesn't contain hydrogenated fat, sugar, or sodium. Before measuring, you'll want to stir the peanut butter to incorporate any oil on the surface.

coconut
sweet potatoes
and wild rice

prep: 30 minutes **bake:** 30 minutes **oven:** 375°F
makes: 6 servings **dish:** 2-quart

1   8.5-ounce pouch cooked brown and wild rice
4   small sweet potatoes (1½ pounds), peeled and cut into ¼-inch slices
1   cup frozen edamame or peas, thawed
1   14-ounce can unsweetened light coconut milk
½   cup chopped onion (1 medium)
⅓   cup creamy natural peanut butter
1   tablespoon red curry paste
2   teaspoons packed brown sugar
    Fresh snipped basil (optional)

1 Preheat oven to 375°F. Lightly grease a 2-quart casserole; set aside. Prepare rice according to package directions.

2 In a medium saucepan cook sweet potato slices, covered, in enough boiling water to cover about 8 minutes or just until tender; drain well. Gently combine sweet potato slices, rice, and edamame. Transfer to casserole dish.

3 In a large skillet combine coconut milk and onion. Bring to boiling; reduce heat. Simmer, uncovered, about 3 minutes or just until onion is tender. Whisk in peanut butter, red curry paste, and brown sugar. Continue to whisk until peanut butter is melted and smooth.

4 Pour coconut milk mixture over vegetables and rice. Bake, covered, for 15 minutes. Uncover and bake about 15 minutes more or until mixture is heated through. If desired, top with snipped basil.

nutrition facts per serving: 325 cal., 14 g total fat (4 g sat. fat), 0 mg chol., 421 mg sodium, 40 g carb., 5 g dietary fiber, 10 g protein.

Polenta is usually eaten as a savory side dish, but this recipe illustrates how good it can be in a golden casserole made with eggs and fresh veggies. Find tubes of polenta in the refrigerator case of your supermarket.

corn and polenta bake

prep: 25 minutes **bake:** 50 minutes **oven:** 325°F
makes: 6 servings **dish:** 2-quart

2 cups fresh corn kernels (4 ears) or frozen whole kernel corn
1 cup chopped green sweet pepper
½ cup chopped onion (1 medium)
2 cloves garlic, minced
¼ to ½ teaspoon ground black pepper
2 tablespoons vegetable oil
2 16-ounce tubes refrigerated cooked polenta
6 eggs, lightly beaten
1 tablespoon stone-ground mustard or Dijon mustard
1 teaspoon sugar
¾ teaspoon salt
1½ cups soft bread crumbs (2 slices)
2 tablespoons butter, melted

1 Preheat oven to 325°F. Lightly grease a 2-quart rectangular baking dish; set aside. In a large saucepan cook corn, sweet pepper, onion, garlic, and black pepper in hot oil about 5 minutes or just until tender.

2 Crumble polenta (you should have about 7 cups). In a large bowl combine eggs, mustard, sugar, and salt. Stir in corn mixture and crumbled polenta. Transfer mixture to the prepared baking dish.

3 In a small bowl combine bread crumbs and melted butter. Sprinkle over polenta mixture. Bake, uncovered, about 50 minutes or until a knife inserted near the center comes out clean.

nutrition facts per serving: 336 cal., 20 g total fat (3 g sat. fat), 32 mg chol., 277 mg sodium, 48 g carb., 12 g dietary fiber, 11 g protein.

Ready-to-use crepes, found in the produce section of the supermarket near the refrigerated tortillas, make a quick and savory weeknight dinner. Here, they're filled with a spinach and ricotta cheese filling and topped with both marinara and Alfredo sauces.

spinach cannelloni
with fontina

prep: 35 minutes **bake:** 25 minutes **stand:** 10 minutes
oven: 375°F **makes:** 5 servings **dish:** 3-quart

1   medium fennel bulb, cored and chopped (1 cup)
3   cloves garlic, minced
1   tablespoon olive oil
1   6-ounce package baby spinach (about 5 cups)
1   egg, lightly beaten
1   15-ounce carton ricotta cheese
²/₃ cup finely shredded Parmesan cheese
½   teaspoon dried Italian seasoning, crushed
½   teaspoon finely shredded lemon zest
1   17-ounce jar marinara sauce (2 cups)
1   4.5- to 5-ounce package ready-to-use crepes (10)
1   10-ounce container refrigerated Alfredo pasta sauce
1   cup shredded fontina cheese (4 ounces)

1 Preheat oven to 375°F. For filling, in an extra-large skillet cook fennel and garlic in hot oil over medium heat for 3 to 4 minutes or until tender. Add spinach; cook, covered, about 2 minutes or until wilted. Transfer spinach mixture to a sieve; press out excess liquid with the back of a spoon. In a large bowl combine egg, ricotta cheese, Parmesan cheese, Italian seasoning, and lemon zest. Stir in spinach mixture.

2 Spread half of the marinara sauce over the bottom of an ungreased 3-quart rectangular baking dish. Spoon about ⅓ cup of the filling along the center of each crepe; roll up crepe. Arrange crepes, seam sides down, on top of marinara sauce in dish. Spoon the remaining marinara sauce over crepes down center of dish. Pour Alfredo sauce over crepes, spreading evenly. Sprinkle with fontina cheese.

3 Bake, uncovered, for 25 to 30 minutes or until bubbly around the edges. Let stand for 10 minutes before serving.

nutrition facts per serving: 672 cal., 47 g total fat (15 g sat. fat), 159 mg chol., 1297 mg sodium, 36 g carb., 4 g dietary fiber, 28 g protein.

Because the brown rice takes 30 to 45 minutes to cook, you may want to cook it ahead of time, or even use leftover cooked brown rice here.

creamy curried broccoli and brown rice

prep: 30 minutes   **bake:** 30 minutes   **oven:** 375°F
makes: 4 servings   **dish:** 2-quart

1	cup brown rice
	Nonstick cooking spray
3	cups chopped broccoli
1	cup chopped red sweet peppers (2 small)
2	cups milk
2	tablespoons cornstarch
1¼	teaspoons curry powder
½	teaspoon salt
⅛	teaspoon turmeric
4	ounces reduced-fat cream cheese (Neufchâtel)
¾	cup soft bread crumbs
1	tablespoon butter, melted

1 Cook brown rice according to package directions. Meanwhile, preheat oven to 375°F. Coat a 2-quart casserole with cooking spray. Transfer cooked brown rice to casserole. Top with broccoli and sweet pepper.

2 For sauce, in a small saucepan combine milk, cornstarch, curry powder, salt, and turmeric. Cook and stir over medium heat until cornstarch is dissolved. Bring to boiling; reduce heat. Cook about 5 minutes or until thickened, stirring constantly. Reduce heat to low. Add cream cheese, stirring until melted. Pour sauce over rice and broccoli in casserole.

3 In a small bowl combine bread crumbs and melted butter; sprinkle on top of casserole. Bake, uncovered, for 30 to 40 minutes or until hot in center. To serve, spoon mixture into small bowls.

nutrition facts per serving: 404 cal., 14 g total fat (7 g sat. fat), 38 mg chol., 541 mg sodium, 58 g carb., 5 g dietary fiber, 13 g protein.

Everyone will love this make-ahead dish in which corn is paired with a captivating combination of dried porcini mushrooms, dried tomatoes, toasted English muffin pieces, and dry Jack cheese.

tomato-mushroom corn pudding

prep: 25 minutes **chill:** 4 hours **bake:** 45 minutes **stand:** 10 minutes
oven: 375°F **makes:** 6 servings **dish:** 2-quart

¼ cup dried porcini mushrooms

3 to 6 dried tomatoes (not oil-packed)

4 cups torn lightly toasted English muffins (about 4 muffins) or cubed dried bread

1½ cups frozen whole kernel corn, thawed

½ cup finely shredded aged (dry) Jack or Parmesan cheese (2 ounces)

1 tablespoon snipped fresh basil or 1 teaspoon dried basil, crushed

½ teaspoon salt

¼ teaspoon ground black pepper

4 eggs, lightly beaten

1½ cups milk

1 Place dried mushrooms and tomatoes in separate small bowls. Cover with boiling water. Let stand for 15 minutes; drain. Rinse mushrooms. Drain again, pressing out excess moisture. Chop dried tomatoes.

2 Meanwhile, in an ungreased 2-quart square baking dish, toss together English muffin pieces, corn, cheese, basil, salt, and pepper. Stir in mushrooms and tomatoes.

3 In a medium bowl combine eggs and milk. Pour evenly over ingredients in dish. Press lightly with a rubber spatula or the back of a large spoon to moisten all of the muffin pieces. Cover and chill for 4 to 24 hours.

4 Preheat oven to 375°F. Bake, uncovered, about 45 minutes or until a knife inserted in the center comes out clean. Let stand for 10 minutes before serving.

nutrition facts per serving: 261 cal., 10 g total fat (4 g sat. fat), 150 mg chol., 520 mg sodium, 31 g carb., 3 g dietary fiber, 13 g protein.

This pasta dish is a protein-packed powerhouse. Use whole wheat pasta if you want to increase the nutritional profile even more.

garlic-mushroom pasta

prep: 30 minutes **bake:** 20 minutes **oven:** 375°F
makes: 4 servings **dish:** 2-quart

8 ounces bow tie or penne pasta
2 tablespoons butter
6 ounces fresh baby portobello or button mushrooms, sliced
6 ounces fresh shiitake mushrooms, stemmed and sliced
4 cloves garlic, minced
3 tablespoons all-purpose flour
2 cups milk
1 tablespoon Dijon mustard
½ teaspoon salt
1 15- to 19-ounce can cannellini (white kidney) or navy beans, rinsed and drained
¾ cup finely shredded Parmesan cheese
   Freshly cracked black pepper

1 Preheat oven to 375°F. Cook pasta according to package directions.

2 Meanwhile, in a large skillet melt 1 tablespoon of the butter over medium-high heat. Add mushrooms; cook for 2 to 3 minutes or until mushrooms begin to soften. Add garlic; cook for 1 minute more. Transfer mixture to a large bowl. Place the remaining 1 tablespoon butter in the skillet; melt over medium-low heat. Stir in flour. Gradually add milk, mustard, and salt. Cook and stir for 2 to 3 minutes or until thickened and bubbly. Stir in mushroom mixture. Remove from heat.

3 Drain pasta; add to mushroom mixture. Stir in beans and ½ cup of the cheese. Season to taste with pepper. Transfer to an ungreased 2-quart casserole. Sprinkle with the remaining ¼ cup cheese. Bake, uncovered, about 20 minutes or until heated through.

nutrition facts per serving: 509 cal., 14 g total fat (8 g sat. fat), 36 mg chol., 899 mg sodium, 77 g carb., 8 g dietary fiber, 26 g protein.

*A medley of vegetables adds vibrant color and fresh flavor to good ol'
mac and cheese. A slimmed-down cream sauce makes it healthier.*

vegetable primavera casserole

prep: 30 minutes   **bake:** 30 minutes   **stand:** 5 minutes
oven: 375°F   **makes:** 8 servings   **dish:** 3-quart

1½   cups dried elbow
macaroni (6 ounces)

1   16-ounce package
loose-pack frozen
vegetable blend
(any combination)

2   medium zucchini,
halved lengthwise
and sliced

½   cup chopped red
sweet pepper
(1 small)

2   12-ounce cans
evaporated milk

1   cup vegetable or
chicken broth

⅓   cup all-purpose flour

1   teaspoon dried
oregano, crushed

½   teaspoon garlic
powder

½   teaspoon salt

½   teaspoon ground
black pepper

¾   cup grated Parmesan
or Romano cheese

1   medium tomato,
halved and sliced

1 Lightly grease a 3-quart rectangular baking dish; set aside. Preheat oven to 375°F. In a 4- to 5-quart saucepan cook macaroni in lightly salted boiling water for 8 minutes, adding the frozen vegetables, zucchini, and sweet pepper for the last 3 minutes of cooking; drain well. Return macaroni mixture to pan.

2 Meanwhile, in a medium saucepan whisk together evaporated milk, broth, flour, oregano, garlic powder, salt, and black pepper. Cook and stir over medium heat until thickened and bubbly. Add to macaroni mixture; toss to coat. Stir in ½ cup of the Parmesan cheese. Transfer macaroni mixture to prepared baking dish.

3 Bake, uncovered, for 25 minutes. Top with tomato slices and the remaining ¼ cup Parmesan cheese. Bake about 5 minutes more or until heated through. Let stand for 5 minutes before serving.

nutrition facts per serving: 280 cal., 9 g total fat (5 g sat. fat), 31 mg chol., 499 mg sodium, 35 g carb., 3 g dietary fiber, 13 g protein.

meatless **wonders**

This homemade polenta, layered between a creamy white sauce and a fragrant tomato sauce, is sprinkled with Asiago cheese and baked until bubbly.

polenta with two sauces

prep: 45 minutes   **chill:** 2 to 24 hours   **bake:** 12 minutes
oven: 450°F   **makes:** 4 servings   **dish:** 2-quart/8-ounce dishes

3   cups water
1   cup yellow cornmeal
1   cup water
½   teaspoon salt
¾   cup shredded Asiago
     or Parmesan cheese
     (3 ounces)
1   15-ounce can Italian-
     style tomato sauce
2   tablespoons all-
     purpose flour
½   teaspoon dried basil,
     crushed
¼   teaspoon salt
⅛   teaspoon ground
     black pepper
     Pinch ground nutmeg
1¼ cups milk
     Shaved Asiago or
     Parmesan cheese
     (optional)

1 For polenta, lightly grease a 2-quart square baking dish; set aside. In a medium saucepan bring the 3 cups water to boiling. Meanwhile, in a small bowl combine cornmeal, the 1 cup water, and ½ teaspoon salt. Slowly add cornmeal mixture to the boiling water, stirring constantly. Cook and stir until mixture returns to boiling. Reduce heat to low. Cook, uncovered, for 10 to 15 minutes or until thick, stirring frequently. Remove from heat. Stir in ¼ cup of the shredded cheese.

2 Spread polenta evenly in the prepared baking dish; cool slightly. Cover and chill for 2 to 24 hours. Cut polenta into 1-inch squares; set aside.

3 Preheat oven to 450°F. For red sauce, in a medium saucepan bring tomato sauce to boiling; reduce heat. Simmer, uncovered, about 10 minutes or until slightly thickened and reduced to 1⅓ cups.

4 For white sauce, in another medium saucepan combine flour, basil, ¼ teaspoon salt, pepper, and nutmeg. Gradually stir in milk. Cook and stir over medium heat until thickened and bubbly. Cook and stir for 1 minute more. Remove from heat; stir in ¼ cup of the remaining shredded cheese until melted.

5 To assemble, divide red sauce among four ungreased 8- to 10-ounce au gratin dishes; top with polenta. Spoon white sauce over polenta; sprinkle with the remaining ¼ cup shredded cheese.

6 Bake, uncovered, for 12 to 15 minutes or until edges are bubbly and cheese is starting to brown. If desired, sprinkle with shaved cheese.

nutrition facts per serving: 318 cal., 11 g total fat (6 g sat. fat), 29 mg chol., 1133 mg sodium, 42 g carb., 5 g dietary fiber, 13 g protein.

Zucchini, eggplant, and sweet peppers—the colorful combo used for this meatless dish—ripen together at the peak of the summer season. While sautéing the veggies, keep the pieces moving briskly until crisp-tender.

zucchini and
eggplant bake

prep: 35 minutes bake: 20 minutes stand: 10 minutes
oven: 350°F makes: 6 to 8 servings dish: 3-quart

4	cups thinly sliced zucchini (3 medium)
2	cups coarsely chopped red sweet peppers (2 large)
1	cup coarsely chopped onions (2 medium)
5	cups coarsely chopped, peeled eggplant (1 medium)
2	cloves garlic, minced
½	teaspoon salt
¼	teaspoon ground black pepper
3	tablespoons olive oil
4	eggs
½	cup light mayonnaise
1	cup grated Pecorino Romano cheese (4 ounces)
2	cups shredded mozzarella cheese (8 ounces)
⅔	cup crushed rich round crackers (12)

1 Preheat oven to 350°F. Grease a 3-quart rectangular baking dish; set aside. In a 12-inch skillet cook zucchini, sweet peppers, onions, eggplant, garlic, salt, and black pepper in hot oil over medium-high heat for 10 to 15 minutes or until vegetables are tender, stirring occasionally.

2 Meanwhile, in extra-large bowl whisk together eggs and mayonnaise until combined. Stir in Pecorino-Romano cheese and 1 cup of the mozzarella cheese. Add cooked vegetables; toss to combine. Evenly spread vegetable mixture in prepared baking dish. Top with remaining mozzarella and cracker crumbs.

3 Bake, uncovered, for 20 to 25 minutes or until top is lightly browned and a knife inserted near center comes out clean. Let stand for 10 minutes before serving.

nutrition facts per serving: 440 cal., 32 g total fat (11 g sat. fat), 188 mg chol., 942 mg sodium, 21 g carb., 5 g dietary fiber, 23 g protein.

Roasting vegetables—done quickly under the broiler—gives them a subtle sweetness that enhances most any dish.

roasted vegetable
lasagna

prep: 35 minutes **broil:** 12 minutes **bake:** 50 minutes **stand:** 10 minutes
oven: 375°F **makes:** 9 servings **dish:** 3-quart

12	packaged dried lasagna noodles
4	cups zucchini cut into bite-size pieces
2½	cups thinly sliced carrots (5 medium)
2	cups fresh cremini or button mushrooms, halved
1½	cups coarsely chopped red or green sweet peppers (3 small)
¼	cup olive oil
1	tablespoon dried Italian seasoning, crushed
½	teaspoon salt
½	teaspoon ground black pepper
1	12-ounce carton cottage cheese
1	egg, beaten
½	cup grated Parmesan cheese
1	26-ounce jar marinara sauce
3	cups shredded mozzarella cheese (12 ounces)

1 Cook noodles according to package directions; drain. Rinse with cold water; drain again. Place noodles in a single layer on a sheet of foil; set aside.

2 Meanwhile, preheat broiler. In a large bowl combine zucchini, carrots, mushrooms, and sweet peppers. Drizzle vegetables with oil; sprinkle with Italian seasoning, salt, and black pepper. Toss well to combine. Place vegetable mixture in a shallow roasting pan.

3 Broil vegetables 5 to 6 inches from the heat for 6 minutes. Stir vegetables. Broil for 6 to 8 minutes more or until light brown and tender. Set vegetables aside.

4 In a medium bowl combine cottage cheese, egg, and ¼ cup of the Parmesan cheese. Reduce oven temperature to 375°F.

5 Grease a 3-quart rectangular baking dish. Place one-third of the marinara sauce in prepared baking dish. Layer four of the cooked noodles on top of the sauce. Top with half of the roasted vegetables, one-third of the sauce, and one-third of the mozzarella cheese. Add four more noodles, all of the cottage cheese mixture, and one-third of the mozzarella cheese. Add the remaining four noodles, the remaining vegetables, the remaining sauce, and the remaining mozzarella cheese. Sprinkle with the remaining ¼ cup Parmesan cheese.

6 Cover with foil. Bake for 30 minutes. Uncover. Bake about 20 minutes more or until heated through. Let stand for 10 minutes before serving.

nutrition facts per serving: 420 cal., 21 g total fat (8 g sat. fat), 3 mg chol., 1020 mg sodium, 37 g carb., 3 g dietary fiber, 22 g protein.

Used in place of ricotta, tofu adds protein to this vegetarian version of an Italian favorite. It's so delicious, your family will never notice the difference.

tofu manicotti

prep: 40 minutes **bake:** 32 minutes **stand:** 10 minutes
oven: 350°F **makes:** 4 servings **dish:** 3-quart

8   dried manicotti
      Nonstick cooking
        spray
1   cup chopped fresh
        mushrooms
½   cup chopped
        scallions (4)
1   teaspoon dried Italian
        seasoning, crushed
1   12.3- or 16-ounce
        package soft tofu
        (fresh bean curd),
        drained
1   egg, lightly beaten
¼   cup finely shredded
        Parmesan cheese
        (1 ounce)
1   14.5-ounce can diced
        tomatoes with basil,
        oregano, and garlic,
        undrained
1   11-ounce can
        condensed tomato
        bisque soup
⅛   teaspoon ground
        black pepper
¾   cup shredded Italian
        cheese blend
        (3 ounces)

1 Preheat oven to 350°F. Cook manicotti shells according to package directions; drain. Rinse with cold water; drain again.

2 Meanwhile, coat a medium skillet with cooking spray; heat skillet over medium heat. Add mushrooms and scallions; cook until tender, stirring occasionally. Stir in Italian seasoning.

3 In a medium bowl mash tofu. Stir in mushroom mixture, egg, and Parmesan cheese. Gently spoon about ¼ cup of the tofu mixture into each manicotti shell. Arrange stuffed shells in a single layer in an ungreased 3-quart rectangular baking dish.

4 In a medium bowl combine tomatoes, soup, and pepper. Pour tomato mixture over stuffed shells.

5 Bake, uncovered, about 30 minutes or until heated through. Sprinkle with Italian cheese. Bake, uncovered, about 2 minutes more or until cheese is melted. Let stand for 10 minutes before serving.

nutrition facts per serving: 411 cal., 13 g total fat (6 g sat. fat), 74 mg chol., 1383 mg sodium, 53 g carb., 4 g dietary fiber, 21 g protein.

Though often thought of as a grain, couscous is actually a tiny pasta typically made from semolina wheat.

spiced **butternut squash** with almonds

prep: 30 minutes **bake:** 1 hour 30 minutes **stand:** 10 minutes
oven: 375°F **makes:** 4 to 6 servings **dish:** 2-quart

2	pounds butternut squash, peeled, seeded, and cut into 1-inch pieces
1	14-ounce can vegetable broth
1	cup orange juice
1	cup chopped onion (1 large)
³⁄₄	cup dried cherries
1	tablespoon olive oil
2	teaspoons honey
3	cloves garlic, minced
¹⁄₂	teaspoon ground cumin
¹⁄₂	teaspoon paprika
¹⁄₄	teaspoon ground cinnamon
1	cup quick-cooking couscous
¹⁄₂	cup sliced almonds, toasted

1 Preheat oven to 375°F. Lightly grease a 2- to 2½-quart rectangular baking dish.

2 In a large bowl combine squash, broth, orange juice, onion, dried cherries, oil, honey, garlic, cumin, paprika, and cinnamon. Transfer to prepared baking dish. Cover with foil. Bake for 1 hour.

3 Stir mixture. Bake, uncovered, about 30 minutes more or until squash is tender.

4 Remove from oven. Stir in dry couscous. Cover and let stand for 10 minutes before serving. Garnish with almonds.

nutrition facts per serving: 495 cal., 10 g total fat (1 g sat. fat), 0 mg chol., 408 mg sodium, 98 g carb., 10 g dietary fiber, 12 g protein.

Here's a yummy way to get the kids to eat their vegetables—fettuccine mixed with broccoli and cauliflower and baked in a rich, cheesy sauce.

broccoli-cauliflower
tetrazzini

prep: 35 minutes **bake:** 15 minutes **oven:** 400°F
makes: 4 servings **dish:** 3-quart

8	ounces dried fettuccine or spaghetti, broken
1	16-ounce package loose-pack frozen broccoli, carrots, and cauliflower
2	tablespoons butter or margarine
3	tablespoons all-purpose flour
2½	cups milk
½	cup grated Parmesan cheese
¼	teaspoon salt
¼	teaspoon ground black pepper
1	4.5-ounce jar sliced mushrooms, drained
2	tablespoons grated Parmesan cheese

1 Preheat oven to 400°F. Lightly grease a 3-quart rectangular baking dish; set aside. Cook pasta according to package directions; drain. Cook vegetables according to package directions; drain. Set aside.

2 Meanwhile, for cheese sauce, in a medium saucepan melt butter over medium heat. Stir in flour. Add milk all at once. Cook and stir until slightly thickened and bubbly. Cook and stir for 1 minute more. Remove from heat. Stir in ½ cup Parmesan cheese, salt, and pepper.

3 In a large bowl toss pasta with ½ cup of the cheese sauce. Spread pasta evenly in prepared dish. Top with vegetables and mushrooms. Pour the remaining cheese sauce over all. Sprinkle with the 2 tablespoons Parmesan cheese.

4 Bake, uncovered, about 15 minutes or until heated through.

nutrition facts per serving: 456 cal., 13 g total fat (8 g sat. fat), 38 mg chol., 602 mg sodium, 61 g carb., 5 g dietary fiber, 21 g protein.

make-ahead directions: Prepare as directed through Step 3. Cover and chill in the refrigerator for up to 24 hours. Bake, covered, in a 400°F oven for 15 minutes. Uncover and bake for 10 to 15 minutes more.

To quickly thaw frozen spinach, place it in a colander and run warm water over it until defrosted. Press out as much water as you can before adding the spinach to the cheese mixture.

spinach and feta casserole

prep: 20 minutes **bake:** 45 minutes **oven:** 350°F
makes: 4 servings **dish:** 1½-quart

3 eggs, lightly beaten
2 cups cream-style
    cottage cheese
1 10-ounce package
    frozen chopped
    spinach, thawed
    and well drained
⅓ cup crumbled feta
    cheese
¼ cup butter, melted
3 tablespoons all-
    purpose flour
2 teaspoons dried
    minced onion
    Pinch ground nutmeg

1 Preheat oven to 350°F. Grease a 1½-quart casserole; set aside. In a large bowl combine eggs, cottage cheese, spinach, feta cheese, butter, flour, dried onion, and nutmeg. Transfer mixture to prepared casserole.

2 Bake, uncovered, about 45 minutes or until center is nearly set (160°F).

nutrition facts per serving: 344 cal., 24 g total fat (14 g sat. fat), 218 mg chol., 784 mg sodium, 12 g carb., 22 g protein.

Its fun to go meatless now and then—especially with varied, flavor-packed recipes like this one. Six ounces of spinach may look like a lot at first, but as you stir, it wilts pleasingly to the right amount.

roasted vegetables and spinach with pasta

prep: 30 minutes **bake:** 45 minutes **oven:** 400°F
makes: 6 to 8 servings **dish:** 3-quart

1 pound eggplant, peeled and cut into 1-inch chunks (about 6 cups)
1 large red onion, cut into thin wedges
2 cups coarsely chopped yellow and/or green sweet peppers (2 medium)
1 tablespoon olive oil
½ teaspoon salt
1 teaspoon olive oil
½ teaspoon dried thyme, crushed
¼ teaspoon fennel seeds, crushed
¼ teaspoon ground black pepper
⅛ teaspoon crushed red pepper
2 cloves garlic, minced
1 11-ounce can condensed tomato bisque soup
1 cup water
4 cups dried cut ziti or rotini pasta (12 ounces)
1 6-ounce bag baby spinach (about 8 cups)
1 cup shredded mozzarella cheese (4 ounces)

1 Preheat oven to 400°F. In an ungreased 3-quart rectangular baking dish combine eggplant, red onion, sweet peppers, and 1 tablespoon oil. Sprinkle with salt. Roast, uncovered, for 30 to 35 minutes or until vegetables begin to brown, stirring twice.

2 Meanwhile, in a small saucepan heat 1 teaspoon oil over medium heat. Add thyme, fennel seeds, black pepper, crushed red pepper, and garlic. Cook and stir for 2 minutes. Stir in tomato bisque soup and water. Bring to boiling; reduce heat. Simmer, uncovered, for 5 minutes, stirring occasionally.

3 Meanwhile, cook pasta according to package directions; drain well and return it to saucepan. Add tomato soup mixture and roasted vegetables; toss to coat. Stir in baby spinach.

4 Spoon pasta mixture into the same baking dish. Sprinkle with cheese. Bake, uncovered, for 15 to 20 minutes or until heated through and cheese is melted.

nutrition facts per serving: 382 cal., 8 g total fat (3 g sat. fat), 14 mg chol., 775 mg sodium, 63 g carb., 8 g dietary fiber, 15 g protein.

Festive and full of flavor, this lively dish can tap any combination of canned beans that you enjoy. A medley of toppers—you choose 'em—enlivens the Mexican flavor.

three-bean enchiladas

prep: 25 minutes **bake:** 25 minutes **oven:** 350°F
makes: 8 servings **dish:** 10-ounce dishes

16   6-inch corn tortillas
1   15-ounce can red
      kidney beans,
      rinsed and drained
1   15-ounce can pinto
      beans, rinsed and
      drained
1   15-ounce can navy
      or Great Northern
      beans, rinsed and
      drained
1   10.75-ounce can
      condensed cheddar
      cheese soup or
      nacho cheese soup
1   10-ounce can red or
      green enchilada
      sauce
1   8-ounce can tomato
      sauce
1½   cups shredded
      Monterey Jack or
      cheddar cheese
      (6 ounces)
      Sliced pitted black
      olives (optional)
      Chopped green sweet
      pepper (optional)

1 Preheat oven to 350°F. Stack tortillas and wrap tightly in foil. Bake about 10 minutes or until warm.

2 For filling, in a large bowl stir together beans and soup. Spoon about ¼ cup of the filling onto one edge of each tortilla. Starting at the edge with the filling, roll up tortilla. Arrange tortillas, seam sides down, in eight ungreased 10- to 12-ounce au gratin dishes or two ungreased 2-quart rectangular baking dishes.

3 For sauce, in a small bowl stir together enchilada sauce and tomato sauce. Spoon over tortillas.

4 Bake, covered, about 20 minutes for the small dishes (about 30 minutes for the large dishes) or until heated through. Sprinkle with cheese. Bake, uncovered, about 5 minutes more or until cheese is melted. If desired, sprinkle with olives and sweet pepper.

nutrition facts per serving: 360 cal., 10 g total fat (5 g sat. fat), 22 mg chol., 1139 mg sodium, 55 g carb., 12 g dietary fiber, 20 g protein.

A vegetarian pasta with a little Greek influence describes this hearty one-dish entrée. Plain yogurt gives the sauce some creaminess.

rotini-bean bake

prep: 35 minutes **bake:** 35 minutes **stand:** 10 minutes
oven: 375°F **makes:** 8 servings **dish:** 3-quart

4	cups dried rotini pasta (12 ounces)
½	cup bottled balsamic vinaigrette
1	pound roma tomatoes, coarsely chopped
1	15-ounce can white kidney (cannellini) or garbanzo beans (chickpeas), rinsed and drained
8	ounces feta cheese, crumbled
1	cup coarsely chopped pitted Greek black olives
½	cup seasoned fine dry bread crumbs
1	cup plain low-fat yogurt
¾	cup milk
⅓	cup grated Parmesan cheese
1	tablespoon all-purpose flour

1 Lightly grease a 3-quart rectangular baking dish; set aside. Preheat oven to 375°F. Cook pasta according to package directions; drain. In a very large bowl combine vinaigrette and cooked pasta; toss to coat. Stir in tomatoes, beans, feta cheese, and olives.

2 Sprinkle ¼ cup of the bread crumbs into prepared dish. Spoon pasta mixture into dish. In a medium bowl stir together yogurt, milk, Parmesan cheese, and flour until smooth. Pour evenly over pasta mixture. Sprinkle with the remaining ¼ cup bread crumbs.

3 Bake, covered, for 25 minutes. Uncover; bake for 10 to 15 minutes more or until heated through and top is lightly browned. Let stand for 10 minutes before serving.

nutrition facts per serving: 425 cal., 15 g total fat (6 g sat. fat), 31 mg chol., 1045 mg sodium, 57 g carb., 6 g dietary fiber, 19 g protein.

Fresh veggies and cheese-filled tortellini taste terrific together when baked in a cream cheese sauce flavored with oregano and lemon.

tortellini-vegetable bake

prep: 30 minutes **bake:** 30 minutes **oven:** 350°F
makes: 8 servings **dish:** 3-quart

2 9-ounce packages
refrigerated cheese
tortellini

1½ cups fresh sugar snap
peas, trimmed and
halved crosswise

½ cup thinly sliced
carrot (1 medium)

1 tablespoon butter

1 cup sliced fresh
mushrooms

⅓ cup vegetable broth

2 teaspoons all-purpose
flour

1½ teaspoons dried
oregano, crushed

½ teaspoon garlic salt

½ teaspoon ground
black pepper

1 cup milk

1 8-ounce package
cream cheese,
cubed and softened

1 tablespoon lemon
juice

1 cup halved or
quartered cherry
tomatoes

½ cup coarsely chopped
red or green sweet
pepper (1 small)

2 tablespoons grated
Parmesan cheese

1 Preheat oven to 350°F. Cook tortellini according to package directions, adding sugar snap peas and carrot for the last 1 minute of cooking; drain.

2 Meanwhile, in a 12-inch skillet melt butter over medium heat. Add mushrooms; cook about 5 minutes or until mushrooms are tender, stirring occasionally. Remove from skillet.

3 In a screw-top jar combine broth, flour, oregano, garlic salt, and black pepper. Cover and shake until smooth. Add to the same skillet; add milk. Cook and stir until thickened and bubbly. Add cream cheese; cook and stir until smooth. Remove from heat; stir in lemon juice.

4 Stir tortellini mixture, mushrooms, tomatoes, and sweet pepper into cream cheese mixture. Spoon into an ungreased 3-quart rectangular baking dish. Bake, covered, about 30 minutes or until heated through. Sprinkle with Parmesan cheese.

nutrition facts per serving: 353 cal., 17 g total fat (9 g sat. fat), 69 mg chol., 468 mg sodium, 37 g carb., 1 g dietary fiber, 15 g protein.

Garbanzo beans add a meaty texture to an aromatic mix of vegetables, finished with baked cheese on top.

roasted vegetables
parmigiana

prep: 20 minutes roast: 17 minutes oven: 450°F
makes: 6 servings dish: 3-quart

2 medium zucchini, cut into 1-inch chunks
1 medium yellow summer squash, cut into 1-inch chunks
1 medium red or green sweet pepper, seeded and cut into 1-inch pieces
8 ounces fresh mushrooms (stems removed, if desired)
2 tablespoons olive oil
1/2 teaspoon dried rosemary, crushed
1/4 teaspoon salt
1/4 teaspoon cracked black pepper
1 15-ounce can garbanzo beans (chickpeas), rinsed and drained
1 14.5-ounce can Italian-style stewed tomatoes, undrained
1/3 cup shredded mozzarella cheese
1/3 cup finely shredded Parmesan cheese

1 Preheat oven to 450°F. In an ungreased 3-quart rectangular baking dish combine zucchini, summer squash, sweet pepper, and mushrooms. Drizzle vegetable mixture with oil; sprinkle with rosemary, salt, and pepper. Toss lightly to coat.

2 Roast, uncovered, for 12 minutes. Remove from oven. Gently stir in garbanzo beans and tomatoes. Roast about 5 minutes more or just until vegetables are tender. Transfer vegetable mixture to a serving dish; sprinkle with mozzarella cheese and Parmesan cheese.

nutrition facts per serving: 223 cal., 10 g total fat (3 g sat. fat), 9 mg chol., 558 mg sodium, 26 g carb., 6 g dietary fiber, 10 g protein.

pasta

per

7

Bring a uniquely delicious culinary experience to your family's table with some of the richest, cheesiest, most soul-satisfying lasagnas, mac and cheese bakes, and other pasta delights.

fect

Make this casserole even easier by using frozen chopped onions, thawed. No tears and no chopping. What could be better than that?

easy spaghetti bake

prep: 35 minutes   bake: 30 minutes   oven: 350°F
makes: 6 servings   dish: 2-quart

8	ounces dried thin spaghetti, broken in half
12	ounces lean ground beef
1½	cups chopped onions (3 medium)
1	cup chopped green sweet pepper (1 large)
1	clove garlic, minced
1	10.75-ounce can reduced-fat and reduced-sodium condensed cream of mushroom soup
1	10.75-ounce can reduced-fat and reduced-sodium condensed tomato soup
1⅓	cups water
2	cups shredded cheddar cheese (8 ounces)
½	teaspoon salt
½	teaspoon ground black pepper

1 Preheat oven to 350°F. Lightly grease a 2-quart square baking dish; set aside. Cook spaghetti according to package directions; drain. Return to pan.

2 Meanwhile, in a large skillet cook ground meat, onions, sweet pepper, and garlic over medium heat until meat is brown and onion is tender. Drain off fat. Stir in mushroom soup, tomato soup, and the water.

3 Bring to boiling; reduce heat. Simmer, uncovered, for 10 minutes, stirring occasionally. Stir in 1½ cups of the cheese, the salt, and black pepper. Gently stir in cooked spaghetti.

4 Transfer spaghetti mixture to prepared baking dish. Sprinkle with the remaining cheese. Bake, uncovered, about 30 minutes or until heated through.

nutrition facts per serving: 504 cal., 23 g total fat (11 g sat. fat), 80 mg chol., 871 mg sodium, 46 g carb., 2 g dietary fiber, 26 g protein.

You can't beat the spicy flavor that Italian sausage gives to pasta. Choose mild or spicy or mix them to your liking in this crowd-pleasing dish.

baked cavatelli

prep: 20 minutes bake: 40 minutes oven: 375°F
makes: 6 servings dish: 2-quart

7   ounces dried cavatelli
     or medium shell
     macaroni (1³/₄ cups)
12   ounces bulk Italian
     sausage or ground
     beef
³/₄ cup chopped onion
     (1 large)
¹/₂ cup chopped green
     sweet pepper
     (optional)
2   cloves garlic, minced
1   26-ounce jar tomato
     and basil pasta
     sauce
1¹/₄ cups shredded
     mozzarella cheese
     (5 ounces)
¹/₄ cup sliced pitted
     black olives
     (optional)
¹/₄ teaspoon ground
     black pepper

1 Preheat oven to 375°F. Cook pasta according to package directions. Drain; set aside.

2 Meanwhile, in a large skillet cook sausage, onion, green pepper (if using), and garlic or until sausage is brown. Drain off fat.

3 In a large bowl stir together pasta sauce, 1 cup of the cheese, the olives (if using), and black pepper. Add cooked pasta and drained sausage mixture. Stir gently to combine. Spoon mixture into an ungreased 2-quart casserole.

4 Bake, covered, for 35 to 40 minutes or until heated through. Uncover; sprinkle with the remaining cheese. Bake about 5 minutes more or until cheese melts.

nutrition facts per serving: 468 cal., 20 g total fat (10 g sat. fat), 52 mg chol., 903 mg sodium, 46 g carb., 5 g dietary fiber, 21 g protein.

The traditional way to assemble lasagna is to layer the ingredients. Tossing together the pasta and sauce and adding one cheesy topping cuts preparation time, but not the yummy lusciousness of this dish.

quick lasagna casserole

prep: 25 minutes bake: 35 minutes stand: 10 minutes oven: 375°F
makes: 8 to 10 servings dish: 3-quart

12 ounces dried campanelle or cellantani pasta
1 pound bulk Italian sausage
1 large onion, cut in thin wedges
1 medium yellow sweet pepper, cut in bite-size strips
3 cloves garlic, minced
1 24- to 28-ounce jar marinara sauce
1 teaspoon fennel seeds, crushed
1 15-ounce carton ricotta cheese
1 egg, lightly beaten
2 cups shredded Italian cheese blend (8 ounces)

1 Preheat oven to 375°F. Cook pasta according to package directions; drain.

2 In a large skillet cook sausage, onion, sweet pepper, and garlic until sausage is no longer pink; drain fat. Transfer sausage mixture to a very large bowl. Stir in marinara sauce, fennel seeds, and cooked pasta.

3 Transfer the pasta mixture to an ungreased 3-quart rectangular baking dish. In a medium bowl stir together ricotta cheese, egg, and 1 cup of the Italian blend cheese. Spoon the ricotta cheese over the pasta mixture in large spoonfuls. Sprinkle the remaining shredded Italian cheese over the top. Bake, covered, for 35 to 40 minutes or until heated through. Let stand 10 minutes before serving.

nutrition facts per serving: 636 cal., 35 g total fat (17 g sat. fat), 112 mg chol., 1133 mg sodium, 47 g carb., 5 g dietary fiber, 34 g protein.

make-ahead directions: Spoon mixture into 3-quart rectangular baking dish. Cover with plastic wrap. Chill 2 to 24 hours. Remove plastic wrap. Bake in a 350°F oven for 50 to 60 minutes or until heated through. Let stand 10 minutes before serving.

Here's the mother of all others. This is the everyday dish we grew up loving and the one you'll fall back on time and again.

classic lasagna

prep: 30 minutes bake: 30 minutes cook: 15 minutes stand: 10 minutes
oven: 375°F makes: 12 servings dish: 3-quart

9 dried lasagna noodles
1 pound bulk Italian
   or pork sausage or
   ground beef
1 cup chopped onion
   (1 large)
2 cloves garlic, minced
1 14.5-ounce can diced
   tomatoes, undrained
1 8-ounce can tomato
   sauce
1 tablespoon dried
   Italian seasoning,
   crushed
1 teaspoon fennel
   seeds, crushed
   (optional)
¼ teaspoon ground
   black pepper
1 egg, lightly beaten
1 15-ounce carton ricotta
   cheese or 2 cups
   cream-style cottage
   cheese, drained
¼ cup grated Parmesan
   cheese
2 cups shredded
   mozzarella cheese
   (8 ounces)
   Grated Parmesan
   cheese (optional)

1 Preheat oven to 375°F. Cook lasagna noodles according to package directions; drain well. Rinse with cold water; drain well. Place lasagna noodles in a single layer on a sheet of foil; set aside.

2 For sauce, in a large skillet cook sausage, onion, and garlic until meat is cooked through, using a wooden spoon to break up meat as it cooks; drain off fat. Stir tomatoes, tomato sauce, Italian seasoning, fennel seeds (if using), and pepper into meat mixture. Bring to boiling; reduce heat. Cover and simmer for 15 minutes, stirring occasionally.

3 For filling, in a medium bowl combine egg, ricotta cheese, and ¼ cup Parmesan cheese.

4 Spread about ¼ cup of the sauce over the bottom of an ungreased 3-quart rectangular baking dish. Place three of the cooked lasagna noodles on the sauce in the dish. Spread with one-third of the filling. Top with one-third of the remaining meat sauce and one-third of the mozzarella cheese. Repeat layers two more times, starting with noodles and ending with mozzarella cheese; make sure the top layer of noodles is completely covered with meat sauce. If desired, sprinkle with additional Parmesan cheese.

5 Bake, uncovered, for 30 to 35 minutes or until heated through. Let stand 10 minutes before serving.

nutrition facts per serving: 335 cal., 21 g total fat (10 g sat. fat), 78 mg chol., 623 mg sodium, 19 g carb., 2 g dietary fiber, 18 g protein.

make-ahead directions: Prepare as directed through Step 4. Cover and chill for up to 24 hours. Bake, covered, in 375°F oven for 40 minutes. Uncover; bake about 20 minutes more or until heated through. Let stand 10 minutes before serving.

Make this delightful dish meat-full or meatless by adding or subtracting the Italian sausage. It's perfect for a twist on the old favorite lasagna.

red pepper lasagna

prep: 50 minutes bake: 35 minutes stand: 40 minutes oven: 425°F/350°F
makes: 8 servings dish: 3-quart

4   medium red sweet peppers or two 7-ounce jars roasted red sweet peppers
1   tablespoon olive oil
1   28-ounce can crushed tomatoes, undrained
½   cup snipped fresh basil
4   cloves garlic, minced
¾   teaspoon ground black pepper
1   teaspoon salt
8   ounces sweet or hot bulk Italian sausage, cooked and drained (optional)
⅓   cup butter or margarine
⅓   cup all-purpose flour
½   teaspoon ground nutmeg
3   cups milk
12 no-boil lasagna noodles
1¼ cups finely shredded Parmesan cheese (5 ounces)

1 Preheat oven to 425°F. For red pepper sauce, cut fresh sweet peppers in half; remove stems, seeds, and membranes. Place peppers, cut sides down, on a foil-lined baking sheet. Bake for 20 to 25 minutes or until skin is bubbly and browned. Wrap peppers in foil; let stand for 20 to 30 minutes or until cool enough to handle. Peel skins from peppers. Cut peppers into thin strips. (Or, if using bottled roasted red peppers, drain and cut into thin strips).

2 In a large saucepan heat olive oil over medium heat. Add sweet peppers; cook for 1 minute. Stir in tomatoes, basil, garlic, black pepper, and ½ teaspoon of the salt. Bring to boiling; reduce heat. Simmer, uncovered, for 20 minutes, stirring often. Set aside to cool. Stir in cooked sausage (if using).

3 For béchamel sauce, in a medium saucepan melt butter over medium heat. Stir in flour, nutmeg, and the remaining ½ teaspoon salt until smooth. Add milk all at once. Cook and stir until thickened and bubbly. Let cool.

4 Preheat oven to 350°F. To assemble, grease the bottom of a 3-quart rectangular baking dish. Cover bottom of dish with three lasagna noodles. Spread about 1 cup of the red pepper sauce over the pasta. Top with ¾ cup of the béchamel sauce, spreading evenly; sprinkle with ¼ cup of the Parmesan cheese. Repeat, layering three more times with the remaining pasta, red pepper sauce, béchamel sauce, and ¾ cup Parmesan cheese. Be sure the top layer of noodles is completely covered with sauce. Sprinkle with the remaining ¼ cup Parmesan cheese.

5 Bake, uncovered, for 35 to 40 minutes or until bubbly and light brown on top. Let stand for 20 minutes before serving.

nutrition facts per serving: 451 cal., 24 g total fat (12 g sat. fat), 58 mg chol., 936 mg sodium, 41 g carb., 3 g dietary fiber, 19 g protein.

make-ahead directions: Assemble lasagna as directed. Cover with plastic wrap; refrigerate for up to 24 hours. To serve, remove and discard plastic wrap. Cover lasagna with foil. Bake in 350°F oven for 30 minutes. Remove foil. Bake for 15 to 25 minutes or until bubbly and light brown on top.

Lasagna gets a tasty remake with whole wheat noodles, spinach, chicken, and a creamy white sauce instead of a tomato sauce.

chicken caesar lasagna

prep: 35 minutes bake: 50 minutes stand: 15 minutes
oven: 325°F makes: 9 servings dish: 3-quart

Nonstick cooking
spray
9 dried whole wheat
or regular lasagna
noodles
2 10-ounce containers
refrigerated light
Alfredo pasta sauce
3 tablespoons lemon
juice
½ teaspoon cracked
black pepper
3 cups chopped cooked
chicken breast*
1 10-ounce package
frozen chopped
spinach, thawed
and well drained
1 cup bottled roasted
red sweet peppers,
drained and
chopped
¾ cup shredded Italian
cheese blend
(3 ounces)

1 Preheat oven to 325°F. Lightly coat a 3-quart rectangular baking dish with nonstick cooking spray; set aside. Cook lasagna noodles according to package directions; drain well. Rinse with cold water; drain well. Place lasagna noodles in a single layer on a sheet of foil. Meanwhile, in a large bowl combine Alfredo sauce, lemon juice, and black pepper. Stir in cooked chicken, spinach, and roasted sweet peppers.

2 Arrange three of the cooked lasagna noodles in prepared dish. Top with one-third of the chicken mixture. Repeat layers two more times.

3 Bake, covered, for 45 to 55 minutes or until heated through. Uncover; sprinkle with cheese. Bake, uncovered, about 5 minutes more or until cheese is melted. Let stand for 15 minutes before serving.

nutrition facts per serving: 268 cal., 10 g total fat (6 g sat. fat), 68 mg chol., 557 mg sodium, 20 g carb., 2 g dietary fiber, 24 g protein.

*test kitchen tip: For chopped cooked chicken, season 2 pounds skinless, boneless chicken breasts with ¼ teaspoon salt and ⅛ teaspoon black pepper. In large skillet heat 1 tablespoon olive oil over medium-high heat. Reduce heat to medium. Add chicken. Cook, uncovered, for 8 to 12 minutes or until no longer pink, turning halfway through cooking. Cool chicken slightly before chopping.

The sauce for this white lasagna is flavored with tarragon and Monterey Jack cheese.

lasagna **blanca**

prep: 1 hour bake: 35 minutes stand: 10 minutes oven: 350°F
makes: 12 servings dish: 3-quart

12 dried lasagna noodles
1 pound spicy bulk pork sausage
½ cup chopped scallions (4)
½ cup chopped fresh mushrooms
1 cup cream-style cottage cheese
½ of an 8-ounce package cream cheese, softened and cut up
1½ cups shredded Monterey Jack or cheddar cheese (6 ounces)
½ teaspoon garlic powder
⅛ teaspoon ground black pepper
1 tablespoon butter or margarine
1 tablespoon all-purpose flour
⅛ teaspoon dried tarragon, crushed
⅛ teaspoon ground black pepper
1 cup milk

1 Cook lasagna noodles according to package directions; drain. Place lasagna noodles in a single layer on a sheet of foil; set aside. Meanwhile, in a large skillet cook sausage, scallions, and mushrooms until sausage is no longer pink; drain off fat. Set aside.

2 For cheese filling, in a medium bowl combine cottage cheese, cream cheese, ½ cup of the Monterey Jack cheese, the garlic powder, and ⅛ teaspoon pepper.

3 Preheat oven to 350°F. Lightly grease a 3-quart rectangular baking dish; set aside. Divide and spread cheese filling evenly over noodles. Sprinkle sausage mixture on top. Roll up each noodle into a spiral. Place lasagna roll-ups, seam sides down, in prepared baking dish.

4 For sauce, in a small saucepan melt butter over medium heat. Stir in flour, tarragon, and ⅛ teaspoon pepper. Add milk all at once. Cook and stir until slightly thickened and bubbly. Remove from heat. Stir in another ½ cup of the Monterey Jack cheese. Pour sauce over lasagna roll-ups.

5 Bake, covered, for 25 minutes. Uncover; sprinkle with the remaining ½ cup Monterey Jack cheese. Bake, uncovered, about 10 minutes more or until heated through. Let stand for 10 minutes before serving.

nutrition facts per serving: 317 cal., 17 g total fat (9 g sat. fat), 54 mg chol., 378 mg sodium, 21 g carb., 1 g dietary fiber, 17 g protein.

make-ahead directions: Prepare as directed through Step 4. Cover and refrigerate for up to 24 hours. Bake, covered, in a 350°F oven for 40 minutes. Uncover; sprinkle with the remaining ½ cup Monterey Jack cheese. Bake, uncovered, about 10 minutes more or until heated through.

Prepare this hearty vegetarian pasta dish for a satisfying casual supper. If you prefer a sharper flavor, substitute sharp white cheddar cheese for the Swiss.

baked pasta with
mushrooms and spinach

prep: 45 minutes   **bake:** 30 minutes   **oven:** 350°F
makes: 8 servings   **dish:** 3-quart

12   ounces dried cut ziti or penne pasta (about 4 cups)
1   15-ounce carton whole-milk ricotta cheese
1   cup half-and-half or light cream
1   egg
1   teaspoon sugar
½   teaspoon salt
¼   teaspoon ground black pepper
⅛   teaspoon ground nutmeg
¼   cup snipped fresh thyme, parsley, basil, and/or rosemary
¼   cup cooking oil
10   cups sliced fresh mushrooms
½   cup chopped onion (1 small)
2   cloves garlic, minced
4   cups chopped spinach
2   cups shredded Swiss cheese (8 ounces)
½   cup shredded Parmesan cheese (2 ounces)

1 Preheat oven to 350°F. Cook pasta according to package directions; drain.

2 Meanwhile, place the ricotta cheese in a food processor bowl; cover and process until smooth. Add half-and-half, egg, sugar, salt, pepper, and nutmeg; process until well mixed. Stir in thyme. Stir into cooked pasta.

3 In a large skillet heat oil over medium-high heat. Add mushrooms; cook and stir until tender and liquid is reduced. Remove mushrooms from skillet. Add onion and garlic to skillet. Cook and stir until tender and liquid is reduced. Return mushrooms to skillet. Add spinach. Cook and stir for 2 to 3 minutes or until spinach is wilted. Drain mixture well in a colander or sieve. Stir into pasta mixture; stir in 1 cup of the Swiss cheese. Transfer to an ungreased 3-quart rectangular baking dish.

4 Bake, covered, for 20 minutes. Sprinkle with the remaining Swiss cheese and the Parmesan cheese. Bake, uncovered, for 10 to 15 minutes more or until heated through and the top begins to brown.

nutrition facts per serving: 525 cal., 28 g total fat (14 g sat. fat), 94 mg chol., 371 mg sodium, 43 g carb., 3 g dietary fiber, 27 g protein.

Evaporated milk, a pantry staple, provides smooth richness to the sauce in this savory pasta dish. Find it in your market's baking aisle.

inside-out spaghetti pie

prep: 20 minutes bake: 50 minutes stand: 15 minutes oven: 350°F
makes: 6 servings dish: 9-inch pie plate

1 5-ounce can
    evaporated milk
½ cup fine dry bread
    crumbs
⅓ cup chopped onion
    (1 small)
1 teaspoon salt
1 teaspoon dried Italian
    seasoning, crushed
¼ teaspoon ground
    black pepper
1 pound lean ground
    beef
4 ounces dried spaghetti
1 tablespoon butter
1 egg, lightly beaten
¼ cup grated Parmesan
    cheese
1 8-ounce can pizza
    sauce
1 cup shredded
    mozzarella cheese
    (4 ounces)

1 Preheat oven to 350°F. In a large bowl combine evaporated milk, bread crumbs, onion, salt, Italian seasoning, and pepper. Add ground beef; mix well. Lightly press mixture evenly onto the bottom and up the side of an ungreased 9-inch pie plate. Bake, uncovered, about 30 minutes or until done (160°F). Carefully tilt dish and drain off fat.

2 Meanwhile, cook spaghetti according to package directions; drain. Return to pan. Stir in butter until melted. Stir in egg and Parmesan cheese until spaghetti is coated.

3 Spread half of the pizza sauce over meat mixture. Top with ½ cup of the mozzarella cheese and the spaghetti mixture. Top with the remaining pizza sauce and the remaining ½ cup mozzarella cheese.

4 Bake, uncovered, about 20 minutes or until heated through. (If necessary, cover edges of meat mixture with foil to prevent overbrowning.) Let stand for 15 minutes before serving.

nutrition facts per serving: 373 cal., 17 g total fat (8 g sat. fat), 110 mg chol., 1078 mg sodium, 28 g carb., 2 g dietary fiber, 26 g protein.

Choose a clear, vinaigrette-style Italian salad dressing for this flavor-packed one-dish meal.

pasta, zucchini, and sausage bake

prep: 25 minutes bake: 30 minutes oven: 350°F
makes: 8 servings dish: 3-quart

1 1.29-pound package mild or hot Italian sausage links, sliced ½-inch thick (such as Johnsonville sausage links)

1 tablespoon olive oil

1 12-ounce package dried medium shell macaroni

½ cup bottled Italian salad dressing

1 10.75-ounce can condensed cream of chicken soup

1 8-ounce carton sour cream

1 8-ounce package shredded Italian cheese blend (2 cups)

2 tablespoons all-purpose flour

3 garlic cloves, minced

2 medium zucchini and/or yellow summer squash, halved lengthwise and sliced ½-inch thick

1 Preheat oven to 350°F. In large skillet cook sausage in hot oil until no longer pink, stirring frequently. Drain in a colander. Meanwhile, cook pasta according to package directions; drain over sausage in colander.

2 In large bowl combine salad dressing, soup, sour cream, 1 cup of the cheese, the flour, and garlic. Stir in pasta/sausage mixture and squash. Pour into an ungreased 3-quart rectangular baking dish. Cover with foil and bake 25 minutes. Uncover; sprinkle with remaining 1 cup cheese. Bake 5 minutes more or until hot and bubbly.

nutrition facts per serving: 658 cal., 43 g total fat (17 g sat. fat), 91 mg chol., 1281 mg sodium, 41 g carb., 2 g dietary fiber, 26 g protein.

Using taco cheese with its added seasonings gives extra flavor to this family-style pasta dish.

tacos in pasta shells

prep: 35 minutes bake: 30 minutes oven: 350°F
makes: 12 servings dish: 2-quart

12	ounces dried jumbo pasta shells
2	16-ounce jars salsa
2½	pounds ground beef
6	ounces cream cheese, cut up
2	teaspoons chili powder
1½	cups shredded taco or cheddar cheese (6 ounces)
	Chopped tomato (optional)

1 Preheat oven to 350°F. Cook pasta according to package directions; drain. Rinse with cold water; drain again.

2 Meanwhile, divide about 1 cup of the salsa between two ungreased 2-quart rectangular baking dishes, spreading evenly. In an extra-large skillet cook ground beef over medium heat until brown. Drain off fat. Stir in cream cheese and chili powder. Cool slightly.

3 Spoon meat mixture into cooked pasta shells. Arrange filled shells on top of salsa in dishes. Top with the remaining salsa.

4 Bake, covered, for 15 minutes. Sprinkle with taco cheese. Bake, uncovered, about 15 minutes more or until heated through. If desired, sprinkle with tomato.

nutrition facts per serving: 416 cal., 22 g total fat (11 g sat. fat), 90 mg chol., 513 mg sodium, 27 g carb., 2 g dietary fiber, 27 g protein.

Rich, decadent, and creamy! This cheesy pasta dish bakes in less than 30 minutes for a simple weeknight meal.

cheesy baked penne and sausage

prep: 25 minutes bake: 25 minutes oven: 350°F
makes: 6 servings dish: 2-quart

8 ounces dried penne pasta
8 ounces bulk mild Italian sausage
1/3 cup sliced scallions
2 tablespoons all-purpose flour
2 tablespoons whole-grain mustard
1 1/4 cups milk
1/4 teaspoon ground black pepper
1/2 of an 8-ounce carton mascarpone cheese
1 cup shredded fontina cheese (4 ounces)
1 cup shredded provolone cheese (4 ounces)

1 Preheat oven to 350°F. Cook pasta according to package directions; drain. Meanwhile, in very large skillet cook sausage until browned; drain fat well. Stir in scallions; cook 1 minute. Add flour and mustard; gradually stir in milk and pepper. Cook and stir until slightly thickened and bubbly. Reduce heat; stir in mascarpone cheese until blended. Add fontina cheese, provolone cheese, and pasta.

2 Transfer pasta mixture to an ungreased 2-quart rectangular baking dish. Bake, uncovered, for 25 to 30 minutes or until heated through.

nutrition facts per serving: 461 cal., 24 g total fat (14 g sat. fat), 74 mg chol., 687 mg sodium, 36 g carb., 1.4 g dietary fiber, 26 g protein.

This basil-enhanced shrimp spectacular will impress sophisticated diners who may not recognize this as macaroni and cheese.

macaroni with pesto shrimp

prep: 25 minutes   bake: 40 minutes   stand: 10 minutes   oven: 350°F
makes: 6 servings   dish: 2-quart

1	pound fresh or frozen medium shrimp in shells
2	cups dried elbow macaroni (8 ounces)
2	eggs, lightly beaten
1	cup half-and-half or light cream
¼	cup butter, melted
1½	cups lightly packed fresh basil leaves, snipped
1¼	cups shredded fontina cheese (5 ounces)
½	cup grated Parmesan cheese
2	tablespoons pine nuts, toasted (optional)
2	cloves garlic, minced
½	teaspoon salt
¼	teaspoon ground black pepper
1	ounce Parmesan cheese, shaved (optional)
	Fresh basil leaves (optional)

1 Thaw shrimp, if frozen. Peel and devein shrimp, removing tails. Rinse shrimp; pat dry with paper towels. Chop shrimp and set aside. Preheat oven to 350°F. Grease a 2-quart casserole; set aside.

2 Cook macaroni according to package directions. Drain and keep warm.

3 Meanwhile, for cheese sauce, in a large bowl combine eggs, half-and-half, and butter. Stir in 1½ cups basil, 1 cup of the fontina cheese, ¼ cup of the Parmesan cheese, the pine nuts (if using), garlic, salt, and pepper. Stir in shrimp and cooked macaroni. Transfer mixture to prepared casserole. Sprinkle with the remaining ¼ cup fontina cheese and the remaining ¼ cup Parmesan cheese.

4 Bake, uncovered, for 40 to 45 minutes or until heated through and shrimp are opaque. Let stand for 10 minutes before serving. If desired, garnish with shaved Parmesan cheese and additional fresh basil.

nutrition facts per serving: 489 cal., 25 g total fat (14 g sat. fat), 254 mg chol., 694 mg sodium, 32 g carb., 1 g dietary fiber, 33 g protein.

Here's an all-new take on a comfort food classic, with sausage for heartiness, two kinds of cheeses for richness, and some chipotle to liven things up.

chipotle mac and cheese

prep: 25 minutes   bake: 30 minutes   stand: 10 minutes   oven: 350°F
makes: 6 to 8 servings   dish: 2-quart

12	ounces dried medium shell pasta
2	tablespoons butter
2	tablespoons all-purpose flour
1	12-ounce can evaporated milk
1	cup milk
1½	cups shredded Monterey Jack cheese (6 ounces)
1½	cups shredded sharp cheddar cheese (6 ounces)
1	tablespoon chopped canned chipotle chile pepper in adobo sauce
¼	teaspoon salt
1	pound bulk pork sausage or uncooked chorizo sausage, cooked and drained, or 2 cups diced cooked ham

1 Preheat oven to 350°F. Lightly grease a 2- to 2½-quart casserole; set aside. Cook pasta according to package directions; drain. Return to pan.

2 Meanwhile, in a medium saucepan melt butter over medium heat. Stir in flour; cook and stir for 1 minute. Gradually stir in evaporated milk and milk. Cook and stir until slightly thickened and bubbly. Remove from heat. Stir in 1 cup of the Monterey Jack cheese, 1 cup of the cheddar cheese, the chipotle pepper, and salt. Stir cheese mixture into cooked pasta. Stir in cooked sausage.

3 Transfer mixture to the prepared casserole. Sprinkle with the remaining ½ cup Monterey Jack cheese and the remaining ½ cup cheddar cheese. Place casserole on a baking sheet. Bake, covered, about 30 minutes or until bubbly. Let stand for 10 minutes before serving.

nutrition facts per serving: 348 cal., 19 g total fat (11 g sat. fat), 64 mg chol., 401 mg sodium, 28 g carb., 1 g dietary fiber, 16 g protein.

Brie cheese and lump crabmeat make this casserole a rich dish for special occasions.

macaroni and brie
with crab

prep: 20 minutes   bake: 20 minutes   cook: 15 minutes   stand: 5 minutes
oven: 350°F   makes: 8 servings   dish: 14-ounce dishes

Nonstick cooking
   spray
1 pound dried medium
   shell pasta
5 tablespoons butter
1 medium sweet onion
   (such as Vidalia or
   Maui), halved and
   thinly sliced
1/3 cup all-purpose flour
3/4 teaspoon salt
1/2 teaspoon ground
   black pepper
3 cups milk
1 pound Brie cheese,
   trimmed, cut into
   small wedges, and
   chopped (reserve
   8 small wedges for
   topping)
12 ounces fresh cooked
   crabmeat or canned
   lump crabmeat,
   drained, flaked, and
   cartilage removed
3 slices firm white
   bread, torn into
   large pieces

1 Preheat oven to 350°F. Lightly coat eight 14- to 16-ounce individual baking dishes with cooking spray; set aside. In a Dutch oven cook pasta according to package directions; drain. Return pasta to Dutch oven.

2 Meanwhile, in a large skillet melt butter over medium-low heat. Add onion and cook about 15 minutes or until tender and golden brown, stirring occasionally. Add flour, salt, and pepper; cook and stir about 1 minute or until combined. Add milk all at once. Cook and stir until slightly thickened and bubbly. Gradually add the chopped Brie cheese; cook and stir over medium-low heat until cheese is melted. Stir cheese mixture into cooked pasta. Fold in crab. Transfer to prepared baking dishes.

3 Place bread pieces in a food processor; cover and process until in coarse crumbs. Sprinkle crumbs over pasta mixture. Bake, uncovered, for 20 to 25 minutes or until heated through and crumbs are golden brown. For the last 5 minutes of baking, top each dish with one of the reserved small Brie wedges. Let stand for 5 minutes before serving.

nutrition facts per serving: 595 cal., 27 g total fat (16 g sat. fat), 137 mg chol., 905 mg sodium, 57 g carb., 2 g dietary fiber, 31 g protein.

Smoked mozzarella takes these manicotti from okay to awesome. It's easy to find in the cheese case—just look for the mozzarella with the caramel-color rind.

stuffed manicotti

prep: 30 minutes bake: 35 minutes oven: 350°F
makes: 6 servings dish: 3-quart

12 packaged dried manicotti
8 ounces lean ground beef
8 ounces bulk Italian sausage
½ of a 15-ounce carton ricotta cheese (about 1 cup)
2 cups shredded smoked mozzarella cheese (8 ounces)
½ cup finely shredded Parmesan cheese (2 ounces)
1½ teaspoons dried Italian seasoning, crushed
3 cups purchased marinara sauce

1 Preheat oven to 350°F. Cook pasta according to package directions; drain. Place pasta in a single layer on a sheet of greased foil.

2 Meanwhile, in a large skillet cook ground beef and Italian sausage over medium heat until brown. Drain off fat. In a medium bowl combine ricotta cheese, 1 cup of the mozzarella cheese, the Parmesan cheese, and Italian seasoning. Stir in cooked meat mixture. Using a small spoon, fill pasta with meat mixture. Arrange filled pasta in an ungreased 3-quart rectangular baking dish. Pour marinara sauce over pasta. Sprinkle with the remaining 1 cup mozzarella cheese.

3 Bake, covered, for 25 minutes. Uncover and bake about 10 minutes more or until mixture is heated through and cheese is melted.

nutrition facts per serving: 646 cal., 36 g total fat (16 g sat. fat), 109 mg chol., 1203 mg sodium, 44 g carb., 3 g dietary fiber, 34 g protein.

Although this smoky version has nearly half the calories and fat of classic macaroni and cheese, the flavor is all there and then some.

macaroni
and smoked cheddar

prep: 25 minutes   bake: 20 minutes   stand: 5 minutes   oven: 350°F
makes: 4 servings   dish: 1½-quart

8   ounces packaged dried large elbow pasta
3   ounces smoked cheddar or smoked Gouda cheese
1   cup reduced-sodium chicken broth
½   cup chopped onion (1 medium)
¾   cup fat-free half-and-half
1   tablespoon all-purpose flour
½   teaspoon dry mustard
¼   teaspoon ground black pepper
1   medium tart apple, coarsely chopped
1   tablespoon finely shredded Parmesan cheese

1 In a Dutch oven cook pasta according to package directions; drain and return to Dutch oven. If desired, use a vegetable peeler to remove any dark outer layer from the smoked cheese. Shred cheese (you should have about ¾ cup).

2 Preheat oven to 350°F. For cheese sauce, in a medium saucepan combine broth and onion; cook, covered, over medium-high heat about 5 minutes or until onion is tender. In a screw-top jar combine half-and-half, flour, dry mustard, and pepper. Cover and shake well. Add to broth mixture in saucepan. Cook and stir over medium heat just until bubbly. Remove from heat; add cheddar cheese, stirring until most of the cheese is melted. Pour cheese sauce over cooked pasta, stirring until combined. Transfer pasta mixture to an ungreased 1½-quart casserole.

3 Bake, covered, for 10 minutes. Uncover and bake about 10 minutes more or until bubbly. Let stand for 5 minutes before serving. Top with apple and Parmesan cheese.

nutrition facts per serving: 376 cal., 8 g total fat (4 g sat. fat), 24 mg chol., 564 mg sodium, 59 g carb., 3 g dietary fiber, 15 g protein.

The secret to this ultra-creamy macaroni and cheese? A little processed cheese mixed in with the other cheeses.

baked macaroni and cheese

prep: 25 minutes   bake: 40 minutes   stand: 10 minutes   oven: 325°F
makes: 8 to 10 servings   dish: 3-quart

16 ounces dried elbow macaroni (4 cups)
1   8-ounce package shredded sharp cheddar cheese (2 cups)
1   8-ounce package pasteurized prepared cheese product, cut up
¼   cup butter, cut up
3   eggs, lightly beaten
1   12-ounce can evaporated milk
1   cup process cheese dip or one 10.75-ounce can condensed cheddar cheese soup
¼   teaspoon ground white pepper

1 Preheat oven to 325°F. Cook macaroni according to package directions. Meanwhile, let the cheeses and butter stand at room temperature. Drain macaroni; transfer to a very large bowl. Add 1½ cups of the shredded cheddar, the cheese product, and the butter to the hot pasta, stirring well.

2 In a medium bowl whisk together eggs, milk, cheese dip, and white pepper until combined. Stir egg mixture into macaroni mixture. Transfer mixture to an ungreased 3-quart rectangular baking dish, spreading evenly. Cover dish with foil.

3 Bake for 25 minutes. Uncover and stir well. Sprinkle with the remaining ½ cup cheddar cheese. Bake, uncovered, for 15 to 20 minutes more or until cheese is melted and mixture is heated through. Let stand 10 minutes before serving.

nutrition facts per serving: 635 cal., 35 g total fat (21 g sat. fat), 189 mg chol., 1207 mg sodium, 54 g carb., 2 g dietary fiber, 27 g protein.

lightened-up macaroni and cheese: Prepare as directed except substitute reduced-fat cheddar cheese and reduced-fat pasteurized prepared cheese product for the cheese and cheese product. Decrease butter to 2 tablespoons, decrease eggs to 2, and substitute evaporated fat-free milk for the evaporated milk.

Broccoli and mushrooms kick up the nutrition profile in this cheesy one-dish meal.

loaded macaroni and cheese

prep: 25 minutes bake: 30 minutes stand: 10 minutes oven: 375°F
makes: 6 servings dish: 2-quart

2 cups dried macaroni
   (8 ounces)
1 cup cottage cheese
½ of an 8-ounce
   package cream
   cheese, softened
1 tablespoon yellow
   mustard
½ teaspoon salt
½ teaspoon ground
   black pepper
   Dash bottled hot
   pepper sauce
2 cups cooked broccoli
   florets
1 cup sliced fresh
   mushrooms
½ cup finely chopped
   onion (1 medium)
1 cup shredded
   mozzarella cheese
   (4 ounces)
1 cup shredded
   cheddar cheese
   (4 ounces)
¼ cup freshly grated
   Parmesan cheese

1 Cook macaroni according to package directions; drain. Set aside. Meanwhile, preheat oven to 375°F. Grease a 2-quart square baking dish; set aside.

2 In a large bowl combine cottage cheese, cream cheese, mustard, salt, black pepper, and bottled hot pepper sauce; mix well. Stir in broccoli, mushrooms, and onion. Stir in mozzarella cheese and ¼ cup of the cheddar cheese. Gently stir in cooked macaroni. Transfer mixture to prepared baking dish.

3 Bake, covered, for 20 minutes. Uncover and sprinkle with the remaining ¾ cup cheddar cheese and the Parmesan cheese. Bake, uncovered, about 10 minutes more or until cheese is melted. Let stand for 10 minutes before serving.

nutrition facts per serving: 400 cal., 18 g total fat (11 g sat. fat), 59 mg chol., 730 mg sodium, 35 g carb., 3 g dietary fiber, 24 g protein.

Tuscany is a well-known region in Italy from where this mac 'n' cheese dish draws its name. The Italian influence can been seen in the hearty nature of this bake, as well as the addition of mozzarella cheese, sliced tomato, Italian sausage, and kalamata olives.

tuscan mac 'n' cheese

prep: 45 minutes bake: 50 minutes stand: 15 minutes oven: 350°F
makes: 6 to 8 servings. dish: 2-quart

8 ounces dried gemelli pasta or elbow macaroni (2 cups)
8 ounces sweet or hot bulk Italian sausage
1 8-ounce package cream cheese, cut into cubes and softened
4 ounces crusty Italian bread, cut into 1-inch cubes (about 2 cups)
1 cup pitted kalamata olives, halved
1 cup shredded mozzarella cheese (4 ounces)
1 tablespoon butter or margarine
1 tablespoon all-purpose flour
1 teaspoon dried sage, crushed
½ teaspoon salt
¼ teaspoon dried thyme, crushed
⅛ teaspoon cayenne pepper
1½ cups milk
1 medium tomato, sliced
½ cup finely shredded Asiago, Parmesan, or Romano cheese (2 ounces)
   Snipped fresh thyme (optional)

1 Cook pasta according to package directions; drain and set aside.

2 Meanwhile, in a large skillet cook sausage over medium heat until brown; drain off fat. In an extra-large bowl combine cooked sausage, pasta, cream cheese, bread cubes, olives, and mozzarella cheese.

3 Preheat oven to 350°F. In a medium saucepan melt butter over medium heat. Stir in flour, sage, salt, dried thyme, and cayenne. Add milk all at once. Cook and stir until slightly thickened and bubbly. Pour over pasta mixture in bowl; stir gently to mix. Transfer to an ungreased 2-quart casserole.

4 Bake, covered, for 35 minutes. Top with tomato slices and Asiago cheese. Bake, uncovered, about 15 minutes more or until heated through. Let stand for 15 minutes before serving. If desired, sprinkle with fresh thyme.

nutrition facts per serving: 637 cal., 39 g total fat (19 g sat. fat), 101 mg chol., 1187 mg sodium, 46 g carb., 3 g dietary fiber, 24 g protein.

Take your mac 'n' cheese to the Mediterranean simply by stirring in kalamata olives and topping with feta cheese. Pictured on page 178.

greek-style mac 'n' cheese

prep: 25 minutes bake: 25 minutes stand: 10 minutes oven: 350°F
makes: 4 servings dish: 2-quart

2 cups dried elbow
   macaroni (8 ounces)
1/2 cup chopped onion
   (1 medium)
2 tablespoons butter
   or margarine
2 tablespoons all-
   purpose flour
1/8 teaspoon ground
   black pepper
2 1/2 cups milk
1 1/2 cups shredded
   cheddar cheese
   (6 ounces)
1 1/2 cups shredded
   American cheese
   (6 ounces)
1/2 cup pitted Kalamata
   olives, halved
2 tablespoons crumbled
   feta cheese
   Snipped fresh
   oregano

1 Preheat oven to 350°F. Cook macaroni according to package directions; drain.

2 For cheese sauce, in a medium saucepan cook onion in hot butter until tender. Stir in flour and pepper. Add milk all at once. Cook and stir over medium heat until slightly thickened and bubbly. Add cheeses, stirring until melted. Stir in cooked macaroni and olives. Transfer mixture to an ungreased 2-quart casserole.

3 Bake, uncovered, for 25 to 30 minutes or until bubbly. Top with feta cheese and oregano. Let stand for 10 minutes before serving.

nutrition facts per serving: 717 cal., 39 g total fat (24 g sat. fat), 116 mg chol., 1149 mg sodium, 57 g carb., 3 g dietary fiber, 34 g protein.

Gorgonzola, an Italian-style blue cheese, ranges in taste from mild to pungent, depending on how long it aged. You may also want to try other styles of blue cheese, such as Roquefort, American blue, or Stilton.

nutty gorgonzola roll-ups

prep: 40 minutes   bake: 40 minutes   oven: 375°F
makes: 8 servings   dish: 2-quart

8   dried lasagna noodles
12 ounces cream cheese, softened
2   cups shredded Italian cheese blend (8 ounces)
1   cup crumbled Gorgonzola or other blue cheese (4 ounces)
1   cup chopped walnuts, toasted
2   tablespoons snipped fresh basil or 2 teaspoons dried basil, crushed
1   26-ounce jar tomato-basil pasta sauce
    Freshly ground black pepper (optional)
    Shredded fresh basil (optional)
6   cups shredded fresh spinach

1 Preheat oven to 375°F. Cook lasagna noodles according to package directions; drain. Rinse with cold water; drain again. Place noodles in a single layer on a sheet of foil.

2 Meanwhile, in a large bowl combine cream cheese, Italian cheese, Gorgonzola cheese, ¾ cup of the walnuts, and the snipped fresh basil. Spread cheese mixture evenly over lasagna noodles. Roll up each noodle into a spiral.

3 Place lasagna rolls, seam sides down, in an ungreased 2-quart rectangular baking dish. Top with pasta sauce. Bake, covered, about 40 minutes or until heated through.

4 Sprinkle with the remaining ¼ cup walnuts. If desired, sprinkle with pepper and shredded fresh basil. Serve lasagna rolls on top of spinach, spooning sauce in dish over rolls.

nutrition facts per serving: 513 cal., 37 g total fat (17 g sat. fat), 77 mg chol., 813 mg sodium, 28 g carb., 4 g dietary fiber, 21 g protein.

Kids will dive into these pasta shell "bowls" filled with cheesy vegetables and topped with red sauce.

broccoli-and-cheese-stuffed shells

prep: 25 minutes   bake: 15 minutes   oven: 350°F
makes: 4 to 5 servings   dish: 2-quart

16   dried jumbo pasta
       shells
2   cups chopped
       broccoli florets
1   tablespoon water
1   15-ounce carton light
       ricotta cheese
½   cup shredded part-
       skim mozzarella
       cheese (2 ounces)
⅔   cup tomato pasta
       sauce
2   tablespoons
       shredded part-skim
       mozzarella cheese

1 Preheat oven to 350°F. Cook shells according to package directions; drain and rinse with cold water.

2 Meanwhile, in a medium microwave-safe bowl combine broccoli and the water. Cover with waxed paper. Microwave on 100 percent power (high) for 2 minutes. Drain. Stir ricotta and ½ cup mozzarella cheese into cooked broccoli. Spoon mixture into shells. Arrange in an ungreased 2-quart rectangular baking dish. Spoon pasta sauce over shells. Sprinkle with 2 tablespoons shredded cheese.

3 Bake, uncovered, about 15 minutes or until heated through.

nutrition facts per serving: 388 cal., 8 g total fat (4 g sat. fat), 348 mg sodium, 52 g carb., 4 g dietary fiber, 20 g protein.

Walnuts add crunch to these mozzarella-and-Parmesan-cheese–filled pasta shells.

cheese-and-nut-stuffed shells

prep: 45 minutes bake: 45 minutes oven: 350°F
makes: 6 servings dish: 3-quart

24   dried jumbo pasta
       shells*
2   eggs, lightly beaten
1   15-ounce carton
       ricotta cheese
1½   cups shredded
       mozzarella cheese
       (6 ounces)
1   cup shredded
       Parmesan cheese
       (4 ounces)
1   cup chopped walnuts
1   tablespoon snipped
       fresh parsley
½   teaspoon salt
¼   teaspoon ground
       black pepper
⅛   teaspoon ground
       nutmeg
1   26-ounce jar thick-
       and-chunky tomato
       pasta sauce

1 Cook pasta shells according to package directions; drain and set aside.

2 Preheat oven to 350°F. For filling, in a large bowl stir together eggs, ricotta cheese, 1 cup of the mozzarella, ¾ cup of the Parmesan cheese, the walnuts, parsley, salt, pepper, and nutmeg.

3 Spread 1 cup of the pasta sauce in the bottom of an ungreased 3-quart rectangular baking dish. Spoon a heaping tablespoon of filling into each cooked shell. Arrange the filled shells in the baking dish. Pour the remaining sauce over shells. Sprinkle with the remaining ½ cup mozzarella cheese and the remaining ¼ cup Parmesan cheese.

4 Bake, covered, about 45 minutes or until shells are heated through.

nutrition facts per serving: 549 cal., 32 g total fat (12 g sat. fat), 132 mg chol., 1072 mg sodium, 36 g carb., 4 g dietary fiber, 30 g protein.

*test kitchen tip: Cook a few extra shells to replace any that may tear during cooking.

make-ahead directions: Prepare shells as directed through Step 3. Cover with plastic wrap, then foil, and refrigerate for up to 24 hours. To serve, remove plastic wrap. Bake, covered with foil, in a 350°F oven for 50 to 55 minutes or until shells are heated through.

This three-cheese macaroni makes perfect family fare but is elegant enough to serve to company, along with a green salad and chilled dry white wine.

modern macaroni and cheese

prep: 25 minutes bake: 20 minutes oven: 350°F
makes: 4 servings dish: 1½-quart

7	ounces dried elbow macaroni (about 2 cups)
2	tablespoons butter or margarine
2	tablespoons finely chopped shallot (1 medium)
2	cloves garlic, minced
1⅓	cups milk
1	cup shredded Gruyère cheese (4 ounces)
1	cup shredded fontina cheese (4 ounces)
1	cup shredded Emmentaler cheese (4 ounces)
1	tablespoon cornstarch
1	tablespoon Dijon-style mustard
¼	teaspoon ground black pepper
⅛	teaspoon ground nutmeg (optional)
¼	cup seasoned fine dry bread crumbs or fine cracker crumbs
1	tablespoon butter or margarine, melted

1 Preheat oven to 350°F. Cook macaroni according to package directions; drain and set aside.

2 Meanwhile, in a large saucepan melt the 2 tablespoons butter over medium heat. Add shallot and garlic; cook about 3 minutes or until tender. Carefully stir in milk; heat through.

3 In a medium bowl toss together Gruyène cheese, fontina cheese, and Emmentaler cheese and cornstarch until cheese is evenly coated. Reduce heat under large saucepan to medium-low. Add cheese mixture to saucepan, about one-fourth at a time, stirring until cheeses are melted after each addition. Cook and stir until thickened and bubbly. (Mixture may appear to curdle at first but should become smooth with continued cooking.) Add mustard, pepper, and nutmeg (if using). Stir in macaroni.

4 Transfer macaroni mixture to an ungreased 1½-quart casserole. In a small bowl combine bread crumbs and 1 tablespoon melted butter. Sprinkle over macaroni mixture in casserole.

5 Bake, uncovered, for 20 to 25 minutes or until heated through and bubbly.

nutrition facts per serving: 682 cal., 37 g total fat (21 g sat. fat), 120 mg chol., 774 mg sodium, 52 g carb., 1 g dietary fiber, 35 g protein.

The corn chip topping clinches it for this winning dish that is irresistible to kids.

chili-style macaroni and cheese

prep: 25 minutes bake: 25 minutes stand: 10 minutes oven: 350°F
makes: 4 servings dish: 2-quart

2	cups dried elbow macaroni (8 ounces)
½	cup chopped onion (1 medium)
2	tablespoons butter or margarine
2	tablespoons all-purpose flour
⅛	teaspoon ground black pepper
2½	cups milk
1½	cups shredded cheddar cheese (6 ounces)
1½	cups shredded American cheese (6 ounces)
1	15-ounce can chili beans in chili gravy
½	cup corn chips

1 Preheat oven to 350°F. Cook macaroni according to package directions; drain.

2 Meanwhile, for cheese sauce, in a medium saucepan cook onion in hot butter until tender. Stir in flour and pepper. Add milk all at once. Cook and stir over medium heat until slightly thickened and bubbly. Add cheeses, stirring until melted. Stir in cooked macaroni and chili beans in gravy. Transfer mixture to an ungreased 2-quart casserole. Top with corn chips.

3 Bake, uncovered, for 25 to 30 minutes or until bubbly. Let stand for 10 minutes before serving.

nutrition facts per serving: 869 cal., 43 g total fat (24 g sat. fat), 112 mg chol., 1358 mg sodium, 80 g carb., 8 g dietary fiber, 40 g protein.

mac 'n' cheese toppers

Tweak the flavor of the Modern Macaroni and Cheese, opposite, with one of these tasty toppers.

- *Pesto: Add 2 tablespoons purchased basil pesto to the pasta mixture.*

- *Smoky apple: Use smoked cheddar cheese in place of the cheeses. Add 4 slices crisp-cooked crumbled bacon to pasta mixture. After baking, top with thinly sliced apple and cheese.*

- *Chili-style: Stir one 15-ounce can chili beans in chili gravy into pasta mixture. Instead of crumb topping, top with crushed corn chips.*

- *Meat lovers: Add 1½ cups crumbled cooked sausage to pasta mixture. Omit crumb crust. After baking, top with chopped red sweet pepper and fresh basil.*

baked ziti with three cheeses

prep: 30 minutes bake: 30 minutes oven: 425°F
makes: 6 servings dish: 3-quart

12 ounces dried ziti or
    penne pasta
    (4 cups)
1   14.5-ounce can fire-
    roasted crushed
    tomatoes or one
    14.5-ounce can
    diced tomatoes,
    undrained
1   cup chopped onions
    (2 medium)
12 cloves garlic, minced
2   tablespoons olive oil
½   cup dry white wine
2   cups whipping cream
1   cup shredded
    Parmesan cheese
    (4 ounces)
¾   cup crumbled
    Gorgonzola or
    other blue cheese
    (3 ounces)
½   cup shredded fontina
    cheese (2 ounces)
¾   teaspoon salt
¼   teaspoon ground
    black pepper
    Snipped fresh Italian
    parsley (optional)

1 Preheat oven to 425°F. In a large saucepan cook pasta according to package directions; drain. Place in an ungreased 3-quart rectangular baking dish; stir in tomatoes. Set aside.

2 Meanwhile, in a large saucepan cook onion and garlic in hot oil over medium heat just until tender. Carefully stir in wine and cook about 3 minutes or until liquid reduces by half. Add cream; heat to boiling. Boil gently, uncovered, about 5 minutes or until mixture thickens slightly, stirring frequently. Remove from heat. Stir in Parmesan cheese, ½ cup of the Gorgonzola cheese, the fontina cheese, salt, and pepper.

3 Pour cheese mixture over pasta. Bake, covered, for 30 to 35 minutes or until sauce is bubbly. Stir pasta to coat. Sprinkle with the remaining Gorgonzola cheese.

nutrition facts per serving: 741 cal., 48 g total fat (28 g sat. fat), 141 mg chol., 970 mg sodium, 53 g carb., 3 g dietary fiber, 24 g protein.

Blue cheese offers up a tang that's a treat when added to this creamy casserole.

mac and blue cheese

prep: 25 minutes bake: 25 minutes stand: 10 minutes oven: 350°F
makes: 4 serving dish: 2-quart

2 cups dried elbow macaroni (8 ounces)
½ cup chopped onion (1 medium)
4 cloves garlic, minced
2 tablespoons butter or margarine
2 tablespoons all-purpose flour
⅛ teaspoon ground black pepper
2½ cups milk
1½ cups shredded American cheese (6 ounces)
1 cup shredded cheddar cheese (4 ounces)
½ cup crumbled blue cheese (2 ounces)

1 Cook macaroni according to package directions; drain.

2 Meanwhile, preheat oven to 350°F. For cheese sauce, in a medium saucepan cook onion and garlic in hot butter until tender. Stir in flour and pepper. Add milk all at once. Cook and stir over medium heat until slightly thickened and bubbly. Add cheeses, stirring until melted. Stir in cooked macaroni. Transfer mixture to an ungreased 2-quart casserole.

3 Bake, uncovered, for 25 to 30 minutes or until bubbly. Let stand for 10 minutes before serving.

nutrition facts per serving: 698 cal., 37 g total fat (23 g sat. fat), 110 mg chol., 1151 mg sodium, 57 g carb., 2 g dietary fiber, 33 g protein.

'round

the

wo

Turn your table into a hot travel destination with oven-baked dishes that capture the vibrant flavors of Italy, Spain, Greece, Mexico, and Asia. The spicy, robust characteristics that define each cuisine translate beautifully into earthy, satisfying one-dish meals.

8

rld

In Spanish, enchilada *means "spiced with chile," a requisite step in preparing a one-dish meal that's ideal for dinner at home or toting to a potluck.*

shredded beef and chile enchiladas

prep: 35 minutes **bake:** 40 minutes **oven:** 350°F
makes: 12 servings **dish:** 3-quart

2 4-ounce cans diced green chile peppers, undrained

½ teaspoon chile powder

1 tablespoon all-purpose flour

1 8-ounce carton sour cream

2 cups shredded Monterey Jack cheese (8 ounces)

5 cups shredded beef*

12 7- to 8-inch flour tortillas

1 cup salsa verde or desired salsa

1 Preheat oven to 350°F. Grease a 3-quart rectangular baking dish; set aside. In a medium saucepan combine chile peppers and chili powder; cook about 1 minute or until heated through. Stir in flour. Cook and stir for 1 minute more. Remove from heat. Stir in sour cream and ½ cup of the cheese.

2 Divide beef among tortillas. Top with sour cream mixture. Roll up tortillas. Arrange rolled tortillas, seam sides down, in prepared baking dish.

3 Bake, covered, for 30 minutes. Uncover. Sprinkle with half of the remaining 1½ cups cheese. Spoon salsa verde over; sprinkle with the remaining cheese. Bake, uncovered, about 10 minutes more or until cheese is melted and enchiladas are heated through.

nutrition facts per serving: 490 cal., 33 g total fat (15 g sat. fat), 103 mg chol., 572 mg sodium, 21 g carb., 2 g dietary fiber, 25 g protein.

*test kitchen tip: Roast a 3½-pound boneless beef chuck pot roast until tender. Using two forks, shred the beef.

Tubes of prepared polenta, an Italian version of cooked cornmeal, can be found in the refrigerated or produce section of large supermarkets. Here it's used in place of pasta for a flavorful change of pace.

meatball and polenta
casserole

prep: 20 minutes bake: 45 minutes stand: 5 minutes oven: 350°F
makes: 8 servings dish: 3-quart

1   16-ounce package refrigerated polenta
2   16-ounce packages frozen cooked Italian meatballs
1   10.75-ounce can condensed golden mushroom soup
3/4 cup water
1   4-ounce jar sliced mushrooms, drained
1   teaspoon dried Italian seasoning, crushed
1/4 teaspoon garlic powder
1/8 teaspoon ground black pepper
1/2 cup shredded Parmesan cheese (2 ounces)

1 Preheat oven to 350°F. Grease a 3-quart rectangular baking dish; set aside. Cut polenta crosswise into 12 slices. Arrange polenta slices in prepared dish. Arrange meatballs on polenta. In a medium bowl combine soup, the water, mushrooms, Italian seasoning, garlic powder, and pepper. Pour evenly over meatballs.

2 Bake, uncovered, about 45 minutes or until heated through. Sprinkle with Parmesan cheese. Let stand for 5 minutes before serving.

nutrition facts per serving: 551 cal., 35 g total fat (18 g sat. fat), 98 mg chol., 1963 mg sodium, 22 g carb., 6 g dietary fiber, 34 g protein.

Called Kjottkaker *in Norwegian, these nutmeg-accented meatballs are terrific served over buttered noodles with the creamy mushroom sauce on top.*

norwegian meatballs

prep: 25 minutes bake: 30 minutes oven: 350°F
makes: 5 or 6 servings dish: 3-quart

2 eggs
½ cup milk
⅔ cup crushed saltine crackers (about 18 crackers)
⅓ cup finely chopped onion
½ teaspoon celery salt
½ teaspoon ground nutmeg
½ teaspoon ground black pepper
2 pounds lean ground beef
1 10.75-ounce can condensed cream of mushroom soup
¾ cup milk

1 Preheat oven to 350°F. Grease a 3-quart rectangular baking dish; set aside. In a large bowl beat eggs with a fork; stir in ½ cup milk. Stir in crushed crackers, onion, celery salt, ¼ teaspoon of the nutmeg, and the pepper. Add ground beef; mix well. Shape mixture into 20 meatballs. Arrange meatballs in prepared dish. Bake about 30 minutes or until done (160°F).*

2 For sauce, in a medium saucepan combine cream of mushroom soup, ¾ cup milk, and the remaining ¼ teaspoon nutmeg. Cook and stir over medium heat until heated through.

3 To serve, transfer meatballs to a serving bowl. Spoon sauce over meatballs.

nutrition facts per serving: 469 cal., 26 g total fat (10 g sat. fat), 204 mg chol., 842 mg sodium, 17 g carb., 1 g dietary fiber, 39 g protein.

*test kitchen tip: To measure the doneness of a meatball, insert an instant-read thermometer into the center of the meatball. If it reads 160°F, the meatballs are done.

The ground beef forms the "shell" and tortilla chips form the top crust of this spicy pie.

mexican meat loaf pie

prep: 30 minutes bake: 1 hour stand: 15 minutes oven: 350°F
makes: 6 servings dish: 10-inch pie plate

1¼ pounds lean ground beef
1 cup finely crushed tortilla chips or corn chips
1 envelope (½ of a 2-ounce package) onion soup mix
¾ cup bottled taco sauce
2 eggs, lightly beaten
½ teaspoon ground black pepper
1 8.8-ounce pouch cooked Spanish-style rice (such as Uncle Ben's Ready Rice)
1 15.5-ounce can golden hominy, rinsed and drained
1 14.5-ounce can diced tomatoes with green chiles, drained
1 cup shredded Monterey Jack cheese with jalapeño chile peppers (4 ounces)
1 medium fresh Anaheim chile pepper, seeded and chopped* (½ cup)
¼ cup snipped fresh cilantro
Tortilla chips and/ or sliced fresh jalapeño chile pepper*

1 Preheat oven to 350°F. In a large bowl combine beef, crushed chips, dry soup mix, ½ cup of the taco sauce, one of the eggs, and the black pepper. Press mixture into a 10-inch deep-dish pie plate.

2 Heat rice according to package directions. In a large bowl combine rice, the remaining ¼ cup taco sauce, the remaining egg, hominy, tomatoes, cheese, the Anaheim chile pepper, and the snipped cilantro. Spoon mixture into the meat shell. Place pie plate on a baking sheet. Cover loosely with foil.

3 Bake for 40 minutes. Remove foil; bake about 20 minutes more or until an instant-read thermometer inserted in center of meat mixture registers 160°F. Let stand for 15 minutes before serving. Top with additional chips and/or the jalapeño chile pepper.

nutrition facts per serving: 493 cal., 21 g total fat (8 g sat. fat), 150 mg chol., 1355 mg sodium, 41 g carb., 4 g dietary fiber, 29 g protein.

*test kitchen tip: Because chile peppers contain volatile oils that can burn your skin and eyes, avoid direct contact with them as much as possible. When working with chile peppers, wear plastic or rubber gloves. If your bare hands do touch the peppers, wash your hands and nails well with soap and warm water.

Some call pastitsio (pronounced pah-STEET-see-oh) the Greek lasagna. Cinnamon is an integral ingredient in this classic dish, and it provides an enticing flavor. Also try making it with ground lamb instead of beef.

pastitsio

prep: 45 minutes bake: 30 minutes stand: 15 minutes oven: 350°F
makes: 8 servings dish: 3-quart

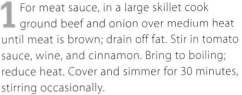

1 pound lean ground beef
1 cup chopped onion (1 large)
1 8-ounce can tomato sauce
¼ cup dry white wine, beef broth, or water
⅛ teaspoon ground cinnamon
8 ounces dried penne pasta (about 2⅔ cups)
¾ cup milk
2 eggs, lightly beaten
4 tablespoons butter or margarine
2 tablespoons all-purpose flour
¼ teaspoon salt
⅛ teaspoon ground black pepper
1½ cups milk
2 eggs, lightly beaten
1 cup shredded kefalotiri, kasseri, or Romano cheese* (4 ounces)
   Ground cinnamon (optional)

1 For meat sauce, in a large skillet cook ground beef and onion over medium heat until meat is brown; drain off fat. Stir in tomato sauce, wine, and cinnamon. Bring to boiling; reduce heat. Cover and simmer for 30 minutes, stirring occasionally.

2 Meanwhile, cook pasta according to package directions; drain. In a large bowl toss cooked pasta with ¾ cup milk, 2 beaten eggs, and 2 tablespoons of the butter. Set pasta mixture aside.

3 For cream sauce, in a small saucepan melt the remaining 2 tablespoons butter over medium heat. Stir in flour, salt, and pepper until smooth. Gradually add 1½ cups milk. Cook and stir until mixture is thickened and bubbly. Gradually stir milk mixture into 2 beaten eggs.

4 Preheat oven to 350°F. Spread half of the pasta mixture in a greased 3-quart rectangular baking dish. Top with meat sauce. Sprinkle with one-third of the cheese. Top with the remaining pasta mixture; sprinkle with another one-third of the cheese. Pour cream sauce over all; sprinkle with the remaining cheese. Cover dish with foil.

5 Bake for 20 minutes. Uncover and bake for 10 to 15 minutes more or until a knife inserted in center comes out clean. Let stand for 15 minutes before serving. If desired, sprinkle each serving with additional ground cinnamon.

nutrition facts per serving: 431 cal., 23 g total fat (12 g sat. fat), 178 mg chol., 537 mg sodium, 30 g carb., 2 g dietary fiber, 23 g protein.

*test kitchen tip: Kefalotiri and kasseri cheeses are both hard cheeses widely used in Greek cooking. They have sharp, salty flavors that are quite similar to Romano cheese, which you may find more readily in your supermarket. You also can substitute grated Parmesan cheese.

This layered lamb-eggplant dish is a classic in Greek cuisine, but it took the adventuresome '80s to make moussaka mainstream. One reason this still ranks as a favorite is its crowd-pleasing appeal.

moussaka

prep: 50 minutes bake: 35 minutes stand: 10 minutes oven: 325°F
makes: 4 to 6 servings dish: 2-quart

2	tablespoons vegetable oil
1	medium eggplant (1 pound), peeled and cut into ½-inch slices
1	pound ground lamb or ground beef
½	cup chopped onion (1 medium)
1	clove garlic, minced
1	8-ounce can tomato sauce
¼	cup dry red wine or beef broth
½	teaspoon salt
¼	teaspoon dried oregano, crushed
⅛	teaspoon ground cinnamon
1	egg, lightly beaten
2	tablespoons butter
2	tablespoons all-purpose flour
	Pinch ground black pepper
1	cup milk
1	egg
¼	cup shredded Parmesan cheese (1 ounce)

1 In a large skillet heat oil over medium-high heat. Add half of the eggplant slices; cook about 4 minutes or until browned, turning once. Using a slotted spatula, remove from skillet. Repeat with the remaining eggplant slices, adding more oil if necessary.

2 In the same skillet cook ground lamb, onion, and garlic over medium-high heat until meat is brown, using a wooden spoon to break up meat as it cooks. Drain off fat. Stir in tomato sauce, wine, ¼ teaspoon of the salt, the oregano, and cinnamon. Bring to boiling; reduce heat. Simmer, uncovered, about 10 minutes or until most of the liquid is absorbed. Cool mixture slightly. Gradually stir ½ cup of the meat mixture into 1 beaten egg. Return to meat mixture in skillet.

3 Meanwhile, in a medium saucepan melt butter over medium heat. Stir in flour, pepper, and the remaining ¼ teaspoon salt. Add milk all at once. Cook and stir until thickened and bubbly. In a medium bowl lightly beat 1 egg with a fork. Gradually stir hot milk mixture into beaten egg.

4 Preheat oven to 325°F. Arrange half of the eggplant slices in an ungreased 2-quart rectangular baking dish. Spread meat mixture over eggplant in dish; top with the remaining eggplant slices. Pour the hot milk mixture over top. Sprinkle with Parmesan cheese.

5 Bake, uncovered, for 35 to 40 minutes or until edges are bubbly. Let stand for 10 minutes before serving.

nutrition facts per serving: 499 cal., 34 g total fat (13 g sat. fat), 207 mg chol., 801 mg sodium, 18 g carb., 5 g dietary fiber, 29 g protein.

Eating tortilla roll-ups stuffed with seasoned shredded meat is a favorite of Mexican food lovers everywhere. For extra flavor kick, use spicy salsa.

pork burritos

prep: 25 minutes bake: 30 minutes oven: 350°F
makes: 8 burritos dish: 3-quart

8   8- to 10-inch flour
    tortillas
1½ cups shredded
    cooked pork or beef
    (about 8 ounces)
1   cup purchased salsa
1   3.125-ounce can
    jalapeño-flavored
    bean dip
1   teaspoon fajita
    seasoning
8   ounces Monterey
    Jack or cheddar
    cheese, cut into
    eight 5½-inch
    sticks
    Shredded lettuce
    (optional)
    Sour cream (optional)
    Purchased salsa
    (optional)

1 Preheat oven to 350°F. Wrap tortillas in foil; heat in oven about 10 minutes or until heated through.

2 Meanwhile, in a large bowl stir together shredded meat, 1 cup salsa, bean dip, and fajita seasoning.

3 Grease a 3-quart rectangular baking dish; set aside. To assemble burritos, place ⅓ cup of the meat mixture onto each tortilla near one edge. Top meat mixture on each tortilla with a stick of cheese. Fold in the sides of tortilla and roll up, starting from edge with the filling. Place filled tortillas, seam sides down, in prepared dish.

4 Bake, uncovered, about 30 minutes or until heated through. If desired, serve with lettuce, sour cream, and additional salsa.

nutrition facts per burrito: 261 cal., 13 g total fat (6 g sat. fat), 48 mg chol., 441 mg sodium, 18 g carb., 1 g dietary fiber, 17 g protein.

Layers of fabulous flavor treat your taste buds in every bite of this comfort food casserole.

polenta with pork chops

prep: 35 minutes bake: 15 minutes oven: 350°F
makes: 6 servings dish: 3-quart

Nonstick cooking
  spray
6 boneless pork top loin
   chops (1½ pounds)
1 teaspoon salt
½ teaspoon dried
   thyme, crushed
¼ teaspoon ground
   black pepper
2 teaspoons canola oil
1 15-ounce carton
   ricotta cheese
1 7-ounce container
   refrigerated basil
   pesto
½ cup grated Parmesan
   cheese
1 egg, beaten
4 cups milk
1½ cups yellow cornmeal
   Snipped fresh basil
     (optional)
   Toasted pine nuts
     (optional)

1 Preheat oven to 350°F. Coat a 3-quart rectangular baking dish with cooking spray; set aside. Sprinkle pork chops with ½ teaspoon of the salt, the thyme, and pepper. In a 12-inch skillet heat oil over medium-high heat. Add chops; cook for 4 minutes, turning once to brown evenly.

2 In a small bowl stir together ricotta cheese, pesto, Parmesan cheese, and egg; set aside.

3 For polenta, in a medium saucepan combine 2 cups of the milk and the remaining ½ teaspoon salt. Heat over medium-high heat just until boiling. In a medium bowl whisk together cornmeal and the remaining 2 cups milk. Slowly add cornmeal mixture to milk mixture in saucepan. Cook and stir over medium-low heat until mixture is very thick and bubbly.

4 Spread half of the polenta in the prepared baking dish. Spread half of the ricotta mixture over the polenta. Arrange pork chops in a single layer over ricotta mixture. Spread the remaining ricotta mixture over the pork chops. Dollop the remaining polenta over the ricotta mixture.

5 Bake, uncovered, about 15 minutes or until hot in center and top is light golden brown. If desired, sprinkle with basil and toasted pine nuts.

nutrition facts per serving: 722 cal., 40 g total fat, (6 g sat. fat) 177 mg chol., 972 mg sodium, 41 g carb., 3 g dietary fiber, 48 g protein.

Salty prosciutto, the pride of Italy, lends terrific taste to this casserole. While this dish makes a perfect main course, it also makes 6 to 8 tasty side-size portions.

hearty tuscan bean casserole

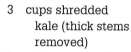

prep: 25 minutes bake: 30 minutes oven: 350°F
makes: 4 servings dish: 2-quart

3	cups shredded kale (thick stems removed)
2	tablespoons olive oil
½	cup chopped onion (1 medium)
½	cup chopped celery (1 medium)
2	19-ounce cans cannellini beans (white kidney beans), rinsed and drained
1	14.5-ounce can diced tomatoes, undrained
4	ounces thinly sliced prosciutto or cooked ham, cut into bite-size strips
¼	cup fine dry bread crumbs
½	teaspoon dried sage, crushed
1	clove garlic, minced
¼	teaspoon ground black pepper

1 Preheat oven to 350°F. In a small saucepan cook kale in a small amount of boiling water for 8 to 10 minutes or until tender. Drain well in a colander.

2 Meanwhile, in a small skillet heat 1 tablespoon of the oil over medium heat. Add onion and celery. Cook for 4 to 5 minutes or until tender.

3 In a large bowl combine cooked kale, onion mixture, beans, tomatoes, prosciutto, 2 tablespoons of the bread crumbs, the sage, garlic, and pepper. Transfer mixture to an ungreased 2-quart casserole. In a small bowl combine the remaining 2 tablespoons bread crumbs and the remaining 1 tablespoon oil; sprinkle over bean mixture.

4 Bake, covered, for 20 minutes. Bake, uncovered, about 10 minutes more or until heated through.

nutrition facts per serving: 353 cal., 11 g total fat (2 g sat. fat), 20 mg chol., 1560 mg sodium, 53 g carb., 14 g dietary fiber, 26 g protein.

'round **the world**

Supermarket freezer cases hold a colorful assortment of Asian-style stir-fry vegetables. Any of them will work in this recipe, so choose your favorite.

chinese pork bake

prep: 30 minutes bake: 35 minutes oven: 350°F
makes: 4 to 6 servings dish: 2-quart

1 pound boneless
   pork loin
¼ cup all-purpose flour
¼ teaspoon ground
   black pepper
2 tablespoons
   vegetable oil
1 16-ounce package
   frozen pepper
   and onion stir-fry
   vegetables, thawed
1 10.75-ounce can
   condensed cream of
   mushroom soup
1 4-ounce can (drained
   weight) sliced
   mushrooms, drained
2 tablespoons
   soy sauce
¼ teaspoon ground
   ginger
1 3-ounce package
   Oriental-flavor
   ramen noodles
¼ cup slivered
   almonds

1 Preheat oven to 350°F. Grease a 2-quart casserole; set aside. Trim fat from meat. Thinly slice meat across the grain into bite-size strips. In a medium bowl combine flour and pepper. Add meat, half at a time, tossing gently to coat.

2 In a large skillet heat oil over medium-high heat. Cook meat, half at a time, in hot oil until brown (add additional oil, if necessary). Return all of the meat to skillet. Stir in stir-fry vegetables, soup, mushrooms, soy sauce, and ginger.

3 Meanwhile, cook noodles in boiling water about 3 minutes or just until tender; drain. Stir cooked noodles into meat mixture; stir in the seasoning packet from noodles. Transfer mixture to the prepared casserole. Sprinkle with almonds.

4 Bake, uncovered, about 35 minutes or until heated through.

nutrition facts per serving: 530 cal., 28 g total fat (7 g sat. fat), 63 mg chol., 1592 mg sodium, 34 g carb., 5 g dietary fiber, 35 g protein.

Cuban chorizo typically is full of cilantro instead of the hot chile peppers that are found in Mexican chorizo. It's worth seeking out in specialty food stores, but any uncooked chorizo—or even bulk pork sausage—can be substituted.

cuban casserole

prep: 25 minutes   bake: 55 minutes   oven: 350°F
makes: 6 servings   dish: 3-quart

4	ounces uncooked chorizo (casings removed if present)
1	15-ounce can black beans, rinsed and drained
1½	cups uncooked long grain white rice
8	ounces ham steak, cut into ½-inch pieces (about 1⅓ cups)
½	teaspoon crushed red pepper
¼	teaspoon ground black pepper
5	cups chicken broth
1½	cups soft bread crumbs
2	tablespoons butter, melted
8	slices Swiss cheese (6 ounces)
2	tablespoons snipped fresh cilantro (optional)
	Dill pickle spears (optional)

1 Preheat oven to 350°F. In a large skillet cook chorizo over medium-high heat until brown, using a wooden spoon to break up meat as it cooks. Add beans, rice, ham, crushed red pepper, and black pepper to skillet. Toss to combine. Add broth; bring to boiling.

2 Transfer bean mixture to an ungreased 3-quart rectangular baking dish. Bake, covered, for 45 minutes, stirring once, then cover again.

3 Meanwhile, in a small bowl toss bread crumbs with melted butter. Remove casserole from oven; stir. Top with cheese; sprinkle with bread crumb mixture. Bake about 10 minutes more or until cheese is melted and bread crumbs are browned. If desired, sprinkle with cilantro and serve with dill pickle spears.

nutrition facts per serving: 546 cal., 23 g total fat, 76 mg chol., 1862 mg sodium, 56 g carb., 5 g dietary fiber, 28 g protein.

This dish salutes Tuscany, a region in Italy known for delicious ways with cannellini beans. The recipe also salutes the busy American cook by calling on easy-to-use canned beans instead of dried beans, which require long soaking times.

white **bean** and
sausage rigatoni

prep: 20 minutes bake: 25 minutes oven: 350°F
makes: 6 servings dish: 2-quart

8 ounces dried rigatoni
   pasta
1 15-ounce can
   cannellini (white
   kidney), Great
   Northern, or navy
   beans, rinsed and
   drained
1 15-ounce can tomato
   sauce
1 14.5-ounce can
   Italian-style
   stewed tomatoes,
   undrained
8 ounces cooked
   smoked turkey
   sausage, halved
   lengthwise and cut
   into 1-inch pieces
⅓ cup snipped
   fresh basil or
   1 tablespoon dried
   basil, crushed
¼ cup shredded Asiago
   or Parmesan cheese
   (1 ounce)

1 Preheat oven to 350°F. Lightly grease a 2-quart casserole; set aside. Cook pasta according to package directions; drain. Return to pan. Stir in beans, tomato sauce, tomatoes, sausage, and basil. Transfer mixture to the prepared casserole. Sprinkle with cheese.

2 Bake, uncovered, for 25 to 30 minutes or until mixture is heated through and cheese is lightly browned.

nutrition facts per serving: 304 cal., 6 g total fat (2 g sat. fat), 30 mg chol., 1246 mg sodium, 50 g carb., 7 g dietary fiber, 18 g protein.

A vibrant mixture of spicy Italian sausage, mushrooms, and onions is mellowed out by rich and creamy polenta in this family-pleasing dish.

italian polenta casserole

prep: 45 minutes bake: 20 minutes oven: 400°F
makes: 8 servings dish: 3-quart

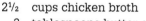

2½	cups chicken broth
3	tablespoons butter or margarine
2	cups milk
1½	cups quick-cooking polenta mix
1	3-ounce package cream cheese, cut up
1	cup shredded mozzarella or provolone cheese (4 ounces)
½	cup finely shredded or grated Parmesan cheese (2 ounces)
12	ounces sweet or hot bulk Italian sausage
1	cup quartered fresh mushrooms
1	medium onion, cut into thin wedges
2	cloves garlic, minced
2	cups purchased pasta sauce

1 Preheat oven to 400°F. Lightly grease a 3-quart rectangular baking dish; set aside.

2 In a large saucepan bring broth and butter to boiling. Meanwhile, stir together milk and polenta. Add polenta mixture to boiling broth. Cook and stir until bubbly; cook and stir 3 to 5 minutes more or until very thick. Remove from heat. Stir in cream cheese, ¾ cup of the mozzarella cheese, and ¼ cup of the Parmesan cheese. Spread two-thirds of the polenta mixture in the prepared baking dish.

3 In a large skillet cook sausage, mushrooms, onion, and garlic until meat is brown and onion is tender, using a wooden spoon to break up meat as it cooks. Drain off fat. Stir pasta sauce into meat mixture; heat through. Spoon meat mixture over polenta in dish, spreading evenly. Spoon remaining polenta on sauce and sprinkle with the remaining ¼ cup mozzarella cheese and ¼ cup Parmesan cheese.

4 Bake, uncovered, about 20 minutes or until heated through and top is light golden brown.

nutrition facts per serving: 584 cal., 34 g total fat (18 g sat. fat), 93 mg chol., 1879 mg sodium, 36 g carb., 4 g dietary fiber, 31 g protein.

This homey casserole contains many of the most popular pizza ingredients—marinara sauce, mushrooms, onion, green sweet pepper, pepperoni, and lots of cheese.

italian **penne** bake

prep: 25 minutes bake: 30 minutes oven: 350°F
makes: 4 servings dish: 2-quart

Nonstick cooking
  spray
1½ cups dried penne
  pasta
1 medium green or red
  sweet pepper, cut
  into thin, bite-size
  strips
3 ounces sliced
  pepperoni or
  Canadian-style
  bacon, cut up
½ cup sliced fresh
  mushrooms
½ cup quartered, thinly
  sliced onion
1½ teaspoons bottled
  minced garlic
  (3 cloves)
1½ teaspoons olive oil or
  cooking oil
1½ cups purchased
  marinara sauce
⅔ cup shredded Italian
  cheese blend

1 Preheat oven to 350°F. Lightly coat a 2-quart square baking dish with nonstick cooking spray; set dish aside.

2 Cook pasta according to package directions; drain well. Return pasta to saucepan. Meanwhile, in a medium skillet cook sweet pepper, pepperoni, mushrooms, onion, and garlic in hot oil for 3 minutes. Add vegetable mixture and marinara sauce to pasta; toss to coat. Spread pasta mixture evenly in prepared baking dish.

3 Bake, covered, about 25 minutes or until heated through. Uncover and sprinkle with cheese. Bake, uncovered, about 5 minutes more or until cheese is melted.

nutrition facts per serving: 390 cal., 19 g total fat (7 g sat. fat), 31 mg chol., 848 mg sodium, 41 g carb., 3 g dietary fiber, 15 g protein.

Duck legs confit lend flavor intrigue to this hearty bean and pork dish. Traditionally, curing and cooking duck legs in duck fat make the confit extremely flavorful. Find confit in the gourmet section of the supermarket.

country french
cassoulet

prep: 40 minutes bake: 2 hours 20 minutes cook: 1 hour stand: 1 hour 15 minutes
oven: 325°F/400°F makes: 8 servings dish: Dutch oven

1½ pounds dry Great Northern beans (3¾ cups)
5 fresh parsley sprigs
3 celery leaves
2 fresh thyme sprigs
2 bay leaves
5 whole cloves
½ teaspoon whole black peppercorns
1 8-ounce portion unsmoked bacon, ham, or pancetta
1 medium onion, cut in half
½ cup coarsely chopped carrot (1 medium)
10 cloves garlic
4 cups beef broth or 2 cups duck and veal demi-glace dissolved in 2 cups water
3 cups peeled, seeded, and chopped tomatoes (6 medium)
½ cup chopped onion (1 medium)
Pinch ground black pepper
4 duck legs confit
1 pound garlic sausage, halved crosswise or cut into thick slices
Kosher salt, sea salt, or salt
Ground black pepper

1 Rinse beans. In a 4-quart Dutch oven combine beans and 8 cups water. Bring to boiling; reduce heat. Simmer, uncovered, for 2 minutes. Remove from heat. Cover and let stand for 1 hour. (Or place beans in the water in Dutch oven. Cover and let soak in a cool place for 6 to 8 hours or overnight.) Drain and rinse beans. Return beans to Dutch oven.

2 For bouquet garni, place parsley, celery leaves, thyme, bay leaves, cloves, and peppercorns in the center of a double-thick, 6-inch square of 100-percent-cotton cheesecloth. Bring up corners and tie closed with clean kitchen string. Add bouquet garni, 10 cups fresh water, bacon, onion halves, carrot, and garlic to beans in Dutch oven.

3 Bring to boiling; reduce heat. Simmer, covered, about 1 hour or just until beans are tender, stirring frequently. Drain in a colander; remove and discard onion halves and bouquet garni. Return bean mixture to Dutch oven. Add broth, tomatoes, ½ cup chopped onion, and pinch pepper. Bring to boiling.

4 Meanwhile, preheat oven to 325°F. Remove duck meat from bones or cut each duck leg in half at the joint.

5 Remove half of the bean mixture from Dutch oven. Add duck legs and sausage; cover with the removed bean mixture. Bake, covered, about 2 hours or until bubbly.

6 Increase oven temperature to 400°F. Bake, uncovered, about 20 minutes more or until top is browned. Remove from oven; let stand for 15 minutes before serving. Season to taste with salt and additional pepper.

nutrition facts per serving: 648 cal., 24 g total fat (8 g sat. fat), 102 mg chol., 1359 mg sodium, 63 g carb., 20 g dietary fiber, 45 g protein.

Northern Italy, home of the Emilia-Romagna region, produces superlative dairy products, some of which contribute to this dish's glory.

tortellini emilia

prep: 25 minutes bake: 20 minutes stand: 10 minutes oven: 400°F
makes: 8 servings dish: 2-quart

2 8-ounce packages dried cheese-filled tortellini
3 tablespoons finely chopped red onion
2 tablespoons finely chopped shallot
1 tablespoon butter
2 cups half-and-half or light cream
1/2 cup milk
2 egg yolks
1/4 cup grated Parmesan cheese
1 tablespoon snipped fresh sage or 1 teaspoon dried sage, crushed
1/4 teaspoon ground black pepper
1/2 cup shredded Gruyère or Swiss cheese (2 ounces)
1/2 cup broken walnuts
2 ounces thinly sliced prosciutto or cooked ham, finely chopped

1 Preheat oven to 400°F. Cook tortellini according to package directions; drain.

2 Meanwhile, for sauce, in a medium saucepan cook onion and shallot in hot butter over medium heat until tender. Stir in half-and-half and milk. Bring just to boiling. Remove from heat. Gradually stir about 1 cup of the hot mixture into egg yolks. Stir yolk mixture into the remaining mixture in saucepan. Cook and stir over medium-low heat about 10 minutes or until slightly thickened and just starting to bubble. Stir in Parmesan cheese, sage, and pepper.

3 Spread half of the cooked tortellini in the bottom of an ungreased 2-quart rectangular baking dish. Sprinkle with Gruyère cheese. Add half of the sauce. Top with the remaining tortellini, the walnuts, prosciutto, and the remaining sauce.

4 Bake, uncovered, about 20 minutes or until mixture is heated through and top is lightly browned. Let stand for 10 minutes before serving.

nutrition facts per serving: 455 cal., 25 g total fat (8 g sat. fat), 96 mg chol., 824 mg sodium, 38 g carb., 1 g dietary fiber, 21 g protein.

Israeli couscous consists of large round balls of semolina and resembles whole tapioca.

moroccan lamb casserole with preserved lemons

prep: 30 minutes   bake: 30 minutes   oven: 350°F
makes: 6 servings   dish: 2-quart

1	6.3-ounce package (1⅓ cups) Israeli couscous
⅓	cup finely chopped preserved lemons or 1 tablespoon finely shredded lemon peel
1	teaspoon ground cumin
2	cloves garlic, minced
½	teaspoon ground ginger
¼	teaspoon ground cinnamon
1½	pounds ground lamb or ground beef
1	cup chopped carrots (2 medium)
1	medium onion, cut into thin wedges
1	14.5-ounce can diced tomatoes, undrained
¼	cup golden raisins
½	teaspoon salt
¼	teaspoon ground black pepper
⅓	cup sliced almonds, toasted
	Snipped fresh cilantro

1 Preheat oven to 350°F. Cook couscous according to package directions. Meanwhile, in a small bowl combine preserved lemons, cumin, garlic, ginger, and cinnamon.

2 In a large skillet cook ground lamb, carrots, and onion over medium heat until meat is brown. Drain off fat. Stir in cooked couscous, lemon mixture, tomatoes, raisins, salt, and pepper.

3 Transfer mixture to an ungreased 2- to 2½-quart casserole. Bake, covered, about 30 minutes or until heated through. Sprinkle with almonds and cilantro.

nutrition facts per serving: 517 cal., 29 g total fat (12 g sat. fat), 83 mg chol., 657 mg sodium, 39 g carb., 5 g dietary fiber, 25 g protein.

Many of us do not make curries often enough to quickly use up a container of curry powder. The flavor is best when the yellow blend of spices is used within a year. If your curry has been in the cupboard for longer than you remember, replace it with a fresh supply.

indian-style lamb curry

prep: 30 minutes bake: 25 minutes oven: 350°F
makes: 8 servings dish: 3-quart

1½	pounds ground lamb
1	large red onion, halved and thinly sliced
2	cloves garlic, minced
2	medium potatoes (12 ounces), cut into ½-inch pieces
2	cups cauliflower florets
1	cup apple juice
½	cup sliced carrot (1 medium)
1	tablespoon curry powder
1	teaspoon salt
¼	teaspoon ground ginger
¼	cup cold water
2	tablespoons cornstarch
1	medium zucchini, halved lengthwise and sliced (about 1¼ cups)
1	cup frozen peas
⅓	cup golden raisins
3	cups hot cooked rice
	Chutney (optional)

1 Preheat oven to 350°F. Grease a 3-quart rectangular baking dish; set aside. In an extra-large skillet or Dutch oven cook ground lamb, onion, and garlic over medium heat until meat is brown and onion is tender. Drain off fat. Stir in potatoes, cauliflower, apple juice, carrot, curry powder, salt, and ginger. Bring to boiling; reduce heat. Simmer, covered, for 10 minutes.

2 In a small bowl combine water and cornstarch; stir into meat mixture. Cook and stir just until mixture comes to boiling. Stir in zucchini, peas, and raisins. Transfer to prepared dish. Cover dish with foil.

3 Bake for 25 to 30 minutes or until potatoes and cauliflower are tender. Serve over hot cooked rice. If desired, serve with chutney.

nutrition facts per serving: 337 cal., 12 g total fat (5 g sat. fat), 57 mg chol., 378 mg sodium, 39 g carb., 3 g dietary fiber, 19 g protein.

The name of this classic French recipe literally means "chicken in wine." Serve this chicken, smothered in a rich, wine-flavored gravy, with a lettuce salad and a loaf of French bread.

coq au vin

prep: 40 minutes   bake: 45 minutes   oven: 350°F
makes: 6 servings   dish: 3-quart

2½   to 3 pounds chicken drumsticks and/or thighs, skin removed
2   tablespoons vegetable oil
    Salt and ground black pepper
2   tablespoons butter
3   tablespoons all-purpose flour
1¼   cups Pinot Noir or Burgundy wine
¼   cup chicken broth or water
1   cup whole fresh mushrooms
1   cup very thinly sliced carrots (2 medium)
⅔   cup frozen small whole onions, thawed (18)
1½   teaspoons snipped fresh marjoram or ½ teaspoon dried marjoram, crushed
1½   teaspoons snipped fresh thyme or ½ teaspoon dried thyme, crushed
2   cloves garlic, minced
2   slices bacon, crisp-cooked, drained, and crumbled
    Snipped fresh parsley (optional)
3   cups hot cooked noodles (optional)

1 Preheat oven to 350°F. In an extra-large skillet cook chicken, half at a time, in hot oil over medium heat for 10 to 15 minutes or until brown, turning occasionally. Transfer chicken to an ungreased 3-quart rectangular baking dish. Sprinkle chicken with salt and pepper.

2 In the same skillet heat butter over medium heat until melted. Stir in flour until smooth. Gradually stir in wine and broth. Cook and stir until mixture comes to boiling. Cut any large mushrooms in half. Stir mushrooms, carrots, onions, marjoram, thyme, and garlic into wine mixture. Return mixture just to boiling. Pour vegetable mixture over chicken.

3 Bake, covered, about 45 minutes or until chicken is no longer pink (180°F). Transfer chicken and vegetable mixture to a serving platter. Top with bacon. If desired, sprinkle with parsley and serve with hot cooked noodles.

nutrition facts per serving: 286 cal., 13 g total fat (4 g sat. fat), 95 mg chol., 321 mg sodium, 8 g carb., 1 g dietary fiber, 24 g protein.

Marsala is an Italian wine fortified with brandy. It adds a rich, smoky flavor to chicken that's baked to perfection with a mozzarella and Parmesan cheese topping.

baked **chicken marsala**

prep: 30 minutes bake: 20 minutes oven: 375°F
makes: 8 servings dish: 3-quart

8 skinless, boneless chicken breast halves (about 2 pounds)
1/3 cup all-purpose flour
6 tablespoons butter or margarine
2 cups sliced fresh mushrooms
1 cup dry Marsala
2/3 cup chicken broth
1/8 teaspoon salt
1/8 teaspoon ground black pepper
1 cup shredded mozzarella or fontina cheese (4 ounces)
2/3 cup grated Parmesan cheese
1/2 cup thinly sliced scallions

1 Preheat oven to 375°F. Cut each chicken breast half in half lengthwise. Place each chicken breast piece, boned side down, between two pieces of plastic wrap. Using the flat side of a meat mallet and working from the center out, pound each piece to 1/8-inch thickness. Remove plastic wrap. Coat chicken lightly with flour.

2 In a 12-inch skillet melt 2 tablespoons of the butter over medium heat. Add half of the chicken. Cook for 4 minutes, turning once. Transfer to an ungreased 3-quart rectangular baking dish. Repeat with 2 tablespoons butter and the remaining chicken pieces.

3 Melt remaining 2 tablespoons butter in the skillet; add mushrooms. Cook and stir until tender; stir in Marsala, broth, salt, and pepper. Bring to boiling; boil gently about 5 minutes or until mixture is reduced to 1 cup (including the mushrooms). Pour reduced mixture over the chicken.

4 In a medium bowl combine mozzarella cheese, Parmesan cheese, and scallions; sprinkle over the chicken. Bake, uncovered, about 20 minutes or until chicken is no longer pink (170°F).

nutrition facts per serving: 364 cal., 17 g total fat (9 g sat. fat), 121 mg chol., 496 mg sodium, 6 g carb., 0 g dietary fiber, 42 g protein.

This dish scores well among people who enjoy Asian foods but prefer them mildly spiced. For a lower-sodium version, use reduced-fat and reduced-sodium condensed cream of chicken soup.

chicken
chow mein casserole

prep: 25 minutes   bake: 50 minutes   oven: 350°F
makes: 8 servings   dish: 3-quart

4	cups chopped cooked chicken*
2	cups chopped celery (4 stalks)
1	cup shredded carrots (2 medium)
1	cup chopped red sweet pepper
2	4-ounce cans (drained weight) sliced mushrooms, drained
⅔	cup sliced or slivered almonds, toasted
2	tablespoons diced pimiento, drained
2	10.75-ounce cans condensed cream of chicken soup
2	cups chow mein noodles

1 Preheat oven to 350°F. In an extra-large bowl stir together chicken, celery, carrots, sweet pepper, mushrooms, almonds, and pimiento. Add soup to chicken mixture; mix well.

2 Transfer chicken mixture to an ungreased 3-quart rectangular baking dish. Bake, covered, for 45 minutes. Sprinkle with chow mein noodles. Bake, uncovered, for 5 to 10 minutes more or until heated through.

nutrition facts per serving: 366 cal., 19 g total fat (4 g sat. fat), 68 mg chol., 921 mg sodium, 21 g carb., 4 g dietary fiber, 27 g protein.

*test kitchen tip: If you don't have cooked chicken on hand, use frozen chopped cooked chicken, thawed. Or, purchase deli-roasted chicken; remove chicken from bones, discard skin, chop chicken.

This delicious Asian-inspired recipe calls for specialty ingredients, such as red curry paste and unsweetened coconut milk, that may not be available at your local supermarket. Check at a nearby Asian food store.

thai peanut
chicken

prep: 40 minutes bake: 1 hour 20 minutes oven: 300°F
makes: 4 servings dish: 3-quart

1	13.5- or 14-ounce can unsweetened coconut milk
1/4	cup creamy peanut butter
1/3	cup chicken broth
2	tablespoons soy sauce
2	tablespoons rice vinegar
1	tablespoon packed brown sugar
1	tablespoon toasted sesame oil
2	teaspoons red curry paste
1	teaspoon grated fresh ginger
1	clove garlic, minced
1/8	to 1/4 teaspoon cayenne pepper
1/2	cup all-purpose flour
1/2	teaspoon salt
1/2	teaspoon ground black pepper
4	chicken legs (thigh-drumstick pieces) or two 1- to 1½-pound Cornish game hens, halved
2	tablespoons vegetable oil
2	tablespoons snipped fresh cilantro
2	cups hot cooked rice

1 In a medium saucepan whisk together coconut milk and peanut butter until nearly smooth. Whisk in broth, soy sauce, vinegar, brown sugar, sesame oil, curry paste, ginger, garlic, and cayenne. Bring just to boiling over medium-high heat; reduce heat. Simmer, uncovered, for 15 minutes, stirring occasionally.

2 Preheat oven to 300°F. In a plastic bag, combine flour, salt, and black pepper. If desired, remove skin from chicken. Add chicken pieces, one at a time, to flour mixture, shaking to coat.

3 In a large skillet cook chicken, half at a time, in hot vegetable oil until brown, turning occasionally. Transfer chicken to an ungreased 3-quart rectangular baking dish. Pour peanut butter mixture over chicken. Cover loosely with foil. Bake for 1 hour for chicken (1½ hours for Cornish hens), spooning sauce over chicken occasionally. Bake, uncovered, for 20 to 30 minutes more or until chicken is very tender.

4 Transfer chicken to a serving platter. Skim fat from sauce in dish. Spoon some of the sauce over chicken. Sprinkle with cilantro. Serve with the remaining sauce and hot cooked rice.

nutrition facts per serving: 725 cal., 38 g total fat (15 g sat. fat), 155 mg chol., 968 mg sodium, 35 g carb., 1 g dietary fiber, 38 g protein.

Greek seasoning varies from brand to brand, but most include a great variety of herbs and spices, including parsley, oregano, onion powder, nutmeg, and pepper. The product makes it easy to bring a load of flavor to a recipe—without a lengthy recipe list.

greek chicken and pita casserole

prep: 20 minutes bake: 20 minutes oven: 350°F
makes: 6 servings dish: 3-quart

4 cups chopped cooked chicken or turkey
3 medium zucchini, halved lengthwise and cut into ½-inch pieces (4 cups)
1 10.75-ounce can condensed cream of chicken soup
½ cup chopped red onion (1 medium)
½ cup chicken broth
1½ teaspoons Greek seasoning*
2 cloves garlic, minced
2 6-inch pita bread rounds, cut into bite-size wedges
  Nonstick cooking spray
1 cup chopped roma tomatoes (3 medium)
1 cup crumbled feta cheese (4 ounces)
½ cup pitted Kalamata olives, sliced

1 Preheat oven to 350°F. In a large bowl combine chicken, zucchini, soup, onion, broth, 1 teaspoon of the Greek seasoning, and the garlic. Transfer mixture to an ungreased 3-quart rectangular baking dish.

2 Coat pita wedges with cooking spray; sprinkle with the remaining ½ teaspoon Greek seasoning. Sprinkle pita wedges, tomatoes, cheese, and olives on top of chicken mixture. Bake, uncovered, about 20 minutes or until heated through.

nutrition facts per serving: 388 cal., 17 g total fat (6 g sat. fat), 109 mg chol., 1068 mg sodium, 23 g carb., 3 g dietary fiber, 35 g protein.

*test kitchen tip: If you can't find Greek seasoning, make your own by combining 2 teaspoons oregano, 1½ teaspoons onion powder, 1½ teaspoons garlic powder, 1 teaspoon dried parsley, 1 teaspoon ground black pepper, ½ teaspoon ground cinnamon, and ½ teaspoon ground nutmeg.

Tomatillos, considered to be staples in Mexican cooking, look like green cherry tomatoes in papery husks. Discard the husks before using the tomatillos.

chicken and **tortillas** with **tomatillo** sauce

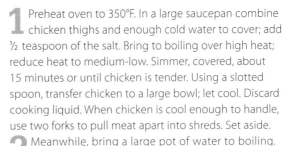

prep: 40 minutes   bake: 30 minutes   oven: 350°F
makes: 8 servings   dish: 3-quart

1   pound skinless, boneless chicken thighs
1   teaspoon salt
2½ pounds fresh tomatillos, husked and quartered*
3   cloves garlic, halved
2   fresh jalapeño chile peppers, stemmed, seeded, and cut up**
2   cups shredded Mexican cheese blend
½   of an 8-ounce package cream cheese, softened
1½ teaspoons chili powder
    Nonstick cooking spray
8   8-inch flour tortillas
    Cherry tomatoes, quartered (optional)
    Fresh snipped cilantro (optional)

1 Preheat oven to 350°F. In a large saucepan combine chicken thighs and enough cold water to cover; add ½ teaspoon of the salt. Bring to boiling over high heat; reduce heat to medium-low. Simmer, covered, about 15 minutes or until chicken is tender. Using a slotted spoon, transfer chicken to a large bowl; let cool. Discard cooking liquid. When chicken is cool enough to handle, use two forks to pull meat apart into shreds. Set aside.

2 Meanwhile, bring a large pot of water to boiling. Add tomatillos and cook for 3 minutes; drain. Transfer tomatillos to a food processor or blender; add garlic, chile peppers, and the remaining ½ teaspoon salt. Cover and process or blend until smooth.

3 In a medium bowl combine shredded cheese, cream cheese, and chili powder, stirring with a wooden spoon until combined.

4 Coat a 3-quart rectangular baking dish with cooking spray. Spoon one-third of the tomatillo mixture into the prepared baking dish. Lay 2 of the tortillas over the tomatillo mixture. Top with half of the chicken and half of the cheese mixture. Top with another 2 tortillas, another one-third of the tomatillo mixture, and 2 more tortillas. Top with the remaining chicken and the remaining cheese mixture. Top with the remaining 2 tortillas and the remaining tomatillo mixture. Cover with foil.

5 Bake about 30 minutes or until heated through and bubbly around the edges. If desired, top with cherry tomatoes and cilantro.

nutrition facts per serving: 445 cal., 23 g total fat (0 g sat. fat), 94 mg chol., 790 mg sodium, 36 g carb., 3 g dietary fiber, 24 g protein.

*test kitchen tip: If you can't find fresh tomatillos, use 5 cups quartered canned tomatillos. Do not cook in boiling water. Combine in food processor with garlic, chile peppers, and the remaining ½ teaspoon salt. Continue as directed.

**test kitchen tip: See tip on handling chile peppers, page 80.

You'll love the spinach-and-feta stuffing—the same flavorful combo that's layered between phyllo in the classic Greek pie called spanakopita.

spanakopita stuffed
chicken breasts

prep: 30 minutes bake: 35 minutes oven: 375°F
makes: 4 servings dish: 3-quart

Nonstick cooking
  spray
1 small lemon
3 tablespoons olive oil
½ cup finely chopped
  onion (1 medium)
2 cloves garlic, minced
1 10-ounce package
  frozen chopped
  spinach, thawed
  and well drained
⅓ cup crumbled feta
  cheese
3 tablespoons snipped
  fresh dill
¼ teaspoon ground
  nutmeg
¼ teaspoon ground
  black pepper
4 chicken breast halves
  (about 2 pounds)
½ teaspoon salt
2 medium lemons,
  halved
Snipped fresh dill
  (optional)

1 Preheat oven to 375°F. Lightly coat a 3-quart rectangular baking dish with cooking spray; set aside. Squeeze juice from small lemon (you should have 2 tablespoons). In a medium skillet heat 2 tablespoons of the oil over medium heat. Add onion and garlic; cook for 4 to 6 minutes or until tender. Remove from heat. Add spinach, cheese, 3 tablespoons dill, 1 tablespoon of the reserved lemon juice, the nutmeg, and pepper to skillet; stir to combine.

2 Using your fingers, gently separate chicken skin from breast halves along the rib edges to make a pocket. Season chicken with salt. Spoon one-fourth of the stuffing mixture under skin of each breast half; press down to create an even layer.

3 Place chicken, bone side down, in prepared baking dish. Add lemon halves. Combine the remaining oil and remaining lemon juice; drizzle over chicken. Bake, uncovered, for 35 to 40 minutes or until chicken is no longer pink (170°F). If desired, sprinkle with additional dill.

nutrition facts per serving: 468 cal., 30 g total fat (8 g sat. fat), 127 mg chol., 598 mg sodium, 7 g carb., 3 g dietary fiber, 43 g protein.

It's a fiesta of flavor in every bite when layers of tortillas, chicken, and a spicy sauce featuring tomatoes combine in this sure-to-please casserole.

mexican-style chicken

prep: 25 minutes   bake: 45 minutes   stand: 10 minutes   oven: 350°F
makes: 8 servings   dish: 3-quart

2   10.75-ounce cans reduced-fat and reduced-sodium condensed cream of chicken soup
1   10-ounce can diced tomatoes with green chile peppers, undrained
¾   cup chopped green sweet pepper (1 medium)
½   cup chopped onion (1 medium)
1½ teaspoons chili powder
¼   teaspoon ground black pepper
12 6- or 7-inch corn tortillas, cut into thin, bite-size strips
3   cups cubed cooked chicken (about 1 pound)
2   cups shredded cheddar cheese (8 ounces)
    Sliced tomatoes (optional)
    Sliced scallions (optional)

1 Preheat oven to 350°F. In a medium bowl combine cream of chicken soup, tomatoes with chile peppers, sweet pepper, onion, chili powder, and black pepper.

2 To assemble, sprinkle about one-third of the tortilla strips into an ungreased 3-quart rectangular baking dish. Layer half of the chicken over tortilla strips; spoon half of soup mixture on top. Sprinkle half of the cheddar cheese and another one-third of the tortilla strips over the soup mixture. Layer with the remaining chicken, soup mixture, and tortilla strips.

3 Bake, uncovered, about 45 minutes or until bubbly around edges and center is hot. Remove from oven; sprinkle with the remaining cheese. Let stand for 10 minutes before serving. If desired, top with sliced tomatoes and scallions.

nutrition facts per serving: 380 cal., 16 g total fat (7 g sat. fat), 83 mg chol., 702 mg sodium, 33 g carb., 2 g dietary fiber, 27 g protein.

Mole sauce, a key ingredient that adds complex flavors to Mexican dishes like this one, is a smooth, cooked blend of onion, garlic, chiles, and chocolate.

mole enchiladas

prep: 45 minutes bake: 40 minutes oven: 350°F
makes: 12 enchiladas dish: 2-quart

Nonstick cooking
  spray
12 6- or 7-inch flour
  tortillas
1/2 cup chopped onion
  (1 medium)
2 cloves garlic, minced
1 medium fresh
  jalapeño or serrano
  chile pepper,
  seeded and finely
  chopped*
1 tablespoon
  vegetable oil
1/3 cup sour cream
1/4 cup purchased mole
  sauce
2 tablespoons water
2 15-ounce cans black
  or pinto beans,
  rinsed and drained
2 cups shredded
  asadero, Monterey
  Jack, or sharp
  cheddar cheese
  (8 ounces)
1 8-ounce carton sour
  cream
2 tablespoons all-
  purpose flour
1 teaspoon ground
  cumin
1/4 teaspoon salt
3/4 cup milk
1 recipe Mango Salsa

1 Preheat oven to 350°F. Coat two 2-quart rectangular baking dishes with cooking spray; set aside. Stack tortillas and wrap tightly in foil. Bake about 10 minutes or until heated through.

2 Meanwhile, for filling, in a large skillet cook onion, garlic, and chile pepper in hot oil over medium heat until tender; remove from heat. In a small bowl stir together the 1/3 cup sour cream, mole sauce, and the water; add to skillet along with the beans and half of the cheese.

3 Spoon 1/3 cup of the filling onto one edge of each tortilla; roll up. Place, seam sides down, in prepared baking dishes.

4 For sauce, in a medium bowl combine 8-ounce carton sour cream, flour, cumin, and salt; whisk in milk. Pour sauce down center of filled tortillas.

5 Bake, covered, about 25 minutes until heated through. Uncover; top with the remaining cheese. Bake, uncovered, about 5 minutes more or until cheese is melted. Top with Mango Salsa.

nutrition facts per enchilada: 299 cal., 15 g total fat (5 g sat. fat), 29 mg chol., 458 mg sodium, 30 g carb., 4 g dietary fiber, 14 g protein.

*test kitchen tip: Because chile peppers contain volatile oils that can burn your skin and eyes, avoid direct contact with chiles as much as possible. When working with chile peppers, wear plastic or rubber gloves. If your bare hands do touch the chiles, wash your hands well with soap and water.

mango salsa: In a small bowl combine 1 large mango, seeded, peeled, and chopped; 2 fresh jalapeño or serrano chile peppers, seeded and finely chopped; 2 tablespoons snipped fresh cilantro; and 1 tablespoon lemon or lime juice. Place in an airtight storage container in the refrigerator until serving time or for up to 2 days.

This Greek-style potpie gets blanketed with a buttery phyllo cover-up. Make it easy by taking advantage of frozen phyllo dough, which is readily available and speeds up the process of producing amazing pastry.

chicken and spinach phyllo bake

prep: 35 minutes   bake: 45 minutes   oven: 375°F
makes: 8 servings   dish: 3-quart

Nonstick cooking
    spray
2   tablespoons butter
2½ pounds ground
    chicken
1   cup chopped onion
    (1 large)
3   10-ounce packages
    frozen chopped
    spinach, thawed
    and squeezed dry
1   teaspoon ground
    black pepper
½   teaspoon salt
½   teaspoon ground
    nutmeg
¼   teaspoon crushed red
    pepper
4   eggs, lightly beaten
1½ cups crumbled feta
    cheese* (6 ounces)
1   tablespoon snipped
    fresh oregano
16 sheets frozen phyllo
    dough (14×9-inch
    rectangles), thawed

1 Preheat oven to 375°F. Lightly coat a 3-quart rectangular baking dish with cooking spray; set aside. In an extra-large skillet melt butter over medium-high heat. Add ground chicken and onion; cook about 8 minutes or until chicken is brown and onion is tender, using a wooden spoon to break up meat as it cooks. Drain off fat. Stir spinach, black pepper, salt, nutmeg, and crushed red pepper into chicken mixture in skillet; cook and stir for 5 minutes. Transfer mixture to a large bowl. Stir in eggs, cheese, and oregano.

2 Unfold phyllo dough. Using a sharp knife, cut a 1-inch strip off one of the short ends of the phyllo stack; discard. Place a phyllo sheet in the bottom of the prepared baking dish. Lightly coat phyllo sheet with cooking spray. (As you work, cover the remaining phyllo dough with plastic wrap to prevent it from drying out.) Top with seven more sheets, coating each sheet with cooking spray. Spread chicken mixture over phyllo in dish. Top with the remaining eight phyllo sheets, coating each sheet with cooking spray and casually crumpling the top few sheets.

3 Bake, uncovered, about 45 minutes or until mixture is heated through and top is brown.

nutrition facts per serving: 530 cal., 29 g total fat (13 g sat. fat), 273 mg chol., 1024 mg sodium, 29 g carb., 4 g dietary fiber, 41 g protein.

*test kitchen tip: Feta cheese is available in a variety of flavors, any of which would work well in this dish.

Poblano peppers are chopped instead of stuffed in this shrimp-filled spin on chiles rellenos.

shrimp
rellenos
casserole

prep: 40 minutes   bake: 35 minutes
oven: 350°F   makes: 10 servings   dish: 3-quart

1   pound fresh or frozen peeled, cooked medium shrimp
4   large fresh poblano chile peppers, stemmed, seeded, and chopped* (4 cups)
1   cup finely chopped onion (1 large)
4   cloves garlic, minced
3   tablespoons butter
1   8-ounce package cream cheese, cut up
1   cup chopped roma tomatoes (3 medium)
2   cups shredded Monterey Jack cheese (8 ounces)
2   cups shredded cheddar cheese (8 ounces)
1   cup all-purpose flour
1   teaspoon baking powder
1   teaspoon baking soda
½   teaspoon salt
1   egg, lightly beaten
1   cup milk
2   tablespoons vegetable oil

1 Thaw shrimp, if frozen. Preheat oven to 350°F. Grease a 3-quart rectangular baking dish; set aside. In a large skillet cook chile peppers, onion, and garlic in hot butter about 5 minutes or until onion is tender. Add cream cheese, stirring until smooth. Stir in shrimp and tomatoes. Remove from heat. Stir in 1 cup of the Monterey Jack cheese and 1 cup of the cheddar cheese. Transfer mixture to prepared baking dish.

2 In a medium bowl combine flour, baking powder, baking soda, and salt. In a small bowl combine egg, milk, and oil. Add egg mixture to flour mixture, stirring until smooth. Pour over shrimp mixture. Sprinkle with the remaining 1 cup Monterey Jack cheese and the remaining 1 cup cheddar cheese.

3 Bake, uncovered, for 35 to 40 minutes or until golden brown and set in the center.

nutrition facts per serving: 449 cal., 30 g total fat (17 g sat. fat), 190 mg chol., 742 mg sodium, 18 g carb., 1 g dietary fiber, 26 g protein.

*test kitchen tip: Because chile peppers contain volatile oils that can burn your skin and eyes, avoid direct contact with them as much as possible. When working with chile peppers, wear plastic or rubber gloves. If your bare hands do touch the peppers, wash your hands and nails well with soap and warm water.

The green salsa used in Mexican dishes is typically based on tomatillos, green chiles, and cilantro. In this shrimp and corn casserole, it provides the heat.

fiesta tortilla-shrimp casserole

prep: 20 minutes   bake: 45 minutes   oven: 350°F
makes: 4 servings   dish: 2-quart

6 6-inch corn tortillas
1 cup green salsa
½ cup sour cream
3 tablespoons all-
   purpose flour
4 teaspoons dried
   cilantro, crushed
1 12-ounce package
   frozen peeled and
   deveined cooked
   shrimp, thawed
1 cup frozen whole
   kernel corn
1 cup shredded
   Mexican Chihuahua
   or farmer cheese
   (4 ounces)
   Snipped fresh
   cilantro, sour cream,
   and/or chopped
   tomato (optional)

1 Preheat oven to 350°F. Lightly grease a 2-quart baking dish. Cut each of three tortillas into six wedges; place in the bottom of the prepared baking dish. Cut the remaining three tortillas into thin bite-size strips; place on a baking sheet. Bake, uncovered, about 10 minutes or until crisp.

2 Meanwhile, in a medium bowl combine salsa, ½ cup sour cream, flour, and dried cilantro. Stir in shrimp and corn. Spoon shrimp mixture over tortillas in dish.

3 Bake, uncovered, for 40 to 45 minutes or until heated through. Top with baked tortilla strips and cheese. Bake, uncovered, about 5 minutes more or until cheese is melted. If desired, garnish with fresh cilantro, additional sour cream, and/or tomato.

nutrition facts per serving: 408 cal., 15 g total fat (9 g sat. fat), 208 mg chol., 581 mg sodium, 39 g carb., 2 g dietary fiber, 29 g protein.

This meatless Mexican specialty is easy to assemble and needs to bake right away so that the tortillas remain crisp.

chilaquiles casserole

prep: 20 minutes bake: 35 minutes stand: 15 minutes oven: 375°F
makes: 8 servings dish: 2-quart

1 cup chopped onion
   (1 large)
2 cloves garlic, minced
1 tablespoon
   vegetable oil
12 6-inch corn tortillas,
   cut into 1-inch
   pieces
2 cups shredded
   Monterey Jack
   cheese (8 ounces)
2 4-ounce cans diced
   green chile peppers,
   undrained
4 eggs, lightly beaten
2 cups buttermilk or
   sour milk*
1/2 teaspoon salt
1/4 teaspoon ground
   black pepper
1/8 teaspoon ground
   cumin
1/8 teaspoon dried
   oregano, crushed
   Refrigerated
   prepared salsa
   (optional)

1 Preheat oven to 375°F. In a large skillet cook onion and garlic in hot oil over medium heat until onion is tender.

2 Meanwhile, grease a 2-quart rectangular baking dish. Spread half of the tortillas in the bottom of the prepared baking dish. Top with half of the cheese and one can of the chile peppers. Sprinkle with onion mixture. Top with the remaining tortillas, cheese, and chile peppers.

3 In a large bowl combine eggs, buttermilk, salt, black pepper, cumin, and oregano. Pour evenly over ingredients in dish.

4 Bake, uncovered, for 35 to 40 minutes or until center is set and edges are lightly browned. Let stand for 15 minutes before serving. If desired, top with salsa.

nutrition facts per serving: 284 cal., 15 g total fat (7 g sat. fat), 133 mg chol., 507 mg sodium, 25 g carb., 4 g dietary fiber, 15 g protein.

*test kitchen tip: To make 2 cups sour milk, place 2 tablespoons lemon juice or vinegar in a glass measuring cup. Add enough milk to make 2 cups total liquid; stir. Let the mixture stand for 5 minutes before using.

This layered dish has a unique flavor combination with corn tortillas, sautéed fresh vegetables, and Cotija (ko-TEE-hah), a dry grating Mexican cheese. Feta cheese is another tasty option for the cheese filling.

lasagna olé

prep: 35 minutes bake: 30 minutes stand: 10 minutes oven: 375°F
makes: 6 to 8 servings dish: 2-quart

½	cup chopped onion (1 medium)
2	tablespoons olive oil
6	cloves garlic, minced
5	cups sliced fresh mushrooms
1¼	cups sliced yellow summer squash (1 medium)
¾	cup chopped red sweet pepper (1 medium)
½	cup frozen whole kernel corn
1	6-ounce package (about 5 cups) baby spinach
3	eggs
2	cups cream-style cottage cheese
1½	cups crumbled Cotija or shredded mozzarella cheese (6 ounces)
½	cup fresh cilantro leaves
10	6-inch corn tortillas
1¾	cups salsa

1 Preheat oven to 375°F. Lightly grease a 2-quart baking dish; set aside. In a 12-inch skillet cook onion in hot oil over medium heat about 5 minutes or until tender. Stir in garlic. Cook and stir for 30 seconds. Add mushrooms, squash, sweet pepper, and corn. Cook and stir for 5 to 7 minutes or until mushrooms are tender and squash is crisp-tender. Stir in spinach. Cook and stir just until spinach starts to wilt. Set aside.

2 In a food processor or blender, combine eggs, cottage cheese, and 1¼ cups of the Cojita cheese. Cover and process or blend until well mixed. Add cilantro. Cover and process or blend with several on/off pulses until cilantro is chopped.

3 Arrange five of the tortillas in the bottom of the prepared baking dish, cutting as necessary to fit. Spread with cheese mixture and vegetable mixture. Top with the remaining tortillas, cutting as necessary to fit. Spread with salsa. Sprinkle with the remaining ¼ cup Cojita cheese.

4 Bake, uncovered, for 30 to 40 minutes or until mixture is set. Let stand for 10 minutes before serving.

nutrition facts per serving: 441 cal., 22 g total fat (9 g sat. fat), 152 mg chol., 1163 mg sodium, 39 g carb., 7 g dietary fiber, 26 g protein.

Take pot stickers out of the appetizer category and serve them up for dinner in a vegetable-filled casserole with a spicy sauce. Pictured on page 208.

asian vegetables and pot stickers

prep: 35 minutes   bake: 40 minutes   oven: 350°F
makes: 6 servings   dish: 2½-quart

2   9- to 13-ounce packages frozen shrimp, pork, or chicken pot stickers
1   16-ounce package frozen sugar snap stir-fry vegetables, thawed
1   8-ounce can sliced water chestnuts, drained
1   tablespoon finely chopped peeled fresh ginger
1   14-ounce can beef broth
2   tablespoons cornstarch
2   tablespoons soy sauce
2   tablespoons honey
1   teaspoon Chinese-style hot mustard
1   tablespoon sesame seeds, toasted
    Chile oil (optional)

1 Preheat oven to 350°F. Cook pot stickers according to package directions; drain, if necessary. Place pot stickers in an ungreased 2½-quart casserole. Stir in vegetables, water chestnuts, and ginger.

2 In a medium saucepan combine broth, cornstarch, soy sauce, honey, and mustard. Cook and stir over medium heat until thickened and bubbly. Pour broth mixture over pot stickers in casserole.

3 Bake, covered, for 40 to 45 minutes or until heated through. Sprinkle with sesame seeds before serving. If desired, pass chile oil.

nutrition facts per serving: 272 cal., 5 g total fat (1 g sat. fat), 12 mg chol., 1038 mg sodium, 46 g carb., 3 g dietary fiber, 9 g protein.

global ingredients

Give your pantry continental flair with the amazing flavors these ingredients offer:

- *Serrano peppers look like small jalapeño peppers but have a much spicier kick.*

- *Peppercorns are the dried fruit of the black pepper plant, which is native to India, but used in many cultures.*

- *Chili paste is made from fermented fava beans, hot red chiles, and garlic.*

- *Tomatillos are slightly tart cousins of the tomato. Tomatillos form the base of Latin American green sauces. Discard the papery husks before using.*

- *Ginger is a tropical root that intensifies dishes with a pungent peppery sweetness. It's a mainstay in the pantries of Asian and India.*

9

Make one of these showstoppers the centerpiece for a dinner party. Assembling the dish ahead of time makes it easy. While it bakes, you'll have plenty of time to pour the wine, toss a salad, and enjoy your guests.

made for com

pany

made for company

Tawny port infuses a smooth caramel flavor and nutty aroma into the savory cooking liquid that yields a tender, flavorful roast. As you are nearing the end of roasting time, fresh carrots and parsnips are added to lend color and more flavor appeal.

tawny beef with parsnips

prep: 30 minutes bake: 2 hours 30 minutes oven: 350°F
makes: 6 servings dish: Dutch oven

1	3-pound boneless beef chuck roast, trimmed and cut into 1½- to 2-inch pieces
	Salt and ground black pepper
2	tablespoons olive oil
½	cup beef broth
½	cup tawny port or Belgian-style beer
2	large red onions, cut into wedges
1	clove garlic, minced
1½	pounds parsnips, peeled and quartered
4	carrots, quartered
⅓	cup crumbled Stilton cheese
	Fresh thyme sprigs

1 Preheat oven to 350°F. Season meat with salt and pepper. In an ovenproof 4-quart Dutch oven cook beef in hot oil, half at a time, until browned. Drain off fat. Pour broth and port over beef. Top with onions and garlic. Bake, covered, for 1½ hours. Add parsnips and carrots. Bake, covered, about 1 hour more or until meat and vegetables are tender.

2 Using a slotted spoon, transfer meat and vegetables to a shallow bowl or serving platter. Skim fat from cooking liquid. Spoon some of the cooking liquid over the meat and vegetables. Sprinkle with cheese. Garnish with fresh thyme. Serve the remaining cooking liquid with the meat and vegetables.

nutrition facts per serving: 660 cal., 39 g total fat (15 g sat. fat), 124 mg chol., 429 mg sodium, 33 g carb., 7 g dietary fiber, 39 g protein.

A creamy walnut-garlic and tarragon vinaigrette infuses the layers of this make-ahead dish. Whether you serve this at a sit-down dinner or tote it to a potluck, it's an intriguing combination.

pork and potato stack

prep: 45 minutes   roast: 35 minutes   stand: 10 minutes   chill: 2 hours
oven: 425°F   makes: 6 servings   dish: 2-quart

1   1-pound pork tenderloin
    Salt and ground black pepper
1   pound Yukon gold or other yellow-flesh potatoes
1   cup frozen shelled sweet soybeans (edamame)
1   medium zucchini or yellow summer squash
1   recipe Creamy Walnut-Garlic Vinaigrette
1   cup frozen whole kernel corn, thawed
½   cup sliced scallions (4)
    Shredded carrots (optional)
    Fresh tarragon and thyme (optional)

1 Preheat oven to 425°F. Place pork on rack in roasting pan; sprinkle with salt and pepper. Roast, uncovered, for 35 to 40 minutes or until thermometer registers 155°F. Cover; let stand for 10 minutes. Cut pork into bite-size pieces.

2 Meanwhile, cut potatoes into ¼-inch slices. In a large saucepan cook potatoes and soybeans in lightly salted boiling water, covered, for 5 to 8 minutes or until potatoes are tender; drain.

3 Cut zucchini into 1½- to 2-inch-long sections. Slice sections lengthwise into planks.

4 In a lightly greased 2-quart rectangular baking dish layer half of the potatoes and soybeans. Drizzle with ⅓ cup vinaigrette. Arrange zucchini in an even layer over top; drizzle with ⅓ cup vinaigrette. Evenly arrange pork and remaining potatoes and soybeans over zucchini; drizzle with ⅓ cup vinaigrette. In a small bowl combine corn, scallions, and the remaining vinaigrette; spoon over layers in baking dish.

5 Cover and refrigerate for 2 to 24 hours to allow flavors to blend. If desired, top with carrots and fresh tarragon.

nutrition facts per serving: 355 cal., 19 g total fat (3 g sat. fat), 49 mg chol., 576 mg sodium, 24 g carb., 4 g dietary fiber, 23 g protein.

creamy walnut-garlic vinaigrette: In a food processor combine ¼ cup refrigerated or frozen egg product, thawed; ¼ cup white wine vinegar; 1 teaspoon Dijon mustard; 1 teaspoon snipped fresh tarragon or thyme or ¼ teaspoon dried tarragon or thyme, crushed; 1 teaspoon salt; ¼ teaspoon ground black pepper; and 3 cloves garlic, quartered. With food processor running, gradually add ⅓ cup olive oil through feed tube. Process until mixture is slightly thickened. Stir in ⅓ cup finely chopped toasted walnuts. Makes about 1¼ cups.

These succulent pork chops are marinated in soy sauce, peanut oil, and Asian spices, then baked with apples. Serve with mashed potatoes and steamed green vegetables.

spiced pork and apples

prep: 25 minutes marinate: 4 hours bake: 20 minutes
oven: 425°F makes: 4 servings dish: 3-quart

4	thin-cut (about ½-inch-thick) boneless pork chops (about 1¼ pounds)
¼	cup peanut oil or vegetable oil
¼	cup honey or packed brown sugar
¼	cup reduced-sodium soy sauce
2	tablespoons rice wine or sherry
1	teaspoon toasted sesame oil
1	teaspoon five-spice powder
1	2-inch piece fresh ginger, peeled and thinly sliced
2	large baking apples (such as Cortland, Pippin, Rome Beauty, or Winesap), cored and cut in thick slices
¼	teaspoon ground cinnamon or five-spice powder
4	scallions, diagonally sliced into 2-inch pieces
1	tablespoon honey

1 Place pork chops in a resealable plastic bag set in a shallow dish. For marinade, in a small bowl combine peanut oil, honey, soy sauce, rice wine, sesame oil, five-spice powder, and ginger. Pour marinade over pork chops. Seal bag; turn to coat chops. Marinate in the refrigerator for 4 to 12 hours, turning occasionally.

2 Preheat oven to 425°F. Drain chops, reserving ¼ cup marinade. Arrange chops in an ungreased 3-quart rectangular baking dish. Arrange apples around chops. Drizzle apples with the reserved ¼ cup marinade. Sprinkle apples with cinnamon.

3 Bake, uncovered, for 10 minutes. Add scallions. Bake, uncovered, for 10 to 15 minutes more or until chops are cooked through (160°F) and apples are tender. Arrange chops and apples on a serving platter. Drizzle apples with honey.

nutrition facts per serving: 539 cal., 28 g total fat (7 g sat. fat), 98 mg chol., 473 mg sodium, 42 g carb., 3 g dietary fiber, 31 g protein.

For a change of pace, try this satisfying stuffing, studded with dried cranberries and crunchy pistachios. Packaged stuffing mix gives it a nice texture.

chorizo corn bread stuffing

prep: 40 minutes bake: 30 minutes oven: 350°F
makes: 12 servings dish: 3-quart

15 to 16 ounces uncooked chorizo sausage, casings removed if present
½ cup butter
2 cups chopped onions (2 large)
2 medium fennel bulbs, trimmed, cored, and cut into thin wedges (reserve feathery tops for garnish) or 2 large apples, cored and chopped (2 cups)
¾ cup chopped celery
2 cloves garlic, minced
1 16-ounce package corn bread stuffing mix
1 cup dry-roasted salted pistachio nuts
¾ cup dried cranberries
2 eggs, lightly beaten
1 14-ounce can reduced-sodium chicken broth

1 Preheat oven to 350°F. Grease a 3-quart baking dish; set aside. In a large skillet cook sausage until cooked through, stirring to break up sausage as it cooks. Drain off fat. Transfer sausage to an extra-large bowl. Set aside.

2 Carefully wipe out skillet. Melt butter in the skillet over medium heat. Add onions, fennel (if using), celery, and garlic. Cook for 10 to 15 minutes or until tender, stirring occasionally. Add apple (if using). Cook and stir for 2 minutes more.

3 Add onion mixture, stuffing mix, nuts, and cranberries to sausage in bowl; toss to combine. In a medium bowl combine eggs and broth. Drizzle broth mixture over onion-stuffing mixture to moisten, tossing lightly to combine. (For moister stuffing, add ½ cup water.) Spoon into prepared dish.

4 Bake, covered, for 35 minutes. Uncover and bake for 10 to 15 minutes more or until heated through and top is light brown. (Stuffing is done when an instant-read thermometer inserted in center of stuffing mixture registers 165°F.) If desired, garnish with fennel tops.

nutrition facts per serving: 504 cal., 30 g total fat (11 g sat. fat), 356 mg chol., 1054 mg sodium, 42 g carb., 3 g dietary fiber, 17 g protein.

Bits of biscuit over a fabulous filling will remind you of a savory cobbler.

italian sausage potpie

prep: 25 minutes bake: 30 minutes stand: 20 minutes oven: 400°F
makes: 6 servings dish: 2-quart

1½ pounds bulk Italian
    sausage
1½ cups chopped carrots
12 ounces fresh green
    beans, trimmed
    and cut into 2-inch
    lengths
 2 cups purchased
    Alfredo pasta sauce
 2 teaspoons dried
    Italian seasoning,
    crushed
 1 cup shredded
    mozzarella cheese
    (4 ounces)
 1 7.5-ounce package
    refrigerated biscuits
    (10 biscuits)
    Milk
    Dried Italian
    seasoning and/or
    grated Parmesan
    cheese (optional)

1 Preheat oven to 400°F. In a large skillet cook sausage and carrots until sausage is brown and carrot is just tender, using a wooden spoon to break up sausage as it cooks. Drain off fat. Stir green beans, Alfredo sauce, and 2 teaspoons Italian seasoning into meat mixture in skillet. Heat through. Stir in cheese.

2 Transfer meat and vegetable mixture to a greased 2-quart casserole or baking dish. Quarter each biscuit; arrange biscuit pieces over filling.

3 Brush biscuits lightly with milk and sprinkle with additional Italian seasoning and/or Parmesan cheese (if using). Bake, uncovered, about 30 minutes or until golden brown and bubbly. Let stand for 20 minutes before serving.

nutrition facts per serving: 709 cal., 54 g total fat (20 g sat. fat), 130 mg chol., 1751 mg sodium, 29 g carb., 3 g dietary fiber, 26 g protein.

baked risotto with sausage and artichokes

prep: 40 minutes bake: 70 minutes stand: 5 minutes oven: 350°F
makes: 6 to 8 servings dish: 2½-quart

1   pound bulk Italian
    sausage
1   cup chopped fennel
    bulb (1 medium)
½   cup chopped onion
2   cloves garlic, minced
¾   cup arborio or long
    grain rice
2   9-ounce packages
    frozen artichoke
    hearts, thawed,
    drained, and halved
1   cup coarsely
    shredded carrots
2   teaspoons snipped
    fresh thyme or
    ½ teaspoon dried
    thyme, crushed
½   teaspoon ground
    black pepper
2   cups chicken broth
⅓   cup dry white wine
    or chicken broth
½   cup panko (Japanese-
    style bread crumbs)
¼   cup finely shredded
    Asiago or Parmesan
    cheese
1   tablespoon butter or
    margarine, melted
½   teaspoon finely
    shredded lemon
    zest

1 Preheat oven to 350°F. In a 12-inch skillet cook and stir sausage, fennel, onion, and garlic over medium-high heat until vegetables are tender but not brown. Drain fat; discard. Add rice; cook and stir 1 minute more.

2 Add artichoke hearts, carrots, thyme, and pepper. Stir in broth and wine. Bring just to boiling. Transfer to a 2½-quart casserole. Bake, covered, about 1 hour or until rice is tender, stirring once.

3 Meanwhile, in a small bowl combine panko, cheese, butter, and lemon zest. Uncover casserole and top with crumb mixture. Bake, uncovered, 10 minutes more. Let stand for 5 minutes before serving.

nutrition facts per serving: 476 cal., 28 g total fat (11 g sat. fat), 68 mg chol., 1038 mg sodium, 36 g carb., 8 g dietary fiber, 17 g protein.

The best tool to use for pounding the chicken breast is the flat side of a meat mallet or the bottom of a small skillet. Because chicken breast is tender, be sure not to pound too long or it will begin to fall apart.

crab-stuffed
chicken

prep: 45 minutes bake: 37 minutes oven: 350°F
makes: 8 servings dish: 3-quart

8	skinless, boneless chicken breast halves (about 2½ pounds)
3	tablespoons butter
¼	cup all-purpose flour
¾	cup milk
¾	cup chicken broth
⅓	cup dry white wine
1	tablespoon butter
1	cup chopped fresh mushrooms
¼	cup chopped onion
1	6-ounce can crabmeat, drained, flaked, and cartilage removed
½	cup coarsely crushed saltine crackers (10 crackers)
2	tablespoons snipped fresh parsley
½	teaspoon salt Pinch ground black pepper
2	tablespoons butter
1	cup shredded Swiss cheese (4 ounces)
½	teaspoon paprika

1 Preheat oven to 350°F. Place each chicken breast half between two pieces of plastic wrap. Using the flat side of a meat mallet, pound chicken lightly until about ⅛ inch thick. Remove plastic wrap.

2 For sauce, in a medium saucepan melt 3 tablespoons butter over medium heat. Stir in flour. Gradually stir in milk, broth, and wine. Cook and stir until thickened and bubbly.

3 For filling, in a medium skillet heat 1 tablespoon butter over medium heat. Add mushrooms and onion; cook until tender. Stir in crabmeat, crackers, parsley, salt, and pepper. Stir in 2 tablespoons of the sauce. Place about ¼ cup of the filling on each piece of chicken. Fold in sides; roll up. Secure with wooden toothpicks, if necessary. In a large skillet heat the 2 tablespoons butter over medium heat. Cook chicken rolls, half at a time, in hot butter until brown on all sides.

4 Arrange chicken rolls, seam sides down, in an ungreased 3-quart rectangular baking dish. Top with the remaining sauce. Bake, covered, about 35 minutes or until chicken is no longer pink. Sprinkle with cheese and paprika. Bake, uncovered, about 2 minutes more or until cheese is melted. Remove toothpicks, if using.

5 Transfer chicken to a serving platter. Whisk mixture in baking dish; pass with chicken.

nutrition facts per serving: 367 cal., 16 g total fat (9 g sat. fat), 140 mg chol., 542 mg sodium, 9 g carb., 1 g dietary fiber, 43 g protein.

When you're in a hurry to present a special main dish, this little number satisfies. It takes just a half an hour in the oven to create a melding of fantastic flavors.

roast chicken with
olive-raisin sauce

prep: 25 minutes   roast: 25 minutes   oven: 425°F
makes: 4 servings   dish: 3-quart

4   bone-in chicken breast halves (about 2¼ pounds)
8   to 12 fresh sage leaves or 24 sprigs fresh marjoram
¼   teaspoon salt
¼   teaspoon ground black pepper
½   cup sliced celery
½   cup chopped onion (1 small)
2   large cloves garlic, minced
2   tablespoons olive oil
½   cup chicken broth
½   cup dry red wine or ⅓ cup chicken broth plus 2 tablespoons balsamic vinegar
½   cup pitted and halved mixed olives or Kalamata olives
½   cup golden raisins
⅛   teaspoon cayenne pepper (optional)
1   tablespoon snipped fresh marjoram

1 Preheat oven to 425°F. Using your fingers, gently separate the chicken skin from the meat of the breasts along rib edges. Place two or three of the sage leaves or six sprigs of the marjoram under the skin of each piece of chicken. Sprinkle chicken with salt and black pepper.

2 Place chicken, skin sides up, in an ungreased 3-quart rectangular baking dish. Roast, uncovered, for 25 to 30 minutes or until chicken is golden brown and no longer pink (170°F).

3 Meanwhile, in a large skillet cook celery, onion, and garlic in hot oil until tender. Add broth, wine, olives, raisins, and cayenne (if using). Bring mixture to boiling; reduce heat. Simmer, uncovered, about 7 minutes or until slightly thickened. Stir in the snipped marjoram; simmer for 1 minute more.

4 Spoon the sauce over roasted chicken breast halves.

nutrition facts per serving: 542 cal., 28 g total fat (6 g sat. fat), 131 mg chol., 601 mg sodium, 21 g carb., 2 g dietary fiber, 44 g protein.

A velvety three-cheese cream sauce enrobes smoked chicken, while a subtle drizzle of white truffle oil adds opulence. Look for white truffle oil at gourmet shops or Internet sources.

three-cheese ziti and smoked chicken casserole

prep: 25 minutes bake: 25 minutes stand: 10 minutes
oven: 375°F makes: 6 servings dish: 2-quart

12	ounces dried ziti pasta
3	tablespoons butter
2	cloves garlic, minced
3	tablespoons all-purpose flour
¼	teaspoon salt
¼	teaspoon ground white pepper
3½	cups milk
1½	cups finely shredded Asiago cheese (6 ounces)
1	cup finely shredded fontina cheese (4 ounces)
½	cup crumbled blue cheese (2 ounces)
2	cups chopped smoked chicken or shredded purchased roasted chicken
⅓	cup panko (Japanese-style bread crumbs) or fine dry bread crumbs
2	teaspoons truffle-flavor oil or melted butter

1 Preheat oven to 375°F. Grease a 2-quart casserole; set aside. Cook pasta according to package directions; drain. Return to pan.

2 Meanwhile, in a medium saucepan heat butter over medium heat. Add garlic; cook and stir for 30 seconds. Stir in flour, salt, and white pepper. Gradually stir in milk. Cook and stir until thickened and bubbly. Gradually add Asiago cheese, fontina cheese, and blue cheese, stirring until melted. Stir in chicken. Stir chicken mixture into cooked pasta.

3 Transfer mixture to the prepared casserole. In a small bowl combine panko and truffle oil; sprinkle over pasta mixture. Bake, uncovered, about 25 minutes or until mixture is heated through and crumbs are lightly browned. Let stand for 10 minutes before serving.

nutrition facts per serving: 753 cal., 39 g total fat (22 g sat. fat), 141 mg chol., 953 mg sodium, 56 g carb., 2 g dietary fiber, 43 g protein.

In this baked dish, chicken breasts are rolled up with mozzarella cheese and a lively mix of Italian flavors. Brushing on sherry just before baking intensifies the flavor.

chicken-mozzarella
roll-ups

prep: 30 minutes bake: 20 minutes oven: 375°F
makes: 6 servings dish: 3-quart

2 tablespoons olive oil or cooking oil
1/3 cup chopped onion
6 skinless, boneless chicken breast halves (about 2 pounds)
6 mozzarella cheese slices (about 4 1/2 ounces)
3/4 teaspoon garlic powder
1/4 teaspoon ground black pepper
3 tablespoons dry sherry or chicken broth
1/2 cup fine dry bread crumbs
3 tablespoons grated Romano cheese
3/4 teaspoon dried oregano, crushed
1/2 teaspoon onion salt
3 tablespoons butter, melted
3 cups purchased tomato pasta sauce
Hot cooked fettuccine (optional)

1 Preheat oven to 375°F. Grease a 3-quart rectangular baking dish; set aside. In a small saucepan heat 1 tablespoon of the oil over medium heat. Add onion; cook for 3 to 5 minutes or until tender.

2 Place each chicken breast half, boned side down, between two pieces of plastic wrap. Using the flat side of a meat mallet and working from the center out, pound each half lightly into a rectangle about 1/8 inch thick. Remove plastic wrap.

3 Brush tops of chicken breast halves with the remaining 1 tablespoon oil. On boned side of each breast half, place a slice of mozzarella cheese and some of the cooked onion.

4 In a small bowl combine garlic powder and pepper; sprinkle evenly over cheese and onion on chicken breast halves.

5 Fold in sides and bottoms of chicken breast halves; roll up each piece into a spiral, pressing edges to seal. Brush chicken rolls with sherry. In a shallow bowl combine bread crumbs, Romano cheese, oregano, and onion salt. Roll chicken roll-ups in bread crumb mixture to coat. Place in prepared baking dish. Drizzle with melted butter.

6 Bake, uncovered, for 20 to 25 minutes or until chicken is no longer pink. Meanwhile, in a medium saucepan cook and stir the pasta sauce over medium heat until heated through. Serve chicken roll-ups with warmed pasta sauce and hot cooked fettuccine (if using).

nutrition facts per serving: 429 cal., 18 g total fat (8 g sat. fat), 122 mg chol., 1257 mg sodium, 19 g carb., 4 g dietary fiber, 44 g protein.

made for company

A roasted-lemon vinaigrette replaces a cream-laden sauce, lending a bright flavor to both the casserole and the side salad.

chicken and potatoes
with lemon

prep: 20 minutes bake: 30 minutes oven: 450°F
makes: 4 servings dish: 3-quart

4   bone-in chicken breast halves (about 1½ pounds)
1   pound fingerling or baby Yukon gold potatoes
3   lemons, halved crosswise
⅓   cup pitted green and/or black olives
6   tablespoons olive oil
    Salt and ground black pepper
1   tablespoon honey
6   cups arugula and/or mixed salad greens

1 Preheat oven to 450°F. Place chicken, potatoes, lemons, and olives in an ungreased 3-quart rectangular baking dish. Drizzle 2 tablespoons of the oil over the mixture; toss to coat. Spread mixture in a single layer in baking dish, arranging chicken skin sides up and lemons cut sides up. Sprinkle with salt and pepper.

2 Bake, uncovered, about 30 minutes or until chicken is no longer pink (170°F), potatoes are tender, and lemons are browned at the edges and soft throughout.

3 When lemons are cool enough to handle, squeeze juice and pulp into a small bowl. Discard any seeds. Whisk in the remaining 4 tablespoons oil and the honey. Season to taste with salt and pepper. Meanwhile, cover chicken, potatoes, and olives to keep warm.

4 Divide arugula among four salad plates. Top with chicken, potatoes, and olives. Drizzle with honey mixture. Sprinkle with additional pepper.

nutrition facts per serving: 573 cal., 40 g total fat (8 g sat. fat), 87 mg chol., 435 mg sodium, 34 g carb., 7 g dietary fiber, 26 g protein.

Originating in the Netherlands, gouda cheese adds a delightfully smoky flavor and creamy texture to this classic pasta. Pair this dish with a spicier wine, such as Zinfandel or Pinot Noir.

smokin' turkey **tetrazzini**

prep: 30 minutes   bake: 30 minutes   stand: 5 minutes
oven: 350°F   makes: 6 servings   dish: 3-quart

12   ounces dried multigrain, spinach, or whole wheat fettuccine or linguine

¾   cup dried tomatoes (not oil-packed), snipped

3   cups sliced fresh mushrooms (8 ounces)

2   cups red sweet pepper strips (2 medium)

½   cup chopped onion (1 medium)

2   tablespoons olive oil

2   tablespoons all-purpose flour

1⅓   cups milk

1   cup water

2   cups shredded smoked gouda or smoked cheddar cheese (8 ounces)
     Salt and ground black pepper

2   cups shredded roasted turkey or chicken

2   tablespoons sliced almonds, toasted
     Shredded smoked gouda or smoked cheddar cheese (optional)

1 Preheat oven to 350°F. Grease a 3-quart baking dish; set aside. Cook pasta according to package directions, adding dried tomatoes to boiling water with the pasta; drain.

2 For sauce, in a large skillet cook mushrooms, sweet peppers, and onion in hot oil over medium heat until tender. Stir in flour. Gradually stir in milk and the water. Cook and stir until slightly thickened and bubbly. Gradually add 2 cups cheese, stirring until melted. Season to taste with salt and pepper.

3 In a large bowl combine cooked pasta mixture, sauce, and turkey. Transfer mixture to the prepared baking dish. Sprinkle with almonds.

4 Bake, covered, about 30 minutes or until heated through. Let stand for 5 minutes before serving. If desired, sprinkle each serving with additional cheese.

nutrition facts per serving: 526 cal., 19 g total fat (9 g sat. fat), 70 mg chol., 908 mg sodium, 54 g carb., 7 g dietary fiber, 36 g protein.

A delicious Parmesan-and-sherry-flavored asparagus sauce enrobes the prosciutto-stuffed chicken, making this dish worthy of any special occasion.

prosciutto-stuffed
chicken bake

prep: 40 minutes   bake: 50 minutes   oven: 375°F
makes: 8 servings   dish: 3-quart

8   medium skinless, boneless chicken breast halves (about 2½ pounds)
8   thin slices prosciutto or 4 pieces Canadian-style bacon, halved
6   cups cooked long grain white and wild rice blend* or cooked white rice
¼   cup butter
1   cup sliced scallions (8)
¼   cup all-purpose flour
¼   teaspoon ground black pepper
2   cups milk
1   cup coarsely chopped asparagus (about 12 spears) or chopped broccoli
¾   cup grated Parmesan cheese
¼   cup dry sherry, white wine, or milk
¾   cup panko (Japanese-style bread crumbs)
½   teaspoon dried Italian seasoning, crushed

1 Preheat oven to 375°F. With a small sharp knife, make a 2-inch-wide horizontal slit in the side of each chicken breast to create a deep pocket. Stuff each pocket with 1 piece of the prosciutto or half of a piece of the Canadian bacon, folding or cutting as needed to fit.

2 Spread rice in an ungreased 3-quart rectangular baking dish. Top with chicken. Bake, covered, for 25 minutes.

3 Meanwhile, for sauce, in a medium saucepan melt butter over medium heat. Add scallions; cook for 3 to 5 minutes or until tender. Whisk in flour and pepper until well mixed. Add milk all at once, whisking to combine. Cook and stir over medium-high heat until thickened and bubbly. Stir in asparagus, ½ cup of the Parmesan cheese, and the sherry. In a small bowl combine the remaining ¼ cup Parmesan cheese, the panko, and Italian seasoning.

4 Pour sauce over chicken; sprinkle with crumb mixture. Bake, uncovered, for 25 to 30 minutes more or until chicken is no longer pink (170°F).

nutrition facts per serving: 547 cal., 17 g total fat (6 g sat. fat), 109 mg chol., 899 mg sodium, 45 g carb., 47 g protein.

*test kitchen tip: If cooking packaged long grain and wild rice blend, do not use the seasoning packet.

make-ahead directions: Prepare as directed. Cover and chill for up to 2 days or freeze for up to 3 months. To serve, thaw casserole in refrigerator for 48 hours, if frozen. Bake, covered, in a 375°F oven for 1 hour. Bake, uncovered, about 30 minutes more or until heated through.

Based on whole wheat bread, this distinctive stuffing blends sweet, fruity orange and cranberries with savory fresh herbs. Serve it alongside ham or turkey.

orange-cranberry
stuffing

prep: 15 minutes   bake: 40 minutes   oven: 350°F
makes: 6 servings   dish: 1½-quart

- ⅓ cup butter
- ½ cup chopped red onion
- 2 teaspoons chopped pickled ginger or 1 tablespoon grated fresh ginger (optional)
- 1 teaspoon dried thyme, crushed
- 1 teaspoon snipped fresh rosemary
- 1 teaspoon Dijon mustard
- ½ teaspoon salt
- ¼ teaspoon ground black pepper
- 8 slices whole wheat bread, cubed and dried*
- ½ cup orange-flavored sweetened dried cranberries, chopped
- ¾ to 1¼ cups orange juice

1 Preheat oven to 350°F. In a large saucepan melt butter over medium heat. Add onion; cook and stir about 5 minutes or until tender. Stir in ginger (if desired), thyme, rosemary, mustard, salt, and pepper; cook and stir for 1 minute. Remove from heat.

2 In a very large bowl combine bread cubes and cranberries; stir in onion mixture. Drizzle with enough orange juice to moisten, tossing lightly to combine. Transfer to an ungreased 1½-quart casserole.

3 Bake, covered, for 30 minutes. Uncover and bake 10 to 15 minutes more or until heated through (170°F) and top is slightly crisp.

nutrition facts per serving: 314 cal., 14 g total fat (7 g sat. fat), 27 mg chol., 499 mg sodium, 44 g carb., 5 g dietary fiber, 6 g protein.

*test kitchen tip: To dry bread cubes, preheat oven to 300°F. Spread bread cubes in a shallow baking or roasting pan. Bake for 10 to 15 minutes or until cubes are dry, stirring twice. Cool. (Cubes will continue to dry and crisp as they cool.) Or let bread cubes stand, loosely covered, at room temperature for 8 to 12 hours.

For this simple yet sophisticated dish, salmon, shrimp, and scallops marry well with the mild acidity of a dry white wine such as Chardonnay. Serve the same wine at the table as you use for roasting.

seafood casseroles

bake: 20 minutes   oven: 25 minutes   oven: 450°F
makes: 4 servings   dish: 10-ounce dishes

12   ounces fresh or
     frozen skinless
     salmon or haddock
     fillets, thawed and
     cut into 1-inch
     chunks
1   pound fresh or
     frozen sea scallops,
     thawed and halved
     or quartered if large
12   fresh or frozen large
     shrimp in shells
     (10 ounces),
     thawed, peeled,
     and deveined
2   cups thinly sliced
     zucchini (2 small)
2   cups thinly sliced
     yellow summer
     squash (2 small)
½   cup thinly sliced
     shallots (2 small)
¼   teaspoon salt
⅛   teaspoon ground
     black pepper
¼   cup olive oil
¼   cup dry white wine
1   tablespoon snipped
     fresh lemon thyme,
     thyme, or dill
     Cooked long grain
     and/or wild rice
     (optional)
     Lemon wedges

1 Rinse fish, scallops, and shrimp; pat dry with paper towels.

2 Preheat oven to 450°F. Divide salmon, scallops, and shrimp among four 10- to 12-ounce au gratin dishes. Add sliced zucchini, squash, and shallots; sprinkle with salt and pepper. Whisk together oil and wine; spoon over mixture in dishes. Sprinkle each with herb.

3 Bake, uncovered, about 20 minutes or until fish flakes easily when tested with a fork and scallops and shrimp are opaque. If desired, serve with long grain and/or wild rice and lemon wedges to squeeze over.

nutrition facts per serving: 533 cal., 28 g total fat (5 g sat. fat), 213 mg chol., 514 mg sodium, 13 g carb., 2 g dietary fiber, 56 g protein.

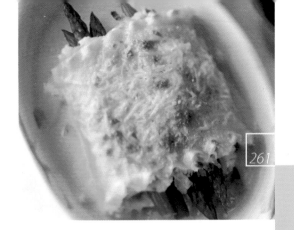

Pecorino Romano, a classic Italian sheep's milk cheese, highlights the delicate sauce that pairs wonderfully with asparagus, salmon, and pasta.

salmon-asparagus
lasagna rolls

prep: 45 minutes   bake: 45 minutes   stand: 10 minutes
oven: 350°F   makes: 4 servings   dish: 2-quart

8   dried lasagna noodles
12   ounces fresh asparagus or one 8-ounce package frozen asparagus spears
1   8-ounce tub cream cheese spread with chives and onion
1   cup finely shredded Pecorino Romano or Parmesan cheese (4 ounces)
2   tablespoons milk
1   4-ounce piece smoked salmon, flaked and skin and bones removed
1   10.75-ounce can condensed cream of celery soup
1/4   cup milk
1   teaspoon finely shredded lemon zest

1 Preheat oven to 350°F. Lightly grease a 2-quart rectangular baking dish; set aside. Cook lasagna noodles according to package directions, adding fresh or frozen asparagus for the last 3 minutes of cooking. Using tongs, transfer asparagus to a colander; drain. Rinse with cold water; drain again. Remove from colander. Drain noodles in colander. Rinse with cold water; drain again. Place noodles in a single layer on a sheet of foil.

2 Meanwhile, for filling, in a medium bowl combine cream cheese, ½ cup of the Pecorino Romano cheese, and the 2 tablespoons milk. Gently stir in salmon. Spread about 2 tablespoons of the filling over each lasagna noodle. Place 3 or 4 stalks of asparagus at one end; roll up each noodle into a spiral. Place lasagna rolls, seam sides down, in the prepared baking dish.

3 For sauce, in another medium bowl combine soup, ¼ cup milk, and lemon zest. Pour over lasagna rolls. Sprinkle with the remaining ½ cup Pecorino Romano cheese.

4 Bake, covered, for 35 minutes. Bake, uncovered, about 10 minutes more or until mixture is heated through and cheese is lightly browned. Let stand for 10 minutes before serving.

nutrition facts per serving: 561 cal., 30 g total fat (18 g sat. fat), 92 mg chol., 1245 mg sodium, 48 g carb., 3 g dietary fiber, 23 g protein.

made for company

Roasted squash takes the place of meat in this lasagna that has autumn written all over it, but it's a recipe you'll relish year-round.

butternut squash
lasagna

prep: 45 minutes bake: 50 minutes stand: 10 minutes
oven: 425°F/375°F makes: 8 to 10 servings dish: 3-quart

3   pounds butternut
    squash, peeled,
    seeded, and cut into
    ¼ - to ½ -inch slices
3   tablespoons olive oil
½   teaspoon salt
¼   cup butter or
    margarine
6   cloves garlic, minced
¼   cup all-purpose flour
½   teaspoon salt
4   cups milk
1   tablespoon snipped
    fresh rosemary
9   no-boil lasagna
    noodles
1⅓ cups finely shredded
    Parmesan cheese
    (5½ ounces)
1   cup whipping cream

1 Preheat oven to 425°F. Lightly grease a 15×10×1-inch baking pan. Place squash in the prepared baking pan. Add oil and ½ teaspoon salt; toss gently to coat. Spread in an even layer. Roast, uncovered, for 25 to 30 minutes or until squash is tender, stirring once. Reduce oven temperature to 375°F.

2 Meanwhile, for sauce, in a large saucepan heat butter over medium heat. Add garlic; cook and stir for 1 minute. Stir in flour and ½ teaspoon salt. Gradually stir in milk. Cook and stir until thickened and bubbly. Stir in roasted squash and rosemary.

3 Lightly grease a 3-quart rectangular baking dish. To assemble, spread about 1 cup of the sauce over the bottom of the prepared baking dish. Layer three of the noodles in dish. Spread with one-third of the remaining sauce. Sprinkle with ⅓ cup of the Parmesan cheese. Repeat layering noodles, sauce, and Parmesan cheese two more times. Pour whipping cream evenly over layers in dish. Sprinkle with the remaining ⅓ cup Parmesan cheese.

4 Bake, covered, for 40 minutes. Bake, uncovered, about 10 minutes more or until edges are bubbly and top is lightly browned. Let stand for 10 minutes before serving.

nutrition facts per serving: 525 cal., 29 g total fat (15 g sat. fat), 76 mg chol., 628 mg sodium, 53 g carb., 4 g dietary fiber, 16 g protein.

make-ahead directions: Prepare as directed through Step 3. Cover unbaked lasagna with foil; chill for 2 to 24 hours. To serve, bake, covered, in a 375°F oven for 45 minutes. Bake, uncovered, for 10 to 15 minutes more or until edges are bubbly and top is lightly browned. Let stand for 10 minutes before serving.

Cinnamon-raisin bread is the base of this festive, fruity stuffing. Earthy celery, onions, and walnuts balance the sweetness of apples and dried fruit bits.

tropical fruit stuffing

prep: 20 minutes bake: 45 minutes oven: 350°F
makes: 8 servings dish: 2-quart

1/3 cup butter
2 medium Granny
    Smith apples, cored
    and chopped
    (2 cups)
1 cup sliced celery
    (2 stalks)
1/2 cup chopped onion
    (1 medium)
1 teaspoon poultry
    seasoning
1 teaspoon ground
    sage
1/2 teaspoon seasoned
    salt
9 cups dried cinnamon-
    raisin bread cubes*
    (12 slices)
1/2 cup chopped walnuts,
    toasted
3/4 cup tropical blend
    mixed dried fruit
    bits
2 tablespoons cider
    vinegar
3/4 to 1 cup chicken
    broth

1 Preheat oven to 350°F. In a large saucepan melt butter over medium heat. Add apples, celery, and onion; cook about 5 minutes or until tender. Stir in poultry seasoning, sage, and seasoned salt.

2 In a very large bowl combine bread cubes, walnuts, and dried fruits. Add apple mixture to bread cube mixture; toss to combine. Drizzle vinegar and enough chicken broth over mixture to moisten, tossing lightly to combine. Transfer to an ungreased 2-quart baking dish. Bake, covered, about 45 minutes or until heated through (170°F).

nutrition facts per serving: 346 cal., 15 g total fat (6 g sat. fat), 28 mg chol., 463 mg sodium, 47 g carb., 4 g dietary fiber, 7 g protein.

*test kitchen tip: To dry bread cubes, cut fresh bread into ½-inch cubes. Spread in two 15×10×1-inch baking pans. Bake in a 300°F oven for 10 to 15 minutes or until cubes are dry, stirring twice; cool. (Cubes will continue to dry and crisp as they cool.) Or let bread cubes stand, loosely covered, at room temperature for 8 to 12 hours.

Full of potatoes, rich cheese, and smoky bacon, this decadent dish originates in the French Alps. Although the classic dish often features Reblochon, a local cheese, you'll get a similar creamy texture and nutty taste with Brie. Pictured on page 245.

tartiflette

prep: 45 minutes   bake: 40 minutes   oven: 350°F
makes: 12 servings   dish: 2-quart

3   pounds Yukon gold potatoes
½   teaspoon salt
¼   teaspoon ground black pepper
5   slices thick-sliced bacon, chopped
1   large onion, thinly sliced
2   cloves garlic, minced
⅓   cup dry white wine
2   teaspoons snipped fresh thyme
¼   cup chicken broth
¼   cup whipping cream
2   8-ounce rounds Brie cheese

1 Preheat oven to 350°F. Grease a 2-quart au gratin dish or rectangular baking dish. In a covered Dutch oven cook potatoes in enough boiling water to cover for 25 minutes; drain. Rinse with cold water; drain again. Slice potatoes. Sprinkle with salt and pepper. Place half of the potatoes in the bottom of the prepared au gratin dish.

2 Meanwhile, in a large skillet cook bacon over medium heat for 1 minute. Add onion and garlic; cook about 5 minutes or until bacon is crisp and onion is tender. Drain off fat. Carefully add wine to bacon mixture. Simmer, uncovered, until wine is nearly evaporated. Stir in thyme.

3 Spoon bacon mixture over potatoes in dish. Top with the remaining potatoes. Pour broth and cream over potato mixture.

4 Using a sharp knife, score both sides of cheese rounds in a diamond pattern by making shallow diagonal cuts at 1-inch intervals. Cut rounds in half horizontally, then in half crosswise. Arrange cheese, rind sides up, on top of potato mixture.

5 Bake, uncovered, about 40 minutes or until potatoes are tender and cheese is lightly browned.

nutrition facts per serving: 268 cal., 15 g total fat (8 g sat. fat), 49 mg chol., 468 mg sodium, 22 g carb., 3 g dietary fiber, 12 g protein.

No need to hollow a pumpkin. Pumpkin seeds, or pepitas, can be found in most grocery stores or Latino markets.

sweet potato–rice
casserole

prep: 30 minutes   bake: 30 minutes   oven: 350°F
makes: 6 to 8 servings   dish: 2-quart

2	cups water
1½	cups chopped peeled sweet potato (1 large)
1	cup long grain white rice
½	teaspoon salt
1	15-ounce can black beans, rinsed and drained
1½	cups frozen sweet soybeans (edamame), thawed
1	cup shredded Monterey Jack cheese (4 ounces)
1	8-ounce carton sour cream
1	4-ounce can diced green chile peppers, undrained
¼	cup chopped scallions (2)
2	tablespoons all-purpose flour
1	tablespoon snipped fresh sage
2	cloves garlic, minced
½	teaspoon salt
	Toasted pumpkin seeds (pepitas, optional)*

1 Preheat oven to 350°F. In a medium saucepan bring the water to boiling. Stir in sweet potato, rice, and ½ teaspoon salt. Return to boiling; reduce heat. Simmer, covered, about 20 minutes or until liquid is absorbed.

2 Meanwhile, in a large bowl combine black beans, soybeans, ½ cup of the cheese, the sour cream, chile peppers, scallions, flour, sage, garlic, and ½ teaspoon salt. Stir in rice mixture.

3 Transfer mixture to an ungreased 2-quart casserole. Sprinkle with the remaining ½ cup cheese. Bake, uncovered, about 30 minutes or until heated through. If desired, sprinkle each serving with pumpkin seeds.

nutrition facts per serving: 378 cal., 15 g total fat (8 g sat. fat), 36 mg chol., 773 mg sodium, 48 g carb., 7 g dietary fiber, 16 g protein.

*test kitchen tip: To toast pumpkin seeds, place them in a shallow dry skillet over medium heat. Shake the pan gently until the seeds turn golden and release a rich pumpkin aroma.

made for company

Mild and juicy, sweet onions such as Vidalia or Walla Walla are ideal for this delicious side. Serve this with pork, beef, or lamb.

cheddar and
onion puddings

prep: 30 minutes bake: 20 minutes stand: 10 minutes
oven: 400°F makes: 10 to 12 servings dish: 5-ounce dishes

2 medium onions, cut into 8 wedges each, root end attached
1 tablespoon olive oil
   Salt and ground black pepper
3 tablespoons butter
1 clove garlic, minced
3 eggs
1½ cups milk
⅓ cup all-purpose flour
4 ounces white cheddar cheese, shredded (1 cup)
1 tablespoon snipped fresh sage
   Fresh sage leaves (optional)

1 Preheat oven to 400°F. In a large skillet place onions in hot oil; season with salt and pepper. Cook for 5 minutes over medium-low heat, stirring occasionally. Add 2 tablespoons of the butter and the garlic; cook until onions are tender, about 8 minutes more, stirring occasionally. Remove from heat; set aside.

2 Grease ten to twelve 5- to 7-ounce individual ramekins or custard cups. Arrange in a 15×10×1-inch baking pan or two 13×9×2-inch baking pans and set aside. In a large bowl whisk together the eggs and milk. Whisk in the flour until smooth. Add cheese and snipped sage; stir to combine.

3 Spoon onion mixture into prepared dishes. Pour about ¼ cup batter over each dish. Bake for 20 to 25 minutes or until puffed and golden brown. Remove puddings from oven. Let stand for 10 minutes before serving. Serve warm garnished with additional fresh sage (if using).

nutrition facts per serving: 150 cal., 11 g total fat (6 g sat. fat), 87 mg chol., 190 mg sodium, 7 g carb., 0 g dietary fiber, 6 g protein.

Shallots lend superb flavor to these individual puddings, but if you do not have them, use ¹/₄ cup chopped scallions.

wild mushroom
bread pudding

prep: 30 minutes   chill: 2 to 24 hours   bake: 35 minutes
oven: 325°F   makes: 8 servings   dish: 10-ounce dishes

3   cups sliced assorted fresh wild mushrooms (such as cremini, portobello, chanterelle, and/or stemmed shiitake or oyster; 8 ounces)

2   medium shallots, sliced (¹/₄ cup)

3   cloves garlic, minced

2   tablespoons olive oil

¹/₄   cup dry sherry or dry white wine

8   ounces rosemary or onion focaccia, cut into 1-inch pieces (about 6 cups)

4   eggs, lightly beaten

2   cups half-and-half or light cream

1   cup shredded Gruyère cheese (4 ounces)

1   tablespoon snipped fresh thyme

1   tablespoon snipped fresh rosemary

¹/₂   teaspoon salt

¹/₂   teaspoon coarsely ground black pepper

1 Grease eight 10-ounce individual casseroles; set aside. In a large skillet cook mushrooms, shallots, and garlic in hot oil over medium heat about 5 minutes or until tender. Carefully add sherry. Simmer, uncovered, until liquid is nearly evaporated. Transfer mixture to a large bowl. Stir in focaccia pieces.

2 In a medium bowl combine eggs, half-and-half, cheese, thyme, rosemary, salt, and pepper. Pour egg mixture over focaccia mixture, pressing with a wooden spoon to moisten all of the bread.

3 Divide mixture among the prepared casseroles. Cover and chill for 2 to 24 hours.

4 Preheat oven to 325°F. Bake, uncovered, for 35 to 40 minutes or until a knife inserted near the centers comes out clean.

nutrition facts per serving: 289 cal., 18 g total fat (8 g sat. fat), 146 mg chol., 366 mg sodium, 18 g carb., 1 g dietary fiber, 13 g protein.

10

great

amer
dish

North to South, East to West, every region of the United States adds its own touch to one-dish meals, utilizing foods and flavors reflective of the land and the people that live in the region. Use these diverse recipes as a road map to delicious dinners ahead.

ican

es

This hearty dish has all the great tastes of traditional enchiladas—cumin, chiles, and sour cream—without the frying, filling, and rolling. Pictured on page 269.

bean-and-beef enchilada casserole

prep: 35 minutes bake: 40 minutes oven: 350°F
makes: 12 servings dish: 3-quart

12   ounces lean ground
       beef
1   cup chopped onion
       (1 large)
1½   teaspoons chili
       powder
¾   teaspoon ground
       cumin
2   15-ounce cans pinto
       beans, rinsed and
       drained
2   4-ounce cans diced
       green chile peppers,
       undrained
1½   cups sour cream
3   tablespoons all-
       purpose flour
½   teaspoon garlic
       powder
12   6-inch corn tortillas
2   10-ounce cans
       enchilada sauce
1   cup shredded
       cheddar cheese
       (4 ounces)

1 Preheat oven to 350°F. Lightly grease a 3-quart rectangular baking dish; set aside. In a large skillet cook beef and onion until meat is brown and onion is tender; drain off fat. Stir chili powder and cumin into meat mixture; cook and stir for 1 minute. Stir pinto beans and chiles into meat mixture; set aside.

2 In a small bowl stir together sour cream, flour, and garlic powder until combined.

3 Place half of the tortillas in the prepared baking dish, cutting to fit and overlapping as necessary. Top with half of the meat mixture, half of the sour cream mixture, and half of the enchilada sauce; repeat layers.

4 Bake, covered, for 30 to 40 minutes or until heated through. Uncover; sprinkle casserole with cheese and bake about 5 minutes more or until cheese is melted. If desired, garnish with chopped tomato and sliced green onion.

nutrition facts per serving: 304 cal., 14 g total fat (7 g sat. fat), 38 mg chol., 682 mg sodium, 32 g carb., 6 g dietary fiber, 15 g protein.

make-ahead directions: Prepare as directed through Step 3. Cover with plastic wrap and chill for up to 24 hours. Remove plastic wrap. Cover dish with foil. Bake in a 350°F oven for 35 minutes or until heated through. Uncover; sprinkle with cheese. Return to oven and bake about 5 minutes more or until cheese is melted.

A savory American classic, meat loaf has been around as long as there has been ground meat. Baking the meat loaf in a dish that is larger than the loaf improves browning and allows excess fat to escape.

classic meat loaf

prep: 40 minutes   bake: 1 hour   stand: 10 minutes
oven: 350°F   makes: 8 servings   dish: 3-quart

2   tablespoons unsalted butter
1¼ cups onions, finely diced
1¼ cups fresh portobello or other mushrooms, finely chopped
½   cup celery, finely diced
½   teaspoon dried thyme
1   teaspoon finely chopped garlic
½   cup grated carrot
1   cup fresh bread crumbs
½   cup half-and-half or milk
2   eggs
1½ pounds ground beef chuck
8   ounces ground pork
4   slices bacon, finely chopped
1¾ teaspoon kosher salt
½   teaspoon ground black pepper
½   cup ketchup
2   tablespoons brown sugar
2   teaspoons cider vinegar

1 Preheat oven to 350°F. In a large skillet heat butter until melted. Add onions, mushrooms, and celery. Season to taste with salt and pepper. Cook for 3 minutes, being careful not to brown.

2 Sprinkle thyme over onion mixture. Rub garlic and a pinch of salt into paste; add garlic mixture to vegetables. Cook and stir until onions are tender. Stir in carrot; remove from heat. Cool completely. Meanwhile, soak bread crumbs in half-and-half; lightly beat in the eggs.

3 In a large mixing bowl combine ground meats, bacon, cooled vegetables, and bread crumb mixture. Sprinkle with kosher salt and ½ teaspoon pepper. Using hands, mix until well blended.

4 Transfer mixture to an ungreased 3-quart rectangular baking dish. Using your hands, shape into a 9×5-inch loaf. Make shallow indentation around sides.

5 For ketchup topping, combine ketchup, brown sugar, and vinegar. Spoon over top of meat loaf. Bake, uncovered, about 1 hour or until meat thermometer reaches 155°F. Let stand 10 minutes before serving.

nutrition facts per serving: 518 cal., 38 g total fat (15 g sat. fat), 160 mg chol., 1013 mg sodium, 19 g carb., 1.5 g dietary fiber, 26 g protein.

This dish is a little Italian, a little Mexican, and a whole lot of oohs and aahs. Cooked spaghetti forms the crust for a spicy meat and cheese topping.

southwest spaghetti pie

prep: 40 minutes bake: 10 minutes stand: 5 minutes
oven: 425°F makes: 8 servings dish: 3-quart

8	ounces dried spaghetti
1	egg
½	cup milk
1	pound ground pork
1	cup chopped onion (1 large)
¾	cup chopped green sweet pepper (1 medium)
1	clove garlic, minced
1	tablespoon chili powder
½	teaspoon salt
½	teaspoon ground cumin
½	teaspoon dried oregano, crushed
¼	teaspoon ground black pepper
1	15-ounce can tomato sauce
1	cup shredded Monterey Jack cheese with jalapeño chile peppers (4 ounces)
1	cup shredded cheddar cheese (4 ounces)

1 Preheat oven to 425°F. Grease a 3-quart rectangular baking dish; set aside. Cook pasta according to package directions; drain well. Return to pan. In a small bowl combine egg and milk; stir into hot pasta. Transfer mixture to prepared baking dish (there will be some free liquid). Using a rubber spatula or the back of a large spoon, press spaghetti mixture into an even layer.

2 In a large skillet cook pork, onion, sweet pepper, and garlic until meat is brown; drain off fat. Stir in chili powder, salt, cumin, oregano, and black pepper. Cook and stir for 2 minutes. Stir in tomato sauce. Bring to boiling; reduce heat. Simmer, uncovered, for 2 minutes. Spoon meat mixture over pasta mixture in baking dish. Sprinkle with cheeses.

3 Bake, uncovered, about 10 minutes or until bubbly around the edges. Let stand for 5 minutes before serving.

nutrition facts per serving: 330 cal., 15 g total fat (8 g sat. fat), 84 mg chol., 621 mg sodium, 29 g carb., 2 g dietary fiber, 20 g protein.

Layers of herb-seasoned croutons, cream-sauced zucchini, and juicy pork chops create a tasty one-dish meal.

zucchini and pork chop supper

prep: 30 minutes bake: 50 minutes oven: 350°F
makes: 6 servings dish: 3-quart

1   14-ounce package herb-seasoned stuffing croutons

¼   cup butter or margarine, melted

4   cups coarsely chopped zucchini

1   10.75-ounce can condensed cream of celery soup

1   8-ounce carton light sour cream

¾   cup milk

½   cup shredded carrot (1 medium)

1   tablespoon snipped fresh parsley or 1 teaspoon dried parsley flakes

¼   to ½ teaspoon ground black pepper

6   bone-in pork loin chops, cut ¾ inch thick

1 Preheat oven to 350°F. Grease a 3-quart rectangular baking dish; set aside. In a large bowl combine 7½ cups of the croutons and the melted butter; toss gently to coat. Spread half of the buttered croutons in the prepared baking dish.

2 In another large bowl combine zucchini, soup, sour cream, ½ cup of the milk, the carrot, parsley, and pepper. Spoon evenly over croutons in dish. Sprinkle with the remaining buttered croutons.

3 Pour the remaining ¼ cup milk into a shallow dish. Coarsely crush the remaining croutons; place in another shallow dish. Trim fat from chops. Dip chops into milk, then into crushed croutons, turning to coat. Place chops on top of layers in baking dish. Sprinkle with any remaining crushed croutons.

4 Bake, uncovered, for 50 to 60 minutes or until chops are slightly pink in center and juices run clear (160°F).

nutrition facts per serving: 639 cal., 24 g total fat (10 g sat. fat), 130 mg chol., 1417 mg sodium, 57 g carb., 4 g dietary fiber, 46 g protein.

In Cincinnati chili parlors, meaty chili is spooned over spaghetti and topped with cheddar cheese and chopped onion. Great for potluck dinners, this saucy version uses ziti (thick tube-shape pasta) instead of spaghetti.

cincinnati-style chili

prep: 25 minutes bake: 1 hour oven: 350°F
makes: 16 servings dish: Dutch oven

2 pounds lean ground beef
2 cups chopped onion (2 large)
1 26-ounce jar tomato and garlic pasta sauce
1 15-ounce can red kidney beans, rinsed and drained
½ cup water
2 tablespoons chili powder
2 tablespoons semisweet chocolate pieces
1 tablespoon vinegar
1 teaspoon ground cinnamon
¼ teaspoon cayenne pepper
¼ teaspoon ground allspice
16 ounces dried ziti or gemelli pasta
Shredded cheddar cheese (optional)
Chopped onion (optional)

1 Preheat oven to 350°F. In an ovenproof 4- to 5-quart Dutch oven cook ground beef and 2 cups onion until meat is brown and onion is tender, using a wooden spoon to break up meat as it cooks. Drain off fat. Return meat to Dutch oven.

2 Stir in pasta sauce, beans, the water, chili powder, chocolate pieces, vinegar, cinnamon, cayenne, and allspice.

3 Bake, covered, for 1 hour, stirring once halfway through baking.

4 To serve, cook pasta according to package directions; drain. Serve chili over cooked pasta. If desired, sprinkle with cheese and additional onion.

nutrition facts per serving: 257 cal., 7 g total fat (2 g sat. fat), 36 mg chol., 277 mg sodium, 33 g carb., 4 g dietary fiber, 17 g protein.

When browning chops for this hearty bake, be sure to work in batches so that each chop has a chance to become beautifully browned and caramelized.

pork chop casserole

prep: 25 minutes   bake: 30 minutes   oven: 350°F
makes: 8 servings   dish: 3-quart

8	boneless pork loin chops, cut about ³/₄ inch thick
¹/₃	cup all-purpose flour
¹/₄	teaspoon salt
¹/₄	teaspoon ground black pepper
2	tablespoons vegetable oil
1	10.75-ounce can condensed cream of mushroom soup
²/₃	cup chicken broth
¹/₂	cup sour cream
¹/₂	teaspoon ground ginger
¹/₂	teaspoon dried rosemary, crushed
1¹/₂	cups french-fried onions
	Thick slices of toasted bread or hot cooked noodles

1 Preheat oven to 350°F. Trim fat from chops. In a shallow dish combine flour, salt, and pepper. Dip chops in flour mixture, turning to coat evenly.

2 In a large skillet heat oil over medium-high heat. Cook chops, half at a time, in hot oil until brown on both sides. Remove from heat.

3 For sauce, in a medium bowl combine soup, broth, sour cream, ginger, and rosemary. Stir in half of the french-fried onions. Pour sauce into an ungreased 3-quart rectangular baking dish, spreading evenly. Top with chops.

4 Bake, covered, for 25 minutes. Sprinkle with the remaining french-fried onions. Bake, uncovered, for 5 to 10 minutes more or until chops are tender and juices run clear (160°F). Serve on toasted bread or hot cooked noodles.

nutrition facts per serving: 411 cal., 19 g total fat (5 g sat. fat), 95 mg chol., 536 mg sodium, 31 g carb., 1 g dietary fiber, 28 g protein.

Black-eyed peas, an essential ingredient in Hoppin' John, are a popular legume in the South. The small beige bean has a black circular "eye" at its inner curve. If using dried peas, you'll need to soak them before cooking.

soufflé hoppin' john

prep: 25 minutes   bake: 20 minutes   oven: 400°F
makes: 10 to 12 servings   dish: 2-quart

½ cup chopped onion
(1 medium)
½ cup finely chopped
red sweet pepper
(1 small)
1 clove garlic, minced
2 tablespoons butter
2 tablespoons all-
purpose flour
⅛ to ¼ teaspoon
cayenne pepper
or several dashes
bottled hot pepper
sauce
⅛ teaspoon salt
2 cups milk, half-and-
half, or light cream
2 egg yolks
2 cups cooked white
rice
2 cups cooked black-
eyed peas; 2 cups
frozen black-eyed
peas, thawed; or
one 15-ounce can
black-eyed peas,
rinsed and drained
¼ cup finely chopped
prosciutto or cooked
ham
2 egg whites
⅓ cup snipped fresh
parsley

1 Preheat oven to 400°F. Lightly grease a 2-quart square baking dish; set aside.

2 For sauce, in a large saucepan cook onion, sweet pepper, and garlic in hot butter over medium heat until onion is tender. Stir in flour, cayenne, and salt. Gradually stir in milk. Cook and stir until thickened and bubbly. Cook and stir for 1 minute more. Remove from heat.

3 Gradually stir about ¼ cup of the sauce into egg yolks. Stir yolk mixture into the remaining sauce in saucepan. Stir in cooked rice, black-eyed peas, and prosciutto.

4 In a small bowl beat egg whites with an electric mixer on high speed until stiff peaks form (tips stand straight). Gently fold beaten egg whites into rice mixture. Transfer mixture to the prepared baking dish.

5 Bake, uncovered, about 20 minutes or until puffed and golden and a knife inserted in the center comes out clean. Sprinkle with parsley.

nutrition facts per serving: 175 cal., 6 g total fat (2 g sat. fat), 52 mg chol., 353 mg sodium, 22 g carb., 2 g dietary fiber, 8 g protein.

A can of black beans stretches a pound and a half of pork into a dish that serves eight. The cream of chicken soup makes it extra-satisfying.

pork and green chile
casserole

prep: 20 minutes bake: 30 minutes stand: 10 minutes
oven: 350°F makes: 8 servings dish: 2-quart

1½ pounds boneless pork
1 tablespoon vegetable oil
1 15-ounce can black beans, rinsed and drained
1 14.5-ounce can diced tomatoes, undrained
1 10.75-ounce can condensed cream of chicken soup
2 4-ounce cans diced green chile peppers, undrained
1 cup instant brown rice
¼ cup water
2 to 3 tablespoons bottled salsa
½ cup shredded cheddar cheese (2 ounces)

1 Preheat oven to 350°F. Trim fat from pork. Cut pork into ½-inch pieces. In a large skillet brown pork, half at a time, in hot oil. Drain off fat. Return pork to skillet.

2 Stir in black beans, tomatoes, cream of chicken soup, chiles, brown rice, the water, and salsa. Bring to boiling. Carefully pour mixture into an ungreased 2-quart square baking dish.

3 Bake, uncovered, for 30 minutes. Sprinkle with cheese. Let stand for 10 minutes before serving.

nutrition facts per serving: 271 cal., 13 g total fat (4 g sat. fat), 49 mg chol., 717 mg sodium, 22 g carb., 4 g dietary fiber, 20 g protein.

This curried chicken dish is a Southern classic whose name harks back to the days when ships' captains in port cities such as Charleston, South Carolina, and Savannah, Georgia, traded in spices acquired during their travels abroad.

baked country captain

prep: 30 minutes **bake:** 1 hour **oven:** 350°F
makes: 4 servings **dish:** 2-quart

2 pounds chicken drumsticks and/or thighs, skin removed
1 large onion, cut into thin wedges
1 small green sweet pepper, cut into 1-inch pieces
2 tablespoons dried currants or raisins
2 cloves garlic, minced
1 tablespoon vegetable oil
1 tablespoon curry powder
1 14.5-ounce can tomatoes, undrained, cut up
½ teaspoon sugar
½ teaspoon salt
½ teaspoon ground mace
¼ teaspoon dried thyme, crushed
¼ teaspoon ground black pepper
2 tablespoons cornstarch
2 tablespoons cold water
3 cups hot cooked rice
2 tablespoons chopped scallion (optional)
2 tablespoons sliced almonds, toasted (optional)

1 Preheat oven to 350°F. Arrange chicken, onion wedges, sweet pepper, and currants in an ungreased 2-quart rectangular baking dish.

2 In a small saucepan cook garlic in hot oil for 15 seconds. Add curry powder. Cook and stir for 1 minute more. Stir in the tomatoes, sugar, salt, mace, thyme, and black pepper. Bring to boiling; pour over ingredients in dish.

3 Bake, covered, about 1 hour or until chicken is tender. Using a slotted spoon, transfer chicken, vegetables, and currants to a platter.

4 For sauce, measure pan juices; add enough water to equal 2 cups if necessary. Transfer to a saucepan. In a small bowl combine cornstarch and the cold water; add to saucepan. Cook and stir until thickened and bubbly. Cook and stir for 2 minutes more.

5 Serve chicken mixture and sauce over hot cooked rice. If desired, top with scallion and almonds.

nutrition facts per serving: 548 cal., 18 g total fat (4 g sat. fat), 87 mg chol., 538 mg sodium, 62 g carb., 33 g protein.

Use chicken leftover from a weekend roast, buy a deli chicken, or keep frozen cooked chicken strips on hand for super-easy, super-tasty roll-ups.

tex-mex chicken roll-ups

prep: 20 minutes bake: 25 minutes oven: 350°F
makes: 6 servings dish: 3-quart

1 3-ounce package cream cheese, softened
¼ cup snipped dried tomatoes
1 tablespoon snipped fresh cilantro
6 7- or 8-inch flour tortillas
1 4.5-ounce can whole green chiles, drained and cut into thin strips
1½ cups cooked chicken strips
½ cup shredded Monterey Jack cheese (2 ounces)
   Salsa

1 Preheat oven to 350°F. Lightly grease a 3-quart rectangular baking dish; set aside. In a small bowl stir together cream cheese, dried tomatoes, and cilantro. Spread mixture over tortillas. Place some of the chile strips near an edge of each tortilla. Top each tortilla with chicken and cheese. Roll up tortillas. Place tortilla rolls in prepared baking dish.

2 Bake, covered, for 25 to 30 minutes or until heated through. Serve with salsa.

nutrition facts per serving: 252 cal., 13 g total fat (6 g sat. fat), 55 mg chol., 377 mg sodium, 17 g carb., 1 g dietary fiber, 16 g protein.

The supportive cast of ingredients contributing to the Tex-Mex flavor includes chile peppers, chili powder, and cumin.

tex-mex chicken
and rice casserole

prep: 35 minutes bake: 25 minutes stand: 5 minutes
oven: 425°F makes: 6 servings dish: 2-quart

½ cup chopped onion
    (1 medium)
1   tablespoon olive oil
1   6.9-ounce package
    chicken-flavored
    rice and vermicelli
    mix
2   cups water
1   14-ounce can chicken
    broth
2   cups chopped cooked
    chicken or turkey
2   medium tomatoes,
    seeded and
    chopped (1 cup)
3   tablespoons canned
    diced green chile
    peppers, drained
1½ teaspoons chili
    powder
1   teaspoon dried basil,
    crushed
⅛   teaspoon ground
    cumin
⅛   teaspoon ground
    black pepper
½   cup shredded
    cheddar cheese
    (2 ounces)

1 Preheat oven to 425°F. In a medium saucepan cook onion in hot oil over medium heat until tender. Stir in rice and vermicelli mix (including seasoning packet); cook and stir for 2 minutes. Stir in water and broth. Bring to boiling; reduce heat. Simmer, covered, for 20 minutes (liquid will not be fully absorbed).

2 In a large bowl combine chicken, tomatoes, chile peppers, chili powder, basil, cumin, and black pepper. Stir in cooked rice mixture. Transfer mixture to an ungreased 2-quart casserole.

3 Bake, covered, about 25 minutes or until heated through. Sprinkle with cheese. Let stand for 5 minutes before serving.

nutrition facts per serving: 280 cal., 10 g total fat (4 g sat. fat), 52 mg chol., 931 mg sodium, 28 g carb., 2 g dietary fiber, 20 g protein.

This one's got a definite kick to it! Cajun seasoning turns chicken and pasta into a mouthwatering and festive dish. If you want less intensity, ease up on the seasoning.

cajun chicken pasta

prep: 50 minutes   bake: 25 minutes   oven: 350°F
makes: 8 to 10 servings   dish: 3-quart

1   pound dried bow tie or rotini pasta
1½ pounds skinless, boneless chicken breasts, cut into 2-inch pieces
2   tablespoons all-purpose flour
2   tablespoons salt-free Cajun seasoning
1   tablespoon cooking oil
2   cups whipping cream
2   cups shredded cheddar and Monterey Jack cheese blend (8 ounces)
½   teaspoon salt
3   cups diced seeded tomatoes
¼   cup sliced scallions (2)
    Bottled hot pepper sauce (optional)

1 Cook pasta according to package directions; drain. Place in a very large bowl.

2 In a large resealable plastic bag combine chicken, flour, and 1 tablespoon of the Cajun seasoning. Seal bag; toss to coat. In a large skillet heat oil over medium-high heat. Add chicken; cook and stir until chicken is no longer pink. Place in bowl with pasta.

3 Preheat oven to 350°F. Grease a 3-quart rectangular baking dish; set aside. For cheese sauce, in a medium saucepan bring whipping cream just to boiling over medium heat, stirring occasionally. Remove from heat. Whisk in 1 cup of the cheese, the remaining 1 tablespoon Cajun seasoning, and the salt until cheese is melted and mixture is smooth.

4 Add cheese sauce, tomatoes, and the remaining 1 cup cheese to chicken mixture; toss to combine. Transfer to prepared dish.

5 Bake, covered, for 25 to 30 minutes or until heated through. Sprinkle with scallions. If desired, pass hot pepper sauce.

nutrition facts per serving: 656 cal., 37 g total fat (21 g sat. fat), 207 mg chol., 395 mg sodium, 47 g carb., 2 g dietary fiber, 34 g protein.

make-ahead directions: Prepare as directed through Step 4. Cover with plastic wrap, then foil, and chill for up to 24 hours. Remove plastic wrap. Bake, covered with foil, in a 350°F oven for 35 to 40 minutes or until heated through. Sprinkle with scallions. If desired, pass hot pepper sauce.

Patterned after a popular Texas recipe, this irresistible main dish includes seasoned chicken layered with chile peppers, tortillas, sour cream sauce, and cheese.

texas-style casserole

prep: 30 minutes **bake:** 35 minutes **stand:** 10 minutes
oven: 350°F **makes:** 12 servings **dish:** 3-quart

2   tablespoons
    vegetable oil
1   cup chopped onion
    (1 large)
½   cup finely chopped
    husked tomatillos
    (2 medium;
    optional)
1   clove garlic, minced
2   4-ounce jars diced
    pimientos, drained
2   4-ounce cans diced
    green chile peppers,
    undrained
2   fresh jalapeño chile
    peppers, seeded
    and finely chopped*
¼   cup butter
¼   cup all-purpose flour
4   teaspoons chili powder
¼   teaspoon salt
    Pinch ground black
    pepper
2   cups canned chicken
    broth
1   8-ounce carton sour
    cream
12 6-inch tostada shells
3   cups chopped cooked
    chicken
2   cups shredded
    mozzarella cheese
    (8 ounces)
    Purchased pico
    de gallo or salsa
    (optional)

1 Preheat oven to 350°F. In a medium saucepan heat the 2 tablespoons oil over medium heat. Add onion, tomatillos (if using), and garlic; cook until onion is tender. Remove from heat. Stir in pimientos, green chile peppers, and jalapeño chile peppers. Set aside.

2 In a small saucepan melt butter over medium heat. Stir in flour, chili powder, salt, and black pepper. Gradually stir in broth. Cook and stir until thickened and bubbly. Cook and stir for 1 minute more. Remove from heat. Stir in sour cream.

3 In an ungreased 3-quart rectangular baking dish, arrange six of the tostada shells, overlapping slightly. Top with half of the chicken, half of the onion mixture, half of the sour cream mixture, and half of the cheese. Top with the remaining tortillas, chicken, onion mixture, sour cream mixture, and cheese.

4 Cover loosely with foil. Bake for 35 to 40 minutes or until heated through. Let stand for 10 minutes before serving. If desired, serve with pico de gallo.

nutrition facts per serving: 462 cal., 33 g total fat (10 g sat. fat), 63 mg chol., 577 mg sodium, 22 g carb., 2 g dietary fiber, 21 g protein.

✳test kitchen tip: Because chile peppers contain volatile oils that can burn your skin and eyes, avoid direct contact with them as much as possible. When working with chile peppers, wear plastic or rubber gloves. If your bare hands do touch the pepper, wash your hands and nails well with soap and warm water.

Creole flavors—bright and robust—burst from this savory concoction of mixed meats, summer vegetables, and tender white rice.

smoked turkey
jambalaya

prep: 30 minutes bake: 55 minutes oven: 350°F
makes: 6 servings dish: 2-quart

2 cups water
1 cup long grain rice
1 16-ounce package
   frozen sweet
   pepper stir-fry
   vegetables
1 14.5-ounce can
   diced tomatoes
   with green pepper,
   celery, and onion,
   undrained
1 10-ounce can diced
   tomatoes with
   green chiles,
   undrained
8 ounces cooked turkey
   kielbasa or smoked
   turkey sausage,
   sliced ¼ inch thick
½ cup sliced
   scallions (4)
½ teaspoon Cajun
   seasoning
1 clove garlic, minced
   Bottled hot pepper
   sauce

1 In a medium saucepan combine the water and rice. Bring to boiling; reduce heat. Simmer, covered, for 15 to 18 minutes or until rice is tender and water is absorbed.

2 Meanwhile, preheat oven to 350°F. In a large bowl combine frozen vegetables, tomatoes, kielbasa, scallions, Cajun seasoning, and garlic. Stir in cooked rice. Transfer mixture to an ungreased 2-quart square baking dish.

3 Bake, uncovered, about 55 minutes or until heated through, stirring once. Pass hot pepper sauce.

nutrition facts per serving: 219 cal., 3 g total fat (0 g sat. fat), 0 mg chol., 842 mg sodium, 35 g carb., 3 g dietary fiber, 12 g protein.

Paella is a Spanish meat and seafood specialty that can take hours to prepare. This easy Americanized version uses chicken and shrimp with onion soup mix for added flavor.

mixed paella

prep: 25 minutes bake: 45 minutes stand: 10 minutes
oven: 350°F makes: 4 to 6 servings dish: 3-quart

Nonstick cooking
    spray
2½ to 3 pounds chicken
    thighs, skinned
2   tablespoons cooking
    oil
1   14-ounce can chicken
    broth
1   cup long grain rice
1   cup loose-pack frozen
    peas, thawed
1   cup peeled and
    deveined cooked
    shrimp
1   4-ounce can sliced
    mushrooms,
    drained
2   tablespoons dried
    onion soup mix
    Salt and ground black
    pepper
    Paprika

1 Preheat oven to 350°F. Lightly coat a 3-quart rectangular baking dish with nonstick cooking spray; set aside.

2 In a large skillet brown chicken thighs in hot oil, turning to brown evenly. In a large bowl combine broth, uncooked rice, peas, shrimp, mushrooms, and dried soup mix. Spread in prepared dish. Arrange chicken thighs on rice mixture. Sprinkle chicken lightly with salt, pepper, and paprika.

3 Bake, covered, about 45 minutes or until chicken is tender and no longer pink (180°F). Let stand, covered, for 10 minutes before serving.

nutrition facts per serving: 500 cal., 12 g total fat (2 g sat. fat), 212 mg chol., 1101 mg sodium, 47 g carb., 3 g dietary fiber, 49 g protein.

great **american dishes**

284

Shred leftover roast chicken to use in place of the tuna to vary this quick-as-lightning weeknight supper.

southwestern tuna bake

prep: 25 minutes bake: 30 minutes oven: 350°F
makes: 6 servings dish: 2-quart

12 ounces dried bow tie pasta
2   10.75-ounce cans condensed cream of mushroom soup
1   cup milk
2   teaspoons chili powder
1   teaspoon ground cumin
¼   teaspoon salt
1   12-ounce can tuna (water pack), drained and flaked
1   11-ounce can whole kernel corn with sweet peppers, drained
4   cups nacho-flavor tortilla chips, coarsely crushed

1 Preheat oven to 350°F. In a Dutch oven cook pasta according to package directions; drain. Return to pan. Stir in soup, milk, chili powder, cumin, and salt. Gently fold in tuna and corn. Transfer mixture to an ungreased 2-quart rectangular baking dish.

2 Bake, covered, for 20 minutes. Sprinkle with chips. Bake, uncovered, for 10 to 15 minutes more or until heated through.

nutrition facts per serving: 511 cal., 12 g total fat (3 g sat. fat), 27 mg chol., 1322 mg sodium, 75 g carb., 5 g dietary fiber, 26 g protein.

Cape Cod cooks would use the prized East Coast bay scallops to make these luscious cheese-sauced enchiladas. But if you can't find bay scallops in your area, use quartered sea scallops instead.

bayside enchiladas

prep: 30 minutes **bake:** 25 minutes **oven:** 350°F
makes: 6 servings **dish:** 3-quart

8	ounces fresh or frozen medium shrimp
8	ounces fresh or frozen bay scallops
1	8-ounce carton sour cream
½	cup salsa
2	cups shredded Monterey Jack cheese (8 ounces)
6	7- to 8-inch flour tortillas
¼	cup cottage cheese
¼	cup milk
2	tablespoons grated Parmesan cheese
¼	cup chopped scallions (2)
¼	cup sliced black olives

1 Preheat oven to 350°F. Thaw shrimp and scallops, if frozen. Peel and devein shrimp. Rinse shrimp and scallops; pat dry with paper towels.

2 In a small bowl combine sour cream and salsa. Stir in shrimp, scallops, and half of the Monterey Jack cheese. Spread about ⅓ cup of the shrimp mixture onto each tortilla near an edge; roll up. Place filled tortillas, seam sides down, in an ungreased 3-quart rectangular baking dish.

3 In a blender container or food processor bowl combine cottage cheese, milk, and Parmesan cheese. Cover and blend or process until almost smooth. Spoon mixture over prepared enchiladas. Sprinkle with onions and olives. Bake, uncovered, for 25 minutes. Sprinkle with the remaining Monterey Jack cheese. Bake about 5 minutes more or until cheese is melted.

nutrition facts per serving: 401 cal., 24 g total fat (13 g sat. fat), 105 mg chol., 674 mg sodium, 20 g carb., 1 g dietary fiber, 25 g protein.

Dry sherry, a common ingredient in Cajun and Creole cooking, adds a smoky-sweet flavor to dishes. If you don't have the fortified wine, substitute an equal amount of dry white wine and a pinch of sugar.

shrimp new orleans

prep: 30 minutes **bake:** 30 minutes **oven:** 350°F
makes: 6 servings **dish:** 2-quart

12	ounces fresh or frozen peeled and deveined cooked shrimp
½	cup chopped onion (1 medium)
¼	cup chopped green or red sweet pepper
2	tablespoons butter
2	cups cooked white rice*
1	10.75-ounce can condensed cream of shrimp soup
½	cup half-and-half or light cream
2	tablespoons dry sherry
1	teaspoon lemon juice
¼	teaspoon salt
⅛	teaspoon cayenne pepper
3	tablespoons sliced almonds, toasted
	Snipped fresh cilantro

1 Thaw shrimp, if frozen. Preheat oven to 350°F. In a medium saucepan cook onion and sweet pepper in hot butter over medium heat until tender. Remove from heat.

2 Stir in shrimp, cooked rice, soup, half-and-half, sherry, lemon juice, salt, and cayenne. Transfer mixture to an ungreased 2-quart square baking dish.

3 Bake, uncovered, about 30 minutes or until heated through. Sprinkle with almonds and cilantro.

nutrition facts per serving: 290 cal., 13 g total fat (5 g sat. fat), 141 mg chol., 624 mg sodium, 23 g carb., 1 g dietary fiber, 19 g protein.

*test kitchen tip: To prepare 2 cups cooked rice, in a medium saucepan combine 1⅓ cups water and ⅔ cup long grain white rice. Bring to boiling; reduce heat. Simmer, covered, for 15 to 18 minutes or until rice is tender.

Like the famous dance named after this Southern city, this recipe for potpie is full of twists and kicks! The Cajun seasoning in the luscious crab-and-leek filling and ultrathin layers of crisp phyllo dough add intriguing flavors.

charleston crab potpie

prep: 35 minutes bake: 25 minutes oven: 375°F
makes: 6 servings dish: 2-quart

3 tablespoons butter
1⅓ cups chopped leeks
   (4 medium)
⅓ cup all-purpose flour
2½ cups milk
1 pound cooked
   crabmeat, flaked and
   cartilage removed
1 cup frozen peas
¼ cup dry sherry
   (optional)
1½ teaspoons Cajun
   seasoning
⅛ to ¼ teaspoon
   cayenne pepper
   (optional)
3 tablespoons butter,
   melted
1 teaspoon Dijon-style
   mustard (optional)
4 sheets (14×9-inch
   rectangles) frozen
   phyllo dough,
   thawed
Paprika (optional)

1 Preheat oven to 375°F. In a large skillet heat 3 tablespoons butter over medium heat. Add leeks; cook and stir for 2 to 3 minutes or until tender. Add flour; cook and stir for 1 minute. Gradually stir in milk; cook and stir until mixture starts to boil. Stir in crabmeat, peas, sherry (if using), Cajun seasoning, and cayenne (if using). Transfer mixture to an ungreased 2-quart square baking dish.

2 In a small bowl stir together 3 tablespoons melted butter and mustard (if using). Unfold phyllo dough; remove one phyllo sheet. (While you work, keep the remaining phyllo dough covered with plastic wrap to prevent it from drying out.) Lightly brush phyllo sheet with some of the butter mixture. Place another sheet on top; brush with butter mixture. Top with two more sheets, brushing each sheet with butter mixture. Using a sharp knife, cut a small circle in the center of the phyllo stack to allow steam to escape. Place phyllo stack on top of crab mixture. Brush with any remaining butter mixture.

3 Bake, uncovered, for 25 to 30 minutes or until mixture is heated through and phyllo is lightly browned. If desired, sprinkle with paprika.

nutrition facts per serving: 297 cal., 13 g total fat (7 g sat. fat), 109 mg chol., 461 mg sodium, 23 g carb., 4 g dietary fiber, 22 g protein.

Seasoned cooked red sweet peppers make a tangy relish for traditional grits. To save time, make the relish ahead and chill for up to 8 hours.

southern grits casserole with red pepper relish

prep: 20 minutes   bake: 45 minutes   stand: 30 minutes
oven: 350°F   makes: 4 servings   dish: 2-quart

4   cups water
1   cup quick-cooking grits
4   eggs, beaten
2   cups shredded cheddar cheese (8 ounces)
½   cup milk
¼   cup scallions, sliced (2)
1   to 2 fresh jalapeño chile peppers, seeded (optional) and chopped*
½   teaspoon garlic salt
¼   teaspoon ground white pepper
2   cups chopped red sweet peppers (2 medium)
½   cup chopped red onion (1 small)
2   cloves garlic, minced
1   tablespoon butter
⅓   cup snipped fresh parsley
1   tablespoon white wine vinegar

1 Preheat oven to 350°F. In a large saucepan bring the water to a boil. Slowly stir in grits. Gradually stir about 1 cup of the hot mixture into the eggs. Add egg mixture to saucepan. Stir in cheese, milk, scallions, jalapeño peppers (if using), garlic salt, and white pepper.

2 Spoon grits mixture into an ungreased 2-quart casserole. Bake, uncovered, for 45 to 50 minutes or until a knife inserted near the center comes out clean.

3 Meanwhile, for relish, in a medium saucepan cook sweet peppers, red onion, and garlic in hot butter until sweet peppers are just tender. Remove from heat and stir in parsley and vinegar. Let stand at room temperature at least 30 minutes. Serve with grits.

nutrition facts per serving: 403 cal., 27 g total fat (14 g sat. fat), 275 mg chol., 731 mg sodium, 16 g carb., 23 g protein.

*test kitchen tip: Because chile peppers contain volatile oils that can burn your skin and eyes, avoid direct contact with them as much as possible. When working with chile peppers, wear plastic or rubber gloves. If your bare hands do touch the peppers, wash your hands and nails well with soap and warm water.

Everyone will ask for seconds when you serve this down-home treat that is similar to corn pudding or spoon bread.

corn belt special

prep: 10 minutes bake: 1 hour 15 minutes stand: 5 minutes
oven: 350°F makes: 8 to 10 servings dish: 2-quart

2	eggs, lightly beaten
1	14.75-ounce can cream-style corn
1	8-ounce carton sour cream
¼	cup butter, melted
1	15.25-ounce can whole kernel corn, drained
1½	cups shredded cheddar cheese (6 ounces)
½	cup chopped onion (1 medium)
1	4-ounce can diced green chile peppers, drained
1	8.5-ounce package corn muffin mix Shredded cheddar cheese (optional)

1 Preheat oven to 350°F. Grease a 2-quart casserole; set aside. In a large bowl combine eggs, cream-style corn, sour cream, and melted butter. Stir in whole kernel corn, cheese, onion, and chile peppers. Add muffin mix, stirring just until moistened. Transfer mixture to the prepared casserole.

2 Bake, uncovered, about 1¼ hours or until a knife inserted in the center comes out clean and top is golden. If desired, sprinkle with additional cheddar cheese. Let stand for 5 minutes before serving.

nutrition facts per serving: 407 cal., 24 g total fat (12 g sat. fat), 104 mg chol., 730 mg sodium, 40 g carb., 1 g dietary fiber, 12 g protein.

Zesty Cajun spices gives this mac and cheese a lot of spunk, while American cheese makes it extra-creamy.

cajun mac and cheese

prep: 30 minutes   bake: 35 minutes   stand: 5 minutes
oven: 350°F   makes: 6 servings   dish: 3-quart

3   cups dried tricolor
    or plain elbow
    macaroni
    (12 ounces)
2   cups shredded
    cheddar cheese
    (8 ounces)
4   ounces American
    cheese, cubed
2   tablespoons butter or
    margarine
³/₄ cup chopped sweet
    onion (such as
    Vidalia, Walla
    Walla, or Maui)
12 cloves garlic, minced
    (2 tablespoons)
¹/₂ cup sliced
    scallions (4)
1   cup chopped sweet
    red and/or green
    pepper (1 large)
2   eggs, lightly beaten
1   12-ounce can
    evaporated milk
2   tablespoons all-
    purpose flour
2   teaspoons yellow
    mustard
2   teaspoons bottled hot
    pepper sauce
¹/₂ teaspoon paprika
¹/₂ teaspoon salt

1 Preheat oven to 350°F. Grease a 3-quart rectangular baking dish; set aside.

2 In a large saucepan cook macaroni according to package directions; drain. Return to hot pan. Stir in cheeses.

3 Meanwhile, in a medium skillet melt butter over medium heat. Add sweet onion and garlic; cook until tender. Stir in scallions and sweet pepper. Cook and stir for 1 minute more; stir into cooked pasta mixture. Spoon into prepared baking dish.

4 In a medium bowl whisk together eggs, evaporated milk, flour, mustard, hot pepper sauce, paprika, and salt until smooth; pour evenly over pasta mixture.

5 Cover with foil. Bake for 20 minutes. Uncover. Bake for 15 to 20 minutes more or until bubbly and heated through. Let stand for 5 minutes before serving.

nutrition facts per serving: 600 cal., 29 g total fat (17 g sat. fat), 154 mg chol., 846 mg sodium, 56 g carb., 3 g dietary fiber, 28 g protein.

Although safe to eat and available year-round, oysters are always best in the winter months, when waters are cold.

carolina low country dressing

prep: 45 minutes bake: 45 minutes oven: 350°F
makes: 16 servings dish: 3-quart

1 pint shucked oysters
½ cup butter
1 stalk celery, chopped (½ cup)
1 medium onion, chopped (½ cup)
1 teaspoon dried sage, crushed
½ teaspoon salt
½ teaspoon ground black pepper
8 cups crumbled corn bread*
6 2¼-inch baked flaky biscuits, torn into bite-size pieces (about 3 cups)
1 cup cooked white or brown rice
2 eggs, lightly beaten
½ to 1 cup chicken broth

1 Preheat oven to 350°F. Drain oysters; reserving liquid. Coarsely chop oysters.

2 In a large skillet melt butter over medium heat. Add celery, onion, sage, salt, and pepper; cook about 5 minutes or until tender. Add chopped oysters; cook and stir for 2 minutes more.

3 In an extra-large bowl combine oyster mixture, corn bread, biscuits, rice, and eggs. Toss just until combined. Drizzle with reserved oyster liquid and enough broth to moisten, tossing lightly to combine. Spoon into an ungreased 3-quart rectangular baking dish.

4 Cover with foil. Bake for 45 minutes. Uncover. Bake about 15 minutes more or until heated through and light brown. (Stuffing is done when an instant-read thermometer inserted in center of stuffing mixture registers 170°F.)

nutrition facts per serving: 319 cal., 14 g total fat (6 g sat. fat), 90 mg chol., 808 mg sodium, 39 g carb., 2 g dietary fiber, 9 g protein.

*test kitchen tip: To make 8 cups of crumbled corn bread, prepare and bake two 8.5-ounce packages corn bread according to package directions.

Shave calories and fat from indulgent favorites, such as spaghetti pie. Or serve up tasty one-dish meals packed with "better-for-you" ingredients, including fresh vegetables, lean meats, and whole grains. Let these lightened-up meals put you and your family on the road to eating more nutritiously.

light &

health

ful

Reduced-fat cheese and light sour cream join other healthful ingredients in this spiced-up casserole.

mexican beef bake with cilantro-lime cream

prep: 25 minutes **bake:** 33 minutes **oven:** 350°F
makes: 6 servings **dish:** 1½-quart

4   ounces dried
    multigrain rotini
    or elbow macaroni
    (1⅓ cups)
12 ounces extra-lean
    ground beef
2   cloves garlic, minced
1   15-ounce can black
    beans or pinto beans,
    rinsed and drained
1   14.5-ounce can
    no-salt-added
    diced tomatoes,
    undrained
¾   cup bottled picante
    sauce or salsa
1   teaspoon dried
    oregano, crushed
½   teaspoon ground
    cumin
½   teaspoon chili powder
½   cup shredded
    reduced-fat Colby
    and Monterey Jack
    cheese (2 ounces)
⅓   cup light sour cream
3   tablespoons sliced
    scallions
2   teaspoons coarsely
    snipped fresh
    cilantro (optional)
½   teaspoon finely
    shredded lime zest
    Lime wedges
    (optional)

1 Preheat oven to 350°F. In a large saucepan cook pasta according to package directions; drain well. Return pasta to saucepan; set aside.

2 Meanwhile, in a large skillet cook meat and garlic until meat is brown, using a wooden spoon to break up meat as it cooks. Drain off fat.

3 Stir cooked meat into pasta. Stir in beans, tomatoes, picante sauce, oregano, cumin, and chili powder. Transfer mixture to an ungreased 1½- or 2-quart baking dish or casserole.

4 Bake, covered, about 30 minutes or until heated through. Sprinkle with cheese. Bake, uncovered, about 3 minutes more or until cheese is melted.

5 Meanwhile, in a small bowl stir together sour cream, 2 tablespoons of the scallions, the cilantro, and lime zest. Serve beef mixture with sour cream mixture, the remaining 1 tablespoon scallions, and, if desired, lime wedges.

nutrition facts per serving: 283 cal., 10 g total fat (4 g sat. fat), 45 mg chol., 520 mg sodium, 29 g carb., 7 g dietary fiber, 23 g protein.

Seasoning the pork and rice with a low-fat curry sauce, tart apple, and fresh cilantro means this hearty dish is loaded with flavor but still fits into a sensible meal plan.

curried pork and rice

prep: 20 minutes **bake:** 45 minutes **stand:** 5 minutes **oven:** 350°F
makes: 4 servings **dish:** 1½-quart

1	teaspoon vegetable oil
12	ounces boneless pork loin, cut into thin bite-size strips
2	cups fat-free milk
2	tablespoons all-purpose flour
1½	teaspoons curry powder
¼	teaspoon salt
¾	cup instant brown rice
1	medium green apple (such as Granny Smith), cored and chopped
1	medium carrot, coarsely shredded
3	scallions, bias-sliced
2	tablespoons chopped peanuts
2	tablespoons snipped fresh cilantro

1 Preheat oven to 350°F. In a large nonstick skillet heat oil over medium heat. Add pork; cook for 3 to 5 minutes or until done. Drain off fat. Set aside.

2 In a screw-top jar combine ½ cup of the milk, the flour, curry powder, and salt; cover and shake until well mixed. Transfer to a medium saucepan; add the remaining milk. Cook and stir over medium heat until thickened and bubbly. Stir in pork, uncooked rice, apple, carrot, and scallions. Transfer to an ungreased 1½-quart casserole. Place casserole on a baking sheet.

3 Bake, covered, about 45 minutes or until rice is tender and most of the liquid is absorbed. Let stand, covered, on a wire rack for 5 minutes. Sprinkle with peanuts and cilantro before serving.

nutrition facts per serving: 275 cal., 7 g total fat (2 g sat. fat), 56 mg chol., 289 mg sodium, 27 g carb., 3 g dietary fiber, 25 g protein.

Lighten Up

Cook up healthier casseroles—without sacrificing flavor—by swapping one ingredient for another. The following suggestions can help lower fat and sodium and increase fiber in your family-favorite recipes.

- *Use reduced-fat cheeses, light cream cheese and sour cream, evaporated skim milk, and reduced-fat canned condensed soups.*

- *Cook with healthy fats and oils, such as olive and canola oils.*

- *Choose intensely flavored cheeses, such as aged Parmesan or tangy, crumbly feta or blue cheese, to top a casserole. Because of the strong flavor, you might get by with using less.*

- *Season sensibly, using garlic or onion powder instead of seasoning salt and boosting flavor with finely chopped fresh herbs, garlic, celery, onions, or grated citrus zest.*

Using prepared pastry, refrigerated potatoes, and frozen veggies makes preparation a snap for this favorite of kids young and old.

lattice-topped oven stew

prep: 20 minutes **bake:** 18 minutes **stand:** 10 minutes
oven: 400°F **makes:** 8 servings **dish:** 3-quart

½   of a 15-ounce package (1 crust) rolled refrigerated unbaked piecrust

1   teaspoon sesame seeds

1½ pounds lean ground beef

2   cups refrigerated diced potatoes with onions or loose-pack frozen diced hash brown potatoes with onions and peppers

2   cups loose-pack frozen mixed vegetables

1   15-ounce can Italian-style or regular tomato sauce

1   14.5-ounce can Italian-style stewed tomatoes, undrained

1 Preheat oven to 400°F. Let refrigerated piecrust stand according to package directions. Unfold piecrust. Using a pizza cutter or sharp knife, cut piecrust into strips ½- to 1-inch wide. Brush strips lightly with water. Place strips on a foil-lined baking sheet, forming a loose lattice pattern. Sprinkle with sesame seeds. Bake for 7 to 9 minutes or until pastry is golden. Cool on baking sheet.

2 In a large skillet cook ground beef over medium heat until cooked through, using a wooden spoon to break up meat as it cooks. Drain off fat. In a large bowl stir together meat, potatoes, mixed vegetables, tomato sauce, and tomatoes. Spoon into an ungreased 3-quart rectangular baking dish. Bake, uncovered, about 20 minutes or until heated through.

3 Gently break or cut pastry into 8 portions. Spoon beef mixture into bowls. Top with pieces of pastry.

nutrition facts per serving: 342 cal., 16 g total fat (6 g sat. fat), 59 mg chol., 669 mg sodium, 32 g carb., 3 g dietary fiber, 19 g protein.

Making the crust with egg whites gives you all the cooking power of whole eggs without the cholesterol. In addition, using lean ground beef instead of the traditional sausage and low-fat cottage cheese lowers the fat in the filling.

lightened-up spaghetti pie

prep: 35 minutes **bake:** 25 minutes **stand:** 15 minutes
oven: 350°F **makes:** 6 servings **dish:** 9-inch pie plate

Nonstick cooking
spray
4 ounces dried
spaghetti
2 egg whites, lightly
beaten
1/3 cup grated Parmesan
cheese
1 tablespoon olive oil
2 egg whites, lightly
beaten
1 12-ounce container
(1¼ cups) low-fat
cottage cheese,
drained
8 ounces ground turkey
breast or 90% or
higher lean ground
beef
1 cup sliced fresh
mushrooms
1/2 cup chopped onion
1/2 cup chopped green
and/or red sweet
pepper
2 cloves garlic, minced
1 8-ounce can no-salt-
added tomato sauce
1½ teaspoons dried
Italian seasoning,
crushed
1/8 teaspoon salt
1/2 cup shredded part-
skim mozzarella
cheese (2 ounces)

1 Preheat oven to 350°F. Coat a 9-inch pie plate with nonstick cooking spray; set aside. For crust, cook spaghetti according to package directions, except omit cooking oil and salt; drain well. Meanwhile, in a medium bowl stir together 2 egg whites, Parmesan cheese, and oil. Add spaghetti to egg white mixture; toss to coat. Transfer spaghetti mixture to prepared pie plate and press spaghetti mixture evenly into the bottom and up the side of pie plate.

2 In a small bowl stir together 2 egg whites and cottage cheese. Spread cottage cheese mixture over spaghetti crust in pie plate.

3 In a large skillet cook turkey, mushrooms, onion, sweet pepper, and garlic until meat is browned. Drain off fat. Stir tomato sauce, Italian seasoning, and salt into meat mixture in skillet. Spoon over cottage cheese mixture in crust.

4 Bake, uncovered, about 20 minutes or until heated through. Sprinkle with mozzarella cheese. Bake about 5 minutes more or until the cheese is melted. Let stand for 15 minutes before serving. Cut into wedges.

nutrition facts per serving: 256 cal., 7 g total fat (3 g sat. fat), 27 mg chol., 479 mg sodium, 23 g carb., 2 g dietary fiber, 26 g protein.

Turn a meal into a fiesta with zesty corn tortillas layered with spicy sausage and cheese and topped with an egg mixture and fresh tomatoes. If you'd like this to be on the milder side, use regular sausage and omit one can of chiles.

layered fiesta casserole

prep: 30 minutes **bake:** 45 minutes **stand:** 20 minutes
oven: 350°F **makes:** 16 servings **dish:** 3-quart

1 pound bulk hot pork
   sausage or bulk
   pork sausage
½ cup chopped onion
   (1 small)
2 cloves garlic, minced
2 4-ounce cans diced
   green chile peppers,
   undrained
8 6-inch corn tortillas,
   cut into 1-inch
   strips
4 cups shredded
   Monterey Jack
   cheese (1 pound)
8 eggs, beaten
½ cup fat-free milk
¾ teaspoon ground
   cumin
½ teaspoon ground
   black pepper
¼ teaspoon salt
3 large tomatoes, sliced
1 teaspoon paprika
   Sour cream, salsa,
   and/or guacamole
   (optional)

1 In a large skillet cook sausage, onion, and garlic until sausage is brown. Drain off fat.

2 Spread half of the chile peppers in a greased 3-quart rectangular baking dish. Top with half of the tortilla strips, half of the cooked sausage mixture, and half of the cheese. Repeat layers.

3 In a large bowl whisk together eggs, milk, cumin, pepper, and salt. Carefully pour over layers. Top with tomato slices and sprinkle with paprika. Cover and chill overnight.

4 Preheat oven to 350°F. Bake, uncovered, for 45 to 50 minutes or until set. Let stand for 20 minutes before serving. If desired, serve warm with sour cream, salsa, and/or guacamole.

nutrition facts per serving: 262 cal., 17 g total fat (8 g sat. fat), 150 mg chol., 402 mg sodium, 11 g carb., 2 g dietary fiber, 15 g protein.

Rich in fiber and protein, red lentils are legumes that have a mild earthy flavor, soft textures, and deep orange-red color. Compared to dried beans, they cook faster and do not require soaking.

dijon lentil and sausage casserole

prep: 40 minutes **bake:** 35 minutes **oven:** 400°F
makes: 8 servings **dish:** 2-quart

1 14-ounce can reduced-sodium chicken broth
1 cup water
8 ounces green beans, trimmed and cut into 2-inch pieces (about 2 cups)
2 medium parsnips, peeled and cut into ½-inch slices
3 medium shallots, halved, or 1 medium onion, cut into thin wedges
8 ounces cooked smoked turkey sausage, coarsely chopped
1¼ cups dried red lentils, rinsed and drained
⅓ cup dry white wine or reduced-sodium chicken broth
2 tablespoons Dijon mustard
2 teaspoons snipped fresh thyme or ½ teaspoon dried thyme, crushed
4 cloves garlic, minced
1½ cups coarse soft whole wheat bread crumbs
1 tablespoon canola oil
¼ cup snipped fresh Italian parsley
2 teaspoons finely shredded lemon zest
Lemon slices (optional)

1 Preheat oven to 400°F. In a large saucepan combine broth and the water. Bring to boiling. Add green beans, parsnips, and shallots. Return to boiling; reduce heat. Simmer, covered, for 8 to 10 minutes or just until vegetables are tender. Remove from heat. Stir in sausage and lentils. In a small bowl combine wine, mustard, thyme, and 2 cloves of the garlic; stir into sausage mixture.

2 Transfer sausage mixture to an ungreased 2-quart casserole. Bake, covered, for 25 to 30 minutes or just until lentils are tender.

3 Meanwhile, in a medium bowl toss together bread crumbs and oil. Sprinkle over sausage mixture. Bake, uncovered, about 10 minutes more or until mixture is heated through and crumbs are lightly browned.

4 In a small bowl combine the remaining 2 cloves garlic, parsley, and lemon zest. Sprinkle over casserole before serving. If desired, garnish with lemon slices.

nutrition facts per serving: 236 cal., 5 g total fat (1 g sat. fat), 20 mg chol., 577 mg sodium, 31 g carb., 12 g dietary fiber, 15 g protein.

Good-for-You Beans and Legumes

- *Black beans: These mild, slightly sweet legumes contain a lot of iron and potassium.*

- *Lentils: Humble lentils pack a punch with folate and provide generous quantities of potassium and iron.*

Potatoes get some healthy company, including sweet potatoes and turnips, in this revised family favorite.

rosemary scalloped
potatoes and ham

prep: 40 minutes   **bake:** 30 minutes   **stand:** 10 minutes
oven: 350°F   **makes:** 6 servings   **dish:** 2-quart

½ cup chopped onion (1 medium)
1½ cups fat-free milk
3 tablespoons all-purpose flour
⅛ teaspoon ground black pepper
1 teaspoon snipped fresh rosemary or ½ teaspoon dried rosemary, crushed
1 medium round red potato, peeled and cut into ¼-inch slices
1 medium sweet potato, peeled and cut into ¼-inch slices
1 medium turnip, peeled and cut into ¼-inch slices
¼ cup water
8 ounces low-fat, reduced-sodium cooked boneless ham, cut into thin strips
Paprika
Fresh rosemary sprigs (optional)

1 Preheat oven to 350°F. For sauce, in a medium saucepan cook onion in a small amount of boiling water over medium heat for 3 to 5 minutes or until tender. Drain; return onion to saucepan. In a screw-top jar combine milk, flour, and pepper; cover and shake until well mixed. Add milk mixture to onion in saucepan. Cook and stir over medium heat until thickened and bubbly. Stir in snipped rosemary.

2 Meanwhile, in a 2-quart microwave-safe baking dish combine potatoes, turnip, and the ¼ cup water. Cover with vented plastic wrap. Microwave on 100 percent power (high) about 8 minutes or just until vegetables are tender. Carefully drain in a colander.

3 In the same ungreased 2-quart baking dish layer half of the ham, half of the potato mixture, and half of the sauce. Top with the remaining potatoes and the remaining ham. Spoon the remaining sauce over. Sprinkle with paprika. Bake, uncovered, about 30 minutes or until heated through. Let stand for 10 minutes before serving. If desired, garnish with rosemary sprigs.

nutrition facts per serving: 120 cal., 2 g total fat (1 g sat. fat), 17 mg chol., 466 mg sodium, 17 g carb., 2 g dietary fiber, 10 g protein.

High-fiber whole grain pasta, Italian-style turkey sausage, and part-skim mozzarella cheese stand in for more traditional—but less healthful—ingredients.

baked sausage and mushroom rotini

prep: 30 minutes **bake:** 30 minutes **oven:** 350°F
makes: 6 servings **dish:** 3-quart

3½ cups packaged dried whole grain rotini or penne

12 ounces uncooked Italian-style turkey sausage links (casings removed), ground turkey, or lean ground beef

1 8-ounce package sliced fresh mushrooms

½ cup chopped onion (1 medium)

2 cloves garlic, minced

2 14.5-ounce cans diced tomatoes with basil, oregano, and garlic, undrained

1 6-ounce can no-salt-added tomato paste

⅓ cup water

¼ teaspoon crushed red pepper

¼ cup shredded part-skim mozzarella cheese (1 ounce)

¼ cup finely shredded Parmesan cheese

1 Preheat oven to 350°F. Lightly grease a 3-quart casserole; set aside. Cook pasta according to package directions; drain well.

2 Meanwhile, in a 4-quart Dutch oven combine sausage, mushrooms, onion, and garlic; cook over medium heat until sausage is brown and vegetables are tender, stirring with a wooden spoon to break up meat as it cooks. Drain off fat. Add cooked pasta, tomatoes, tomato paste, the water, and crushed red pepper to sausage mixture in Dutch oven, stirring until combined. Transfer pasta mixture to prepared casserole.

3 Bake, covered, for 20 minutes. Sprinkle with mozzarella cheese and Parmesan cheese. Bake, uncovered, about 10 minutes more or until heated through.

nutrition facts per serving: 406 cal., 6 g total fat (2 g sat. fat), 43 mg chol., 1276 mg sodium, 60 g carb., 6 g dietary fiber, 29 g protein.

Good-for-You Veggies

- *Garlic: The pungent bulb contains phytochemicals and phenolic compounds that enhance the immune system.*

- *Peppers: In all of their many colors, sweet peppers offer a good source of vitamin C. Red sweet peppers are extra-high in the phytochemical beta-carotene, which routes free radicals out of the body.*

- *Spinach: Cooked spinach possesses plenty of vitamin A and folate and good amounts of vitamin C and calcium.*

- *Sweet potatoes: Fresh sweet potatoes are higher in vitamins A and C than their canned counterparts. They also contain plenty of fiber.*

Evaporated fat-free milk gives this Alfredo-style dish just-like-cream flavor without the fat. Serve this with a side salad tossed with reduced-calorie Italian dressing.

low-fat chicken tetrazzini

prep: 30 minutes   bake: 10 minutes   oven: 400°F
makes: 6 servings   dish: 2-quart

4   ounces dried whole
     wheat spaghetti
2   cups sliced fresh
     cremini, stemmed
     shiitake, and/or
     button mushrooms
³/₄ cup chopped red
     and/or green
     sweet pepper
½   cup cold water
3   tablespoons all-
     purpose flour
1   12-ounce can
     (1½ cups) evaporated
     fat-free milk
½   teaspoon instant
     chicken bouillon
     granules
⅛   teaspoon salt
⅛   teaspoon ground
     black pepper
     Pinch ground nutmeg
1   cup chopped cooked
     chicken or turkey
     breast (5 ounces)
¼   cup finely shredded
     Parmesan cheese
     (1 ounce)
2   tablespoons snipped
     fresh parsley
     Nonstick cooking
     spray

1 Preheat oven to 400°F. Cook the spaghetti according to package directions, except omit any cooking oil and only lightly salt the water. Drain well.

2 Meanwhile, in a covered large saucepan cook the mushrooms and sweet pepper in a small amount of boiling water for 3 to 6 minutes or until the vegetables are tender. Drain well; return to saucepan.

3 In a screw-top jar combine the ½ cup cold water and the flour; cover and shake until well mixed. Stir flour mixture into the vegetable mixture in saucepan. Stir in evaporated milk, bouillon granules, salt, black pepper, and nutmeg. Cook and stir until thickened and bubbly. Stir in the cooked spaghetti, chicken, Parmesan cheese, and parsley.

4 Lightly coat a 2-quart square baking dish with nonstick cooking spray. Spoon spaghetti mixture into dish. Bake, covered, for 10 to 15 minutes or until heated through.

nutrition facts per serving: 202 cal., 2 g total fat (1 g sat. fat), 24 mg chol., 253 mg sodium, 32 g carb., 2 g dietary fiber, 17 g protein.

Turkey sausage links and whole wheat lasagna noodles add a healthful spin, while onion, garlic, and seasonings provide a zesty flavor profile to the meaty sauce.

turkey-zucchini lasagna

prep: 25 minutes **bake:** 40 minutes **stand:** 10 minutes
oven: 375°F **makes:** 6 servings **dish:** 2-quart

8 ounces uncooked Italian turkey sausage links (casings removed)
³/₄ cup chopped onion
3 cloves garlic, minced
1 15-ounce can tomato sauce
2 teaspoons dried Italian seasoning, crushed
1 medium zucchini, coarsely shredded (optional)
6 dried whole wheat lasagna noodles
1 cup light ricotta cheese
1 egg white, lightly beaten
1 cup shredded reduced-fat mozzarella cheese (4 ounces)

1 Preheat oven to 375°F. In a large skillet cook sausage, onion, and garlic until meat is brown and onion is tender, using a wooden spoon to break up meat as it cooks. Drain off fat. Stir tomato sauce and Italian seasoning into meat mixture in skillet. Bring to boiling; remove from heat. Stir in zucchini (if using).

2 Meanwhile, cook lasagna noodles according to package directions. Drain well. In a small bowl combine ricotta cheese and egg white.

3 Spread about ½ cup of the meat mixture in the bottom of an ungreased 2-quart rectangular baking dish. Layer half of the cooked noodles in the dish, trimming and overlapping as necessary to fit. Spread with half of the ricotta mixture. Top with half of the remaining meat mixture and half of the mozzarella cheese. Repeat layers, starting with cooked noodles.

4 Bake, covered, for 30 minutes. Uncover and bake about 10 minutes more or until heated through. Let stand for 10 minutes before serving.

nutrition facts per serving: 262 cal., 9 g total fat (4 g sat. fat), 44 mg chol., 781 mg sodium, 26 g carb., 5 g dietary fiber, 19 g protein.

Turkey and sweet potatoes make this casserole a bit healthier than the classic shepherd's pie.

turkey and sweet potato shepherd's pies

prep: 40 minutes bake: 20 minutes oven: 375°F
makes: 4 servings dish: 10-ounce dishes

1½   pounds sweet potatoes, peeled and cut into 2-inch pieces
2   cloves garlic, halved
¼   cup fat-free milk
½   teaspoon salt
12   ounces uncooked ground turkey breast
½   cup chopped onion (1 medium)
1¼   cups coarsely chopped zucchini (1 medium)
1   cup chopped carrots (2 medium)
½   cup frozen whole kernel corn
¼   cup water
1   8-ounce can tomato sauce
2   tablespoons Worcestershire sauce
2   teaspoons snipped fresh sage or ½ teaspoon dried sage, crushed
⅛   teaspoon ground black pepper
Fresh sage leaves (optional)

1 Preheat oven to 375°F. In a covered medium saucepan cook sweet potatoes and garlic in enough lightly salted boiling water to cover for 15 to 20 minutes or until tender; drain. Mash with a potato masher or beat with an electric mixer on low speed. Gradually add milk and salt, mashing or beating to make potato mixture light and fluffy. Cover and keep warm.

2 Meanwhile, in a large skillet cook turkey and onion over medium heat until meat is brown, stirring with a wooden spoon to break up turkey as it cooks. Drain, if needed. Stir in zucchini, carrots, corn, and the water. Bring to boiling; reduce heat. Simmer, covered, for 5 to 10 minutes or until vegetables are tender.

3 Add tomato sauce, Worcestershire sauce, snipped sage, and pepper to turkey mixture; heat through. Divide turkey mixture among four ungreased 10-ounce ramekins, spreading evenly. Spoon mashed sweet potato mixture in mounds onto turkey mixture.

4 Bake, uncovered, for 20 to 25 minutes or until heated through. If desired, garnish with fresh sage leaves.

nutrition facts per serving: 268 cal., 1 g total fat (0 g sat. fat), 42 mg chol., 824 mg sodium, 41 g carb., 7 g dietary fiber, 24 g protein.

We refreshed this classic by lightening up the ingredients without sacrificing flavor. Whole wheat linguine makes it even more healthful.

turkey
primavera
casserole

prep: 40 minutes bake: 35 minutes stand: 5 minutes
oven: 350°F makes: 6 to 8 servings dish: 3-quart

Nonstick cooking
  spray
8 ounces packaged
    dried whole wheat
    linguine or spaghetti,
    broken in half
1 pound broccoli,
    trimmed and cut
    into 1-inch pieces
2 tablespoons butter
3 medium red
    and/or yellow sweet
    peppers, stemmed,
    seeded, and cut into
    1-inch pieces
2 cloves garlic, minced
¼ cup all-purpose flour
¼ teaspoon salt
⅛ teaspoon ground
    black pepper
1 14-ounce can
    reduced-sodium
    chicken broth
¾ cup fat-free milk
½ cup light sour cream
3 cups shredded
    cooked turkey
¾ cup shredded white
    cheddar cheese
    (3 ounces)
1 recipe Bread Crumb
    Topper

1 Preheat oven to 350°F. Coat a 3-quart casserole with cooking spray; set aside.

2 In a large pot cook linguine according to package directions, adding broccoli for the last 2 minutes of cooking time. Drain. Return linguine and broccoli to Dutch oven.

3 Meanwhile, for sauce, in a large skillet melt butter over medium heat. Add sweet peppers and garlic; cook about 5 minutes or just until peppers are tender, stirring occasionally. Stir in flour, salt, and black pepper until combined. Add broth and milk all at once. Cook and stir until thickened and bubbly. Stir in sour cream.

4 Add sauce, turkey, and cheese to linguine mixture; toss to coat. Spoon into prepared casserole. Bake, covered, for 25 minutes.

5 Sprinkle with Bread Crumb Topper. Bake, uncovered, for 10 to 15 minutes more or until heated through and topper is lightly browned. Let stand for 5 minutes before serving.

nutrition facts per serving: 473 cal., 17 g total fat (8 g sat. fat), 84 mg chol., 515 mg sodium, 46 g carb., 6 g dietary fiber, 35 g protein.

bread crumb topper: In a small bowl toss together 1 cup soft bread crumbs, 1 tablespoon snipped fresh parsley, 1 to 2 teaspoons finely shredded lemon zest, and 1 tablespoon olive oil.

An easy makeover for many pasta dishes can be achieved simply by reaching for whole grain or multigrain pasta and loading up on the vegetables.

mediterranean
pasta gratin

prep: 30 minutes bake: 30 minutes stand: 5 minutes
oven: 375°F makes: 8 servings dish: 12-ounce dishes

8   ounces dried multigrain or whole grain penne pasta
4   cups baby spinach
2   cups fresh cremini mushrooms, quartered
½   cup coarsely chopped oil-packed dried tomatoes*
¼   cup chopped pitted kalamata olives
½   cup basil pesto
2   tablespoons balsamic vinegar
1   4-inch ball (about 8 ounces) fresh mozzarella cheese, cut into chunks or thinly sliced
½   cup shredded fresh basil (optional)

1 Preheat oven to 375°F. Lightly grease four 12-ounce individual casseroles or one 1½-quart au gratin dish; set aside. In a large pot cook pasta according to package directions, adding spinach and mushrooms for the last 1 minute of cooking; drain.

2 Transfer pasta mixture to an extra-large bowl. Stir in dried tomatoes and olives. Add pesto and vinegar; toss gently to coat. Transfer mixture to the prepared casseroles or au gratin dish.

3 Bake, covered, for 20 to 25 minutes or until heated through. Top with cheese. Bake, uncovered, about 10 minutes more or until cheese is melted. Let stand for 5 minutes before serving. If desired, sprinkle with basil. If using individual casseroles, each dish will serve two.

nutrition facts per serving: 324 cal., 18 g total fat (4 g sat. fat), 25 mg chol., 438 mg sodium, 27 g carb., 3 g dietary fiber, 15 g protein.

＊test kitchen tip: If the dried tomatoes are very firm, add them to some of the hot pasta cooking water and let stand for 5 minutes. Drain well, then add to the pasta mixture as directed.

Lentils and fresh vegetables wrapped in tortillas make these enchiladas a meal unto themselves. Serve them with a cool, crunchy salad.

zesty vegetable
enchiladas

prep: 40 minutes **bake:** 15 minutes **oven:** 350°F
makes: 4 servings **dish:** 2-quart

1⅓ cups water
½ cup dried brown lentils, rinsed and drained
Nonstick cooking spray
8 7- to 8-inch flour tortillas
2 medium carrots, thinly sliced (1 cup)
2 small zucchini or yellow summer squash, quartered lengthwise and sliced (2 cups)
1 teaspoon ground cumin
1 8-ounce can tomato sauce
1 cup shredded reduced-fat Monterey Jack cheese (4 ounces)
Dash bottled hot pepper sauce (optional)
1 14.5-ounce can Mexican-style stewed tomatoes, undrained and cut up
Fresh cilantro sprigs (optional)

1 In a medium saucepan combine the water and lentils. Bring to boiling; reduce heat. Simmer, covered, about 30 minutes or until tender; drain.

2 Meanwhile, preheat oven to 350°F. Coat a 2-quart rectangular baking dish with cooking spray; set aside. Stack tortillas and wrap tightly in foil. Bake about 10 minutes or until warm.

3 Lightly coat a large skillet with cooking spray; heat over medium heat. Add carrots; cook and stir for 2 minutes. Add zucchini and cumin; cook and stir for 2 to 3 minutes or until vegetables are crisp-tender. Remove from heat. Stir in cooked lentils, tomato sauce, ¾ cup of the cheese, and hot pepper sauce (if using).

4 Divide lentil mixture among warm tortillas; roll up tortillas. Arrange tortillas, seam sides down, in the prepared baking dish. Sprinkle with the remaining ¼ cup cheese. Spoon tomatoes over tortillas.

5 Bake, uncovered, for 15 to 20 minutes or until heated through. If desired, garnish with cilantro.

nutrition facts per serving: 450 cal., 15 g total fat (4 g sat. fat), 20 mg chol., 929 mg sodium, 57 g carb., 11 g dietary fiber, 22 g protein.

The ingredients for these cheesy potatoes have been updated to help keep the fat in check.

light and cheesy potatoes

prep: 20 minutes **bake:** 1 hour 5 minutes **stand:** 10 minutes
oven: 350°F **makes:** 6 servings **dish:** 2-quart

1   10.75-ounce can
    reduced-fat and
    reduced-sodium
    condensed cream of
    chicken soup
1   cup shredded
    reduced-fat sharp
    cheddar cheese
    (4 ounces)
½   cup fat-free milk
½   cup light sour cream
⅓   cup finely chopped
    onion (1 small) or
    2 tablespoons dried
    minced onion
½   teaspoon ground
    black pepper
1   30- or 32-ounce
    package frozen
    shredded or
    diced hash brown
    potatoes, thawed
½   cup crushed wheat
    cereal flakes
    Sliced scallions
    (optional)

1 Preheat oven to 350°F. Lightly grease a 2-quart casserole; set aside. In a very large bowl combine soup, cheese, milk, sour cream, chopped onion, and pepper. Stir in hash brown potatoes. Spoon mixture into prepared casserole.

2 Bake, covered, for 45 minutes. Stir potatoes, sprinkle with cereal. Bake, uncovered, for 20 to 25 minutes more or until heated through and bubbly. Let stand for 10 minutes before serving. If desired, garnish with scallions.

nutrition facts per serving: 259 cal., 6 g total fat (4 g sat. fat), 23 mg chol., 471 mg sodium, 40 g carb., 2 g dietary fiber, 11 g protein.

Quinoa (KEEN-wah) is a nutrient-packed grain as versatile as rice. When combined with barley and vegetables, it elevates this stuffed pepper side dish to tantalizing heights.

peppers stuffed with quinoa and spinach

prep: 35 minutes **bake:** 45 minutes **oven:** 400°F
makes: 6 servings **dish:** 3-quart

1 14-ounce can vegetable broth
¼ cup quick-cooking barley
¼ cup quinoa, rinsed and drained
2 tablespoons olive oil
½ cup chopped onion (1 medium)
2 cloves garlic, minced
2 cups sliced fresh mushrooms
1 14.5-ounce can diced tomatoes, undrained
½ of a 10-ounce package frozen chopped spinach, thawed and well drained
¼ teaspoon salt
¼ teaspoon ground black pepper
1 cup shredded Monterey Jack cheese with jalapeño chile peppers or regular Monterey Jack cheese (4 ounces)
3 large red sweet peppers
   Salt and ground black pepper

1 Preheat oven to 400°F. In a medium saucepan bring broth to boiling. Add barley and quinoa. Return to boiling; reduce heat. Simmer, covered, about 12 minutes or until tender. Drain, reserving cooking liquid.

2 In a large skillet heat oil over medium-high heat. Add onion and garlic; cook and stir for 2 minutes. Add mushrooms; cook and stir for 4 to 5 minutes more or until mushrooms and onion are tender. Stir in tomatoes, spinach, ¼ teaspoon salt, and ¼ teaspoon black pepper. Add quinoa mixture and ½ cup of the cheese; stir to combine. Remove from heat.

3 Cut sweet peppers in half lengthwise; remove and discard seeds and membranes. Sprinkle insides of the sweet peppers lightly with additional salt and pepper. Fill sweet pepper halves with quinoa mixture. Place sweet peppers, filled sides up, in an ungreased 3-quart oval or rectangular baking dish. Pour reserved cooking liquid into baking dish around peppers.

4 Bake, covered, for 35 minutes. Sprinkle the remaining ½ cup cheese over filled sweet peppers. Bake, uncovered, about 10 minutes more or until sweet peppers are crisp-tender and cheese is browned.

nutrition facts per serving: 230 cal., 12 g total fat (5 g sat. fat), 20 mg chol., 739 mg sodium, 24 g carb., 5 g dietary fiber, 10 g protein.

Polenta—humble, versatile, and satisfying—is a staple in the northern part of Italy, where it is more common than pasta. It is the ultimate comfort food and costs just pennies per serving.

vegetable-polenta
lasagna

prep: 20 minutes **chill:** 30 minutes **bake:** 40 minutes
oven: 350°F **makes:** 8 servings **dish:** 3-quart

2½   cups water
1½   cups yellow cornmeal
1½   cups water
1   teaspoon salt
1   small onion, thinly
        sliced
1   tablespoon olive oil
4   cups fresh
        mushrooms, halved
¼   teaspoon salt
¼   teaspoon ground
        black pepper
2   12-ounce jars roasted
        red sweet peppers,
        drained and cut into
        thin strips
1¼   cups marinara sauce
1   cup shredded
        mozzarella cheese
        (4 ounces)
        Snipped fresh Italian
        parsley (optional)

1 For polenta, in a medium saucepan bring the 2½ cups water to boiling. Meanwhile, in a small bowl combine cornmeal, the 1½ cups water, and 1 teaspoon salt. Slowly add cornmeal mixture to the boiling water, stirring constantly. Cook and stir until mixture returns to boiling. Reduce heat to low. Cook, uncovered, for 10 to 15 minutes or until very thick, stirring frequently. Spread evenly in an ungreased 3-quart rectangular baking dish; cool. Cover and chill about 30 minutes or until firm.

2 Preheat oven to 350°F. In a large nonstick skillet cook onion in hot oil over medium heat for 3 to 4 minutes or until tender. Add mushrooms, ¼ teaspoon salt, and black pepper. Cook and stir about 5 minutes or until mushrooms are tender. Remove from heat. Stir in roasted peppers.

3 Spread marinara sauce over chilled polenta. Top with vegetable mixture; sprinkle with cheese.

4 Bake, covered, for 30 minutes. Bake, uncovered, for 10 to 15 minutes more or until edges are bubbly. If desired, sprinkle with parsley.

nutrition facts per serving: 188 cal., 7 g total fat (2 g sat. fat), 8 mg chol., 649 mg sodium, 27 g carb., 4 g dietary fiber, 8 g protein.

Packed full of vitamins with broccoli and carrots, this layered masterpiece makes a deliciously healthy meal.

broccoli lasagna

prep: 30 minutes bake: 35 minutes stand: 15 minutes
oven: 350°F makes: 8 servings dish: 3-quart

9 dried lasagna noodles
3½ cups milk
½ cup all-purpose flour
1 teaspoon salt
½ teaspoon dry mustard
¼ teaspoon ground black pepper
¼ teaspoon bottled hot pepper sauce
¼ cup grated Parmesan cheese
1 16-ounce package frozen cut broccoli, thawed and drained
2 medium carrots, shredded (1 cup)
2 cups shredded cheddar cheese (8 ounces)

1 Preheat oven to 350°F. Lightly grease a 3-quart rectangular baking dish; set aside. Cook lasagna noodles according to package directions; drain well. Rinse with cold water; drain well. Place noodles in a single layer on a sheet of foil; set aside.

2 Meanwhile, for sauce, in a medium saucepan whisk together about 1 cup of the milk and the flour until smooth. Stir in the remaining milk, salt, dry mustard, black pepper, and hot pepper sauce. Cook and stir over medium heat until thickened and bubbly. Remove from heat; stir in Parmesan cheese.

3 Arrange three of the cooked lasagna noodles in the prepared baking dish. Top with half of the broccoli, half of the carrots, ¾ cup of the cheddar cheese, and 1 cup of the sauce. Repeat layering noodles, broccoli, carrots, cheese, and sauce. Top with the remaining noodles, sauce, and cheese.

4 Bake, uncovered, for 35 to 40 minutes or until heated through. Let stand for 15 minutes before serving.

nutrition facts per serving: 325 cal., 13 g total fat (8 g sat. fat), 41 mg chol., 574 mg sodium, 35 g carb., 3 g dietary fiber, 17 g protein.

These stuffed peppers use barley filling instead of Mom's old-fashioned hamburger stuffing, but they're just as comforting. For an eye-catching presentation, use two different colored sweet peppers.

barley-stuffed peppers

prep: 25 minutes **bake:** 22 minutes **oven:** 350°F
makes: 4 servings **dish:** 2-quart

1 cup sliced fresh mushrooms
1 cup water
2/3 cup quick-cooking barley
1/2 of a vegetable bouillon cube
2 large red, yellow, and/or green sweet peppers
1 egg, lightly beaten
1 large tomato, peeled, seeded, and chopped (about 3/4 cup)
3/4 cup shredded reduced-fat mozzarella cheese (3 ounces)
1/2 cup shredded zucchini
1/3 cup soft bread crumbs
1 tablespoon snipped fresh basil or 1/2 teaspoon dried basil, crushed
1 teaspoon snipped fresh rosemary or 1/8 teaspoon dried rosemary, crushed
1/4 teaspoon onion salt
Several dashes bottled hot pepper sauce

1 Preheat oven to 350°F. In a medium saucepan combine mushrooms, the water, barley, and bouillon cube. Bring to boiling; reduce heat. Simmer, covered, for 12 to 15 minutes or until barley is tender; drain.

2 Meanwhile, halve sweet peppers lengthwise; remove seeds and membranes. If desired, precook peppers in boiling water for 3 minutes. Invert onto paper towels; drain.

3 In a medium bowl combine egg, tomato, 1/2 cup of the cheese, the zucchini, bread crumbs, basil, rosemary, onion salt, and hot pepper sauce. Stir in cooked barley. Place peppers, cut sides up, in an ungreased 2-quart baking dish. Spoon barley mixture into peppers.

4 Bake, covered, for 20 to 25 minutes or until barley mixture is heated through. Sprinkle with the remaining 1/4 cup cheese. Bake, uncovered, about 2 minutes more or until cheese is melted.

nutrition facts per serving: 231 cal., 5 g total fat (3 g sat. fat), 65 mg chol., 514 mg sodium, 33 g carb., 4 g dietary fiber, 13 g protein.

With barley, bulgur, black beans, and a lentil soup base, this aromatic meatless bake is as flavorful as it is nutritious.

vegetable casserole with
barley and bulgur

prep: 15 minutes   bake: 1 hour 15 minutes   stand: 5 minutes
oven: 350°F   makes: 4 servings   dish: 2-quart

1 Preheat oven to 350°F. In an ungreased 2-quart casserole combine soup, beans, carrots, mushrooms, corn, barley, the water, bulgur, onion, pepper, and salt.

2 Bake, covered, about 1¼ hours or until barley and bulgur are tender, stirring twice. Stir again; sprinkle with cheese. Let stand, covered, about 5 minutes or until cheese is melted.

1   14.5- to 18.5-ounce can ready-to-serve lentil soup
1   15-ounce can black beans, rinsed and drained
1   cup sliced carrots (2 medium)
1   cup small fresh mushrooms, quartered
1   cup frozen whole kernel corn
½   cup regular barley
½   cup water
⅓   cup bulgur
¼   cup chopped onion
½   teaspoon ground black pepper
¼   teaspoon salt
½   cup shredded cheddar cheese (2 ounces)

nutrition facts per serving: 384 cal., 8 g total fat (3 g sat. fat), 15 mg chol., 929 mg sodium, 66 g carb., 17 g dietary fiber, 22 g protein.

Good-for-You Grains

- *Bulgur: A steam-cooked and dried type of cracked wheat, bulgur offers all of the benefits of whole grain, including protein, fiber, and B vitamins.*

- *Polenta: The ground corn in polenta acts as a relatively low-calorie provider of fiber and vitamin C.*

- *Whole grain pasta: Complex carbohydrates in nutty, toothsome whole wheat noodles help the body fight obesity, diabetes, and heart disease.*

The green bean casserole gets a new slim profile with the help of reduced-fat and reduced-sodium cream of mushroom soup. Almonds replace the standard fried onion rings on top.

light green bean casserole

prep: 15 minutes bake: 30 minutes oven: 350°F
makes: 6 servings dish: 2-quart

1	10.75-ounce can reduced-fat and reduced-sodium cream of mushroom soup
¼	cup bottled roasted red sweet peppers, chopped, or one 2-ounce jar diced pimientos, drained
¼	teaspoon salt
¼	teaspoon ground black pepper
3	9-ounce packages frozen French-cut green beans, thawed and drained
½	cup sliced almonds, toasted

1 Preheat oven to 350°F. In a large bowl combine soup, roasted sweet peppers, salt, and black pepper. Stir in green beans. Transfer mixture to an ungreased 2-quart rectangular baking dish. Sprinkle with toasted almonds.

2 Bake, uncovered, for 30 to 35 minutes or until heated through.

nutrition facts per serving: 128 cal., 5 g total fat (1 g sat. fat), 1 mg chol., 286 mg sodium, 14 g carb., 5 g dietary fiber, 4 g protein.

pantry

qu

12

Put an easy oven meal on the table pronto! The best quality convenience ingredients keep these family-favorite dishes simple without sacrificing flavor. In 30 minutes or less, it's ready for the oven.

ick

Refrigerated biscuits top the ground beef mixture in this "pizza."

upside-down pizza casserole

prep: 20 minutes   bake: 15 minutes   oven: 400°F
makes: 5 servings   dish: 2-quart

1½   pounds lean ground beef or bulk Italian sausage
1   15-ounce can Italian-style tomato sauce
1   4-ounce can sliced mushrooms, drained
¼   cup sliced pitted black olives (optional)
1   to 1½ cups shredded mozzarella cheese or four-cheese pizza blend (4 to 6 ounces)
1   10-ounce package refrigerated biscuits (10 biscuits)

1 Preheat oven to 400°F. In a large skillet cook beef until brown. Drain off fat. Stir in tomato sauce, mushrooms, and olives (if using); heat through. Transfer meat mixture to an ungreased 2-quart rectangular baking dish or 10-inch deep-dish pie plate. Sprinkle with cheese.

2 Flatten each biscuit with your hands. Arrange biscuits on top of cheese. Bake, uncovered, for 15 to 17 minutes or until biscuits are golden.

nutrition facts per serving: 565 cal., 33 g total fat (13 g sat. fat), 105 mg chol., 1351 mg sodium, 32 g carb., 2 g dietary fiber, 36 g protein.

Baked pasta is a crowd-pleaser, especially when it's partnered with Italian meatballs, tangy pasta sauce, and luscious cheeses.

cheesy italian meatball casserole

prep: 30 minutes bake: 45 minutes oven: 350°F
makes: 8 to 10 servings dish: 3-quart

16 ounces packaged dried ziti or penne pasta
1   26-ounce jar tomato pasta sauce
1   16-ounce package frozen cooked Italian-style meatballs (32 meatballs), thawed
1   15-ounce can Italian-style tomato sauce
1   15-ounce carton ricotta cheese
½   cup grated Parmesan cheese (2 ounces)
2   cups shredded mozzarella cheese (8 ounces)

1 Preheat oven to 350°F. Cook pasta according to package directions; drain. Return to pan. Stir in pasta sauce, meatballs, and tomato sauce. Transfer to an ungreased 3-quart rectangular baking dish. Bake, covered, for 30 minutes.

2 Meanwhile, in a small bowl combine ricotta cheese and Parmesan cheese. Spoon ricotta mixture in mounds on top of pasta mixture. Bake, covered, about 10 minutes more or until heated through. Top with mozzarella cheese. Bake, uncovered, about 5 minutes more or until cheese is melted.

nutrition facts per serving: 636 cal., 30 g total fat (16 g sat. fat), 91 mg chol., 1371 mg sodium, 59 g carb., 6 g dietary fiber, 32 g protein.

Blah!

Here's a comfort food casserole with appeal for the whole family.
Add a simple greens salad and this delightful dinner is a done deal.

beef and noodle casserole

prep: 20 minutes   bake: 25-30 minutes   stand: 5 minutes   oven: 350°F
makes: 4 servings   dish: 1½-quart

1   4.6-ounce package vermicelli with garlic and olive oil or one 4.8-ounce package angel hair pasta with herbs
1   pound lean ground beef
½   cup shredded carrot (1 medium)
½   of an 8-ounce tub cream cheese spread with chives and onion (½ cup)
½   cup milk
    Small fresh basil leaves (optional)

1 Preheat oven to 350°F. Grease a 1½-quart casserole; set aside. Cook pasta according to package directions (including the standing time).

2 Meanwhile, in a large skillet cook ground meat over medium heat until brown. Drain off fat. Stir in carrot, cream cheese, and milk. Stir in cooked vermicelli and a few basil leaves (if using). Transfer mixture to the prepared casserole.

3 Bake, uncovered, for 25 to 30 minutes or until heated through, stirring once halfway through baking. Let stand, covered, for 5 minutes before serving.

nutrition facts per serving: 369 cal., 23 g total fat (12 g sat. fat), 104 mg chol., 359 mg sodium, 11 g carb., 1 g dietary fiber, 26 g protein.

Clever Shortcuts

It's amazing how much prep time can be eliminated thanks to convenience products. Try these for your casseroles.

- *preshredded cheese*
- *jarred pasta sauces*
- *frozen meatballs*
- *presliced mushrooms and other veggies*
- *prepeeled carrots and other veggies*
- *frozen chopped sweet peppers and onions*
- *bottled roasted red sweet peppers*
- *prepared salsas*
- *sauce mixes*
- *seasoning blends*

Stock up on a few convenience items, and you can have this comforting dinner ready for the oven in just a few minutes. Homemade goodness doesn't get any easier!

creamy meatball casserole

prep: 15 minutes bake: 1 hour oven: 350°F
makes: 6 servings dish: 3-quart

1 Preheat oven to 350°F. In a large bowl combine soup, milk, sour cream, salt, and pepper. Stir in potatoes, meatballs, and frozen vegetables.

2 Transfer mixture to an ungreased 3-quart casserole. Bake, covered, about 1 hour or until heated through.

1   10.75-ounce can condensed cream of mushroom or cream of onion soup
1   cup milk
½   cup sour cream
½   teaspoon salt
⅛   teaspoon ground black pepper
1   20-ounce package refrigerated red-skinned potato wedges
1   16-ounce package frozen cooked meatballs (32 meatballs)
1   16-ounce package frozen stir-fry vegetables (any combination)

nutrition facts per serving: 423 cal., 28 g total fat (12 g sat. fat), 37 mg chol., 1291 mg sodium, 28 g carb., 6 g dietary fiber, 17 g protein.

All you need to serve with a hearty family favorite like this is a simple green salad. Add a crusty loaf of French bread and this delightful dinner is a done deal.

baked beef ravioli

prep: 20 minutes bake: 20 minutes oven: 375°F
makes: 8 to 10 servings dish: 3-quart

2   9-ounce packages refrigerated cheese-filled ravioli
1½ pounds ground beef
1   large onion, chopped (1 cup)
6   cloves garlic, minced
1   14.5-ounce can diced tomatoes, undrained
1   10.75-ounce can condensed tomato soup
1   teaspoon dried basil, crushed
1   teaspoon dried oregano, crushed
1½ cups shredded mozzarella cheese (6 ounces)
½   cup finely shredded Parmesan cheese (2 ounces)

1 Preheat oven to 375°F. Cook ravioli according to package directions; drain well. Return to pan; cover and keep warm.

2 Meanwhile, in a large skillet cook ground meat, onion, and garlic over medium heat until meat is brown and onion is tender. Drain off fat. Stir in tomatoes, soup, basil, and oregano. Gently stir in cooked ravioli.

3 Transfer mixture to an ungreased 3-quart casserole or rectangular baking dish. Sprinkle with mozzarella cheese and Parmesan cheese. Bake, uncovered, about 20 minutes or until heated through.

nutrition facts per serving: 503 cal., 20 g total fat (9 g sat. fat), 113 mg chol., 854 mg sodium, 40 g carb., 3 g dietary fiber, 40 g protein.

Lovingly referred to as simply "the hotdish" in some parts of the country, this quintessential casserole is hometown cooking at its best and will surely warm your soul.

hamburger, potato, and **bean** casserole

prep: 30 minutes   bake: 55 minutes   stand: 10 minutes
oven: 350°F   makes: 6 servings   dish: 3-quart

1   pound lean ground beef
1   10.75-ounce can condensed golden mushroom soup
1/2   cup milk
1   teaspoon garlic salt
1/2   teaspoon ground black pepper
3   medium potatoes, peeled, if desired, halved lengthwise, and cut into 1/4-inch slices
1   medium onion, halved and sliced
1   15.5-ounce can dark red kidney beans, rinsed and drained
1   4-ounce can sliced mushrooms, drained
1   cup shredded cheddar cheese (4 ounces)

1   Preheat oven to 350°F. In a large skillet cook ground beef over medium heat until cooked through, using a wooden spoon to break up meat as it cooks. Drain off fat.

2   In a medium bowl combine soup, milk, garlic salt, and pepper; spread 1/3 cup of the soup mixture in an ungreased 3-quart rectangular baking dish. Top with half of the potatoes, half of the onion, half of the beans, half of the ground beef, and half of the mushrooms. Drizzle with half of the remaining soup mixture. Repeat layers, starting with potatoes and ending with soup mixture.

3   Bake, covered, for 55 to 60 minutes or until potatoes are tender. Sprinkle with cheese. Let stand for 10 minutes before serving.

nutrition facts per serving: 364 cal., 15 g total fat (7 g sat. fat), 70 mg chol., 903 mg sodium, 32 g carb., 6 g dietary fiber, 27 g protein.

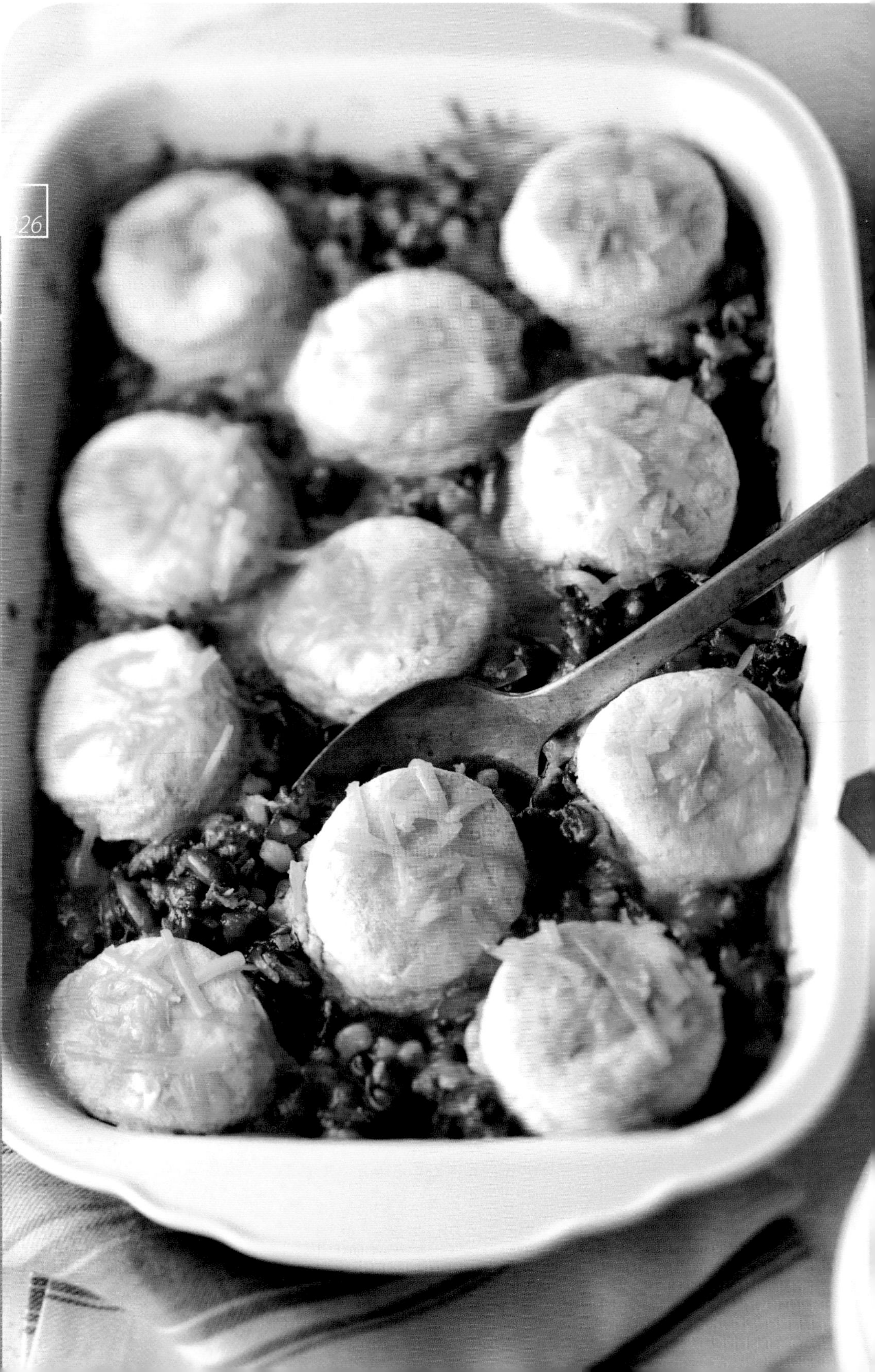

Stirring up a batch of biscuits from packaged biscuit mix is a clever shortcut. Evenly space the biscuits in the dish so the oven heat can circulate around them.

mexican biscuit casserole

prep: 20 minutes bake: 20 minutes stand: 5 minutes
oven: 350°F makes: 8 to 10 servings dish: 3-quart

1½ pounds lean ground
   beef
1 1.25-ounce package
   taco seasoning mix
¾ cup water
1 16-ounce can kidney
   beans, undrained
1 11-ounce can whole-
   kernel corn with
   sweet peppers,
   drained
3¼ cups packaged
   biscuit mix
1 cup milk
3 cups shredded
   cheddar cheese
   (12 ounces)

1 Preheat oven to 350°F. In a large skillet cook ground beef until brown. Drain off fat. Mix taco seasoning according to package directions, except use the ¾ cup water. Add taco seasoning mix, kidney beans and corn to meat in skillet. Bring to boiling.

2 Meanwhile, combine biscuit mix and milk. Stir until moistened. Beat for 30 seconds more. Roll out dough on a lightly floured surface to ½-inch thickness. Cut with a 2-inch round biscuit cutter, making 10 biscuits.

3 Spoon hot meat mixture into an ungreased 3-quart rectangular baking dish and top with 2½ cups of the cheese. Immediately place biscuits on top and bake about 20 minutes or until biscuits are tender. Sprinkle with the remaining cheese. Let stand for 5 minutes before serving.

nutrition facts per serving: 486 cal., 25 g total fat (11 g sat. fat), 81 mg chol., 1365 mg sodium, 40 g carb., 3 g dietary fiber, 29 g protein.

Here's an easy, everyday kind of dish that's sure to bring everyone to the dinner table. Serve with steamed veggies to round out the meal.

mexican beef and macaroni casserole

prep: 20 minutes   bake: 30 minutes   oven: 350°F
makes: 8 servings   dish: 3-quart

2 cups dried elbow macaroni
1½ pounds lean ground beef
2½ cups picante sauce or salsa
1 15-ounce can black beans, rinsed and drained
2 teaspoons dried oregano, crushed
1 teaspoon ground cumin
1 teaspoon chili powder
¾ teaspoon garlic powder
1 16-ounce carton sour cream
¾ cup sliced scallions (6)
1 2.25-ounce can sliced pitted black olives, drained
1 cup shredded Monterey Jack cheese (4 ounces)

1 Preheat oven to 350°F. In a large pot cook macaroni according to package directions; drain. Return to pan.

2 Meanwhile, in a large skillet cook ground meat over medium heat until brown. Drain off fat. Stir meat into cooked macaroni. Stir in picante sauce, beans, oregano, cumin, chili powder, and garlic powder. Transfer mixture to an ungreased 3-quart rectangular baking dish. Bake, covered, about 25 minutes or until heated through.

3 In a medium bowl stir together sour cream, scallions, and olives. Spread sour cream mixture over top of casserole; sprinkle with cheese. Bake, uncovered, about 5 minutes more or until cheese is melted.

nutrition facts per serving: 500 cal., 27 g total fat (14 g sat. fat), 93 mg chol., 744 mg sodium, 36 g carb., 5 g dietary fiber, 31 g protein.

The mashed-potatoes-and-cheese topper makes this savory vegetable-filled favorite a satisfying dinner. Serve it with fresh fruit for dessert and your meal is complete.

hamburger-mash surprise

prep: 25 minutes bake: 30 minutes stand: 5 minutes
oven: 375°F makes: 6 servings dish: 2-quart

³/₄   cup shredded cheddar cheese (3 ounces)
2   cups refrigerated mashed potatoes
12   ounces lean ground beef
½   cup chopped onion
2   cups sliced zucchini or yellow summer squash
1   14.5-ounce can diced tomatoes with basil, oregano, and garlic, undrained
½   of a 6-ounce can (⅓ cup) no-salt-added tomato paste
¼   teaspoon ground black pepper
    Paprika (optional)

1 Preheat oven to 375°F. Stir ½ cup of the cheese into the potatoes. In a large skillet cook ground beef and onion over medium heat until meat is brown and onion is tender. Drain off fat. Stir in squash, tomatoes, tomato paste, and pepper. Bring to boiling. Remove from heat; transfer to an ungreased 2-quart baking dish or casserole.

2 Spoon mashed potato mixture into a large self sealing plastic bag. Seal bag and snip off a corner of the plastic bag. Pipe the potato mixture in rows over meat mixture. (Or spoon mashed potato mixture in mounds on top of hot mixture.) Sprinkle with the remaining cheese. If desired, sprinkle with paprika.

3 Bake, uncovered, about 30 minutes or until mashed potato top is golden brown. Let stand for 5 minutes before serving.

nutrition facts per serving: 254 cal., 12 g total fat (3 g sat. fat), 39 mg chol., 644 mg sodium, 21 g carb., 3 g dietary fiber, 16 g protein.

∗test kitchen tip: If you have an oven-safe skillet, simply top the meat mixture with the mashed potatoes and bake in the skillet.

Refrigerated corn bread twists make a tasty, and easy, topping on this Texas-style casserole.

chili corn pie

prep: 20 minutes bake: 20 minutes stand: 5 minutes oven: 375°F
makes: 4 servings dish: 2-quart

pantry quick

2   11-ounce packages frozen chunky beef and bean chili

1   11.5-ounce package refrigerated corn bread twists

1/3   cup shredded cheddar cheese

1   tablespoon snipped fresh cilantro

1/4   cup sour cream

1 Preheat oven to 375°F. Heat the frozen chili according to microwave package directions.

2 Meanwhile, on a lightly floured surface, unroll sheet of corn bread twist dough (do not separate into strips). Press at perforations to seal. Roll to an 11x7-inch rectangle.

3 Spoon hot chili into an ungreased 2-quart rectangular baking dish. Immediately place corn bread dough on top of chili in baking dish. Using a sharp knife, cut slits in corn bread dough to allow steam to escape.

4 Bake, uncovered, about 20 minutes or until corn bread is lightly browned. Sprinkle with cheese and cilantro. Let stand for 5 minutes before serving. Top individual servings with sour cream.

nutrition facts per serving: 512 cal., 24 g total fat (9 g sat. fat), 44 mg chol., 1429 mg sodium, 50 g carb., 3 g dietary fiber, 22 g protein.

Hot dogs and macaroni are favorite foods with many kids, and they're so easy to cook in a pinch. Here, they're covered with a creamy spaghetti sauce and topped with cheese.

frankfurter-pasta
casserole

prep: 25 minutes bake: 35 minutes oven: 350°F
makes: 6 servings dish: 2-quart

2²/₃ cups dried medium
      shell macaroni
      (8 ounces)
1   tablespoon butter,
      margarine, or
      vegetable oil
1   cup chopped onion
      (1 large)
1   clove garlic, minced
1   16-ounce package
      beef frankfurters,
      halved lengthwise
      and sliced
1½   cups purchased
      spaghetti sauce
1   cup chopped tomato
      (1 large)
1   4-ounce can
      mushroom stems
      and pieces, drained
1   8-ounce carton sour
      cream
1   cup shredded
      provolone and/or
      mozzarella cheese
      (4 ounces)

1 Preheat oven to 350°F. Cook macaroni according to package directions; drain.

2 Meanwhile, in a large skillet, melt butter over medium heat. Add onion and garlic; cook until nearly tender. Stir in frankfurters and cook until light brown. Stir in spaghetti sauce, tomato, and mushrooms. Bring to boiling. Remove from heat. Stir in sour cream and ½ cup of the cheese. Stir mixture into the drained pasta. Transfer mixture to an ungreased 2-quart casserole.

3 Bake, covered, about 30 minutes. Sprinkle with the remaining ½ cup cheese. Bake, uncovered, about 5 minutes more or until cheese melts.

nutrition facts per serving: 600 cal., 38 g total fat (18 g sat. fat), 73 mg chol., 1411 mg sodium, 46 g carb., 4 g dietary fiber, 21 g protein.

When you're looking for a delicious destination for leftover holiday ham, look no further than this simple, inexpensive, bubbly bake.

one-step ham casserole

prep: 15 minutes   **bake:** 50 minutes   **stand:** 10 minutes
oven: 375°F   **makes:** 4 servings.   **dish:** 2-quart

1½ cups milk
1 10.75-ounce can condensed cream of celery soup
2 cups diced cooked ham
1 cup dried elbow macaroni
1 4-ounce can sliced mushrooms, drained
2 tablespoons diced pimiento
1 tablespoon dried minced onion or ½ cup chopped onion
½ cup shredded American cheese (2 ounces)

1 Preheat oven to 375°F. In an ungreased 2-quart casserole gradually stir milk into soup. Stir in ham, macaroni, mushrooms, pimiento, and onion.

2 Bake, covered, about 40 minutes or until macaroni is tender. Sprinkle with cheese. Bake, uncovered, about 10 minutes more or until cheese is melted. Let stand for 10 minutes before serving.

nutrition facts per serving: 341 cal., 12 g total fat (6 g sat. fat), 61 mg chol., 2042 mg sodium, 33 g carb., 2 g dietary fiber, 26 g protein.

Loaded with Mexican flavors, this pork, bean, and rice dish is ideal for busy weeknights.

pork and green chiles
casserole

prep: 15 minutes bake: 30 minutes stand: 5 minutes
oven: 375°F makes: 6 servings dish: 2-quart

1	pound ground pork
1	15-ounce can pinto or black beans, rinsed and drained
1½	cups mild red salsa
1	10.75-ounce can condensed cream of chicken soup
1	cup instant brown rice
1	4-ounce can diced green chile peppers, drained
¼	cup water
1	teaspoon ground cumin
½	cup shredded cheddar or Monterey Jack cheese with jalapeño chile peppers (2 ounces)

1 Preheat oven to 375°F. In a large skillet cook ground meat over medium heat until brown. Drain off fat. Stir in beans, salsa, soup, brown rice, chile peppers, water, and cumin. Cook and stir just until bubbly. Transfer mixture to an ungreased 2-quart casserole.

2 Bake, uncovered, for 30 to 35 minutes or until edges are bubbly. Sprinkle with cheese. Let stand for 5 minutes before serving.

nutrition facts per serving: 314 cal., 13 g total fat (6 g sat. fat), 49 mg chol., 820 mg sodium, 31 g carb., 5 g dietary fiber, 19 g protein.

334

Yukon gold potatoes will also work for this casserole because, like red potatoes, they hold their shape well when baked.

layered potato casserole

prep: 20 minutes bake: 1 hour 5 minutes oven: 350°F
makes: 4 servings dish: 2-quart

4	medium round red potatoes, thinly sliced
1½	cups cubed cooked ham, turkey, chicken, pork, or beef (about 8 ounces)
¾	cup chopped green sweet pepper (1 medium)
⅓	cup chopped onion (1 small)
1	cup shredded Colby–Monterey Jack cheese (4 ounces) Chopped seeded tomato Ground black pepper

1 Preheat oven to 350°F. Grease a 2-quart round or square baking dish. In prepared dish layer half of the potatoes, half of the ham, half of the sweet pepper, half of the onion, and half of the cheese. Repeat layering using the remaining ham, sweet pepper, and onion. Top with the remaining potatoes.

2 Bake, covered, for 45 minutes. Bake, uncovered, about 15 minutes more or until potatoes are tender. Sprinkle with the remaining cheese. Bake, uncovered, 5 minutes more or until cheese is melted. Sprinkle with chopped tomato and black pepper.

nutrition facts per serving: 315 cal., 12 g total fat (6 g sat. fat), 56 mg chol., 1010 mg sodium, 27 g carb., 3 g dietary fiber, 24 g protein.

Apples' crunchy, sweet elements have long made a lovely pairing with pork. Toss them with corn bread stuffing for a fall-flavored dish.

pork and apple casserole

prep: 25 minutes bake: 30 minutes oven: 400°F
makes: 6 servings dish: 2-quart

1 pound bulk pork sausage

1⅓ cups chopped apples (2 medium)

1⅓ cups packaged corn bread stuffing mix

1 tablespoon dried minced onion

2 eggs

1¼ cups apple juice or apple cider

½ cup shredded cheddar cheese (2 ounces)

1 Preheat oven to 400°F. In a large skillet cook sausage until brown. Drain off fat. Stir in chopped apples, dry stuffing mix, and dried minced onion. In a small bowl whisk together eggs and apple juice; add to sausage mixture. Toss to coat. Transfer mixture to a greased 2-quart square baking dish.

2 Bake, covered, for 20 minutes. Uncover; stir stuffing mixture and sprinkle with cheddar cheese. Bake, uncovered, about 10 minutes more or until heated through.

nutrition facts per serving: 429 cal., 29 g total fat (11 g sat. fat), 138 mg chol., 776 mg sodium, 24 g carb., 2 g dietary fiber, 17 g protein.

A corn bread base, browned meat, and beans plus tangy cheddar and green chile peppers look like a party in a pan and taste just as festive. Dollops of sour cream top off the tang.

two-step tamale bake

prep: 20 minutes   bake: 22 minutes   oven: 375°F
makes: 6 servings   dish: 2-quart

1 **8.5-ounce package corn muffin mix**
1 **cup shredded cheddar cheese (4 ounces)**
1 **4-ounce can diced green chile peppers, drained**
1 **pound lean ground beef or bulk pork sausage**
1 **15-ounce can red kidney beans, rinsed and drained**
1 **10-ounce can enchilada sauce**
Sour cream (optional)

1 Preheat oven to 375°F. Grease a 2-quart rectangular baking dish; set aside. Prepare muffin mix according to package directions, except do not bake. Stir in ½ cup of the cheese and the chile peppers. Spread corn muffin mixture into the prepared baking dish. Bake for 12 to 15 minutes or until a wooden toothpick inserted near the center comes out clean.

2 Meanwhile, in a large skillet cook meat until brown. Drain off fat. Stir kidney beans and enchilada sauce into browned meat in skillet. Spread meat mixture over baked corn muffin mixture. Bake for 7 minutes more. Sprinkle with the remaining ½ cup cheese. Bake about 3 minutes more or until cheese melts and mixture is heated through. To serve, cut into squares. If desired, serve with sour cream.

nutrition facts per serving: 464 cal., 21 g total fat (8 g sat. fat), 67 mg chol., 778 mg sodium, 44 g carb., 4 g dietary fiber, 27 g protein.

From cupboard and refrigerator to oven is a 15-minute trip for this layered casserole. While it bakes, toss a simple salad to go with it.

chicken tortilla bake

prep: 15 minutes   bake: 45 minutes   oven: 350°F
makes: 8 servings   dish: 3-quart

2   10.75-ounce cans
    condensed cream of
    chicken soup
1   10-ounce can diced
    tomatoes with
    green chile peppers,
    undrained
12 6- or 7-inch corn
    tortillas, cut into
    thin bite-size strips
3   cups cubed cooked
    chicken (about
    1 pound)
1   cup shredded
    Mexican cheese
    blend (4 ounces)

1 Preheat oven to 350°F. In a medium bowl combine cream of chicken soup and tomatoes. Sprinkle one-third of the tortilla strips into an ungreased 3-quart rectangular baking dish. Layer half of the chicken over tortilla strips; spoon half of the soup mixture on top. Repeat layers. Sprinkle with the remaining tortilla strips.

2 Bake, covered, about 40 minutes or until bubbly around edges and hot in the center. Sprinkle with cheese. Bake, uncovered, about 5 minutes more or until cheese is melted.

nutrition facts per serving: 325 cal., 14 g total fat (6 g sat. fat), 66 mg chol., 819 mg sodium, 26 g carb., 4 g dietary fiber, 23 g protein.

A deli-roasted chicken tops the list of convenience products for family meals. Here we jazz it up with Mexican flavors: salsa, cumin, and chile pepper cheese.

mexican chicken
casserole

prep: 15 minutes bake: 15 minutes oven: 350°F
makes: 4 servings dish: 10-ounce dishes

1 15-ounce can black beans, rinsed and drained
½ cup chunky salsa
½ teaspoon ground cumin
1 2- to 2¼-pound deli-roasted chicken
¼ cup shredded Monterey Jack cheese with jalapeño chile peppers (1 ounce)
Sour cream (optional)

1 Preheat oven to 350°F. In a small bowl stir together beans, ¼ cup of the salsa, and the cumin. Divide bean mixture among four ungreased 10-ounce au gratin dishes or casseroles.

2 Cut chicken into quarters. Place one piece on bean mixture in each dish. Spoon the remaining ¼ cup salsa evenly over chicken pieces. Sprinkle evenly with cheese.

3 Bake for 15 to 20 minutes or until heated through. If desired, serve with sour cream.

nutrition facts per serving: 468 cal., 23 g total fat (7 g sat. fat), 140 mg chol., 596 mg sodium, 16 g carb., 5 g dietary fiber, 50 g protein.

Busy week ahead? Stock these ingredients in your refrigerator and cupboards now, and you'll be less than half an hour away from an incredibly satisfying supper when you need it most. Pictured on page 318.

chicken-biscuit pie

prep: 15 minutes   bake: 12 minutes   oven: 425°F
makes: 4 servings   dish: 1½-quart

1   10.75-ounce can condensed cream of chicken soup
½   cup milk
¼   cup sour cream
1   cup cubed cooked chicken or turkey (5 ounces)
1½   cups frozen mixed vegetables
½   teaspoon dried basil, crushed
⅛   teaspoon ground black pepper
1   package refrigerated biscuits (5 or 6 biscuits), quartered

1 Preheat oven to 425°F. Lightly grease a 1½-quart casserole; set aside.

2 In a medium saucepan stir together soup, milk, and sour cream. Stir in chicken, mixed vegetables, basil, and pepper. Cook and stir over medium heat until boiling.

3 Spoon chicken mixture into prepared casserole. Top with quartered biscuits. Bake, uncovered, for 10 to 12 minutes or until biscuits are light brown.

nutrition facts per serving: 335 cal., 14 g total fat (5 g sat. fat), 49 mg chol., 1049 mg sodium, 33 g carb., 3 g dietary fiber, 20 g protein.

Leftover chicken gets a new life in these sumptuous pastry-topped pies. Give these a whimsical look, using a small rooster-shape cutter, or make simple slits in the top crust to allow steam to escape.

chicken **alfredo** potpies

prep: 25 minutes bake: 12 minutes oven: 450°F
makes: 4 servings dish: 10-ounce dishes

½ of a 15-ounce
  package rolled
  refrigerated
  unbaked piecrust
  (1 crust)
3 cups frozen vegetable
  blend
  (any combination)
3 cups cubed cooked
  chicken or turkey
1 10-ounce container
  refrigerated Alfredo
  pasta sauce
1 teaspoon dried
  thyme, marjoram, or
  sage, crushed
  Milk or water
  Snipped fresh thyme
  or marjoram sprigs
  (optional)

1 Let piecrust stand according to package directions. Preheat oven to 450°F. In a large skillet cook frozen vegetables in a small amount of boiling water for 5 minutes; drain. Return to skillet. Stir in chicken, Alfredo sauce, and dried thyme. Cook and stir until bubbly. Divide mixture among four ungreased 10-ounce individual casseroles or custard cups.

2 On a lightly floured surface, roll piecrust into a 13-inch circle. Cut four 5-inch circles. If desired, use a small cutter to cut out a shape in the centers for steam to escape. Place pastry circles on top of casseroles. Press edges of pastry firmly against sides of casseroles. Brush pastry with a little milk and top with pastry cutouts.

3 Place casseroles in a foil-lined shallow baking pan. Bake, uncovered, for 12 to 15 minutes or until mixture is heated through and pastry is golden. If desired, garnish with fresh thyme.

nutrition facts per serving: 709 cal., 41 g total fat (19 g sat. fat), 143 mg chol., 596 mg sodium, 45 g carb., 4 g dietary fiber, 38 g protein.

*test kitchen tip: Instead of cutting slits for steam to escape, use a small cookie cutter to cut shapes from pastry. Brush pastry with a little milk or water and top with pastry cutouts.

Turn to this casserole for a meal on a harried weeknight. You can even assemble it in the morning and refrigerate so it's ready to pop in the oven when you get home.

turkey-ravioli bake

prep: 10 minutes bake: 35 minutes stand: 10 minutes oven: 375°F
makes: 8 servings dish: 2-quart

1   6-ounce package
    baby spinach,
    chopped (about
    5 cups)
1   12-ounce package
    refrigerated cooked
    Italian-style
    turkey meatballs
    (12 meatballs),
    quartered
1   24- to 26-ounce jar
    marinara sauce
1   cup water
2   9-ounce packages
    refrigerated cheese-
    filled ravioli
2   cups shredded
    mozzarella cheese
    (8 ounces)

1 Preheat oven to 375°F. In an extra-large bowl stir together spinach, meatballs, marinara sauce, and the water.

2 Spread 2 cups of the spinach mixture in the bottom of an ungreased 2-quart rectangular baking dish. Top with one package of the uncooked ravioli. Spread another 2 cups of the spinach mixture over ravioli; sprinkle with 1 cup of the cheese. Top with the remaining uncooked ravioli, spinach mixture, and cheese.

3 Bake, covered, for 30 minutes. Bake, uncovered, for 5 to 10 minutes more or until heated through. Let stand for 10 minutes before serving.

nutrition facts per serving: 415 cal., 20 g total fat (10 g sat. fat), 104 mg chol., 1178 mg sodium, 36 g carb., 3 g dietary fiber, 26 g protein.

Pesto has come a long way in the convenience category! The Italian sauce used to be hand made with a mortar and pestle; today, ready-made versions are widely available, and they add an instant windfall of fresh flavor to everything they touch.

turkey-pesto potpies

prep: 15 minutes bake: 15 minutes oven: 375°F
makes: 6 servings dish: 8-ounce dishes

1   18-ounce jar turkey
    gravy
¼   cup purchased basil
    or dried tomato
    pesto
3   cups cubed cooked
    turkey (about
    1 pound)
1   16-ounce package
    loose-pack frozen
    peas and carrots
1   7-ounce package
    refrigerated
    breadsticks
    (6 breadsticks)
    Grated Parmesan
    cheese (optional)
    Dried basil (optional)

1 Preheat oven to 375°F. In a large saucepan combine turkey gravy and pesto; stir in the turkey and vegetables. Bring to boiling, stirring frequently. Divide turkey mixture evenly among six ungreased 8-ounce casseroles.

2 Unroll and separate breadsticks. Arrange one breadstick on top of each casserole, curling into a spiral to fit. If desired, sprinkle casseroles with cheese and basil.

3 Bake casseroles about 15 minutes or until breadsticks are golden.

nutrition facts per serving: 372 cal., 14 g total fat (2 g sat. fat), 59 mg chol., 988 mg sodium, 30 g carb., 3 g dietary fiber, 30 g protein.

If you grew up loving those saucy, delicious poultry-and-cheese casseroles—but find them too rich and heavy now—this is a light, modern version every bit as comforting.

turkey-potato bake

prep: 15 minutes   bake: 30 minutes   stand: 10 minutes
oven: 400°F   makes: 4 servings   dish: 2-quart

2¼   cups water
1   4.5- to 5-ounce package dried julienne potato mix
2   cups chopped cooked turkey or chicken breast (10 ounces)
1   cup shredded cheddar cheese (4 ounces)
1   teaspoon dried parsley flakes
⅔   cup milk

1 Preheat oven to 400°F. In a medium saucepan bring the water to boiling. Meanwhile, in an ungreased 2-quart square baking dish combine dried potatoes and sauce mix from potato mix. Stir in turkey, ½ cup of the cheese, and the parsley flakes. Stir in the boiling water and milk.

2 Bake, uncovered, for 30 to 35 minutes or until potatoes are tender. Sprinkle with the remaining ½ cup cheese. Let stand for 10 minutes before serving (mixture will thicken while standing).

nutrition facts per serving: 370 cal., 15 g total fat (8 g sat. fat), 87 mg chol., 1050 mg sodium, 27 g carb., 1 g dietary fiber, 32 g protein.

Focus on what's already in your fridge and pantry, and you'll be amazed at the possibilities for creating satisfying casseroles like this one.

catchall casserole

prep: 30 minutes **bake:** 25 minutes **oven:** 350°F
makes: 4 servings **dish:** 2-quart

1 cup water
½ cup long grain rice
2 tablespoons vegetable oil
1 pound boneless meat (such as chicken, turkey, beef, or pork), cut into 1-inch cubes, or ground meat (such as beef, pork, turkey, or sausage)
4 cups cut-up vegetables (such as chopped zucchini or yellow summer squash, small broccoli or cauliflower florets, chopped carrot, celery, onion, cut green beans, chopped potatoes, sliced mushrooms, and/or chopped sweet peppers
1 10.75-ounce can condensed soup (such as cream of chicken or cream of mushroom)
⅔ cup milk or water
½ teaspoon dried herb (such as Italian seasoning, basil, or oregano), crushed, or ¼ teaspoon dried thyme, crushed
1½ cups packaged corn bread stuffing mix, coarsely crushed
3 tablespoons butter, melted

1 In a small saucepan bring the 1 cup water to boiling. Add rice; reduce heat. Cover and simmer for 20 minutes or until liquid is absorbed; set aside.

2 Preheat oven to 350°F. In an extra-large skillet heat 1 tablespoon of the oil over medium-high heat. Add meat; cook and stir for 3 to 5 minutes or until brown and cooked through. If necessary, drain off fat. Remove meat from skillet.

3 Add the remaining 1 tablespoon oil to the skillet. Add vegetables. Cook and stir for 3 to 4 minutes or until crisp-tender. Stir in cooked meat, cooked rice, soup, milk, and herb; heat through. Spoon hot mixture into an ungreased 2-quart casserole.

4 In a medium bowl combine stuffing mix and butter. Sprinkle stuffing mix mixture over meat-vegetable mixture. Bake, uncovered, about 25 minutes or until casserole is bubbly and topping is golden.

nutrition facts per serving: 553 cal., 27 g total fat (9 g sat. fat), 111 mg chol., 1155 mg sodium, 44 g carb., 2 g dietary fiber, 33 g protein.

Smoked cheddar cheese combines with cheddar soup to give extra flavor and richness to this meatless dish.

gardener's pie

prep: 15 minutes   bake: 45 minutes   oven: 350°F
makes: 4 servings   dish: 1½-quart

1   16-ounce package frozen mixed vegetables (any combination), thawed
1   11-ounce can condensed cheddar cheese soup
½   teaspoon dried thyme, crushed
1   16-ounce package refrigerated mashed potatoes
1   cup shredded smoked cheddar cheese (4 ounces)

1 Preheat oven to 350°F. In an ungreased 1½-quart casserole combine vegetables, soup, and thyme. Stir mashed potatoes to soften. Carefully spread mashed potatoes over vegetable mixture to cover surface.

2 Bake, covered, for 30 minutes. Bake, uncovered, about 15 minutes more or until heated through, topping with cheese during the last 5 minutes of baking. Serve in shallow bowls.

nutrition facts per serving: 308 cal., 17 g total fat (8 g sat. fat), 38 mg chol., 872 mg sodium, 31 g carb., 3 g dietary fiber, 14 g protein.

Mayo-inspired snap, sweet red pepper flavor, and a buttery crumb topping transform this dish from standby to standout.

tuna-macaroni casserole

prep: 25 minutes bake: 40 minutes oven: 350°F
makes: 4 servings dish: 1½-quart

4 ounces dried small shell macaroni (1 cup)

1 10.75-ounce can condensed cream of onion soup

⅓ cup milk

¼ cup mayonnaise or salad dressing

½ teaspoon dry mustard

1 6-ounce can tuna, drained and flaked

1 cup shredded American or cheddar cheese (4 ounces)

½ cup chopped bottled roasted red sweet peppers

¼ cup fine dry bread crumbs

1 tablespoon butter or margarine, melted

½ teaspoon paprika
Snipped fresh parsley (optional)

1 Cook macaroni according to package directions; drain.

2 Meanwhile, preheat oven to 350°F. In a large bowl stir together soup, milk, mayonnaise, and mustard. Stir in tuna, cheese, and roasted sweet peppers. Gently fold in cooked macaroni. Spoon into an ungreased 1½-quart casserole.

3 In a small bowl combine bread crumbs, melted butter, and paprika; sprinkle evenly over casserole.

4 Bake, uncovered, for 40 to 45 minutes or until heated through. If desired, sprinkle with parsley.

nutrition facts per serving: 498 cal., 29 g total fat (11 g sat. fat), 72 mg chol., 1394 mg sodium, 36 g carb., 2 g dietary fiber, 23 g protein.

Feta cheese, black olives, and balsamic vinaigrette bring bold flavors to this baked pasta recipe.

rotini bake

prep: 30 minutes   bake: 35 minutes   stand: 10 minutes
oven: 375°F   makes: 8 servings   dish: 3-quart

12   ounces dried rotini pasta

½   cup bottled balsamic vinaigrette

1   15-ounce can white kidney (cannellini) or garbanzo beans (chickpeas), rinsed and drained

8   ounces feta cheese, crumbled

1   cup coarsely chopped pitted Greek black olives

1   pound roma tomatoes, coarsely chopped

½   cup seasoned fine dry bread crumbs

1   8-ounce carton plain low-fat yogurt

¾   cup milk

⅓   cup grated Parmesan cheese

1   tablespoon all-purpose flour

1 Preheat oven to 375°F. Lightly grease a 3-quart rectangular baking dish; set aside. Cook pasta according to package directions. Drain. In a very large bowl combine vinaigrette and pasta; toss to coat. Stir in beans, feta cheese, olives, and tomatoes.

2 Sprinkle ¼ cup of the bread crumbs in prepared dish. Spoon pasta mixture into dish. In a medium bowl stir together yogurt, milk, Parmesan cheese, and flour until smooth. Pour evenly over pasta mixture. Sprinkle with the remaining ¼ cup bread crumbs.

3 Bake, covered, for 25 minutes. Uncover and bake 10 to 15 minutes more until heated through and top is lightly browned. Let stand 10 minutes before serving.

nutrition facts per serving: 425 cal., 15 g total fat (6 g sat. fat), 31 mg chol., 1045 mg sodium, 57 g carb., 6 g dietary fiber, 19 g protein.

The Mediterranean region is known for its full-flavored, satisfying dishes—with or without meat—and this meatless pasta and bean bake doesn't disappoint.

greek pasta casserole

prep: 25 minutes bake: 20 minutes stand: 10 minutes oven: 375°F
makes: 6 servings dish: 3-quart

12 ounces dried rotini pasta (3½ cups)

1 15-ounce can tomato sauce

1 10.75-ounce can condensed tomato soup

1 15-ounce can white kidney (cannellini) or garbanzo beans (chickpeas), rinsed and drained

2 cups crumbled feta cheese (8 ounces)

1 cup coarsely chopped pitted Greek black olives

½ cup seasoned fine dry bread crumbs

2 tablespoons butter, melted

2 tablespoons grated Parmesan cheese

1 Preheat oven to 375°F. Cook pasta according to package directions; drain. Lightly grease a 3-quart rectangular baking dish.

2 In a very large bowl combine cooked pasta, tomato sauce, and soup; toss to coat. Stir in beans, feta cheese, and olives. Spoon pasta mixture into prepared baking dish. In a small bowl combine bread crumbs, melted butter, and Parmesan cheese; sprinkle over pasta mixture.

3 Bake, uncovered, for 20 to 25 minutes or until heated through and top is light brown. Let stand for 10 minutes before serving.

nutrition facts per serving: 553 cal., 19 g total fat (10 g sat. fat), 52 mg chol., 1890 mg sodium, 74 g carb., 7 g dietary fiber, 24 g protein.

You can use cavatelli, gnocchi, or campanelle pasta instead of the elbow macaroni called for in this hearty version of macaroni and cheese.

creamy **macaroni** and **cheese**

prep: 20 minutes bake: 30 minutes stand: 10 minutes
oven: 350°F makes: 6 servings dish: 1½-quart

4	slices bacon
1	large onion, thinly sliced
6	ounces dried elbow macaroni (2 cups)
8	ounces mozzarella cheese, shredded (2 cups)
2	to 4 ounces blue cheese, crumbled (½ to 1 cup)
1	cup half-and-half or light cream
⅛	teaspoon ground black pepper

1 Preheat oven to 350°F. In a large skillet cook bacon over medium heat until crisp, turning once. Drain bacon on paper towels; crumble. Reserve bacon drippings in skillet.

2 Cook onion in reserved bacon drippings for 5 to 8 minutes or until onion is tender and golden brown.

3 Cook elbow macaroni according to package directions. Drain and place in an ungreased 1½-quart casserole dish. Add crumbled bacon, onion, 1½ cups of the mozzarella cheese, the blue cheese, half-and-half, and pepper. Toss gently to combine.

4 Bake, uncovered, for 20 minutes. Stir gently. Top with the remaining mozzarella cheese. Bake about 10 minutes more or until top of casserole is brown and bubbly. Let stand for 10 minutes before serving.

nutrition facts per serving: 331 cal., 18 g total fat (9 g sat. fat), 45 mg chol., 280 mg sodium, 26 g carb., 1 g dietary fiber, 16 g protein.

Give mac and cheese a stylish update with cottage cheese for creaminess and feta cheese for robust flavor.

two-cheese
macaroni bake

prep: 20 minutes   bake: 45 minutes   stand: 10 minutes
oven: 375°F   makes: 8 servings   dish: 2-quart

2	cups dried elbow macaroni (8 ounces)
4	eggs
2½	cups milk
8	ounces feta cheese with basil and tomato or plain feta cheese, crumbled
¾	cup cream-style cottage cheese
½	teaspoon salt

1 Preheat oven to 375°F. Cook macaroni according to package directions; drain well.

2 Place macaroni in a greased 2-quart square baking dish. In a medium bowl lightly beat eggs with a fork; stir in milk, feta cheese, cottage cheese, and salt. Pour over macaroni in dish.

3 Bake, uncovered, for 45 minutes. Let stand for 10 minutes before serving.

nutrition facts per serving: 267 cal., 11 g total fat (6 g sat. fat), 136 mg chol., 609 mg sodium, 26 g carb., 1 g dietary fiber, 17 g protein.

Simple Ways to Jazz Up a Macaroni Bake

- *Pesto: Stir in a spoonful of purchased pesto. Before baking, top with bread crumb topper.*

- *Veggie: Add fresh broccoli florets and/or thinly sliced carrots to pasta water during the last 5 minutes of cooking.*

- *Chicken or Tuna: Add shredded deli roasted chicken or canned tuna to pasta mixture.*

Here's a pantry casserole that fits the bill on a Sunday night. A little festive, a lot easy, a family favorite.

chipotle-bean enchiladas

prep: 25 minutes   bake: 30 minutes   oven: 350°F
makes: 5 servings   dish: 2-quart

10   6-inch corn tortillas
2   10-ounce cans
      enchilada sauce
2   cups shredded
      Mexican cheese
      blend (8 ounces)
1   15-ounce can pinto or
      black beans, rinsed
      and drained
1   tablespoon chopped
      canned chipotle
      chile pepper in
      adobo sauce

1 Preheat oven to 350°F. Stack tortillas and wrap tightly in foil. Bake about 10 minutes or until warm.

2 Meanwhile, grease a 2-quart rectangular baking dish; set aside. For filling, in a medium bowl combine ½ cup of the enchilada sauce, 1 cup of the cheese, the beans, and chipotle pepper. Spoon about ¼ cup of the filling onto one edge of each tortilla. Starting at the edge with the filling, roll up tortilla. Arrange tortillas, seam sides down, in the prepared baking dish. Top with the remaining enchilada sauce.

3 Bake, covered, about 25 minutes or until heated through. Sprinkle with the remaining 1 cup cheese. Bake, uncovered, about 5 minutes more or until cheese is melted.

nutrition facts per serving: 487 cal., 19 g total fat (8 g sat. fat), 40 mg chol., 1091 mg sodium, 63 g carb., 14 g dietary fiber, 23 g protein.

Vary this vegetable-and-rice main dish according to your family's preferences and what you have on hand. Use any color sweet pepper, any variety of pasta sauce, or another Italian-style cheese, such as provolone.

couscous-stuffed peppers

prep: 15 minutes bake: 25 minutes oven: 350°F
makes: 4 servings dish: 2-quart

1	6-ounce package toasted pine nut couscous mix
½	cup shredded carrot (1 medium)
2	large or 4 small red, yellow, green, or orange sweet peppers
½	cup shredded Italian cheese blend (2 ounces)
1½	cups mushroom and olive or tomato-basil pasta sauce

1 Preheat oven to 350°F. Prepare couscous mix according to package directions, omitting oil and adding the shredded carrot with the couscous.

2 Meanwhile, cut large peppers in half lengthwise (for small peppers, cut off tops and reserve). Remove seeds and membranes from peppers. Cook peppers (and tops, if using) in boiling water for 5 minutes. Drain on paper towels. Place peppers, cut sides up, in a 2-quart rectangular baking dish. Spoon cooked couscous mixture into peppers.

3 Bake, covered, for 20 to 25 minutes or until filling is heated through and peppers are tender. Sprinkle cheese over peppers. Bake, uncovered, about 5 minutes more or until cheese is melted.

4 Meanwhile, in a small saucepan heat the pasta sauce. Serve peppers with sauce. (For small peppers, place pepper tops on top of couscous filling.)

nutrition facts per serving: 259 cal., 6 g total fat (3 g sat. fat), 10 mg chol., 801 mg sodium, 42 g carb., 7 g dietary fiber, 11 g protein.

13

one-dish

On weekends and holidays when there's a houseful of guests, share these easy early morning risers, including stratas, French toast casseroles, and savory egg bakes. You'll even find that the do-ahead dishes develop wonderful flavor and texture while sitting overnight in the fridge.

brea

kfasts

Bacon, asparagus, roasted red sweet peppers, and Swiss cheese update this classic breakfast casserole.

bacon-asparagus strata

prep: 45 minutes   chill: 2 to 24 hours   bake: 50 minutes   stand: 10 minutes
oven: 325°F   makes: 12 servings   dish: 3-quart

Nonstick cooking spray
8   slices bacon, crisp-cooked, drained, and chopped
1   9-ounce package frozen cut asparagus, thawed and well drained
¾   cup bottled roasted red sweet peppers, drained and chopped
12 slices dry white bread, cut into ½-inch cubes (about 8 cups)
3   cups shredded Swiss cheese (12 ounces)
8   eggs
3   cups milk
1½ teaspoons dry mustard or 3 tablespoons Dijon mustard
½   teaspoon salt
¼   teaspoon cayenne pepper

1 Lightly coat a 3-quart rectangular baking dish with cooking spray; set aside. In a medium bowl combine bacon, asparagus, and sweet peppers.

2 Place half of the bread cubes in the prepared baking dish. Top with half of the bacon mixture and half of the cheese. Repeat layers with the remaining bread cubes, bacon mixture, and cheese.

3 In a large bowl beat eggs with a rotary beater or whisk. Beat or whisk in milk, mustard, salt, and cayenne. Carefully pour egg mixture evenly over bread mixture in dish. Using the back of a spoon, gently press down on layers to moisten all of the bread. Cover dish with plastic wrap and chill at least 2 to 24 hours.

4 Preheat oven to 325°F. Bake, uncovered, for 50 to 60 minutes or until puffed, golden, and set. Let stand for 10 minutes before serving.

nutrition facts per serving: 365 cal., 22 g total fat (10 g sat. fat), 197 mg chol., 965 mg sodium, 19 g carb., 1 g dietary fiber, 21 g protein.

pork, pepper, and mushroom strata: Prepare as directed, except replace bacon with 1 pound bulk pork or Italian sausage and replace asparagus with 2 cups sliced fresh mushrooms. Cook sausage and mushrooms in a large skillet until sausage is brown; drain off fat. Stir red peppers into mixture in skillet. Use 3 cups shredded American or cheddar cheese in place of the Swiss cheese.

This homey breakfast-style dish is delicious for supper, too. Whip it up in the morning, refrigerate during the day, and pop it in the oven when you get home. Then, relax before dinner!

farmer's casserole

prep: 25 minutes bake: 40 minutes stand: 5 minutes oven: 350°F
makes: 6 servings dish: 2-quart

Nonstick cooking
  spray
3 cups frozen shredded
  hash brown
  potatoes
¾ cup shredded
  Monterey Jack
  cheese with
  jalapeño chile
  peppers or
  shredded cheddar
  cheese (3 ounces)
1 cup diced cooked
  ham, cooked
  breakfast sausage,
  or Canadian-style
  bacon
¼ cup sliced
  scallions (2)
4 eggs, beaten, or
  1 cup refrigerated
  or frozen egg
  product, thawed
1½ cups milk or one
  12-ounce can
  evaporated milk
  or evaporated
  fat-free milk
⅛ teaspoon salt
⅛ teaspoon ground
  black pepper

1 Preheat oven to 350°F. Coat a 2-quart square baking dish with nonstick cooking spray. Arrange hash brown potatoes evenly in the dish. Sprinkle with cheese, ham, and scallions.

2 In a medium bowl combine eggs, milk, salt, and pepper. Pour egg mixture over layers in dish.

3 Bake, uncovered, for 40 to 45 minutes or until a knife inserted near the center comes out clean. Let stand for 5 minutes before serving.

nutrition facts per serving: 263 cal., 12 g total fat (6 g sat. fat), 175 mg chol., 589 mg sodium, 22 g carb., 2 g dietary fiber, 17 g protein.

make-ahead directions: Prepare as directed through Step 2. Cover and chill for up to 24 hours. Bake, uncovered, in a 350°F oven for 50 to 55 minutes or until a knife inserted near the center comes out clean. Let stand 5 minutes before serving.

This do-ahead dish develops wonderful flavor and texture as it sits overnight in the fridge. Even better, you can sleep in because the prep work is already done.

spicy brunch
lasagna

prep: 40 minutes   chill: 8 to 24 hours   bake: 1 hour   stand: 35 minutes
oven: 350°F   makes: 16 servings   dish: 3-quart

1½	pounds bulk Italian sausage
1	24-ounce carton cottage cheese
½	cup finely chopped scallions (4)
¼	cup snipped fresh chives
¼	cup finely shredded carrot
18	eggs
⅓	cup milk
½	teaspoon salt
½	teaspoon ground black pepper
2	tablespoons butter
1	14-ounce jar purchased Alfredo sauce
1	teaspoon dried Italian seasoning, crushed
8	oven-ready lasagna noodles
4	cups frozen shredded hash browns, thawed
2	cups shredded mozzarella cheese (8 ounces)

1 In a large skillet cook sausage until browned. Drain off fat; set aside. Meanwhile, in a medium bowl combine cottage cheese, scallions, chives, and carrot; set aside.

2 In a very large bowl whisk together eggs, milk, salt, and pepper. In a large skillet melt butter over medium heat; pour in egg mixture. Cook over medium heat, without stirring, until mixture begins to set on the bottom and around the edges. Lift and fold the partially cooked egg mixture so that the uncooked portion flows underneath. Continue cooking over medium heat for 2 to 3 minutes or until egg mixture is cooked through but is still glossy and moist. Immediately remove from heat.

3 In a small bowl combine the Alfredo sauce and Italian seasoning. Spread about ½ cup of the sauce mixture over the bottom of an ungreased 3-quart rectangular baking dish. Layer half of the lasagna noodles in the dish, overlapping as necessary. Top with half of the remaining sauce, half of the cottage cheese mixture, half of the hash browns, half of the scrambled egg mixture, and half of the sausage mixture. Sprinkle with half of the cheese. Repeat layers.

4 Cover dish tightly with plastic wrap. Refrigerate for 8 hours or overnight.

5 Remove from refrigerator and let stand at room temperature for 30 minutes before baking. Preheat oven to 350°F. Remove plastic wrap and cover dish with foil. Bake for 45 minutes. Remove foil and bake 15 minutes more or until heated through. Let stand for 5 minutes before cutting into portions.

nutrition facts per serving: 455 cal., 30 g total fat (13 g sat. fat), 312 mg chol., 900 mg sodium, 20 g carb., 1 g dietary fiber, 26 g protein.

This casserole is like a gigantic too-good-to-be-true bacon, egg, and cheese breakfast sandwich. Mix it up by replacing the bacon with crumbled pork sausage.

egg and **bacon** breakfast casserole

prep: 25 minutes chill: 2 to 24 hours bake: 50 minutes stand: 10 minutes
oven: 325°F makes: 6 to 8 servings dish: 2-quart

1 pound bacon, coarsely chopped, or bulk pork sausage
2 tablespoons butter, softened
6 1-inch thick-slices French bread
1 cup shredded Colby and Monterey Jack cheese or American cheese (4 ounces)
6 eggs, lightly beaten
1½ cups whipping cream, half-and-half, light cream, or whole milk
¾ to 1 teaspoon dry mustard
½ teaspoon salt
¼ teaspoon ground black pepper

1 In a large skillet cook bacon over medium-low heat until crisp; drain on paper towels. (If using sausage, cook over medium heat until brown; drain fat.)

2 Meanwhile, butter bread slices on one side. Cut into 1-inch cubes. Place half the bread cubes in a greased 2-quart square baking dish. Top with half the bacon. Top with the remaining bread cubes and remaining bacon; sprinkle with cheese (dish will be full).

3 In a medium bowl whisk together eggs, whipping cream, mustard, salt, and black pepper. Pour evenly over layers in dish. Cover and chill in the refrigerator for 2 to 24 hours.

4 Preheat oven to 325°F. Bake, uncovered, for 50 to 55 minutes or until center is set (170°F). Let stand for 10 minutes before serving.

nutrition facts per serving: 572 cal., 41 g total fat (21 g sat. fat), 267 mg chol., 984 mg sodium, 22 g carb., 2 g dietary fiber, 19 g protein.

This breakfast pie is a delight for a Sunday brunch with a few guests. It's versatile too. Instead of bacon and Swiss cheese, try diced cooked ham or sautéed sliced mushrooms and Gruyère cheese and toss the crumbs with butter.

sunday breakfast pie

prep: 20 minutes   chill: 2 to 24 hours   bake: 50 minutes   oven: 325°F
makes: 6 to 8 servings   dish: 9-inch pie plate

8	slices bacon
½	cup panko (Japanese-style bread crumbs)
5	eggs
2½	cups frozen shredded hash brown potatoes
1	cup shredded Swiss cheese (4 ounces)
½	cup cottage cheese
⅓	cup milk
¼	cup chopped scallions (2)
½	teaspoon salt
¼	teaspoon ground black pepper
4	drops bottled hot pepper sauce

1 In a large skillet cook bacon over medium heat until crisp. Drain bacon on paper towels, reserving 1 tablespoon drippings in skillet. Crumble bacon. Stir bread crumbs into the reserved drippings. Transfer to a small bowl; cover and chill until needed.

2 Lightly grease a 9-inch pie plate; set aside. In a medium bowl beat eggs with a fork until foamy. Stir in bacon, potatoes, Swiss cheese, cottage cheese, milk, scallions, salt, pepper, and hot pepper sauce. Pour mixture into prepared pie plate. Cover and chill for 2 to 24 hours.

3 Preheat oven to 325°F. Sprinkle pie with bread crumb mixture. Bake, uncovered, about 50 minutes or until a knife inserted in the center comes out clean. Cut into six or eight wedges.

nutrition facts per serving: 324 cal., 17 g total fat (7 g sat. fat), 210 mg chol., 640 mg sodium, 22 g carb., 2 g dietary fiber, 20 g protein.

Although chiles rellenos are a south-of-the-border classic, we gave this version a north-of-the-border twist by turning it into a casserole. It features poblano peppers, which are either red or dark green in color and vary in strength from medium to hot.

chile rellenos casserole

prep: 20 minutes bake: 15 minutes stand: 5 minutes oven: 450°F
makes: 4 servings dish: 2-quart

2 large fresh poblano
  or Anaheim chile
  peppers (8 ounces)
1½ cups Monterey
  Jack cheese with
  jalapeño peppers,
  shredded, or
  shredded Mexican
  cheese blend
  (6 ounces)
3 eggs, lightly beaten
¼ cup milk
⅓ cup all-purpose flour
½ teaspoon baking
  powder
¼ teaspoon cayenne
  pepper
⅛ teaspoon salt
  Bottled salsa
    (optional)
  Sour cream (optional)

1 Preheat oven to 450°F. Grease a 2-quart square baking dish; set aside. Quarter the peppers and remove seeds, stems, and veins (see handling tip, page 80). Immerse peppers into boiling water for 3 minutes; drain. Invert peppers onto paper towels to drain well. Place the peppers in prepared baking dish. Top with 1 cup of the cheese.

2 In a medium bowl combine eggs and milk. Add flour, baking powder, cayenne, and salt. Beat until smooth with a rotary beater (or place in a food processor or blender; cover and process or blend until smooth). Pour egg mixture over peppers and cheese.

3 Bake, uncovered, about 15 minutes or until a knife inserted into the egg mixture comes out clean. Sprinkle with the remaining ½ cup cheese. Let stand about 5 minutes or until cheese is melted. If desired, serve with salsa and sour cream.

nutrition facts per serving: 296 cal., 18 g total fat (10 g sat. fat), 205 mg chol., 450 mg sodium, 16 g carb., 1 g dietary fiber, 18 g protein.

This overnight casserole is very versatile and can be made to suit the tastes of your guests. While apple and raisins add unexpected flavors, you may also want to try another cheese, such as Swiss or Gruyère.

ham and cheese strata

prep: 30 minutes   chill: 2 to 24 hours   bake: 55 minutes   oven: 350°F
makes: 8 servings   dish: 3-quart

12   ½-inch slices
    cinnamon-raisin
    bread
6   slices cheddar cheese
    (about 6 ounces)
1   large red or green
    apple, cored and
    thinly sliced
9   ounces thinly sliced
    ham
6   tablespoons butter,
    softened
⅓   cup finely chopped
    onion
3   cups milk
6   eggs
1   tablespoon Dijon
    mustard
1   teaspoon
    Worcestershire
    sauce
¼   teaspoon ground
    black pepper

1 Top 6 bread slices with cheese, apple slices, and ham. Top with the remaining bread slices. Spread outsides of sandwiches with butter. Quarter each sandwich diagonally to form four triangles. Arrange triangles, point sides up, in a buttered 3-quart rectangular baking dish. Sprinkle with onion; set aside.

2 In a large bowl whisk together milk, eggs, mustard, Worcestershire sauce, and pepper. Carefully pour over triangles in dish. Cover chill at least 2 hours or up to 24 hours.

3 Preheat oven to 350°F. Bake, covered, for 25 minutes. Uncover. Bake about 30 minutes more or until a knife inserted near the center comes out clean. Let stand for 10 minutes before serving.

nutrition facts per serving: 483 cal., 26 g total fat (14 g sat. fat), 237 mg chol., 945 mg sodium, 38 g carb., 3 g dietary fiber, 23 g protein.

An old favorite, the Denver omelet, is revitalized in this trendy one-dish meal. Complete with veggies, cheese, meat, and eggs, this new version adds English muffins to the mix to create a complete and convenient breakfast dish.

weekend **denver** strata

prep: 25 minutes bake: 35 minutes stand: 10 minutes oven: 350°F
makes: 10 to 12 servings dish: 3-quart

6   English muffins, split
     and quartered
9   eggs
1   cup milk
1   4.5-ounce can diced
     green chile peppers,
     drained
¼   teaspoon salt
¼   teaspoon ground
     black pepper
1   cup diced cooked ham
     (about 5 ounces)
4   scallions, finely
     chopped (½ cup)
1   2.5-ounce can sliced
     pitted black olives,
     drained
1   7-ounce jar roasted
     red sweet peppers,
     drained and cut into
     strips
1½ cups shredded
     provolone cheese
     (6 ounces)
½   cup shredded
     cheddar cheese
     (2 ounces)

1 Preheat oven to 350°F. Arrange English muffin quarters in a single layer in a greased 3-quart rectangular baking dish.

2 In a large bowl beat together eggs, milk, chile peppers, salt, and black pepper with a rotary beater or whisk until well mixed. Pour egg mixture over muffin quarters; sprinkle with ham, scallions, and olives. Top with roasted sweet peppers, provolone cheese, and cheddar cheese.

3 Bake, uncovered, about 35 minutes or until a knife inserted near the center comes out clean. Let stand for 10 minutes before serving.

nutrition facts per serving: 279 cal., 14 g total fat (6 g sat. fat), 218 mg chol., 744 mg sodium, 20 g carb., 2 g dietary fiber, 18 g protein.

make-ahead directions: Prepare as directed through Step 2; cover with plastic wrap and chill for up to 24 hours. Uncover dish; discard plastic wrap. Cover dish with foil. Bake, uncovered, in 350°F oven about 45 minutes.

Blintzes are a Jewish-American favorite. This one-dish wonder makes preparing them easy by combining all the classic ingredients—cream cheese, sour cream, cottage cheese, and fruit flavoring—into easy-pour layers.

orange blintz casserole

prep: 25 minutes cool: 30 minutes bake: 45 minutes oven: 350°F
makes: 12 to 15 servings dish: 3-quart

6 eggs
2 egg whites
1½ cups sour cream
2 teaspoons finely shredded orange zest
½ cup orange juice
¼ cup butter, softened
1 cup all-purpose flour
½ cup sugar
2 teaspoons baking powder
2 cups cream-style cottage cheese
1 8-ounce package cream cheese, softened
2 egg yolks
2 tablespoons sugar
2 teaspoons vanilla
½ cup orange marmalade, melted

1 Preheat oven to 350°F. Grease a 3-quart rectangular baking dish; set aside. For batter, in a blender or food processor combine eggs, egg whites, sour cream, orange zest, orange juice, and butter. Cover; blend or process until smooth. Add flour, sugar, and baking powder. Cover; blend or process until smooth. Transfer to a medium bowl; set aside. Rinse blender or food processor.

2 For filling, in the blender or food processor combine cottage cheese, cream cheese, egg yolks, sugar, and vanilla. Cover; blend or process until smooth.

3 Pour about 2 cups of the batter into prepared dish. Spoon filling evenly over batter in dish. Using a table knife, swirl filling into batter. Pour the remaining batter evenly over mixture in dish.

4 Bake, uncovered, about 45 minutes or until puffed and lightly golden brown. Cool on a wire rack for 30 minutes before serving (edges may fall during cooling). Drizzle with melted marmalade.

nutrition facts per serving: 357 cal., 21 g total fat (12 g sat. fat), 221 mg chol., 325 mg sodium, 30 g carb., 0 g dietary fiber, 12 g protein.

Kicky Mexican-style eggs cook in a baking dish, perfect for serving at a buffet. The scent of cumin, garlic, and chili powder plus fresh cilantro lets you know what deliciousness lies ahead for your palate.

easy huevos rancheros
casserole

prep: 15 minutes bake: 38 minutes stand: 10 minutes oven: 375°F
makes: 12 servings dish: 3-quart

Nonstick cooking
   spray
1 32-ounce package
   frozen fried potato
   nuggets
12 eggs
1 cup milk
1½ teaspoons dried
   oregano, crushed
1½ teaspoons ground
   cumin
½ teaspoon chili
   powder
¼ teaspoon garlic
   powder
2 cups shredded
   Mexican cheese
   blend (8 ounces)
1 16-ounce jar thick
   and chunky salsa
   Snipped fresh cilantro
1 8-ounce carton sour
   cream

1 Preheat oven to 375°F. Lightly coat a 3-quart rectangular baking dish with nonstick cooking spray. Arrange potato nuggets in dish.

2 In a large mixing bowl combine eggs, milk, oregano, cumin, chili powder, and garlic powder. Beat with a rotary beater or wire whisk until combined. Pour egg mixture over potato nuggets.

3 Bake, uncovered, for 35 to 40 minutes or until a knife inserted near center comes out clean. Sprinkle cheese evenly over egg mixture. Bake about 3 minutes more or until cheese is melted. Let stand for 10 minutes before serving. Top with salsa and cilantro; serve with sour cream.

nutrition facts per serving: 335 cal., 21 g total fat (9 g sat. fat), 240 mg chol., 828 mg sodium, 25 g carb., 2 g dietary fiber, 14 g protein.

A crisp, savory cornflake crust tops this dish. For ease, crush the cornflakes in a resealable plastic bag.

cheesy hash brown
casserole

prep: 15 minutes   bake: 50 minutes   oven: 350°F
makes: 8 to 10 servings   dish: 3-quart

1   16-ounce carton sour
    cream
1   10.75-ounce can
    condensed cream
    of chicken soup
1   32-ounce package
    frozen loose-
    pack hash brown
    potatoes
2   cups cubed cooked
    ham
8   ounces cubed
    American cheese
¼   cup chopped onion
    (optional)
2   cups crushed
    cornflakes
½   cup butter or
    margarine, melted
1   cup shredded
    mozzarella cheese
    (4 ounces)

1 Preheat oven to 350°F. In a large mixing bowl combine sour cream and soup. Stir in the frozen potatoes, ham, American cheese, and onion (if using). Transfer to an ungreased 3-quart rectangular baking dish, spreading mixture evenly.

2 Combine cornflakes and butter. Sprinkle over potato mixture. Bake, uncovered, for 30 minutes. Sprinkle with mozzarella cheese. Return to oven and bake for 20 to 25 minutes more or until bubbly around the edges and heated through.

nutrition facts per serving: 382 cal., 24 g total fat (13 g sat. fat), 64 mg chol., 998 mg sodium, 30 g carb., 1 g dietary fiber, 13 g protein.

make-ahead directions: Prepare as directed in Step 1, except do not preheat oven. Cover and chill for at least 8 hours or up to 24 hours. To serve, continue as directed in Step 2, except bake in a 350°F oven for 50 to 55 minutes or until hot and bubbly.

Nothing enhances egg dishes more than fresh dill, and when you use the herb here, it makes this dish worthy of a special family gathering.

zucchini-brie
breakfast casseroles

prep: 45 minutes chill: 4 to 24 hours bake: 45 minutes stand: 10 minutes
oven: 325°F makes: 6 servings dish: 8-ounce dishes

2 small zucchini and/
or yellow summer
squash, cut
crosswise into
¼-inch slices
(about 2 cups)
Nonstick cooking
spray

4 cups crusty
sourdough bread
cubes (½-inch
cubes; about
8 ounces)

1 4.5-ounce package
Brie cheese, cut into
½-inch cubes

4 eggs, beaten, or
1 cup refrigerated
or frozen egg
product, thawed

⅔ cup evaporated
fat-free milk

⅓ cup sliced scallion

2 tablespoons snipped
fresh dill

¼ teaspoon salt

⅛ teaspoon ground
black pepper
Fresh dill sprigs
(optional)

1 In a medium saucepan cook zucchini, covered, in a small amount of boiling water for 2 to 3 minutes or just until tender. Drain zucchini.

2 Meanwhile, coat six 8- to 10-ounce individual casseroles or ramekins with cooking spray. In a large bowl toss together bread cubes, cheese cubes, and zucchini. Divide equally among prepared casseroles.

3 In a medium bowl combine eggs, milk, scallion, 2 tablespoons dill, salt, and pepper. Pour evenly over mixture in casseroles. Using the back of a large spoon, press bread and cheese pieces down to moisten. Cover with plastic wrap; chill for 4 to 24 hours.

4 Preheat oven to 325°F. Remove plastic wrap; cover casseroles with foil. Bake for 20 minutes. Uncover and bake 25 to 30 minutes more or until a knife inserted near the centers comes out clean. Let stand for 10 minutes before serving. If desired, garnish with fresh dill sprigs.

nutrition facts per serving: 259 cal., 10 g total fat (5 g sat. fat), 163 mg chol., 561 mg sodium, 27 g carb., 2 g dietary fiber, 16 g protein.

Salmon that is cured before it is smoked at low temperatures results in a firm, sliceable fish called lox. Salmon smoked at higher temperatures flakes easily. Both types of smoked salmon work in this strata.

bagel-lox strata

prep: 30 minutes chill: 4 to 24 hours bake: 45 minutes stand: 10 minutes
oven: 350°F makes: 12 servings dish: 3-quart

4 to 6 plain bagels, cut
   into bite-size pieces
   (8 cups)
2 3-ounce packages
   cream cheese, cut
   into ½-inch pieces
1 3-ounce package
   thinly sliced
   smoked salmon
   (lox-style), cut into
   small pieces
¼ cup finely chopped
   red onion
4 teaspoons dried
   chives
8 eggs, lightly beaten
2 cups milk
1 cup cream-style
   cottage cheese
1 tablespoon snipped
   fresh dill or
   ½ teaspoon
   dried dill
¼ teaspoon ground
   black pepper

1 Lightly grease a 3-quart rectangular baking dish. Arrange half of the bagel pieces in the prepared baking dish. Top with cream cheese, salmon, onion, and chives. Arrange the remaining bagel pieces over salmon mixture.

2 In a medium bowl combine eggs, milk, cottage cheese, dill, and pepper. Pour evenly over ingredients in dish. Using a rubber spatula or the back of a large spoon, lightly press down all of the bagel pieces to moisten. Cover with plastic wrap and chill for 4 to 24 hours.

3 Preheat oven to 350°F. Bake, uncovered, for 45 to 50 minutes or until a knife inserted near the center comes out clean and the edges are puffed and golden. Let stand for 10 minutes before serving.

nutrition facts per serving: 204 cal., 10 g total fat (5 g sat. fat), 164 mg chol., 420 mg sodium, 16 g carb., 1 g dietary fiber, 12 g protein.

This is a good all-purpose brunch casserole that's easy to make and will appeal to everyone. Use crusty bread for a firm baked custard or soft bread for a lighter, soufflé-like texture.

overnight egg and sausage strata

prep: 40 minutes   bake: 55 minutes   stand: 1 hour
oven: 350°F   makes: 8 servings   dish: 3-quart

8   ounces sweet or hot bulk Italian sausage
2   teaspoons olive oil
2   cups red sweet pepper strips (2 medium)
2   medium onions, thinly sliced
¼   teaspoon salt
1   1-pound loaf French or Italian bread, cut into ½-inch slices and quartered
1   cup shredded fontina cheese (4 ounces)
4   eggs
5   cups 1% milk
¾   teaspoon salt
⅛   teaspoon ground black pepper

1 In a large nonstick skillet cook sausage over medium-high heat until brown, using a wooden spoon to break up meat as it cooks. Drain sausage in a colander.

2 In the same skillet heat oil over medium heat. Add sweet peppers, onions, and ¼ teaspoon salt. Cook about 15 minutes or until vegetables are lightly browned, stirring occasionally.

3 Place half of the bread in an ungreased 3-quart rectangular baking dish. Top with half of the sausage, half of the sweet pepper mixture, and ½ cup of the cheese. Repeat layers.

4 In a large bowl combine eggs, milk, ¾ teaspoon salt, and black pepper. Pour egg mixture evenly over layers in baking dish. Using the back of a spoon, gently press down on layers to moisten. Cover with plastic wrap and chill overnight.

5 Let strata stand at room temperature for 1 hour before baking. Preheat oven to 350°F. Remove plastic wrap and cover with foil. Bake for 30 minutes. Bake, uncovered, for 25 to 30 minutes more or until lightly browned and set in center.

nutrition facts per serving: 436 cal., 20 g total fat (8 g sat. fat), 151 mg chol., 1046 mg sodium, 41 g carb., 3 g dietary fiber, 21 g protein.

Herbs, onions, and cheese dress up sliced potatoes for breakfast or brunch and fill the kitchen with tantalizing aromas. Serve this hearty dish with scrambled eggs, fresh fruit, and cinnamon rolls.

hearty potato and sausage casserole

prep: 35 minutes bake: 20 minutes oven: 350°F
makes: 8 servings dish: 3-quart

3 large long white potatoes (about 1½ pounds), peeled and cut into ¼-inch slices (about 5 cups)
3 tablespoons butter or margarine
2 large onions, chopped (2 cups)
1 tablespoon dried parsley flakes
½ teaspoon garlic salt
½ teaspoon ground black pepper
½ teaspoon dried thyme, crushed
½ teaspoon dried sage, crushed
¼ teaspoon dried rosemary, crushed
1 pound bulk pork sausage
2 cups shredded Swiss cheese (8 ounces) or 8 ounces sliced Swiss cheese

1 Preheat oven to 350°F. In a covered large saucepan cook potatoes in enough boiling, lightly salted water to cover for 10 to 12 minutes or just until tender; drain.

2 In a large heavy skillet melt butter over medium-high heat. Add potatoes and onions; cook until potatoes are lightly browned, turning frequently. Add parsley, garlic salt, pepper, thyme, sage, and rosemary; toss gently. Transfer mixture to an ungreased 3-quart rectangular baking dish.

3 In the same skillet cook sausage over medium heat until brown. Drain off fat. Spread cooked sausage over potato mixture. Top with cheese.

4 Bake, uncovered, for 20 to 25 minutes or until heated through.

nutrition facts per serving: 423 cal., 29 g total fat (13 g sat. fat), 76 mg chol., 549 mg sodium, 24 g carb., 2 g dietary fiber, 16 g protein.

Horseradish mustard adds a kick of incredible flavor to this popular breakfast dish. Use the condiment another time to flavor grilled salmon, a roast beef sandwich, or a salad dressing.

horseradish
ham-potato bake

prep: 15 minutes   chill: 2 to 24 hours   bake: 55 minutes   stand: 5 minutes
oven: 350°F   makes: 8 servings   dish: 3-quart

Nonstick cooking
  spray
1 28-ounce package
  frozen loose-pack
  diced hash brown
  potatoes with onion
  and peppers
1½ cups diced cooked
  ham (8 ounces)
1 cup shredded Swiss
  cheese (4 ounces)
⅓ cup finely chopped
  red onion
5 eggs, lightly beaten
1½ cups milk
3 tablespoons
  horseradish
  mustard
½ teaspoon salt
¼ teaspoon ground
  black pepper
Chopped scallions
1 recipe Horseradish
  Sour Cream

1 Coat a 3-quart rectangular baking dish with cooking spray. Arrange potatoes evenly in the bottom of the dish. Sprinkle with ham, cheese, and onion.

2 In a medium bowl whisk together eggs, milk, mustard, salt, and pepper. Pour egg mixture over potato mixture. Cover and chill 4 to 24 hours.

3 Preheat oven to 350°F. Bake, uncovered, for 55 to 60 minutes or until a knife inserted near the center comes out clean. Sprinkle with scallion. Let stand 5 minutes before serving. Serve with Horseradish Sour Cream.

nutrition facts per serving: 270 cal., 14 g total fat (6 g sat. fat), 169 mg chol., 651 mg sodium, 21 g carb., 2 g dietary fiber, 16 g protein.

horseradish sour cream: In a small bowl stir together ½ cup sour cream, 1 to 2 tablespoons horseradish mustard, and 1 tablespoon snipped fresh chives.

Baked in individual casseroles, this flavorful strata is perfect for entertaining overnight guests. Serve it with fresh fruit for a satisfying meal.

smoked **chicken** strata

prep: 25 minutes   chill: 2 to 24 hours   bake: 25 minutes   stand: 10 minutes
oven: 325°F   makes: 6 servings   dish: 12-ounce dishes

1 tablespoon canola oil

2 cups cut-up trimmed asparagus or chopped trimmed broccoli

1½ cups sliced fresh mushrooms or halved grape tomatoes

½ cup chopped red or yellow sweet pepper
Nonstick cooking spray

3 whole grain English muffins, torn or cut into bite-size pieces (4 cups)

2 cups shredded smoked chicken or cooked chicken breast (10 ounces)

¾ cup shredded Swiss cheese (3 ounces)

1 cup refrigerated or frozen egg product, thawed, or 4 eggs, lightly beaten

1 cup fat-free milk

⅛ teaspoon ground black pepper

1 In a large nonstick skillet heat oil over medium-high heat. Add asparagus, mushrooms, and sweet pepper; cook about 3 minutes or just until vegetables are crisp-tender.

2 Lightly coat six 12-ounce individual casserole dishes with cooking spray. Divide half of the English muffin pieces among the dishes. Top with the chicken, asparagus mixture, and ½ cup of the cheese. Top with the remaining English muffin pieces.

3 In a medium bowl whisk together eggs, milk, and black pepper. Pour egg mixture evenly over the layers in dishes. Using the back of a large spoon, press muffin pieces down to moisten. Sprinkle with the remaining ¼ cup of the cheese. Cover; chill for 2 to 24 hours.

4 Preheat oven to 325°F. Bake, uncovered, for 25 to 30 minutes or until a knife inserted in the centers comes out clean. Let stand for 10 minutes before serving.

nutrition facts per serving: 243 cal., 8 g total fat (3 g sat. fat), 35 mg chol., 777 mg sodium, 22 g carb., 4 g dietary fiber, 23 g protein.

These mini Mediterranean soufflés rise quite a bit, so using deep, straight-sided dishes helps keep them from spilling over.

zucchini and feta cheese soufflés

prep: 20 minutes bake: 20 minutes stand: 30 minutes oven: 375°F
makes: 6 servings dish: 6-ounce dishes

2 cups shredded zucchini
1 teaspoon salt
3 tablespoons butter
¼ cup all-purpose flour
1 teaspoon dry mustard
¼ cup milk
½ cup crumbled feta cheese (2 ounces)
1 tablespoon grated Parmesan cheese
4 egg yolks
4 egg whites

1 Place zucchini in a colander; sprinkle with salt and toss lightly. Let stand for 30 minutes. Rinse and drain. Squeeze out excess liquid. Preheat oven to 375°F. Grease six 6-ounce soufflé dishes or custard cups; set aside.

2 In a medium saucepan heat butter over medium heat until melted. Stir in flour and dry mustard. Add milk all at once. Cook and stir until thickened and bubbly. Remove from heat. Stir in zucchini, feta cheese, and Parmesan cheese. In a large bowl beat yolks with a fork until combined. Gradually stir in zucchini mixture.

3 In a large bowl beat egg whites with an electric mixer on medium to high until stiff peaks form (tips stand straight). Gently fold about half of the beaten egg whites into zucchini mixture. Gradually add zucchini mixture to the remaining beaten egg whites, folding gently to combine. Spoon into the prepared soufflé dishes.

4 Bake for 20 to 25 minutes or until a knife inserted near centers comes out clean. Serve immediately.

nutrition facts per serving: 174 cal., 12 g total fat (6 g sat. fat), 169 mg chol., 276 mg sodium, 8 g carb., 1 g dietary fiber, 8 g protein.

Using fresh asparagus, spinach, tomato, and basil makes all the difference when it comes to great taste. Reduced-fat feta cheese makes this healthy too.

tomato, spinach, and feta strata

prep: 30 minutes chill: 4 hours bake: 1 hour 10 minutes stand: 10 minutes oven: 325°F makes: 6 servings dish: 2-quart

Nonstick cooking spray
4   cups cubed whole grain bread
1   pound asparagus, trimmed and cut into 1-inch pieces
1   cup chopped onion
2   cups fresh baby spinach
6   eggs
1   cup fat-free milk
1/8   teaspoon sea salt or kosher salt
1/8   teaspoon ground black pepper
2   roma tomatoes, thinly sliced
1/2   cup reduced-fat feta cheese
1/4   cup snipped fresh basil

1 Coat a 2-quart rectangular baking dish with cooking spray. Arrange half of the bread cubes in the prepared baking dish.

2 Cook asparagus and onion in a medium saucepan in a small amount of boiling water for 2 to 3 minutes or just until tender; stir in spinach. Immediately drain well. Spoon half of the asparagus mixture over bread in baking dish. Top with the remaining bread cubes and the remaining asparagus mixture.

3 In a large bowl whisk together eggs, milk, salt, and pepper. Pour evenly over mixture in baking dish. Using the back of a large spoon, lightly press layers down to moisten. Arrange tomato slices on top. Top with feta cheese and basil. Cover with foil and chill for 4 to 24 hours.

4 Preheat oven to 325°F. Bake, covered, for 30 minutes. Uncover; bake about 40 minutes more or until center registers 180°F when tested with an instant-read thermometer (there will be some liquid left in center that will be absorbed during standing). Let stand on a wire rack for 10 minutes before serving.

nutrition facts per serving: 247 cal., 9 g total fat (3 g sat. fat), 216 mg chol., 419 mg sodium, 27 g carb., 7 g dietary fiber, 18 g protein.

To serve this fluffy egg dish, insert two forks back to back in the center of the dish and gently pull the soufflé apart, separating it into serving-size wedges. Use a large spoon to transfer the portions to individual plates.

mock cheese soufflé

prep: 15 minutes   chill: 2 to 24 hours   bake: 45 minutes   oven: 350°F
makes: 6 servings   dish: 1½-quart

6	cups white bread cubes
1½	cups shredded sharp cheddar or Monterey Jack cheese with jalapeño chile peppers (6 ounces)
4	eggs, lightly beaten
1½	cups milk
2	teaspoons Worcestershire sauce
½	teaspoon salt

1 Place half of the bread cubes in an ungreased 1½-quart soufflé dish. Sprinkle with half of the cheese. Repeat layers; press lightly.

2 In a medium bowl combine eggs, milk, Worcestershire sauce, and salt. Pour mixture evenly over layers in soufflé dish. Cover and chill for 2 to 24 hours.

3 Preheat oven to 350°F. Bake, uncovered, for 45 to 50 minutes or until a knife inserted near center comes out clean. Serve immediately.

nutrition facts per serving: 284 cal., 15 g total fat (8 g sat. fat), 176 mg chol., 639 mg sodium, 21 g carb., 1 g dietary fiber, 16 g protein.

Brunch for a Bunch

If you're hosting a brunch, make it a fun and stress-free affair with these tips.

- *Plan your menu around one or two of the time-honored make-ahead recipes in this chapter.*

- *Enlist the help of your favorite bakery for muffins or quick breads and the produce section of your grocery store for cut-up fresh fruit.*

- *Offer a drink that's cold, refreshing, and fruity in addition to coffee or hot cocoa.*

- *Serve buffet style if you are entertaining more than six guests. If space is limited, set up beverages in a separate area.*

With flavors of French toast, this quiche has a cinnamon bread crumb crust. Bake the crust the day before and cover and store at room temperature.

bread pudding quiche with berries and bacon

prep: 40 minutes   cool: 15 minutes   bake: 1 hour 4 minutes
oven: 300°F/375°F/325°F   makes: 8 servings   dish: Springform pan

7   to 8 slices cinnamon swirl bread cut in ½-inch cubes (about 5 cups)
⅓   cup butter, melted
5   eggs
1½   cups milk
1½   cups finely shredded Gruyère cheese (6 ounces)
2   teaspoons all-purpose flour
¼   teaspoon salt
¼   teaspoon ground black pepper
¾   cup chopped cooked ham
½   cup chopped scallions (4)
2   cups assorted fresh berries
4   slices bacon, crisp-cooked, drained, and broken in large pieces

1 Preheat oven to 300°F. Spread bread cubes in single layer on large ungreased baking sheet. Bake 10 to 15 minutes or until dry. Set aside 1 cup of the cubes.

2 For crust, place the remaining bread cubes in food processor. Cover and process until reduced to fine crumbs. With food processor running, pour in melted butter until combined (mixture will be crumbly).

3 Increase oven to 375°F. Press crumb mixture onto bottom and 1½ inches up sides of ungreased 9-inch springform pan or onto bottom and up sides of 10-inch quiche dish. Bake for 4 to 5 minutes or until lightly browned; cool. Reduce oven to 325°F.

4 In a medium bowl whisk together eggs and milk. In a small bowl toss together cheese, flour, salt, and pepper. Add to egg mixture. Fold in reserved bread cubes, ham, and scallions. Pour into prepared crust.

5 Bake for 50 to 60 minutes or until knife inserted near the center comes out clean. If necessary, after 30 minutes tent with foil to prevent overbrowning. Cool on a wire rack for 15 minutes. Remove sides of springform pan, loosening sides with a knife if necessary.

6 To serve, top with assorted berries and bacon pieces.

nutrition facts per serving: 366 cal., 23 g total fat (12 g sat. fat), 191 mg chol., 725 mg sodium, 23 g carb., 3 g dietary fiber, 18 g protein.

With all the lush, sweet flavor and aroma of Mom's apple pie, this strata is well worth getting up for.

apple-almond-cinnamon strata

prep: 20 minutes chill: 2 to 24 hours bake: 50 minutes stand: 15 minutes
oven: 325°F makes: 8 servings. dish: 3-quart

1	1-pound loaf cinnamon-raisin bread, cut into 1-inch pieces
8	eggs, lightly beaten
2	cups milk
$1/4$	teaspoon salt
$1/4$	teaspoon almond extract
1	21-ounce can apple pie filling
$1/2$	cup slivered almonds, toasted
	Ground cinnamon or powdered sugar

1 Spread bread pieces in a greased 3-quart rectangular baking dish; set aside.

2 In a large bowl beat together together eggs, milk, salt, and almond extract with a rotary beater or whisk. Stir in apple pie filling and half of the almonds. Carefully pour apple mixture over the bread in the baking dish. Using a wooden spoon, press bread pieces down to moisten. Sprinkle with the remaining almonds. Cover; refrigerate for 2 to 24 hours.

3 Preheat oven to 325°F. Bake, uncovered, about 50 minutes or until a knife inserted near the center comes out clean. Let stand for 15 minutes before serving. Lightly sprinkle cinnamon or sift powdered sugar over the top before serving.

nutrition facts per serving: 387 cal., 13 g total fat (3 g sat. fat), 216 mg chol., 422 mg sodium, 55 g carb., 4 g dietary fiber, 15 g protein.

Serve this with fresh raspberries, strawberries, or sliced fresh peaches when they are in season. In winter, serve with sliced bananas or oranges. Pictured on page 355.

baked **stuffed** french toast

prep: 25 minutes   chill: 2 to 24 hours   bake: 30 minutes   oven: 375°F
makes: 4 servings   dish: 3-quart

8 ¾-inch slices French bread
1 recipe Cream Cheese Filling
4 eggs, lightly beaten
1 cup milk
1 cup orange juice
   Maple syrup and/or fruit (optional)

1 Place half of the bread slices in a 3-quart baking dish. Spread with Cream Cheese Filling. Top with the remaining bread slices.

2 In a medium bowl combine eggs, milk, and orange juice. Pour egg mixture evenly over bread stacks, covering all of the tops. Cover with plastic wrap and chill for 2 to 24 hours.

3 Preheat oven to 375°F. Line a 15×10×1-inch baking pan with parchment paper or nonstick foil. Arrange bread stacks in the prepared baking pan. Bake, uncovered, for 30 to 35 minutes or until golden, turning once. If desired, serve with syrup and/or fruit.

nutrition facts per serving: 550 cal., 27 g total fat (14 g sat. fat), 279 mg chol., 695 mg sodium, 59 g carb., 3 g dietary fiber, 20 g protein.

cream cheese filling: In a medium bowl combine one 8-ounce package cream cheese, ½ cup snipped dried apricots or golden raisins, and 1 teaspoon ground cinnamon.

Cream cheese is the secret ingredient that dots the mixture, which gets a generous topping of blueberry or maple syrup.

blueberry
surprise french toast casserole

prep: 25 minutes   chill: 2 to 24 hours   bake: 50 minutes   stand: 10 minutes
oven: 375°F   makes: 8 servings   dish: 3-quart

12   slices dried white
      bread, cut into
      ½-inch cubes
      (about 8 cups)*
 2   8-ounce packages
      cream cheese, cut
      into ¾-inch cubes
 1   cup fresh or frozen
      blueberries
12   eggs
 2   cups milk
 ½   cup maple syrup
      Blueberry-flavor or
      maple syrup

1 Place half of the bread cubes over the bottom of a well-buttered 3-quart rectangular baking dish. Sprinkle cream cheese and blueberries over bread cubes. Arrange the remaining bread cubes over blueberries.

2 In a large mixing bowl beat eggs with a rotary beater; beat in milk and ½ cup syrup. Carefully pour egg mixture over the bread mixture. Cover dish with plastic wrap; chill for 2 to 24 hours.

3 Preheat oven to 375°F. Remove plastic wrap and cover dish with foil. Bake for 25 minutes. Uncover and bake about 25 minutes more or until a knife inserted near the center comes out clean and topping is puffed and golden brown. Let stand for 10 minutes before serving. Serve warm with syrup.

nutrition facts per serving: 503 cal., 30 g total fat (13 g sat. fat), 386 mg chol., 497 mg sodium, 40 g carb., 1 g dietary fiber, 19 g protein.

*test kitchen tip: To dry bread slices, arrange bread in a single layer on a wire rack; cover loosely and let stand overnight. Or cut bread with ½-inch cubes; spread in a large baking pan. Bake, uncovered, in a 300°F oven for 10 to 15 minutes or until dry, stirring twice; cool.

380

One favorite becomes another when everything that makes caramel-pecan rolls so yummy shows up in this one-dish breakfast bake.

caramel-pecan french toast

prep: 20 minutes   chill: 2 to 24 hours   stand: 10 minutes   oven: 350°F
makes: 8 servings   dish: 3-quart

1 cup packed brown sugar
½ cup butter
2 tablespoons light corn syrup
1 cup chopped pecans, toasted
16 ½-inch slices French bread
6 eggs, lightly beaten
1½ cups milk
1 teaspoon vanilla
1 tablespoon granulated sugar
1½ teaspoons ground cinnamon
¼ teaspoon ground nutmeg
Raspberries, maple syrup, and/or toasted chopped pecans (optional)

1 In a medium saucepan combine brown sugar, butter, and corn syrup. Cook and stir until butter is melted and brown sugar is dissolved. Pour into an ungreased 3-quart rectangular baking dish. Sprinkle with ½ cup of the pecans.

2 Arrange half of the bread slices in a single layer in the baking dish. Sprinkle with the remaining ½ cup pecans; top with the remaining bread slices.

3 In a medium bowl whisk together eggs, milk, and vanilla. Gradually pour egg mixture over bread. Using the back of a large spoon, press the bread down to moisten lightly. In a small bowl stir together granulated sugar, cinnamon, and nutmeg; sprinkle over bread. Cover and chill for 2 to 24 hours.

4 Preheat oven to 350°F. Bake, uncovered, for 30 to 40 minutes or until lightly browned. Let stand for 10 minutes before serving. To serve, invert French toast onto a large serving platter. If desired, serve with raspberries, maple syrup, and/or additional pecans.

nutrition facts per serving: 579 cal., 27 g total fat (10 g sat. fat), 193 mg chol., 579 mg sodium, 72 g carb., 3 g dietary fiber, 15 g protein.

Brioche (bree-OHSH) is a rich butter and egg French bread with a beautiful burnished crust and golden tender crumb. If you can't find it, soft French bread also works.

amaretto
brioche bake

prep: 20 minutes   chill: 4 to 24 hours   bake: 40 minutes   stand: 15 minutes
oven: 350°F   makes: 8 servings   dish: 3-quart

1	cup packed brown sugar
1/3	cup butter or margarine
1/4	cup amaretto
2	tablespoons light corn syrup
1	12-ounce loaf brioche or other sweet bread, cut into 8 slices
4	eggs, lightly beaten
2	cups half-and-half, light cream, or milk
1 1/2	teaspoons vanilla
1/2	teaspoon salt
1/4	teaspoon ground nutmeg or cardamom
1 1/2	cups fresh blackberries (optional)
2	tablespoons granulated sugar (optional)

1 Lightly grease a 3-quart rectangular baking dish; set aside. In a medium saucepan combine brown sugar, butter, amaretto, and corn syrup. Cook and stir until mixture comes to boiling. Boil, uncovered, for 1 minute. Pour into the prepared baking dish. Arrange bread slices over brown sugar mixture.

2 In a medium bowl combine eggs, half-and-half, vanilla, salt, and nutmeg. Pour evenly over bread slices. Using a rubber spatula or the back of a large spoon, lightly press down on all of the bread to moisten. Cover and chill for 4 to 24 hours.

3 Preheat oven to 350°F. Bake, uncovered, for 40 to 45 minutes or until a knife inserted near the center comes out clean and the top is lightly browned. Let stand for 15 minutes before serving.

4 Meanwhile, if desired, in a small bowl combine blackberries and granulated sugar; lightly crush berries. Let stand until a syrup forms, stirring occasionally. Spoon berry mixture over each serving.

nutrition facts per serving: 470 cal., 23 g total fat (11 g sat. fat), 188 mg chol., 432 mg sodium, 55 g carb., 1 g dietary fiber, 9 g protein.

Buy pears several days before using them. That gives them time to ripen at room temperature in a brown paper bag if they're too firm. If they're ripe enough when purchased, store them in the refrigerator for 3 to 7 days.

maple **baked** stuffed **pears**

prep: 20 minutes   bake: 40 minutes   oven: 350°F
makes: 4 servings   dish: 2-quart

4   medium firm pears
    with stems
¼   cup dried cranberries
    or dried tart red
    cherries
3   tablespoons chopped
    walnuts, toasted
1   tablespoon lemon
    juice
2½ teaspoons sugar
¼   cup water
¼   cup maple syrup

1 Preheat oven to 350°F. Cut a thin slice from the bottom of each pear so the pears stand up. Working through the bottom of each pear, use a melon baller to remove the core.

2 In a small bowl combine cranberries, walnuts, lemon juice, and sugar. Spoon cranberry mixture into the hollowed-out bottoms of pears. Stand pears in an ungreased 2-quart square baking dish. Add the water to baking dish. Pour maple syrup over and around pears. Sprinkle any remaining cranberry mixture into bottom of dish.

3 Bake, covered, for 20 minutes. Uncover; bake for 20 to 25 minutes more or until pears are tender, basting occasionally with cooking liquid.

4 To serve, spoon any remaining cooking liquid over pears. If desired, cut pears in half, topping with the remaining filling from bottom of dish. Serve warm.

nutrition facts per serving: 219 cal., 4 g total fat (0 g sat. fat), 0 mg chol., 4 mg sodium, 49 g carb., 6 g dietary fiber, 1 g protein.

Greek yogurt—as thick as sour cream—is a terrific topper for granola and berries, and when sweetened with a touch of honey, it easily stands in for whipped cream on desserts.

baked apples with
greek yogurt

prep: 30 minutes bake: 1 hour oven: 350°F
makes: 6 to 8 servings dish: 3-quart

- 6 to 8 medium baking apples (such as McIntosh, Rome Beauty, or Granny Smith)
- 1 cup orange juice
- 1 cup rolled oats
- 1/2 cup packed brown sugar
- 1/3 cup slivered almonds, toasted
- 1 tablespoon all-purpose flour
- 3/4 teaspoon ground cinnamon
- 1/4 teaspoon ground nutmeg
- 1/3 cup butter or margarine, melted
  Cinnamon sticks, broken (optional)
- 1/3 cup honey
- 1 6- to 7-ounce carton Greek yogurt or other creamy-style yogurt

1 Preheat oven to 350°F. Remove a 1/2-inch slice from the top of each apple. Using a melon baller, remove core, stopping about 1/2 inch from the bottom of the apple. Arrange apples in an ungreased 3-quart rectangular baking dish. (If necessary, remove a thin slice from the bottoms of each apple so it sits flat.) Brush with 1 tablespoon of the orange juice.

2 In a medium bowl combine oats, brown sugar, almonds, flour, ground cinnamon, and nutmeg. Stir in melted butter. Fill and top apples with oat mixture. Pour the remaining orange juice around apples.

3 Bake, covered, for 50 minutes. If desired, place a piece of cinnamon stick in oat mixture in each apple to resemble a stem. Bake, uncovered, for 10 to 15 minutes more or until apples are tender. Cool slightly. Drizzle apples with honey. Serve with yogurt.

nutrition facts per serving: 487 cal., 18 g total fat (9 g sat. fat), 32 mg chol., 89 mg sodium, 78 g carb., 7 g dietary fiber, 8 g protein.

on the

si

Pop any one of these potato or veggie numbers in the oven for a superlative accompaniment to beef, pork, lamb, poultry, or fish. Flavored with aromatic seasonings, they're so good that everyone will love eating their veggies.

de

Give new life to classic green bean casserole using fresh beans, a silky sauce of cream, Parmesan cheese, and seasonings, and a crunchy topping of crisp-fried shallots.

green bean casserole with crispy shallots

prep: 45 minutes bake: 20 minutes oven: 375°F
makes: 8 servings dish: 2-quart

1½	pounds thin green beans, trimmed
4	tablespoons butter or margarine
12	ounces fresh button mushrooms, sliced
12	ounces fresh shiitake mushrooms, stems discarded and caps sliced
2	tablespoons minced garlic (6 cloves)
1	tablespoon snipped fresh thyme or 1 teaspoon dried thyme, crushed
¼	teaspoon salt
¼	teaspoon ground black pepper
2	tablespoons all-purpose flour
2	cups half-and-half or light cream
½	cup finely shredded Parmesan cheese (2 ounces)
⅛	teaspoon salt
⅛	teaspoon ground black pepper
⅓	cup pine nuts, toasted
½	cup olive oil
4	large shallots, thinly sliced crosswise, or 1 cup thinly sliced sweet onion

1 Preheat oven to 375°F. Grease a 2-quart casserole; set aside. In an extra-large skillet cook beans in lightly salted boiling water about 3 minutes or until crisp-tender; drain. Transfer to a bowl of ice water to stop cooking. Drain again.

2 In the same skillet melt 2 tablespoons of the butter over medium-high heat. Add button and shiitake mushrooms, garlic, and thyme; cook until mushrooms are tender and excess liquid has evaporated. Stir in ¼ teaspoon salt and ¼ teaspoon pepper. Gently toss with beans.

3 For sauce, in a small saucepan melt the remaining 2 tablespoons butter over medium heat. Stir in flour. Stir in half-and-half. Cook and stir over medium heat until thickened and bubbly. Cook and stir for 1 minute more. Stir in the Parmesan cheese, ⅛ teaspoon salt, and ⅛ teaspoon pepper. Pour sauce over green bean mixture, stirring gently just until combined. Transfer green bean mixture to prepared casserole.

4 Bake, uncovered, about 20 minutes or until bubbly. Sprinkle bean mixture with pine nuts.

5 Meanwhile, rinse and dry saucepan. In the saucepan heat oil over medium-high heat. Add sliced shallots in small batches and cook about 1½ minutes or until golden brown and slightly crisp. Using a slotted spoon, transfer shallots to paper towels to drain. Top casserole with fried shallots just before serving.

nutrition facts per serving: 385 cal., 32 g total fat (11 g sat. fat), 41 mg chol., 270 mg sodium, 21 g carb., 4 g dietary fiber, 9 g protein.

make-ahead directions: Prepare as directed through Step 3. Cover and chill for up to 24 hours. Cook shallots as directed in Step 5. Drain and transfer to an airtight container; chill for up to 24 hours. To serve, let casserole stand at room temperature for 30 minutes before baking. Continue as directed.

Hearty oven-roasted sweet potatoes are bathed in a delicious brown sugar and butter mixture. For best results, stir the mixture gently while baking to keep the pieces intact.

candied sweet potatoes

prep: 30 minutes bake: 30 minutes stand: 5 minutes
oven: 375°F makes: 6 servings dish: 2-quart

4   medium sweet potatoes (about 2 pounds) or two 18-ounce cans sweet potatoes, drained
¼   cup packed brown sugar or maple syrup
¼   cup butter, melted
¾   cup chopped pecans or walnuts, toasted if desired, and/or tiny marshmallows

1 Preheat oven to 375°F. Peel fresh sweet potatoes; cut into 1½-inch chunks. Cook fresh sweet potatoes, covered, in enough boiling water to cover for 10 to 12 minutes or just until tender; drain. (Cut up canned sweet potatoes.)

2 Transfer potatoes to an ungreased 2-quart rectangular baking dish. Add brown sugar and melted butter; stir gently to combine.

3 Bake, uncovered, for 30 to 35 minutes or until potatoes are glazed, stirring gently twice. Sprinkle with nuts and/or marshmallows; let stand for 5 minutes before serving.

nutrition facts per serving: 327 cal., 18 g total fat (6 g sat. fat), 20 mg chol., 140 mg sodium, 41 g carb., 6 g dietary fiber, 4 g protein.

candied sweet potatoes with apples: Prepare as directed, except reduce sweet potatoes to 1½ pounds (3 medium). In Step 2, combine prepared sweet potato and 1½ cups sliced apple in a 2-quart rectangular baking dish. Add the brown sugar, the melted butter, and ½ teaspoon ground cinnamon; stir gently to combine. Bake, uncovered, in a 350°F oven for 30 to 35 minutes or until potato and apple are glazed, stirring gently twice. Sprinkle with nuts; let stand for 5 minutes before serving.

make-ahead directions: Prepare as directed through Step 2. Cover and chill for up to 24 hours. Bake, uncovered, in a 375°F oven for 35 to 40 minutes or until potatoes are glazed, stirring gently twice. Continue as directed.

A classic comfort food sparked with cream cheese and chives, this vegetable dish will be a hit at any gathering. It also makes a delicious side for pork chops or roast beef.

creamed corn casserole

prep: 15 minutes   bake: 50 minutes   oven: 375°F
makes: 12 servings   dish: 2-quart

Nonstick cooking
   spray
2   16-ounce packages
   frozen whole kernel
   corn
2   cups chopped red
   and/or green sweet
   peppers (2 large)
1   cup chopped onion
   (1 large)
1   tablespoon butter or
   margarine
¼   teaspoon ground
   black pepper
1   10.75-ounce can
   condensed cream of
   celery soup
1   8-ounce tub cream
   cheese spread with
   chives and onion
   or cream cheese
   spread with garden
   vegetables
¼   cup milk

1 Preheat oven to 375°F. Lightly coat a 2-quart casserole with cooking spray; set aside. Place corn in a colander. Run it under cool water to thaw; drain.

2 In a large saucepan cook sweet pepper and onion in hot butter until tender. Stir in corn and black pepper. In a medium bowl whisk together soup, cream cheese spread, and milk. Stir soup mixture into corn mixture. Transfer to the prepared casserole.

3 Bake, covered, for 50 to 55 minutes or until casserole is heated through, stirring once.

nutrition facts per serving: 169 cal., 9 g total fat (4 g sat. fat), 26 mg chol., 270 mg sodium, 21 g carb., 3 g dietary fiber, 5 g protein.

Retro is revved up with these single-serve sides topped with crushed potato chips. You can also bake this in a 1½-quart casserole for the same amount of time.

corn and broccoli bake

prep: 20 minutes   bake: 35 minutes   oven: 350°F
makes: 6 servings   dish: 6-ounce dishes

1   10-ounce package
    frozen cut broccoli
1   egg, lightly beaten
1   14.75-ounce can
    cream-style corn
2/3 cup crushed rich
    round crackers
    (about 16 crackers)
1/8 teaspoon seasoned
    pepper
3   slices processed
    American cheese
    food (0.75 ounce
    each), halved
1   cup crushed potato
    chips
2   tablespoons butter or
    margarine, melted

1 Preheat oven to 350°F. Place broccoli in a colander and run cold water over broccoli to separate. Drain well. In a medium bowl combine egg, corn, crushed crackers, and pepper. Stir in broccoli.

2 Divide broccoli mixture among six ungreased 6-ounce custard cups or individual baking dishes. Top with cheese. In a small bowl combine crushed potato chips and melted butter; sprinkle over broccoli mixture.

3 Place custard cups in a shallow baking pan. Bake, uncovered, about 35 minutes or until set in center.

nutrition facts per serving: 244 cal., 14 g total fat (6 g sat. fat), 55 mg chol., 528 mg sodium, 25 g carb., 2 g dietary fiber, 7 g protein.

Oven-roasting beets brings out the earthy sweetness of this underground treasure. Drizzling with a lemon-herb mixture and topping with crumbled goat cheese adds a new flavor dimension.

thyme-roasted beets

prep: 20 minutes   cool: 15 minutes   roast: 40 minutes
oven: 400°F   makes: 8 servings   dish: 3-quart

3½   to 4 pounds baby beets (assorted colors) or small beets
6   cloves garlic, peeled
3   sprigs fresh thyme
5   tablespoons olive oil
½   teaspoon kosher salt
¼   teaspoon ground black pepper
2   tablespoons lemon juice
1   tablespoon snipped fresh thyme
3   ounces goat cheese, crumbled (optional)
Snipped fresh thyme (optional)

1 Preheat oven to 400°F. Cut tops off the beets and trim the root ends. Wash beets thoroughly. If using small beets, cut into 1- to 1½-inch wedges. Place beets in a 3-quart rectangular baking dish. Add garlic and thyme sprigs. In a small bowl stir together 3 tablespoons of the oil, the salt, and pepper. Drizzle over vegetables in dish; toss lightly to coat. Cover dish with foil.

2 Roast for 40 to 45 minutes or until tender. Uncover and let beets cool in pan on wire rack about 15 minutes. If using small beets, remove skins by wrapping the wedges, one at a time, in a paper towel and gently rubbing the skins off. (Baby beets do not need to be peeled.)

3 Remove garlic from dish; finely chop. Discard thyme sprigs. In a small bowl combine chopped garlic, the remaining 2 tablespoons oil, lemon juice, and 1 tablespoon snipped thyme. Drizzle oil mixture over beets; toss gently to coat.

4 If desired, sprinkle beets with crumbled goat cheese and additional snipped thyme. Serve warm or at room temperature.

nutrition facts per serving: 165 cal., 9 g total fat (1 g sat. fat), 0 mg chol., 246 mg sodium, 20 g carb., 6 g dietary fiber, 3 g protein.

Gouda, a semi-firm Dutch cheese, adds a distinctive nutty flavor and richness to a classic white sauce that complements broccoli.

gouda-sauced broccoli

prep: 20 minutes   bake: 15 minutes   oven: 425°F
makes: 6 servings   dish: 2-quart

1¼ pounds broccoli, cut into spears
1 tablespoon butter or margarine
½ cup chopped onion (1 medium)
2 cloves garlic, minced
2 tablespoons all-purpose flour
¼ teaspoon salt
⅛ teaspoon ground black pepper
1½ cups milk
¾ cup shredded smoked Gouda cheese (3 ounces)
¾ cup soft bread crumbs (1 slice)
2 teaspoons butter or margarine, melted

1 Preheat oven to 425°F. Place a steamer basket in a large saucepan. Add water to just below the bottom of the steamer basket. Bring water to boiling. Add broccoli to steamer basket. Cover and reduce heat. Steam for 6 to 8 minutes or just until crisp-tender.

2 Meanwhile, for sauce, in a medium saucepan melt 1 tablespoon butter over medium heat. Add onion and garlic; cook until tender. Stir in flour, salt, and pepper. Stir in the milk. Cook and stir until thickened and bubbly. Gradually add cheese, stirring until melted.

3 Transfer broccoli to an ungreased 2-quart square baking dish or a 1½-quart au gratin dish. Pour sauce over broccoli. Combine bread crumbs and 2 teaspoons melted butter; sprinkle over sauce. Bake, uncovered, about 15 minutes or until crumbs are light brown.

nutrition facts per serving: 145 cal., 8 g total fat (5 g sat. fat), 23 mg chol., 429 mg sodium, 13 g carb., 2 g dietary fiber, 7 g protein.

Buttery bread crumbs flavored with Parmesan cheese add a nice crunch to the rich mushroom mix. For speed, use presliced mushrooms that are available from the produce aisle of your market.

mushroom medley au gratin

prep: 35 minutes   bake: 15 minutes   oven: 350°F
makes: 6 servings   dish: 1-quart

on the **side**

2   tablespoons grated Parmesan cheese
2   tablespoons fine dry bread crumbs
2   teaspoons butter, melted
8   ounces fresh shiitake mushrooms
4   ounces fresh oyster mushrooms
1   pound fresh button mushrooms, sliced
1   clove garlic, minced
2   tablespoons butter
2   tablespoons all-purpose flour
2   teaspoons Dijon mustard
1½ teaspoons snipped fresh thyme or
    ½ teaspoon dried thyme, crushed
¼   teaspoon salt
⅔   cup milk

1 Preheat oven to 350°F. In a small bowl stir together Parmesan cheese, bread crumbs, and 2 teaspoons melted butter; set aside.

2 Separate caps and stems from shiitake and oyster mushrooms. (Reserve stems to use in stocks or discard.) Slice mushroom caps.

3 In a large skillet cook button mushrooms and garlic in 2 tablespoons butter over medium-high heat about 5 minutes or until tender and most of the liquid has evaporated, stirring occasionally. Remove mushrooms from skillet and set aside, reserving drippings in skillet.

4 Add shiitake and oyster mushrooms to the skillet. Cook for 7 to 8 minutes or until tender and most of the liquid has evaporated, stirring occasionally. Stir in the flour, mustard, thyme, and salt. Add milk all at once. Cook and stir until thickened and bubbly. Stir in button mushroom mixture.

5 Transfer mushroom mixture to a 1-quart au gratin dish or 1-quart casserole. Sprinkle with the bread crumb mixture. Bake, uncovered, about 15 minutes or until heated through.

nutrition facts per serving: 120 cal., 7 g total fat (4 g sat. fat), 17 mg chol., 237 mg sodium, 10 g carb., 2 g dietary fiber, 6 g protein.

These cheesy potatoes will disappear in a heartbeat from any gathering. You can make them as tongue-tingling or as mild as you like, depending on how much cayenne you add.

easy potluck potatoes

prep: 30 minutes   bake: 30 minutes   stand: 10 minutes
oven: 350°F   makes: 10 servings   dish: 2-quart

6 cups small red potatoes, coarsely chopped (2 to 2¼ pounds)

¾ cup chopped onion (1 medium)

1 8-ounce carton sour cream

1 cup shredded Monterey Jack cheese (4 ounces)

1 cup shredded sharp cheddar cheese (4 ounces)

½ teaspoon salt

¼ to ½ teaspoon cayenne pepper

1 14.5-ounce can diced tomatoes, drained

½ cup sour cream (optional)
   Chopped fresh tomato, chopped avocado, and sliced scallions (optional)

1 Preheat oven to 350°F. In a large covered saucepan cook potatoes and onion in large amount of boiling water about 20 minutes or until tender. Drain; return to saucepan. Stir in 1 cup sour cream, Monterey Jack, and cheddar cheeses, salt, and cayenne. Stir in tomatoes. Spoon potato mixture into an ungreased 2-quart rectangular baking dish.

2 Bake, uncovered, about 30 minutes or until heated through. Cover; let stand for 10 minutes before serving. If desired, top with mounds of ½ cup sour cream, fresh tomato, avocado, and scallions.

nutrition facts per serving: 220 cal., 12 g total fat (8 g sat. fat), 32 mg chol., 333 mg sodium, 20 g carb., 2 g dietary fiber, 9 g protein.

Every mom and grandmother has her favorite recipe for these creamy taters. Here's one more. Feel free to add cheese if you like. Either way, they're hard to beat.

scalloped potatoes

prep: 30 minutes bake: 1 hour 25 minutes stand: 10 minutes
oven: 350°F makes: 10 servings dish: 3-quart

1 cup chopped onion
  (1 large)
2 cloves garlic, minced
¼ cup butter or
  margarine
¼ cup all-purpose flour
½ teaspoon salt
¼ teaspoon ground
  black pepper
2½ cups milk
8 cups thinly sliced red,
  white, long white,
  or yellow potatoes
  (about 2½ pounds)

1 Preheat oven to 350°F. For sauce, in a medium saucepan cook onion and garlic in hot butter over medium heat until tender. Stir in flour, salt, and pepper. Add milk all at once. Cook and stir until thickened and bubbly. Remove from heat.

2 Place half of the sliced potatoes in a greased 3-quart rectangular dish. Top with half the sauce. Repeat with the remaining potatoes and sauce.

3 Bake, covered, for 45 minutes. Bake, uncovered, for 40 to 50 minutes more or until potatoes are tender. Let stand for 10 minutes before serving.

nutrition facts per serving: 182 cal., 6 g total fat (4 g sat. fat), 17 mg chol., 182 mg sodium, 28 g carb., 3 g dietary fiber, 5 g protein.

cheesy scalloped potatoes:
Prepare as directed, except gradually add 1½ cups (6 ounces) shredded cheddar, Gruyère, or Swiss cheese to the thickened sauce, stirring until cheese melts.

Cooks have long appreciated "au gratin" potatoes, meaning "with cheese"—no last-minute mashing needed! Add a few unexpected touches for a whole new tradition.

parmesan potatoes au gratin

prep: 40 minutes bake: 1 hour 10 minutes stand: 10 minutes
oven: 350°F makes: 8 servings dish: 3-quart

6 medium potatoes (2 pounds), peeled, if desired, and thinly sliced (about 6 cups)
1 medium onion, chopped (½ cup)
2 large garlic cloves, minced
2 tablespoons olive oil or cooking oil
¼ cup all-purpose flour
1 teaspoon salt
¼ teaspoon ground black pepper
3 cups milk
1 cup shredded Parmesan cheese (4 ounces)

1 Preheat oven to 350°F. Grease a 3-quart rectangular baking dish; set aside. In a large covered saucepan cook potatoes in lightly salted boiling water for 5 minutes; drain. Set aside.

2 For sauce, in a medium saucepan cook onion and garlic in hot oil over medium heat until tender. Stir in flour, salt, and pepper. Add milk all at once. Cook and stir until thickened and bubbly. Remove from heat.

3 Layer half of the potatoes in the prepared dish. Pour half the sauce over potatoes. Sprinkle with ½ cup cheese. Repeat with the remaining potatoes and remaining sauce.

4 Bake, covered, for 35 minutes. Uncover and sprinkle remaining cheese on top. Bake about 35 minutes more or until potatoes are tender and top is golden. Let stand for 10 minutes before serving.

nutrition facts per serving: 220 cal., 8 g total fat (3 g sat. fat), 15 mg chol., 511 mg sodium, 27 g carb., 2 g dietary fiber, 10 g protein.

mushroom and blue cheese gratin: Prepare as directed, except cook 3 cups sliced cremini mushrooms with the onion and garlic. Add 4 teaspoons snipped fresh sage to sauce. Substitute crumbled blue cheese for Parmesan cheese.

granny smith and smoked cheddar gratin: Prepare as directed, except cut 2 large cored Granny Smith apples into thin wedges. Add 2 teaspoons snipped fresh thyme to sauce. Place half the apples over each layer of potatoes, then pour sauce over. Substitute smoked cheddar or Gouda cheese for Parmesan cheese.

Use one kind of potato, or mix several types for different textures. Yukon gold and round red potatoes work well for scalloped potato dishes because they won't fall apart.

three-cheese
scalloped potatoes

prep: 30 minutes bake: 1 hour 10 minutes stand: 15 minutes oven: 350°F
makes: 6 servings dish: 1½-quart

2 tablespoons butter or margarine
1 large onion, thinly sliced and separated into rings
2 cloves garlic, minced
2 tablespoons all-purpose flour
½ teaspoon salt
¼ teaspoon ground black pepper
1¾ cups milk
1 cup diced ham (5 ounces)
1½ pounds potatoes, such as long white, round white, round red, or Yukon gold, peeled and thinly sliced (4 cups)
¾ cup shredded smoked Gouda cheese (3 ounces)
¾ cup shredded cheddar cheese (3 ounces)
¼ cup grated Parmesan cheese

1 Preheat oven to 350°F. For sauce, in a medium saucepan melt butter over medium heat. Add onion and garlic; cook until tender. Stir in flour, salt, and pepper. Add milk all at once. Cook and stir until thickened and bubbly. Stir in ham. Remove from heat.

2 Place half of the sliced potatoes in a greased 1½-quart square, oval, or round baking dish. Top with half of the sauce. Sprinkle with Gouda and cheddar cheeses. Top with the remaining sliced potatoes and remaining sauce.

3 Bake, covered, for 35 minutes. Uncover and bake for 30 to 35 minutes more or until potatoes are tender and golden. Sprinkle with Parmesan cheese. Bake, uncovered, about 5 minutes more or until cheese is golden. Let stand for 15 minutes before serving.

nutrition facts per serving: 312 cal., 17 g total fat (10 g sat. fat), 58 mg chol., 926 mg sodium, 16 g carb., 2 g dietary fiber, 15 g protein.

Swiss cheese and spinach add appealing flavors to this creamy potato dish. If you're cooking for a crowd, double the ingredients and bake this in a 3-quart rectangular baking dish.

new potato
bake

prep: 25 minutes   bake: 25 minutes   stand: 10 minutes
oven: 375°F   makes: 6 to 8 servings   dish: 2-quart

1½ pounds tiny new potatoes, quartered
1 6-ounce package (about 5 cups) baby spinach
½ cup chopped scallions
1 tablespoon butter or margarine
1 tablespoon all-purpose flour
¼ teaspoon salt
⅛ teaspoon cayenne pepper
   Pinch ground nutmeg
1 cup milk
1 cup shredded Swiss cheese (4 ounces)

1 Preheat oven to 375°F. Lightly grease a 2-quart square baking dish; set aside. In a covered large saucepan cook potatoes in enough lightly salted boiling water to cover for 8 minutes. Stir in spinach; drain well. Return to pan.

2 Meanwhile, in a small saucepan cook scallions in hot butter over medium heat about 3 minutes or until softened. Stir in flour, salt, cayenne, and nutmeg. Gradually stir in milk. Cook and stir until thickened and bubbly. Add ½ cup of the cheese, stirring until melted. Pour over potato mixture; toss gently to combine.

3 Transfer mixture to prepared baking dish. Sprinkle with the remaining ½ cup cheese.

4 Bake, uncovered, for 25 to 30 minutes or until potatoes are tender. Let stand for 10 minutes before serving.

nutrition facts per serving: 210 cal., 8 g total fat (5 g sat. fat), 26 mg chol., 192 mg sodium, 25 g carb., 3 g dietary fiber, 10 g protein.

The distinctive tang of goat cheese plays well against hearty potato slices in this simple, satisfying dish. Serve this with roast chicken, pork, or beef.

potato–goat cheese gratin

prep: 30 minutes   bake: 1 hour 25 minutes   cook: 20 minutes
stand: 10 minutes   oven: 400°F   makes: 8 servings   dish: 2-quart

3	large leeks, (white part only), trimmed, halved lengthwise, and thinly sliced (1¼ cups)
1	tablespoon olive oil
1½	cups fat-free milk
1	tablespoon all-purpose flour
½	teaspoon salt
¼	teaspoon ground black pepper
⅛	teaspoon ground nutmeg
1	clove garlic, minced
	Nonstick cooking spray
2¼	pounds Yukon Gold potatoes (4 to 5 medium), peeled and cut in ⅛-inch slices
4	ounces goat cheese, crumbled (1 cup)
¼	cup panko (Japanese-style bread crumbs) or soft bread crumbs
¼	cup finely shredded Parmesan cheese
	Fresh Italian parsley

1 Preheat oven to 400°F. In a nonstick skillet cook leeks in hot oil over medium-low heat about 20 minutes or until tender and beginning to brown, stirring occasionally. Remove from heat.

2 In a bowl whisk 2 tablespoons of the milk into the flour. Whisk in the remaining milk, the salt, pepper, nutmeg, and garlic.

3 Spray a 2-quart casserole or au gratin dish with nonstick cooking spray. Arrange half the potato slices in dish. Sprinkle with cooked leeks and goat cheese. Top with half of the milk mixture. Layer the remaining potatoes; pour the remaining milk mixture over all.

4 Bake, uncovered, for 45 minutes. Bake about 25 minutes more or until potatoes are tender.

5 In a small bowl stir together the bread crumbs and Parmesan cheese. Sprinkle over potatoes. Bake, uncovered, about 15 minutes more or until topping is browned. Let stand 10 minutes before serving. Top with parsley.

nutrition facts per serving: 209 cal., 6 g total fat (3 g sat. fat), 9 mg chol., 278 mg sodium, 32 g carb., 2 g dietary fiber, 8 g protein.

make-ahead directions: Prepare casserole through Step 3, except do not preheat oven. Cover and chill for up to 24 hours. Remove from refrigerator and let stand at room temperature for 20 minutes. Bake in a 400°F oven as directed.

Gruyére cheese (pronounced groo-YEHR) is a dense, hard cheese with a creamy, nutty, earthy taste. It is comparable to Swiss cheese but sharper and not as sweet. Find it in the specialty cheese section of your supermarket.

creamy potato casserole

prep: 30 minutes bake: 1 hour 10 minutes stand: 10 minutes
oven: 350°F makes: 6 servings dish: 2-quart

1 medium onion, chopped

2 tablespoons butter or margarine

2 tablespoons all-purpose flour

2 tablespoons Dijon-style mustard

1¾ cups milk

½ of an 8-ounce package reduced-fat cream cheese (Neufchâtel), cut up

1 cup Gruyère cheese, shredded (4 ounces)

1 tablespoon snipped fresh chives

1½ pounds Yukon gold or round red potatoes, cut in thin wedges

8 ounces sliced cooked Black Forest or country ham, coarsely chopped

½ cup coarsely crushed bagel chips
Snipped fresh thyme and/or Italian parsley (optional)

1 Preheat oven to 350°F. Grease a 2-quart rectangular baking dish; set aside.

2 For sauce, in medium saucepan cook onion in hot butter over medium heat about 5 minutes or until tender, stirring occasionally. Stir in flour and mustard. Add milk all at once. Cook and stir over medium heat until slightly thickened and bubbly. Reduce heat to low. Whisk in Neufchâtel cheese until smooth. Gradually add ½ cup of the Gruyère cheese, whisking until cheese is melted. Stir in chives; transfer sauce to a large bowl.

3 Add potatoes and ham to sauce in bowl; toss gently to combine. Transfer to prepared baking dish.

4 Bake, covered, about 1 hour or until potatoes are tender. Uncover; stir carefully. Sprinkle with crushed chips and the remaining Gruyère cheese. Bake, uncovered, for 10 to 15 minutes more or until cheese is melted. Let stand for 10 minutes before serving. If desired, sprinkle with thyme and/or parsley.

nutrition facts per serving: 381 cal., 20 g total fat (11 g sat. fat), 73 mg chol., 846 mg sodium, 31 g carb., 3 g dietary fiber, 19 g protein.

This beautiful layered dish depends on thinly sliced potatoes. If your knife skills need work, try slicing on a mandoline—it's a wonderful tool to have.

herbed **yukon gold** and **sweet potato** gratin

prep: 25 minutes   bake: 1 hour 15 minutes   stand: 10 minutes
oven: 350°F   makes: 8 to 10 servings   dish: 3-quart

½ cup chopped
   scallions (4)
1 tablespoon snipped
   fresh sage
1 tablespoon snipped
   fresh thyme
3 cloves garlic, minced
1 teaspoon salt
½ teaspoon ground
   black pepper
1½ pounds sweet
   potatoes, peeled
   and thinly sliced
1½ pounds Yukon gold
   potatoes, peeled
   and thinly sliced
½ cup shredded
   Gruyère or Swiss
   cheese (2 ounces)
¼ cup finely shredded
   Parmesan cheese
   (1 ounce)
½ cup chicken broth
½ cup whipping cream
   Fresh sage leaves
   (optional)

1 Preheat oven to 350°F. Grease a 3-quart rectangular baking dish; set aside. In a small bowl combine scallions, snipped sage, thyme, garlic, salt, and pepper.

2 Layer half of the sweet potatoes and half of the Yukon gold potatoes in prepared baking dish, alternating rows, if desired. Top with half of the herb mixture; sprinkle with half of the Gruyère cheese and half of the Parmesan cheese. Repeat layers. Pour broth and cream over ingredients in dish.

3 Bake, covered, for 1 hour. Bake, uncovered, for 15 to 20 minutes more or until potatoes are tender and top is lightly browned. Let stand for 10 to 15 minutes before serving. If desired, garnish with sage leaves.

nutrition facts per serving: 240 cal., 9 g total fat (5 g sat. fat), 32 mg chol., 480 mg sodium, 34 g carb., 5 g dietary fiber, 7 g protein.

on the **side**

Blue or feta cheese provides an enticingly salty counterpart to the brown sugar–sweetened potato mixture and pineapple topper. Tote this to a holiday gathering and it will win rave reviews.

sweet potato casserole

prep: 40 minutes bake: 30 minutes oven: 350°F
makes: 8 to 12 servings dish: 3-quart

4 pounds sweet potatoes, peeled and quartered
4 eggs, lightly beaten
1 cup packed brown sugar
½ cup butter or margarine, cut up
¼ cup milk
3 to 4 tablespoons lemon juice
1 cup fresh or canned pineapple chunks, drained
½ cup crumbled blue cheese or feta cheese (2 ounces)

1 In a covered Dutch oven cook sweet potatoes in enough salted boiling water to cover for 25 to 30 minutes or until tender; drain. Return to pan.

2 Meanwhile, preheat oven to 350°F. Grease a 3-quart casserole dish; set aside. Slightly mash potatoes with a potato masher. Stir in eggs, brown sugar, butter, milk, and lemon juice. Transfer mixture to the prepared dish. Top with pineapple and cheese.

3 Bake, uncovered, for 30 to 35 minutes or until heated through.

nutrition facts per serving: 482 cal., 17 g total fat (10 g sat. fat), 143 mg chol., 370 mg sodium, 76 g carb., 7 g dietary fiber, 9 g protein.

make-ahead directions: Transfer potato mixture to casserole. Cover with lid or foil and chill up to 24 hours. Bake, covered, in a 350°F oven for 10 minutes. Remove cover; add pineapple and cheese. Bake, uncovered, as directed.

Although tomatoes and okra are a traditional Southern combo, this updated version is distinctive because it includes lima beans and is seasoned with lively crushed red pepper.

baked tomatoes and okra

prep: 25 minutes bake: 1 hour 15 minutes oven: 350°F
makes: 6 servings dish: 2-quart

½ cup frozen lima beans
8 ounces okra, washed, stemmed, and cut into ½-inch slices, or 2 cups frozen cut okra, thawed
2 cups chopped tomatoes (4 medium)
1 medium onion, sliced and separated into rings
½ of a medium yellow or green sweet pepper, seeded and cut into thin strips
¼ to ½ teaspoon crushed red pepper
¼ teaspoon salt

1 Preheat oven to 350°F. Cook lima beans according to package directions; drain.

2 In an ungreased 2-quart casserole combine cooked lima beans, okra, tomatoes, onion, sweet pepper, crushed red pepper, and salt.

3 Bake, covered, for 45 minutes; stir. Bake, uncovered, for 30 minutes more; stir. Serve with a slotted spoon.

nutrition facts per serving: 55 cal., 0 g total fat (0 g sat. fat), 0 mg chol., 112 mg sodium, 12 g carb., 3 g dietary fiber, 3 g protein.

Roasting the butternut squash heightens the flavor before it's paired with mascarpone, a mild, soft, butterlike cheese that adds creamy qualities to this bake.

butternut squash bake

prep: 30 minutes bake: 40 minutes oven: 425°F
makes: 8 to 10 servings dish: 2-quart

1½ pounds butternut squash, peeled, seeded, and cut in 1-inch cubes (3 cups)
2 tablespoons olive oil
8 ounces dried extra-wide noodles
4 tablespoons butter or margarine
6 shallots, chopped
1 tablespoon lemon juice
1 8-ounce carton mascarpone cheese
¾ cup grated Parmesan cheese
½ cup fresh Italian parsley, snipped
¼ teaspoon salt
¼ teaspoon ground black pepper
1 cup panko (Japanese-style bread crumbs) or soft bread crumbs

1 Preheat oven to 425°F. Grease a 2-quart oval gratin dish or baking dish; set aside. In a medium bowl toss squash with oil. Transfer squash to a greased 15×10×1-inch baking pan. Roast, uncovered, about 30 minutes or until lightly browned and tender, stirring twice.

2 Meanwhile, in a 4-quart Dutch oven cook noodles according to package directions. Drain. In same Dutch oven melt 2 tablespoons of the butter. Add shallots; cook and stir over medium heat for 3 to 5 minutes or until shallots are tender and butter just begins to brown. Stir in lemon juice.

3 Add noodles and squash to shallot mixture. Stir in mascarpone, ½ cup of the Parmesan cheese, ¼ cup parsley, salt, and pepper. Transfer to prepared dish.

4 In a small saucepan melt the remaining 2 tablespoons butter; stir in bread crumbs, the remaining Parmesan cheese, and remaining parsley. Sprinkle over noodle mixture. Bake, uncovered, about 10 minutes or until crumbs are golden.

nutrition facts per serving: 413 cal., 26 g total fat (13 g sat. fat), 82 mg chol., 278 mg sodium, 37 g carb., 2 g dietary fiber, 15 g protein.

Bright-colored miniature sweet peppers stuffed with a spicy andouille sausage and rice mixture make a sensational side.

cajun rice-stuffed mini peppers

prep: 50 minutes   bake: 20 minutes   oven: 375°F
makes: 24 to 28 servings   dish: baking pan

12 to 14 miniature red, yellow, and/or orange sweet peppers
¼ cup finely chopped celery
2 tablespoons finely chopped scallion (1)
1 clove garlic, minced
½ teaspoon Cajun seasoning
1 tablespoon olive oil
4 ounces cooked andouille sausage, finely chopped (about 1 cup)
1 cup cooked rice
½ cup shredded cheddar cheese (2 ounces)
2 tablespoons seasoned fine dry bread crumbs
1 tablespoon snipped fresh oregano

1 Preheat oven to 375°F. Halve peppers lengthwise; scoop out seeds and membranes (leave stems intact). In a large saucepan cook peppers in boiling water for 3 minutes; drain. Rinse peppers with cold running water until cool; drain again.

2 For filling, in a small skillet cook celery, scallion, garlic, and Cajun seasoning in hot oil for 3 minutes, stirring often. Remove from heat. In a medium bowl combine sausage, cooked rice, cheese, bread crumbs, oregano, and the cooked celery mixture.

3 Spoon the filling into pepper halves. Using your hands, press the filling firmly into peppers. Place peppers in an ungreased 15×10×1-inch baking pan.

4 Bake, uncovered, about 20 minutes or until heated through and cheese melts.

nutrition facts per serving: 34 cal., 2 g total fat (1 g sat. fat), 6 mg chol., 70 mg sodium, 3 g carb., 0 g dietary fiber, 2 g protein.

make-ahead directions: Prepare the peppers and filling as directed through Step 2. Cover and chill peppers and filling in separate airtight containers or in resealable plastic bags for up to 4 hours before serving. Spoon filling into peppers and bake as directed.

This herb butter is magic on roasted asparagus but would also be wonderful with grilled chicken, broiled fish, or scrambled with eggs.

roasted asparagus with fresh tarragon butter

prep: 15 minutes   chill: 1 hour   roast: 20 minutes   stand: 30 minutes
oven: 400°F   makes: 6 to 8 servings   dish: 3-quart

1 recipe Fresh
    Tarragon Butter
1½ pounds asparagus
1 to 2 tablespoons
    olive oil
1 to 2 cloves garlic,
    minced

1 Preheat oven to 400°F. Wash asparagus; break off woody bases where spears snap easily. If desired, scrape off scales.

2 Line a 3-quart rectangular baking dish with foil. Place asparagus in a large resealable plastic bag. Add oil and garlic to bag. Seal bag. Roll bag to massage the seasonings onto the asparagus spears.

3 Place asparagus in prepared dish. Drizzle oil in the bag over asparagus. Roast, uncovered, about 20 minutes or until crisp-tender.

4 Arrange asparagus on a serving platter. Cut Fresh Tarragon Butter into ½-inch-thick slices. Place desired number of slices of butter on top of asparagus. (Reserve the remaining Fresh Tarragon Butter for another use.)

nutrition facts per serving: 105 cal., 10 g total fat (4 g sat. fat), 22 mg chol., 83 mg sodium, 3 g carb., 1 g dietary fiber, 1 g protein.

fresh tarragon butter: Allow ½ cup butter to stand at room temperature for 30 minutes. In a small bowl stir together the softened butter; 2 tablespoons finely snipped fresh tarragon; 1 teaspoon finely shredded lemon zest; 1 clove garlic, minced; and ⅛ teaspoon salt until well mixed. Transfer to a sheet of waxed paper. Shape into a 4-inch-long roll. Wrap in waxed paper; twist ends to seal. Chill for at least 1 hour or until firm. Makes about ½ cup.

No peeling or chopping the vegetables! An easy-to-use bag of frozen vegetables goes gourmet with a buttery walnut topping.

vegetable medley
au gratin

prep: 20 minutes   bake: 1 hour   oven: 325°F/375°F
makes: 10 servings   dish: 2-quart

- 1   10.75-ounce can condensed cream of chicken soup or cream of mushroom soup
- ½   cup sour cream
- ½   teaspoon dried dill
- 2   16-ounce packages frozen broccoli, cauliflower, and carrots, thawed
- ⅔   cup coarsely crushed stone-ground wheat crackers (about 15 crackers)
- ⅓   cup finely chopped walnuts
- ¼   cup finely shredded Parmesan cheese (1 ounce)
- 2   tablespoons butter or margarine, melted

1 Preheat oven to 325°F. In an extra-large bowl combine soup, sour cream, and dill; stir in vegetables. Transfer mixture to an ungreased 2-quart rectangular baking dish. Bake, covered, for 45 minutes.

2 In a small bowl combine crackers, walnuts, and cheese; stir in melted butter. Sprinkle cracker mixture over vegetable mixture.

3 Increase oven temperature to 375°F. Bake, uncovered, about 15 minutes more or until mixture is heated through and topping is browned.

nutrition facts per serving: 157 cal., 10 g total fat (4 g sat. fat), 16 mg chol., 452 mg sodium, 11 g carb., 3 g dietary fiber, 5 g protein.

Diced green chile peppers and roasted red sweet peppers add a nice bite to this cheesy dish. If you're looking for a great meatless entrée, try this for dinner.

cheese and vegetable
rice casserole

prep: 20 minutes   bake: 35 minutes   stand: 10 minutes
oven: 350°F   makes: 6 servings   dish: 3-quart

1   16-ounce package
     frozen broccoli,
     cauliflower, and
     carrots, thawed
4   cups cooked rice
1   15-ounce can black
     beans, rinsed and
     drained
1   12-ounce jar roasted
     red sweet peppers,
     drained and
     coarsely chopped
1   cup frozen whole
     kernel corn, thawed
2   4-ounce cans diced
     green chile peppers,
     drained
2   cups shredded
     cheddar cheese
     (8 ounces)
1¼ cups chicken broth
½   cup seasoned fine dry
     bread crumbs
2   tablespoons butter or
     margarine, melted

1 Preheat oven to 350°F. Lightly grease a 3-quart rectangular baking dish; set aside.

2 In a large bowl stir together mixed vegetables, cooked rice, beans, roasted sweet peppers, corn, and chile peppers. Stir in 1 cup of the cheese and the broth. Transfer mixture to the prepared baking dish. Sprinkle with the remaining 1 cup cheese.

3 In a small bowl combine bread crumbs and melted butter. Sprinkle over vegetable mixture.

4 Bake, uncovered, for 35 to 40 minutes or until mixture is heated through and crumbs are golden. Let stand for 10 minutes before serving.

nutrition facts per serving: 471 cal., 18 g total fat (10 g sat. fat), 50 mg chol., 1423 mg sodium, 60 g carb., 8 g dietary fiber, 21 g protein.

Green beans and Brussels sprouts are a delectable pair when roasted with aromatic rosemary and smoky pancetta.

rosemary roasted
vegetables

prep: 30 minutes roast: 20 minutes oven: 425°F
makes: 12 servings dish: 3-quart

1 pound Brussels sprouts
12 ounces whole green beans
1 bunch scallions, trimmed and cut up
12 fresh rosemary sprigs
8 slices pancetta or bacon, partially cooked, drained, and cut up
2 tablespoons olive oil
 Salt and ground black pepper
1 lemon, halved

1 Preheat oven to 425°F. Halve any large Brussels sprouts. In a large covered saucepan cook Brussels sprouts in a small amount of lightly salted boiling water for 3 minutes. Add green beans and cook for 5 minutes more. Drain.

2 Transfer Brussels sprouts and green beans to an ungreased 3-quart rectangular baking dish. Add scallions and rosemary sprigs; toss to combine. Top with pancetta. Drizzle vegetable mixture with oil. Sprinkle with salt and pepper.

3 Roast, uncovered, about 20 minutes or until vegetables are crisp-tender and pancetta is crisp. Transfer to a serving platter. Squeeze juice from lemon over vegetables.

nutrition facts per serving: 143 cal., 10 g total fat (4 g sat. fat), 10 mg chol., 275 mg sodium, 6 g carb., 3 g dietary fiber, 4 g protein.

In this recipe, artisanal bread describes any crusty homemade or bakery-fresh loaf. If you wish, choose a loaf with added ingredients such as herbs, dried tomatoes, or cheese.

artisanal bread stuffing

prep: 50 minutes   bake: 1 hour 10 minutes   oven: 350°F
makes: 10 to 12 servings   dish: 3-quart

12   cups ½- to ¾-inch cubes artisanal bread (about a 1¼-pound loaf)
½   cup pine nuts
     Nonstick cooking spray
4½   cups coarsely chopped, cored fennel (reserve leafy green tops)
3   medium onions, chopped (1½ cups)
6   tablespoons butter or margarine
1½   cups pitted kalamata olives, coarsely chopped
3   tablespoons snipped fresh thyme or 1 tablespoon dried thyme, crushed
¾   teaspoon coarsely ground black pepper
2¼   cups chicken broth

1 Preheat oven to 350°F. In a large roasting pan combine bread cubes and pine nuts. Toast for 15 to 20 minutes or until bread cubes are crisp and pine nuts are lightly browned, tossing once. Set aside to cool.

2 Meanwhile, lightly coat a 3-quart rectangular baking dish with cooking spray; set aside. In a large skillet cook fennel and onions in hot butter over medium-high heat about 10 minutes or until vegetables are tender, stirring occasionally. Stir in olives, thyme, and pepper.

3 In a very large bowl combine bread cubes and pine nuts and fennel mixture, tossing to combine. Drizzle with chicken broth to moisten, tossing gently to combine.

4 Spoon stuffing into prepared dish. Bake, covered, for 45 minutes. Uncover and bake about 15 minutes more or until the stuffing is heated through. If desired, chop reserved fennel greens and sprinkle on top.

nutrition facts per serving: 319 cal., 16 g total fat (6 g sat. fat), 20 mg chol., 818 mg sodium, 38 g carb., 5 g dietary fiber, 8 g protein.

make-ahead directions:
Toast the bread cubes and pine nuts in Step 1 and store in an airtight container at room temperature for up to 1 day ahead. Chop the fennel and onion; place in airtight containers. Cover and chill for up to 6 hours ahead of preparing stuffing.

Rustic yet elegant, this gratin combines russet and sweet potatoes, turnips, and parsnips. An herbed cheese mixture complements the earthy flavors of the vegetables.

leek and root vegetable gratin

prep: 35 minutes   bake: 55 minutes   stand: 10 minutes
oven: 350°F/400°F   makes: 8 to 10 servings   dish: 3-quart

8   ounces mild cheddar or Muenster cheese, shredded (2 cups)
1   tablespoon finely chopped fresh herbs, such as Italian parsley, thyme, chives, and/or sage
1   tablespoon extra-virgin olive oil
3   large turnips or rutabagas (about 1 pound), peeled and thinly sliced
1   pound russet potatoes, thinly sliced*
2   cups thinly sliced leeks
1   pound large parsnips, peeled and thinly sliced
1½   pounds sweet potatoes, peeled and thinly sliced
    Assorted fresh herbs (optional)

1 Preheat the oven to 350°F. In a small bowl toss together cheese and chopped herbs; set aside. Coat a 3-quart rectangular baking dish with oil. Layer sliced vegetables in the following order, sprinkling salt, pepper, and 3 to 4 tablespoons the cheese mixture between each layer: half the turnip slices, half the potato slices, half the leek slices, half the parsnip slices, and half the sweet potato slices. Repeat, ending with sweet potato slices. Reserve the remaining cheese mixture.

2 Bake, covered, for 40 to 50 minutes. Remove foil. Sprinkle with the remaining cheese mixture. Increase oven temperature to 400°F. Bake, uncovered, about 15 minutes more or until cheese is melted and starting to brown.

3 Sprinkle with additional fresh herbs. Let stand for 10 minutes before serving.

nutrition facts per serving: 309 cal., 11 g total fat (6 g sat. fat), 27 mg chol., 422 mg sodium, 44 g carb., 8 g dietary fiber, 11 g protein.

*test kitchen tip: To prevent them from discoloring, slice the russet potatoes just before you layer the vegetables in the baking dish.

This tasty recipe calls for eggplant and Parmesan cheese, two Italian favorites. It comes in handy when you have dinner guests who prefer meatless dishes.

eggplant parmigiana

prep: 25 minutes   bake: 10 minutes   oven: 400°F
makes: 4 servings   dish: 2-quart

1   small eggplant
    (12 ounces)
1   egg, lightly beaten
1   tablespoon water
¼   cup all-purpose flour
2   tablespoons
    vegetable oil
⅓   cup grated Parmesan
    cheese
1   cup bottled meatless
    tomato pasta sauce
¾   cup shredded
    mozzarella cheese
    (3 ounces)

1 Preheat oven to 400°F. Peel eggplant; cut crosswise into ½-inch slices. In a shallow bowl combine egg and the water. Place flour in another shallow bowl. Dip eggplant slices into egg mixture, then into flour, turning to coat both sides.

2 In a large skillet heat oil over medium-high heat. Add half of the eggplant slices; cook for 4 to 6 minutes or until golden, turning once. Remove eggplant from skillet. Repeat with the remaining eggplant (if necessary, add additional oil).

3 Place eggplant slices in a single layer in an ungreased 2-quart rectangular baking dish cutting as necessary to fit. Sprinkle with Parmesan cheese. Top with pasta sauce and mozzarella cheese.

4 Bake, uncovered, for 10 to 12 minutes or until heated through.

nutrition facts per serving: 269 cal., 18 g total fat (6 g sat. fat), 76 mg chol., 660 mg sodium, 17 g carb., 3 g dietary fiber, 12 g protein.

While traditional baked beans are seasoned with salt pork and molasses, the pancetta and maple syrup add a lighter flavor. Pancetta is Italian cured bacon—you'll find it at Italian food stores.

boston **baked beans** with **pancetta**

prep: 30 minutes   cook: 1 hour   bake: 1 hour 30 minutes   stand: 1 hour
oven: 300°F   makes: 10 to 12 servings   dish: dutch oven

1 pound dried Great Northern or navy beans (2⅓ cups)*
6 ounces pancetta or bacon, chopped
1 cup chopped onion (1 large)
¼ cup packed brown sugar
⅓ cup maple syrup or molasses
¼ cup Worcestershire sauce
1½ teaspoons dry mustard
½ teaspoon salt
¼ teaspoon ground black pepper
4 ounces pancetta or bacon, chopped, crisp-cooked, and drained (optional)

1 Rinse beans. In a 4- to 5-quart ovenproof Dutch oven combine beans and 8 cups water. Bring to boiling; reduce heat. Simmer, uncovered, for 2 minutes. Remove from heat. Cover and let stand for 1 hour. (Or combine beans and 8 cups water in Dutch oven. Cover and let soak in a cool place overnight.) Drain and rinse beans.

2 Return beans to Dutch oven. Stir in 8 cups fresh water. Bring to boiling; reduce heat. Cover and simmer for 1 to 1¼ hours or until beans are tender, stirring occasionally. Drain beans, reserving liquid.

3 Preheat oven to 300°F. In the same Dutch oven cook 6 ounces pancetta and onion over medium heat until pancetta is slightly crisp and onion is tender, stirring occasionally. Add brown sugar; cook and stir until sugar is dissolved. Stir in maple syrup, Worcestershire sauce, dry mustard, salt, and pepper. Stir in drained beans and 1¼ cups of the reserved bean liquid.

4 Bake, covered, for 1 hour. Uncover and bake for 30 to 45 minutes more or until desired consistency, stirring occasionally. Beans will thicken slightly as they cool. If necessary, stir in additional reserved bean liquid. If desired, sprinkle with the 4 ounces cooked pancetta.

nutrition facts per serving: 275 cal., 6 g total fat (2 g sat. fat), 12 mg chol., 507 mg sodium, 44 g carb., 7 g dietary fiber, 12 g protein.

*test kitchen tip: You may substitute four 15-ounce cans navy beans and/or Great Northern beans, rinsed and drained, for the dried beans. Omit Steps 1 and 2. Prepare as directed in Steps 3 and 4, except add 1¼ cups water to the bean mixture in place of the reserved bean liquid.

Sour cream elevates baked beans to a creamy, rich delight that gets taken to even greater flavor heights with a topping of bacon, parsley, and lemon zest.

baked **butter beans**
with mustard

prep: 25 minutes   bake: 45 minutes   oven: 325°F
makes: 10 servings   dish: 2-quart

8   slices bacon
1   large onion, chopped
    (1 cup)
4   16-ounce cans butter
    beans and/or Great
    Northern beans,
    rinsed and drained
1   8-ounce carton sour
    cream
½   cup chicken or
    vegetable broth
1   tablespoon all-
    purpose flour
1   tablespoon snipped
    fresh rosemary
1   tablespoon Dijon-
    style mustard
¼   teaspoon ground
    black pepper
2   tablespoons chopped
    fresh Italian parsley
2   teaspoons finely
    shredded lemon
    zest

1 Preheat oven to 325°F. In a skillet cook bacon over medium heat until crisp. Remove; drain on paper towels. Crumble bacon. Drain skillet of all but 1 tablespoon drippings. Cook onion in drippings over medium heat until tender. Transfer to a large bowl. Add beans and all but 2 tablespoons of the bacon.

2 In a medium bowl whisk together sour cream, broth, flour, rosemary, mustard, and pepper. Stir into bean mixture. Transfer to an ungreased 2-quart casserole. Bake, covered, for 45 minutes, stirring once halfway through.

3 In a small bowl combine the remaining bacon, parsley, and lemon zest; sprinkle on beans just before serving.

nutrition facts per serving: 247 cal., 10 g total fat (5 g sat. fat), 20 mg chol., 892 mg sodium, 26 g carb., 6 g dietary fiber, 12 g protein.

make-ahead directions: Prepare as directed through Step 2. Cover and chill beans and toppers in separate containers for up to 3 days. Bake beans, covered, in 325°F oven for 1 hour, 15 minutes or until heated through. Sprinkle on toppers.

comfort

des

15

Top off a meal with the sweetest ending of all—
a feel-good dessert. From warm and tender
dumplings, cobblers, and crisps to sweet and
scrumptious bread puddings, these fresh
out-of-the-oven masterpieces are sure to
elicit plenty of smiles and compliments.

serts

For extra sweetness, whisk together ⅓ cup powdered sugar, 2 teaspoons milk, and 1 teaspoon lemon juice. Lightly brush on warm cake. Pictured on page 414.

upside-down berry-cornmeal cake

prep: 20 minutes **cool:** 5 minutes **bake:** 40 minutes **oven:** 350°F
makes: 10 servings **dish:** 8-inch round cake pan

3	cups fresh blueberries, raspberries, and/or blackberries
1⅓	cups all-purpose flour
½	cup yellow cornmeal
1	tablespoon finely snipped fresh basil or mint
2	teaspoons baking powder
¼	teaspoon salt
2	eggs, lightly beaten
½	cup sugar
⅔	cup milk
⅓	cup canola oil
	Fresh basil and/or mint (optional)

1 Preheat oven to 350°F. Lightly grease an 8×1½-inch round cake pan. Line bottom of pan with parchment paper; lightly grease the paper. Arrange 2 cups of the berries in bottom of pan; set side. In a large bowl stir together flour, cornmeal, snipped basil, baking powder, and salt.

2 In a medium bowl whisk together eggs, sugar, milk, and oil. Add egg mixture all at once to flour mixture; stir just until combined. Pour batter over berries in the prepared pan, spreading evenly.

3 Bake for 40 to 45 minutes or until a wooden toothpick inserted near the center comes out clean. Cool cake in pan on a wire rack for 5 minutes. Run a small knife around the edge of the pan to loosen sides of cake. Invert cake onto a serving plate. Remove parchment.

4 Top warm cake with the remaining berries. If desired, top with basil and/or mint.

nutrition facts per serving: 208 cal., 7 g total fat (1 g sat. fat), 43 mg chol., 152 mg sodium, 35 g carb., 2 g dietary fiber, 4 g protein.

Lively lemon and fresh blueberries are sensory delights, and this easy-to-make crisp is a delicious way to combine the flavors. Add a scoop of vanilla ice cream for a creamy sweet finish.

blueberry crisp

prep: 20 minutes   cool: 45 minutes   bake: 30 minutes
oven: 375°F   makes: 8 servings   dish: 3-quart

3   tablespoons all-
      purpose flour
2   tablespoons
      granulated sugar
6   cups fresh
      blueberries
¼   cup lemon juice
1   cup packed brown
      sugar
¾   cup all-purpose flour
¾   cup quick-cooking
      rolled oats
1¼   teaspoons ground
      cinnamon
½   cup cold butter
      Vanilla ice cream
      (optional)

1 Preheat oven to 375°F. In a large bowl stir together 3 tablespoons flour and granulated sugar. Add blueberries and lemon juice; toss gently to combine. Spread berry mixture evenly in an ungreased 3-quart rectangular baking dish.

2 For topping, in a medium bowl combine brown sugar, ¾ cup flour, oats, and cinnamon. Using a pastry blender, cut in butter until mixture resembles coarse crumbs. Sprinkle topping evenly over berry mixture.

3 Bake, uncovered, about 30 minutes or until topping is golden brown and edges are bubbly. Cool on a wire rack about 45 minutes. If desired, serve with ice cream.

nutrition facts per serving: 371 cal., 13 g total fat (8 g sat. fat), 33 mg chol., 142 mg sodium, 63 g carb., 4 g dietary fiber, 4 g protein.

No matter when you bake this homey dessert—in summer when peaches are fresh or at another time, when frozen peaches come to your aid—the aroma of this crumble-topped treasure will permeate every corner of your home.

peach crisp

prep: 30 minutes   cool: 30 minutes   bake: 40 minutes
oven: 375°F   makes: 12 servings   dish: 3-quart

8	cups ½-inch fresh or frozen peach slices (about 2 pounds), peeled (if desired)
⅓	cup granulated sugar
3	tablespoons all-purpose flour
1	teaspoon ground cinnamon
2	tablespoons honey
¾	cup coarsely crushed graham crackers (6 squares)
¾	cup packed brown sugar
½	cup all-purpose flour
¼	cup rolled oats
¼	teaspoon ground cinnamon
½	cup butter, cut up Vanilla ice cream (optional)

1 Thaw peaches, if frozen; do not drain. Preheat oven to 375°F. For filling, in a very large bowl stir together granulated sugar, 3 tablespoons flour, and 1 teaspoon cinnamon. Add peaches; toss to coat. Spread peach mixture in an ungreased 3-quart rectangular baking dish. Drizzle honey over peaches.

2 For topping, in a large bowl stir together crushed graham crackers, brown sugar, ½ cup flour, rolled oats, and ¼ teaspoon cinnamon. Using a pastry blender, cut in butter until mixture resembles coarse crumbs. Sprinkle topping evenly over the peach mixture.

3 Bake, uncovered, about 40 minutes or until topping is golden brown and filling is bubbly. If desired, serve with ice cream.

nutrition facts per serving: 391 cal., 16 g total fat (10 g sat. fat), 52 mg chol., 138 mg sodium, 59 g carb., 3 g dietary fiber, 5 g protein.

A rhubarb filling is rolled into pastry dough for a winning combination that tastes just as delicious as the traditional pie. Plan on about 2 pounds of fresh rhubarb to equal 5 cups sliced.

rhubarb pinwheel dumplings

prep: 40 minutes   cool: 30 minutes   bake: 45 minutes
oven: 350°F   makes: 12 servings   dish: 3-quart

2 cups sugar
2 cups water
1 teaspoon vanilla
2 cups all-purpose flour
2 teaspoons baking powder
1 teaspoon salt
½ teaspoon baking soda
½ cup shortening
½ cup milk
  All-purpose flour
½ cup butter, melted
5 cups sliced fresh rhubarb or frozen unsweetened sliced rhubarb, thawed
½ teaspoon ground cinnamon
¼ teaspoon ground nutmeg
  Vanilla ice cream (optional)

1 For syrup, in a medium saucepan combine sugar and the water. Cook and stir over medium heat until sugar is dissolved; bring to boiling and boil, uncovered, for 5 minutes. Remove saucepan from heat; stir in vanilla. Cover and keep warm.

2 For dough, in a large bowl stir together 2 cups flour, baking powder, salt, and baking soda. Using a pastry blender, cut shortening into flour mixture until pieces are the size of small peas. Make a well in center. Add milk all at once. Stir just until moistened. Turn out dough onto a lightly floured 14×12-inch piece of waxed paper; knead 10 to 12 strokes or until nearly smooth. Lightly sprinkle dough with additional flour. Cover with another 14×12-inch piece of waxed paper. Roll out dough to a 12×10-inch rectangle (about ¼ inch thick).

3 Preheat oven to 350°F. Pour melted butter into a 3-quart rectangular baking dish. For filling, in another large bowl combine rhubarb, cinnamon, and nutmeg. Spoon 3 cups of the rhubarb mixture on top of the melted butter in dish, spreading evenly to form a single layer. Spoon the remaining 2 cups rhubarb mixture evenly over the dough rectangle. Starting from a long side, roll up dough into a spiral. Pinch seam to seal. Cut into twelve 1-inch-wide pieces. Arrange pieces, cut sides down, over the rhubarb mixture in dish. Pour syrup carefully around rolls. (This will look like too much syrup, but the rolls will absorb the liquid during baking.)

4 Bake, uncovered, for 45 to 50 minutes or until golden brown. Cool in dish on a wire rack for 30 minutes. Serve warm. If desired, top with ice cream.

nutrition facts per serving: 369 cal., 16 g total fat (7 g sat. fat), 21 mg chol., 369 mg sodium, 54 g carb., 2 g dietary fiber, 3 g protein.

Dating back to colonial America, betties are baked puddings made of layers of sugared and spiced fruit and soft bread cubes or crumbs.

peach-berry betty

prep: 15 minutes bake: 30 minutes oven: 375°F
makes: 6 servings dish: 2-quart

1 Thaw raspberries and peaches, if frozen. Do not drain. Preheat oven to 375°F.

2 For filling, in a large bowl combine sugar, flour, and ginger. Add berries and peaches and their juices; toss to coat. Add 2 cups of the bread cubes; toss gently until combined. Transfer filling to an ungreased 2-quart casserole or square baking dish.

3 For topping, place the remaining bread cubes in a medium mixing bowl. Drizzle with melted butter; toss to coat. Sprinkle topping over fruit filling. Bake about 30 minutes or until fruit is tender and topping is golden. If desired, serve warm with whipped cream.

nutrition facts per serving: 248 cal., 7 g total fat (4 g sat. fat), 15 mg chol., 251 mg sodium, 45 g carb., 7 g dietary fiber, 4 g protein.

- 3 cups fresh red raspberries or one 12-ounce package frozen red raspberries
- 2 cups sliced, peeled peaches or frozen unsweetened peach slices
- ½ cup sugar
- 1 tablespoon all-purpose flour
- 1 tablespoon finely chopped crystallized ginger or ⅛ teaspoon ground ginger
- 5 cups soft whole wheat bread cubes (about 7 slices)
- 3 tablespoons butter, melted
   Sweetened whipped cream (optional)

apple betty: Prepare as directed, except substitute 5 cups peeled, cored, and sliced cooking apples (5 medium) for the peaches and raspberries, ½ teaspoon ground cinnamon for the ginger, and white bread for the whole wheat bread.

Spicy sweet crystallized ginger in the cherry filling invigorates the senses with every bite. Also known as candied ginger, it's available already chopped in the spice section in many supermarkets.

gingered cherry cobbler

prep: 25 minutes   cool: 30 minutes   bake: 20 minutes
oven: 400°F   makes: 8 to 10 servings   dish: 3-quart

1½	cups all-purpose flour*
½	cup packed brown sugar
½	cup rolled oats
2	teaspoons baking powder
½	teaspoon salt
½	teaspoon baking soda
½	cup butter
8	cups fresh or frozen unsweetened pitted tart red cherries
¾	cup granulated sugar
¼	cup chopped crystallized ginger
3	tablespoons cornstarch
½	teaspoon ground cinnamon
1	egg, lightly beaten
¾	cup milk
½	cup pecan pieces or chopped almonds (optional)
1	tablespoon coarse white decorating sugar
	Sweetened whipped cream (optional)

1 Preheat oven to 400°F. Grease a 3-quart rectangular baking dish; set aside.

2 For topping, in a medium bowl stir together flour, brown sugar, rolled oats, baking powder, salt, and baking soda. Using a pastry blender, cut in butter until mixture resembles coarse crumbs; set aside.

3 For filling, in a large saucepan combine cherries, granulated sugar, ginger, cornstarch, and cinnamon. Cook over medium heat until cherries release juice, stirring occasionally. Continue to cook, stirring constantly, over medium heat until thickened and bubbly. Keep filling hot.

4 In a small bowl stir together egg and milk. Add to flour mixture, stirring just to moisten. Pour hot cherry filling into prepared baking dish. Immediately drop dough in 10 to 12 mounds on top of hot cherry mixture. Sprinkle dough with nuts (if using) and coarse sugar.

5 Bake, uncovered, for 20 to 25 minutes or until topping is golden brown and a wooden toothpick inserted in topping comes out clean. Cool in dish on a wire rack for 30 minutes. If desired, serve with whipped cream.

nutrition facts per serving: 484 cal., 14 g total fat (8 g sat. fat), 59 mg chol., 397 mg sodium, 86 g carb., 4 g dietary fiber, 7 g protein.

*test kitchen tip: If desired, use 1 cup all-purpose flour and ½ cup whole wheat flour.

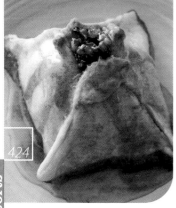

These pretty pastry packages have raisin-filled apples baked inside. Serve warm with the butter sauce for a special autumn dessert.

saucy apple
dumplings

prep: 45 minutes bake: 1 hour oven: 350°F makes: 6 servings dish: 3-quart

2	cups water
1¼	cups sugar
½	teaspoon ground cinnamon
¼	cup butter or margarine
2	cups all-purpose flour
½	teaspoon salt
⅔	cup shortening
⅓	to ½ cup half-and-half or light cream
2	tablespoons chopped golden raisins
2	tablespoons chopped walnuts
1	tablespoon honey
2	tablespoons sugar
½	teaspoon ground cinnamon
6	small cooking apples
1	tablespoon butter or margarine

1 For sauce, in a medium saucepan combine the water, 1¼ cups sugar, and ½ teaspoon cinnamon. Bring to boiling; reduce heat. Simmer, uncovered, for 5 minutes. Stir in the ¼ cup butter; set aside.

2 Meanwhile, for pastry, in a medium bowl combine flour and salt. Using a pastry blender, cut in shortening until pieces are the size of small peas. Sprinkle 1 tablespoon of the half-and-half over part of the mixture; gently toss with a fork. Push moistened dough to the side of the bowl. Repeat moistening dough, using 1 tablespoon of the half-and-half at a time, until all of the dough is moistened. Form dough into a ball. On a lightly floured surface, roll dough into a 12×18-inch rectangle.* Using a pastry wheel or sharp knife, cut into six 6-inch squares.

3 In a small bowl combine raisins, walnuts, and honey. In another small bowl combine the 2 tablespoons sugar and ½ teaspoon cinnamon.

4 Preheat oven to 350°F. Peel and core apples. Place an apple on each pastry square. Fill centers of apples with raisin mixture. Sprinkle with sugar-cinnamon mixture; dot with the 1 tablespoon butter. Moisten edges of each pastry square with water; fold corners to center over apple. Pinch to seal. Place dumplings in an ungreased 3-quart rectangular baking dish. Reheat sauce to boiling and pour over dumplings.

5 Bake, uncovered, about 1 hour or until apples are tender and pastry is golden brown. To serve, spoon sauce from dish over warm dumplings.

nutrition facts per serving: 586 cal., 36 g total fat (18 g sat. fat), 32 mg chol., 306 mg sodium, 68 g carb., 4 g dietary fiber, 1 g protein.

*test kitchen tip: If desired, roll pastry slightly larger so you'll have extra to make pastry leaves for garnishing. Cut the 6-inch squares of pastry; reroll scraps and cut into leaf shapes. Moisten underside of leaf shapes with water; place on top of dumplings, pressing slightly to attach.

Fresh cranberries are available for only a short time, but they freeze beautifully. Buy extra bags and freeze them to use year-round.

apple-cranberry dessert

prep: 30 minutes   cool: 30 minutes   bake: 1 hour
oven: 325°F   makes: 6 servings   dish: 2-quart

1   12-ounce package fresh or frozen cranberries or one 16-ounce package frozen unsweetened pitted tart red cherries*
1   cup chopped peeled cooking apples
1   tablespoon butter, cut up
²/₃ cup sugar
¹/₂ cup chopped walnuts or pecans
1   egg, lightly beaten
¹/₃ cup butter, melted
¹/₂ cup sugar
¹/₃ cup all-purpose flour
    Vanilla ice cream

1 Preheat oven to 325°F. Grease the bottom of a 2-quart baking dish. Toss the cranberries and apples together in prepared dish. Dot cranberry mixture with 1 tablespoon butter. Sprinkle evenly with ²/₃ cup sugar and the chopped walnuts.

2 In a small bowl whisk together egg, melted butter, ¹/₂ cup sugar, and flour until well combined. Pour evenly over cranberry mixture.

3 Bake about 1 hour or until top is golden brown and filling is bubbly. Cool on a wire rack for at least 30 minutes. Serve warm or at room temperature with vanilla ice cream.

nutrition facts per serving: 540 cal., 27 g total fat (13 g sat. fat), 99 mg chol., 157 mg sodium, 72 g carb., 4 g dietary fiber, 6 g protein.

*test kitchen tip: If using frozen cranberries, do not thaw before tossing with the apple. If using frozen cherries, let stand at room temperature for 30 minutes before tossing with the apple.

Pecan-swirled biscuits make a tasty topping for this juicy, crowd-pleasing cobbler.

peach-praline cobbler

prep: 25 minutes bake: 25 minutes oven: 400°F
makes: 12 servings dish: 3-quart

8	cups sliced, peeled fresh or frozen peaches
¾	cup packed brown sugar
¼	cup butter, melted
1½	cups chopped pecans
1	cup granulated sugar
1	cup water
2	tablespoons cornstarch
1	teaspoon ground cinnamon
¾	cup milk
2	teaspoons lemon juice
2¼	cups all-purpose flour
2	teaspoons granulated sugar
2	teaspoons baking powder
½	teaspoon baking soda
½	teaspoon salt
½	cup shortening
	Milk (optional)

1 Thaw frozen peach slices, if using; do not drain. Preheat oven to 400°F. For pecan filling, stir together brown sugar and melted butter. Add pecans; toss to mix. Set aside.

2 In a Dutch oven combine peaches, 1 cup granulated sugar, the water, cornstarch, and cinnamon. Cook and stir until mixture is thickened and bubbly. Keep warm.

3 Combine ¾ cup milk and lemon juice. For dough, in a large bowl stir together flour, 2 teaspoons granulated sugar, baking powder, baking soda, and salt. Cut in shortening until mixture resembles coarse crumbs. Make a well in the center; add milk mixture. Stir just until dough clings together.

4 Turn dough out onto a lightly floured surface. Knead gently for 10 to 12 strokes. Roll dough into a 12×8-inch rectangle; spread with pecan filling. Roll up from one of the long sides. Cut into twelve 1-inch slices.

5 Transfer hot peach mixture to an ungreased 3-quart rectangular baking dish. Place slices, cut side down, on top of the hot peach mixture. Bake about 25 minutes or until topping is golden. Serve warm with additional milk, if desired.

nutrition facts per serving: 511 cal., 23 g total fat (6 g sat. fat), 12 mg chol., 272 mg sodium, 76 g carb., 7 g dietary fiber, 6 g protein.

A sweet and spicy raisin filling is a great way to showcase this fruit's delicious appeal. Choose crisp apples such as Rome Beauty, Granny Smith, or Jonathan because they'll retain their shape while baking.

baked **apples**

prep: 15 minutes bake: 40 minutes oven: 350°F
makes: 4 servings dish: 2-quart

4 medium cooking apples
½ cup raisins, snipped pitted whole dates, or mixed dried fruit bits
2 tablespoons packed brown sugar
½ teaspoon ground cinnamon
¼ teaspoon ground nutmeg
⅓ cup apple juice, apple cider, or water
Caramel ice cream topping (optional)

1 Preheat oven to 350°F. Core apples; peel a strip from the top of each apple. Place apples in an ungreased 2-quart casserole. In a small bowl combine raisins, brown sugar, cinnamon, and nutmeg; spoon into centers of apples. Pour apple juice into casserole.

2 Bake, uncovered, for 40 to 45 minutes or until the apples are tender, basting occasionally with liquid from casserole. If desired, drizzle with caramel topping.

nutrition facts per serving: 164 cal., 1 g total fat (0 g sat. fat), 0 mg chol., 5 mg sodium, 42 g carb., 5 g dietary fiber, 1 g protein.

Sweet yellow apples complement the tart dried cherries in this comforting dessert. Top each serving with vanilla ice cream and drizzle with caramel sauce.

cherry-apple bread pudding

prep: 25 minutes   cool: 30 minutes   bake: 45 minutes   oven: 350°F
makes: 8 to 10 servings   dish: 3-quart

9   slices firm-textured white bread
3   tablespoons butter, softened
3   medium Golden Delicious apples, peeled, cored, and very thinly sliced
2   tablespoons lemon juice
½   cup dried tart red cherries
6   eggs, beaten
3   cups milk
½   cup sugar

1 Preheat oven to 350°F. Lightly butter one side of bread slices; cut bread into quarters. Arrange half of the bread pieces, buttered side down, in an ungreased 3-quart rectangular baking dish. In a large bowl toss together apples and lemon juice. Sprinkle apples and dried cherries over bread in baking dish. Top with the remaining bread, buttered side up.

2 In a large bowl stir together eggs, milk, and sugar. Pour egg mixture evenly over bread in dish. Using the back of a large spoon, press bread mixture down lightly to moisten.

3 Bake, uncovered, for 45 to 50 minutes or until set and a knife inserted near center comes out clean. Cool on a wire rack for 30 minutes. Serve warm.

nutrition facts per serving: 315 cal., 11 g total fat (5 g sat. fat), 178 mg chol., 270 mg sodium, 45 g carb., 2 g dietary fiber, 10 g protein.

Rich cakes with molten chocolate centers have recently emerged as one of the most popular restaurant desserts in years. Their appeal is no surprise—few diners can resist a dessert that oozes with chocolate! What is a surprise is how easy they are to make at home.

mocha lava baby cakes

prep: 15 minutes   chill: 45 minutes   cool: 2 minutes   bake: 13 minutes
oven: 400°F   makes: 6 servings   dish: 6-ounce dishes

¾	cup semisweet chocolate pieces
2	tablespoons whipping cream
½	teaspoon instant espresso coffee powder
1	cup semisweet chocolate pieces
¾	cup butter
1	teaspoon instant espresso coffee powder
3	eggs
3	egg yolks
⅓	cup sugar
1½	teaspoons vanilla
⅓	cup all-purpose flour
3	tablespoons unsweetened cocoa powder
	Caramel ice cream topping (optional)

1 For filling, in a small heavy saucepan combine ¾ cup chocolate pieces, cream, and ½ teaspoon coffee powder, stirring until coffee powder is dissolved. Cook and stir over low heat until chocolate is melted. Cool, stirring occasionally. Cover and chill about 45 minutes or until firm.

2 Meanwhile, in a medium heavy saucepan cook and stir 1 cup chocolate pieces, butter, and 1 teaspoon coffee powder over low heat until smooth; cool.

3 Preheat oven to 400°F. Lightly grease and flour six ¾-cup soufflé dishes or 6-ounce custard cups. Place dishes or cups in a 15×10×1-inch baking pan. Form chilled filling into six balls.

4 In a medium bowl combine eggs, egg yolks, sugar, and vanilla. Beat with an electric mixer on high speed about 5 minutes or until lemon colored. Beat in cooled chocolate-butter mixture on medium speed until combined. Sift flour and cocoa powder over mixture; beat on low speed just until combined. Spoon ⅓ cup of the batter into each prepared dish. Place one ball of filling in each dish. Divide the remaining batter among dishes.

5 Bake about 13 minutes or until edges of cakes are firm. Cool in dishes on a wire rack for 2 to 3 minutes. Using a knife, loosen cakes from sides of dishes. Invert onto six dessert plates. If desired, top with warm caramel ice cream topping. Serve immediately.

nutrition facts per serving: 621 cal., 47 g total fat (27 g sat. fat), 285 mg chol., 291 mg sodium, 50 g carb., 3 g dietary fiber, 8 g protein.

make-ahead directions: Prepare as directed through Step 4, except do not preheat oven. Cover and chill for up to 4 hours. Let stand at room temperature for 30 minutes before baking as directed.

The lightest, most delicate lemon cake imaginable tops off a layer of lemon pudding in this captivating creation.

lemon soufflé dessert

prep: 25 minutes cool: 5 minutes bake: 40 minutes
oven: 350°F makes: 4 servings dish: 1-quart

Nonstick cooking
  spray
6 tablespoons
  granulated sugar
¼ cup all-purpose flour
2 teaspoons finely
  shredded lemon
  zest
¼ cup lemon juice
1 tablespoon butter,
  melted
2 egg yolks
1 cup milk
3 egg whites
  Powdered sugar

1 Preheat oven to 350°F. Lightly coat a 1-quart soufflé dish with cooking spray; set aside. In a large bowl combine 2 tablespoons of the granulated sugar and the flour. Whisk in lemon zest, lemon juice, and melted butter until smooth. In a small bowl whisk together egg yolks and milk. Whisk egg yolk mixture into flour mixture just until combined.

2 In a medium bowl beat egg whites with an electric mixer on medium speed until soft peaks form (tips curl). Gradually add the remaining 4 tablespoons granulated sugar, beating on high speed until stiff peaks form (tips stand straight). Stir a small amount of beaten egg whites into lemon mixture to lighten. Gently fold in the remaining beaten egg whites (batter will be thin).

3 Pour batter into prepared soufflé dish. Place soufflé dish in a 13×9×2-inch baking pan. Place baking pan on an oven rack. Pour boiling water into baking pan around soufflé dish to a depth of 1 inch.

4 Bake about 40 minutes or until top springs back when lightly touched. Carefully remove soufflé dish from baking pan. Cool on a wire rack for 5 minutes. Sprinkle lightly with powdered sugar. Serve warm.

nutrition facts per serving: 190 cal., 5 g total fat (3 g sat. fat), 111 mg chol., 92 mg sodium, 29 g carb., 0 g dietary fiber, 7 g protein.

If you want to serve these fruited custards at room temperature rather than cold out of the refrigerator, let them stand on the counter for 30 minutes before serving.

raspberry
crème brûlée

prep: 25 minutes **chill:** 8 hours **bake:** 1 hour **stand:** 15 minutes
oven: 325°F **makes:** 8 servings **dish:** 4-ounce dishes

2 cups whipping cream
1 vanilla bean,* split lengthwise
5 egg yolks, lightly beaten
½ cup sugar
¾ cup fresh raspberries or sliced small fresh strawberries
   Fresh raspberries or strawberries (optional)

1 Preheat oven to 325°F. In a small heavy saucepan combine cream and vanilla bean. Cook over medium-low heat about 15 minutes or just until mixture starts to simmer, stirring frequently (do not boil). Remove from heat. Cover and let stand about 15 minutes to infuse cream with vanilla flavor. Remove vanilla bean and discard.

2 In a medium mixing bowl combine egg yolks and sugar. Beat with an electric mixer on low speed just until mixture is pale yellow and thick. Gradually whisk about half of the cream mixture into the egg mixture. Pour egg mixture into the remaining cream mixture, stirring until completely combined.

3 Place eight 4-ounce ramekins or six 6-ounce custard cups in a 13×9×2-inch baking pan. Divide the ¾ cup berries among ramekins. Divide cream mixture evenly among ramekins. Place baking pan on rack in oven. Pour boiling water into the baking pan to reach halfway up sides of ramekins.

4 Bake about 1 hour or until a knife inserted near the centers comes out clean. Remove ramekins from water; cool on a wire rack. Cover and chill for 1 to 8 hours. If desired, garnish with additional berries.

*test kitchen tip: You may substitute 2 teaspoons vanilla extract for the vanilla bean. If using the vanilla extract, heat only the whipping cream just until warm; do not cook until simmering or let stand for 15 minutes. Add vanilla extract to warm cream.

nutrition facts per serving: 292 cal., 25 g total fat (15 g sat. fat), 210 mg chol., 28 mg sodium, 15 g carb., 1 g dietary fiber, 3 g protein.

Caramelized sugar is poured into the cups before the custard is added. When the baked flans are unmolded, caramel spills over them like a sauce.

caramel flans

prep: 25 minutes   bake: 30 minutes   stand: 10 minutes   oven: 325°F
makes: 4 servings   dish: 6-ounce dishes

⅓ cup sugar
3 eggs, lightly beaten
1½ cups half-and-half
⅓ cup sugar
1 teaspoon vanilla
   Ground nutmeg
   (optional)

1 To caramelize sugar, in a medium heavy skillet heat ⅓ cup sugar over medium-high heat until it begins to melt, shaking the skillet occasionally; do not stir. When the sugar starts to melt, reduce heat to low and cook about 5 minutes or until all of the sugar is melted, stirring as needed with a wooden spoon. Immediately divide caramelized sugar among four 6-ounce custard cups; tilt cups to coat bottoms. Let stand for 10 minutes.

2 Meanwhile, preheat oven to 325°F. Combine eggs, half-and-half, ⅓ cup sugar, and vanilla. Beat until well combined but not foamy. Place the custard cups in a 2-quart square baking dish. Divide egg mixture among custard cups. Sprinkle with nutmeg (if using). Place baking dish on oven rack. Pour boiling water into baking dish around custard cups to a depth of 1 inch. Bake for 30 to 40 minutes or until a knife inserted near the centers comes out clean.

3 Remove custard cups from water. Cool slightly on a wire rack and unmold. (Or cool completely in custard cups. Cover and chill until serving time.) Using a sharp knife, loosen flan from sides of cups. Invert a plate over each cup; turn plate and cup over together. Remove cups.

nutrition facts per serving: 304 cal., 14 g total fat (8 g sat. fat), 192 mg chol., 89 mg sodium, 38 g carb., 0 g dietary fiber, 7 g protein.

make-ahead directions: Prepare and bake flans as directed. Cool flans completely in custard cups on a wire rack. Cover and chill until serving time.

Lemon curd is really just a very thick lemon sauce. You'll find it shelved along with jams and jellies in larger supermarkets.

lemon-lavender custards

prep: 25 minutes chill: 2 hours bake: 40 minutes oven: 325°F
makes: 6 servings dish: 6-ounce dishes

2	cups milk
2	tablespoons sugar
1½	teaspoons dried lavender buds or 2 sprigs fresh lemon thyme or thyme
3	eggs, lightly beaten
⅓	cup lemon curd
1	teaspoon vanilla

1 Preheat oven to 325°F. In a medium saucepan combine milk, sugar, and lavender. Cook over medium-low heat just until mixture starts to simmer, stirring frequently. Remove from heat. Strain mixture through a fine-mesh sieve into a bowl; discard lavender.

2 In a medium bowl whisk eggs, lemon curd, and vanilla until combined. Gradually whisk the warm strained milk mixture into egg mixture.

3 Place six 6-ounce custard cups in a 13×9×2-inch baking pan. Divide milk mixture evenly among custard cups. Place baking pan on an oven rack. Pour enough boiling water into baking pan to reach halfway up sides of custard cups.

4 Bake, uncovered, about 40 minutes or until edges are set and centers appear nearly set when gently shaken. Remove custard cups from water; cool on a wire rack. Cover and chill for 2 to 24 hours.

5 Using a knife, loosen custards from sides of custard cups and invert onto six dessert plates.

nutrition facts per serving: 117 cal., 1 g total fat (1 g sat. fat), 15 mg chol., 105 mg sodium, 22 g carb., 2 g dietary fiber, 6 g protein.

The apple varieties Jonathan, McIntosh, Braeburn, Pippin, and Winesap are the best tart-sweet baking apples for this ooey-gooey caramel-sauced cake.

upside-down one-bowl
apple cake

prep: 25 minutes cool: 25 minutes bake: 55 minutes oven: 350°F
makes: 9 servings dish: 2-quart

⅓	cup butter, cut up
6	very small red cooking apples (1¼ to 1½ pounds)
⅓	cup packed brown sugar
1⅓	cups all-purpose flour
⅔	cup granulated sugar
2	teaspoons baking powder
1	teaspoon ground ginger
1	teaspoon ground cinnamon
⅔	cup milk
¼	cup butter, softened
1	egg
1	teaspoon vanilla Vanilla ice cream (optional)

1 Preheat oven to 350°F. Place ⅓ cup butter in a 2-quart square baking dish. Place in oven about 5 minutes or until butter is melted. Halve apples; remove stems. With a melon baller or small spoon, scoop out apple cores.

2 Sprinkle brown sugar over melted butter; stir to combine. Spread evenly over bottom of dish. Arrange nine of the apple halves, cut sides down, in butter mixture. Bake for 10 to 15 minutes or until butter mixture is bubbly.

3 Meanwhile, peel and coarsely shred the remaining three apple halves. In a medium bowl stir together flour, granulated sugar, baking powder, ginger, and cinnamon. Add shredded apple, milk, ¼ cup softened butter, egg, and vanilla. Beat with an electric mixer on low speed until combined. Beat on medium speed for 1 minute. Gently spoon batter gently over apples in dish, spreading evenly (some apple may still be exposed and some butter mixture may come to the surface).

4 Bake about 35 minutes or until a wooden toothpick inserted near center comes out clean. Cool in pan on a wire rack for 5 minutes.

5 Using a sharp knife or narrow metal spatula, loosen edges of cake from sides of dish. Carefully invert onto a serving platter. Spoon any butter mixture remaining in pan onto cake. Cool for 20 minutes more. Serve warm. If desired, serve with ice cream.

nutrition facts per serving: 313 cal., 13 g total fat (8 g sat. fat), 56 mg chol., 157 mg sodium, 47 g carb., 2 g dietary fiber, 3 g protein.

comfort **desserts**

Using top ingredients is the surest route to the most delectable cakes. Find fresh pineapple—peeled, cored, and packed in its own juice—in the produce section of grocery stores.

carrot-pineapple
upside-down cake

prep: 30 minutes **cool:** 5 minutes **bake:** 45 minutes **oven:** 350°F
makes: 9 servings **dish:** 2-quart

Nonstick cooking
   spray
⅓ cup packed brown
   sugar
2 tablespoons butter
1 tablespoon water
6 to 8¼-inch slices
   fresh pineapple,
   cored and halved
2 cups all-purpose flour
1 tablespoon baking
   powder
½ teaspoon salt
¼ teaspoon ground
   nutmeg
½ cup butter, softened
1 cup granulated sugar
2 eggs
1 teaspoon vanilla
¾ cup milk
1½ cups finely shredded
   carrots (3 medium)

1 Preheat oven to 350°F. Lightly coat a 2-quart square baking dish with cooking spray; set aside.

2 In a small saucepan combine brown sugar, 2 tablespoons butter, and the water. Cook and stir over medium heat until mixture comes to boiling. Pour into prepared dish; tilt to evenly coat bottom. Arrange pineapple in dish; set aside.

3 In a medium bowl combine flour, baking powder, salt, and nutmeg.

4 In a large bowl beat ½ cup butter with an electric mixer on medium to high speed for 30 seconds. Add granulated sugar. Beat until light and fluffy, scraping side of bowl occasionally. Beat in eggs and vanilla until combined. Alternately add flour mixture and milk, beating on low speed after each addition just until combined. Stir in carrot. Carefully pour batter over pineapple, spreading evenly.

5 Bake about 45 minutes or until top is golden and a toothpick inserted in center comes out clean. Cool in pan on a wire rack for 5 minutes. Using a knife, loosen edges of cake from dish; invert onto a serving platter. Spoon any brown sugar mixture remaining in dish onto cake. Serve warm.

nutrition facts per serving: 374 cal., 15 g total fat (9 g sat. fat), 82 mg chol., 341 mg sodium, 56 g carb., 2 g dietary fiber, 5 g protein.

Luscious berries also add a sweet depth of flavor to this fluffy custardlike cake. Substitute one or more types, including blueberries, raspberries, or sliced strawberries for the other fruit.

mixed fruit clafouti

prep: 30 minutes Cool: 15 minutes bake: 50 minutes
oven: 375°F makes: 8 servings dish: 9-inch pie plate

⅔ cup whipping cream
⅓ cup milk
3 eggs
⅓ cup all-purpose flour
¼ cup granulated sugar
2 tablespoons butter, melted
1 teaspoon vanilla
¼ teaspoon almond extract (optional)
⅛ teaspoon salt
3 cups mixed fruit, such as fresh or frozen sliced plums and/or peaches, thawed, and frozen sweet cherries, thawed
1 tablespoon powdered sugar

1 Preheat oven to 375°F. Butter the bottom and sides of a 9-inch pie plate or eight 6- to 8-ounce custard dishes or ramekins; set aside.

2 In a medium mixing bowl combine whipping cream, milk, eggs, flour, granulated sugar, melted butter, vanilla, almond extract, and salt. Beat with an electric mixer on low speed until smooth. Arrange mixed fruit in prepared pie plate or custard cups. Pour cream mixture over berries. If using custard cups, place on a baking sheet.

3 Bake for 50 to 55 minutes for pie plate, 25 to 30 minutes for custard dishes, or until puffed and light brown. Cool for 15 to 20 minutes on a wire rack. Sift powdered sugar over top(s). Serve warm.

nutrition facts per serving: 204 cal., 13 g total fat (7 g sat. fat), 116 mg chol., 48 mg sodium, 19 g carb., 1 g dietary fiber, 4 g protein.

Love to look inside bakery cases and gaze at all the amazing rolls and pastries? These small wonders create a big splash and rival any pastry shop creation.

sticky pecan
upside-down baby cakes

prep: 30 minutes **cool:** 5 minutes **bake:** 25 minutes **oven:** 350°F
makes: 12 cakes **dish:** jumbo muffin pan

Nonstick cooking
    spray
²/₃ cup packed brown
    sugar
½ cup butter
⅓ cup honey
1½ cups coarsely
    chopped pecans
1 teaspoon finely
    shredded orange
    zest
2½ cups all-purpose flour
1 teaspoon baking
    powder
½ teaspoon baking soda
½ teaspoon salt
3 eggs
2 cups granulated
    sugar
1 cup cooking oil
1 8-ounce carton sour
    cream
2 teaspoons vanilla

1 Preheat oven to 350°F. Lightly coat twelve 3½-inch (jumbo) muffin cups with cooking spray; set aside.

2 In a medium saucepan combine brown sugar, butter, and honey. Cook and stir over medium heat about 2 minutes or until smooth; remove from heat. Stir in pecans and orange zest; set aside. In a medium bowl stir together flour, baking powder, baking soda, and salt.

3 In a large bowl combine eggs and granulated sugar. Beat with an electric mixer on medium to high speed about 3 minutes or until mixture is thick and lemon-colored. Add oil, sour cream, and vanilla; beat until combined. Gradually add flour mixture, beating on low speed until smooth.

4 Place 2 tablespoons of the pecan mixture in the bottom of each muffin cup. Spoon a heaping ⅓ cup batter into each cup. Place muffin cups on a large foil-lined baking sheet.

5 Bake for 25 to 30 minutes or until a wooden toothpick inserted in the centers comes out clean. Cool in muffin cups on wire racks for 5 minutes. Using a narrow metal spatula, loosen edges of cakes from sides of cups. Invert cakes onto racks. Spoon any pecan mixture remaining in muffin cups onto cakes. Serve warm, or cool completely.

nutrition facts per cake: 679 cal., 41 g total fat (10 g sat. fat), 83 mg chol., 271 mg sodium, 76 g carb., 2 g dietary fiber, 6 g protein.

This luscious pudding is a most delicious example of true comfort food. All the good parts of banana bread are put in a baking dish, topped with walnut-oatmeal goodness, and baked until bubbly.

warm banana bread cobbler

prep: 20 minutes cool: 30 minutes bake: 25 minutes
oven: 375°F makes: 12 to 16 servings dish: 3-quart

1   cup self-rising flour*
1   cup granulated sugar
¾   cup milk
½   cup butter, melted
1   teaspoon vanilla
4   medium bananas, peeled and sliced (about 4 cups)
1   cup rolled oats
¾   cup packed brown sugar
½   cup self-rising flour*
½   cup butter
½   cup chopped walnuts
    Vanilla ice cream

1 Preheat oven to 375°F. Grease a 3-quart rectangular baking dish; set aside.

2 In a medium bowl stir together 1 cup flour and granulated sugar. Add milk, melted butter, and vanilla. Stir until smooth. Spread evenly in the prepared dish. Top with sliced bananas.

3 In a large bowl combine oats, brown sugar, and ½ cup flour. Using a pastry blender, cut in ½ cup butter until crumbly. Stir in walnuts. Sprinkle mixture over bananas. Bake, uncovered, for 25 to 30 minutes or until browned and set. Cool in dish on a wire rack for 30 minutes. Serve warm with vanilla ice cream.

nutrition facts per serving: 560 cal., 28 g total fat (15 g sat. fat), 74 mg chol., 378 mg sodium, 75 g carb., 3 g dietary fiber, 7 g protein.

*test kitchen tip: Self-rising flour already contains the leavening and salt needed in this recipe. If you do not have self-rising flour, substitute a mixture of 1½ cups all-purpose flour, 1½ teaspoons baking powder, ¾ teaspoon salt, and ¼ teaspoon baking soda. Use 1 cup of the mixture for Step 2 and the remaining ½ cup of mixture for Step 3.

comfort **desserts**

When baking with pears, choose fruits that have just begun to ripen. To test for ripeness, press your thumb into the top of the pear near the stem. When it gives lightly, it's ready for baking.

upside-down pear gingerbread

prep: 25 minutes cool: 5 minutes bake: 35 minutes oven: 350°F
makes: 9 servings dish: 2-quart baking pan

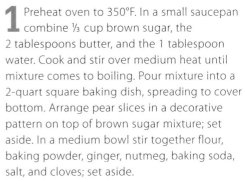

⅓ cup packed brown sugar
2 tablespoons butter
1 tablespoon water
1 Anjou pear or 3 Seckel pears, peeled, cored, and thinly sliced
2 cups all-purpose flour
1 teaspoon baking powder
1 teaspoon ground ginger
½ teaspoon ground nutmeg
¼ teaspoon baking soda
¼ teaspoon salt
¼ teaspoon ground cloves
½ cup butter, softened
⅓ cup packed brown sugar
2 eggs
½ cup molasses
¾ cup water
   Sweetened whipped cream (optional)

1 Preheat oven to 350°F. In a small saucepan combine ⅓ cup brown sugar, the 2 tablespoons butter, and the 1 tablespoon water. Cook and stir over medium heat until mixture comes to boiling. Pour mixture into a 2-quart square baking dish, spreading to cover bottom. Arrange pear slices in a decorative pattern on top of brown sugar mixture; set aside. In a medium bowl stir together flour, baking powder, ginger, nutmeg, baking soda, salt, and cloves; set aside.

2 In a large bowl beat ½ cup butter with an electric mixer on medium to high speed for 30 seconds. Add ⅓ cup brown sugar; beat until combined. Beat in eggs and molasses until combined.

3 Alternately add flour mixture and the ¾ cup water to butter mixture, beating on low speed after each addition just until combined. Pour batter evenly over pear slices in dish, being careful not to disturb pear slices.

4 Bake for 35 to 40 minutes or until center springs back when lightly touched. Cool in pan on a wire rack for 5 minutes. Using a sharp knife or narrow metal spatula, loosen edges of cake from sides of dish. Carefully invert onto a serving platter. Serve warm. If desired, top each serving with whipped cream.

nutrition facts per serving: 315 cal., 14 g total fat (9 g sat. fat), 81 mg chol., 256 mg sodium, 43 g carb., 1 g dietary fiber, 5 g protein.

Frozen puff pastry—miracle worker of the dessert world—makes this coconut custard dessert ultra-rich and wonderful. Following a Greek or Mideastern dinner—with cups of strong coffee—it is pure perfection.

puffed egyptian bread pudding

prep: 25 minutes cool: 20 minutes bake: 15 minutes plus 35 minutes
oven: 400°F/350°F makes: 12 servings dish: 3-quart

1	17.3-ounce package frozen puff pastry sheets (2 sheets), thawed
3/4	cup packed brown sugar
1	teaspoon ground cinnamon
1 1/2	cups flaked coconut
3/4	cup golden raisins
1/2	cup sliced almonds
2	eggs, beaten
2	12-ounce cans evaporated milk
1	tablespoon cornstarch
2	tablespoons honey (optional)

1 Preheat oven to 400°F. Cut puff pastry sheets along creases, cut each piece in half lengthwise. Cut pieces crosswise into about 1½-inch squares. Arrange squares about 1 inch apart on 2 large ungreased baking sheets. Bake on separate oven racks about 15 minutes or until pastry squares are golden, rotating baking sheets once during baking. Reduce oven temperature to 350°F.

2 Place hot baked squares in a 3-quart rectangular baking dish. In a small bowl combine brown sugar and cinnamon; sprinkle about two-thirds of sugar mixture over pastry. Top with coconut, raisins, and almonds. In a 4-cup glass measure whisk together eggs, evaporated milk, and cornstarch; pour evenly over mixture in dish. Sprinkle over the remaining brown sugar mixture.

3 Bake, covered, for 20 minutes. Uncover; bake 15 to 20 minutes more or until top is golden and mixture is set. Remove from oven. Cool in dish on wire rack 20 minutes. Serve warm. Drizzle with honey.

nutrition facts per serving: 450 cal., 25 g total fat (7 g sat. fat), 52 mg chol., 274 mg sodium, 49 g carb., 2 g dietary fiber, 9 g protein.

Look around your cupboards for distinct-tasting ingredients to toss into the classic bread pudding, starting with chocolate chips, snipped dried apricots, or your favorite liqueur.

classic bread pudding

prep: 30 minutes bake: 50 minutes oven: 350°F
makes: 8 servings dish: 1½-quart

4 cups dried white or cinnamon swirl bread cubes (6 to 7 slices)*
⅓ cup raisins or dried cranberries
2 eggs, lightly beaten
2 cups milk
¼ cup butter, melted
½ cup sugar
1 teaspoon ground cinnamon
½ teaspoon ground nutmeg
1 teaspoon vanilla
   Caramel ice cream topping (optional)

1 Preheat oven to 350°F. Grease a 1½-quart casserole; set aside. In a large bowl combine bread cubes and raisins.

2 In a medium bowl combine eggs, milk, melted butter, sugar, cinnamon, nutmeg, and vanilla. Stir into bread mixture. Pour into prepared casserole.

3 Bake, uncovered, for 50 to 55 minutes or until puffed and a knife inserted near the center comes out clean. Cool slightly. If desired, serve with warm caramel ice cream topping.

nutrition facts per serving: 219 cal., 9 g total fat (5 g sat. fat), 73 mg chol., 212 mg sodium, 30 g carb., 1 g dietary fiber, 5 g protein.

*test kitchen tip: To dry bread cubes, cut bread into ½-inch cubes. Spread cubes in a 15×10×1-inch baking pan. Bake in a 300°F oven for 10 to 15 minutes or until dry, stirring twice; cool.

pear-ginger bread pudding: Prepare as above, except substitute snipped dried pears for the raisins, 1 tablespoon finely chopped crystallized ginger for the cinnamon, and 1 teaspoon finely shredded orange peel for the nutmeg.

Once known as "poor man's pudding," this decadent whiskey-laced confection is anything but. A double dose of white chocolate—melted in the soaking liquid and chopped and tossed with the bread—gives this old-fashioned favorite a fancy touch.

white chocolate bread
pudding with hard sauce

prep: 30 minutes   chill: 1 to 8 hours   bake: 1 hour
oven: 350°F   makes: 12 servings   dish: 2-quart

2	cups whole milk, half-and-half, or light cream
10	ounces white baking chocolate with cocoa butter, chopped
1½	teaspoons vanilla
5	eggs
⅔	cup sugar
½	teaspoon ground cinnamon
6	cups dried French bread cubes*
⅓	cup dried tart cherries, cranberries, or raisins
1	recipe Hard Sauce

1 In a medium saucepan heat and stir milk and half of the white chocolate over low heat just until mixture simmers and chocolate is melted. Remove from heat. Stir vanilla into the milk mixture.

2 In a large bowl combine eggs, sugar, and cinnamon. Beat with a wire whisk or rotary beater just until combined. Gradually add milk mixture to egg mixture, stirring constantly.

3 In an ungreased 2-quart square baking dish, toss together the remaining white chocolate, bread cubes, and dried cherries. Pour milk mixture evenly over bread mixture. Press mixture lightly with the back of a large spoon. Cover baking dish with foil and refrigerate for 1 to 8 hours.

4 Preheat oven to 350°F. Place baking dish in another larger pan. Place pan on oven rack. Pour hot water into pan until 1 inch up sides of pan. Bake, covered, about 1 hour or until top appears evenly set. Cool on a wire rack. Serve warm with Hard Sauce.

nutrition facts per serving: 703 cal., 39 g total fat (20 g sat. fat), 277 mg chol., 485 mg sodium, 69 g carb., 1 g dietary fiber, 12 g protein.

*test kitchen tip: To dry bread cubes, place in a large, shallow baking pan. Bake in a 350°F oven about 10 minutes or until dry, stirring twice; cool.

hard sauce: In a bowl lightly beat 4 egg yolks. In a small saucepan cook and stir 1 cup butter and ½ cup sugar over medium heat until butter is melted and mixture is bubbly. Remove from heat. Gradually whisk mixture into yolks; return to saucepan. Cook and stir over medium-low heat about 15 minutes or until mixture reaches 170°F when tested with an instant-read thermometer. Remove from heat. Stir in ¼ cup whiskey or milk. If necessary, stir in hot water, 1 teaspoon at a time, to make sauce the desired consistency. Serve immediately or cover and let stand at room temperature for up to 1 hour (stir in hot water, 1 teaspoon at a time, if sauce becomes too thick).

Complex flavors in bittersweet chocolate combined with refreshing orange deliver pure pleasure in every bite of this warm dessert.

orange-chocolate bread pudding

prep: 25 minutes   bake: 45 minutes   oven: 325°F
makes: 8 servings   dish: 3-quart

8   cups 1-inch cubes
    French or Italian
    bread
4   cups milk
1   cup sugar
6   ounces bittersweet
    chocolate, coarsely
    chopped
8   eggs, lightly beaten
1   tablespoon finely
    shredded orange
    zest
1   teaspoon vanilla
⅛   teaspoon salt
    Whipped cream
    (optional)

1 Preheat oven to 325°F. Butter a 3-quart rectangular baking dish. Spread bread cubes evenly in the prepared baking dish; set aside.

2 In a medium saucepan combine milk, sugar, and chocolate. Cook over medium heat until chocolate is melted, whisking frequently. Remove from heat.

3 In a large bowl combine eggs, orange zest, vanilla, and salt. Gradually whisk in chocolate mixture. Pour evenly over bread in dish. Using a rubber spatula or the back of a large spoon, press all of the bread lightly down to moisten.

4 Bake, uncovered, for 45 to 50 minutes or until evenly puffed and set. Cool on a wire rack for 30 minutes. Serve warm. If desired, serve with whipped cream.

nutrition facts per serving: 434 cal., 18 g total fat (9 g sat. fat), 226 mg chol., 351 mg sodium, 59 g carb., 2 g dietary fiber, 16 g protein.

For flavor richness, use pure maple syrup for this tasty custardlike dessert.

maple bread pudding with pecan praline

prep: 35 minutes   chill: 1 hour   cool: 30 minutes   bake: 40 minutes
oven: 375°F   makes: 12 to 16 servings   dish: 3-quart

1	cup granulated sugar
¼	cup water
½	cup chopped pecans, toasted
8	eggs
4	cups half-and-half or light cream
1	cup packed brown sugar
1	cup maple syrup
1	tablespoon vanilla
1	1-pound loaf egg bread, torn into bite-size pieces (about 14 cups)
	Vanilla ice cream

1 For pecan praline crunch, lightly grease a baking sheet; set aside. In a small saucepan combine granulated sugar and the water. Cook over medium heat, stirring to dissolve sugar. Bring to boiling; reduce heat. Boil gently, uncovered, without stirring about 7 minutes or until mixture turns a deep amber color. Remove from heat. Stir in pecans. Quickly pour onto the prepared baking sheet; cool for 30 minutes. Break or chop praline into small pieces; set aside.

2 In a very large bowl whisk together eggs, half-and-half, brown sugar, maple syrup, and vanilla. Add bread pieces; stir to moisten evenly. Cover and chill for 1 hour.

3 Preheat oven to 375°F. Lightly grease a 3-quart rectangular baking dish. Transfer bread mixture to the prepared baking dish. Bake, uncovered, about 40 minutes or until golden brown and a knife inserted in the center comes out clean. Cool on a wire rack for 30 minutes.

4 Serve warm bread pudding with scoops of ice cream. Sprinkle with pecan praline crunch.

nutrition facts per serving: 647 cal., 26 g total fat (13 g sat. fat), 222 mg chol., 331 mg sodium, 92 g carb., 2 g dietary fiber, 13 g protein.

It's like camping out in your kitchen when you concoct this s'mores dessert casserole.

s'mores bread pudding

prep: 25 minutes cool: 20 minutes bake: 40 minutes
oven: 325°F makes: 9 servings dish: 2-quart

4 cups Hawaiian sweet bread cut in 1-inch pieces
4 eggs
1 14-ounce can sweetened condensed milk
¾ cup milk
1 teaspoon vanilla
¼ teaspoon ground nutmeg
1 cup tiny marshmallows
¾ cup semisweet chocolate pieces
5 graham cracker squares, coarsely crushed (about ½ cup)
2 tablespoons milk

1 Preheat oven to 325°F. Grease a 2-quart square baking dish; set aside. Place bread pieces on a shallow baking sheet. Bake for 7 to 8 minutes or until dry and crisp; cool.

2 In medium bowl lightly beat eggs. Stir in sweetened condensed milk, ¾ cup milk, vanilla, and nutmeg.

3 Place bread pieces in prepared baking dish. Sprinkle with ½ cup each of the marshmallows and chocolate pieces. Evenly pour milk mixture over all. Let stand for 5 minutes. Sprinkle with crushed graham crackers. Bake, uncovered, for 35 minutes. Sprinkle with ¼ cup of the remaining marshmallows. Bake about 5 minutes more or until a knife inserted near center comes out clean. Cool for 20 to 30 minutes.

4 Meanwhile, for chocolate drizzle, in a small saucepan combine the remaining ¼ cup marshmallows, the remaining ¼ cup chocolate pieces, and 2 tablespoons milk. Cook over low heat until melted and smooth, whisking constantly.

5 To serve, spoon bread pudding into glasses or bowls. Top with chocolate drizzle.

nutrition facts per serving: 348 cal., 12 g total fat (6 g sat. fat), 111 mg chol., 221 mg sodium, 52 g carb., 1 g dietary fiber, 10 g protein.

Fluffy and light, a soufflé for dessert always feels decadent. This one offers a bittersweet ending. Melting the chocolate over a hot-water bath ensures the smoothest consistency.

bittersweet soufflés

prep: 40 minutes bake: 14 minutes stand: 30 minutes
oven: 375°F makes: 8 servings dish: 6-ounce dishes

3 egg yolks
4 egg whites
   Sugar
8 ounces bittersweet
      (70% cocoa)
      chocolate or
      semisweet
      chocolate, finely
      chopped*
1 tablespoon butter
1/3 cup chocolate milk or
      milk
1/8 teaspoon cream of
      tartar
1/3 cup sugar*
   Caramel ice cream
      topping
   Chocolate-covered
      espresso beans,
      chopped (optional)

1 Place egg yolks in a small bowl and egg whites in a large bowl; allow to stand at room temperature for 30 minutes. Position a rack in the lower third of the oven; preheat oven to 375°F. Butter eight 6-ounce ramekins, soufflé dishes, or custard cups; sprinkle with sugar.

2 In a large heatproof bowl or small saucepan combine chocolate, butter, and the milk. Place bowl in a large skillet of barely simmering water or heat saucepan over low heat. Stir until the chocolate is melted and the mixture is smooth. Remove the bowl from the water bath or the saucepan from heat. Whisk in egg yolks. (Don't worry if the mixture stiffens slightly or is less than perfectly smooth at this point.)

3 Add cream of tartar to egg whites; beat with an electric mixer on medium speed until soft peaks form (tips curl). Gradually sprinkle in 1/3 cup sugar, beating on high speed until the whites are stiff but not dry (tips stand straight). Fold one-fourth of the egg whites into the chocolate mixture to lighten it, then fold into the remaining egg whites.

4 Divide the mixture evenly among the prepared ramekins, filling each three-fourths full.

5 Place ramekins on a baking sheet. Bake, uncovered, for 14 to 17 minutes or until soufflés rise and crack on tops and a wooden skewer inserted into centers comes out slightly moist and gooey (the centers should not be completely liquid).

6 Remove soufflés from the oven. Drizzle with caramel ice cream topping. If desired, top each serving with chopped espresso beans. Serve immediately.

nutrition facts per serving: 295 cal., 17 g total fat (9 g sat. fat), 88 mg chol., 99 mg sodium, 31 g carb., 3 g dietary fiber, 6 g protein.

make-ahead directions: Prepare as directed through Step 4, except do not preheat oven. Cover and chill for up to 24 hours. Bake and serve as directed in Steps 5 and 6, except bake chilled soufflés for 16 to 20 minutes.

*test kitchen tip: If you prefer a sweeter, less intense chocolate flavor, substitute a lower-percentage bittersweet or semisweet chocolate; if desired, reduce the sugar to 1/4 cup to partially compensate for the sweeter chocolate.

It's well worth the little bit of extra time it takes to play with the eggs in this fluffy fantasy.

swirled **chocolate** and **peanut butter** soufflé

prep: 35 minutes   bake: 42 minutes   oven: 350°F
makes: 6 to 8 servings   dish: 2-quart

Sugar
2   ounces bittersweet or semisweet chocolate, chopped
3   tablespoons butter
¼   cup all-purpose flour
1¼   cups half-and-half, light cream, or milk
¼   cup creamy peanut butter
4   egg yolks
6   egg whites
⅓   cup sugar
Whipped cream (optional)

1 Preheat oven to 350°F. Butter the sides of a 2-quart soufflé dish. For a collar on the dish, measure enough foil to wrap around the top of the dish and add 3 inches. Fold the foil into thirds lengthwise. Lightly grease one side of the foil with butter; sprinkle with sugar. Place foil, sugar side in, around the outside of the dish so foil extends about 2 inches above the dish. Tape ends of foil together. Sprinkle inside of dish with sugar; set aside.

2 In a small saucepan cook and stir chocolate over low heat until melted. In a medium saucepan melt 3 tablespoons butter. Stir in flour; gradually stir in half-and-half. Cook and stir over medium heat until thickened and bubbly. Remove from heat. Stir half of the hot cream mixture into the melted chocolate; set aside. Stir peanut butter into the remaining hot cream mixture in the saucepan.

3 In a medium bowl beat 2 of the egg yolks with a fork just until combined. Gradually stir peanut butter mixture into egg yolks; set aside. In another medium bowl lightly beat the remaining 2 egg yolks. Gradually stir chocolate mixture into egg yolks; set aside.

4 In a large bowl beat egg whites until soft peaks form. Gradually add ⅓ cup sugar, 1 tablespoon at a time, beating until stiff peaks form. Gently fold half of beaten whites into peanut butter mixture. Gently spoon peanut butter mixture into prepared soufflé dish. Gently fold remaining beaten whites into chocolate mixture; spoon over peanut butter mixture in dish. Using a table knife, gently swirl the mixtures to marble.

5 Bake, uncovered, for 45 to 50 minutes or until a knife inserted near the center comes out clean. Serve immediately. If desired, top with whipped cream.

nutrition facts per serving: 366 cal., 26 g total fat (13 g sat. fat), 179 mg chol., 184 mg sodium, 27 g carb., 2 g dietary fiber, 11 g protein.

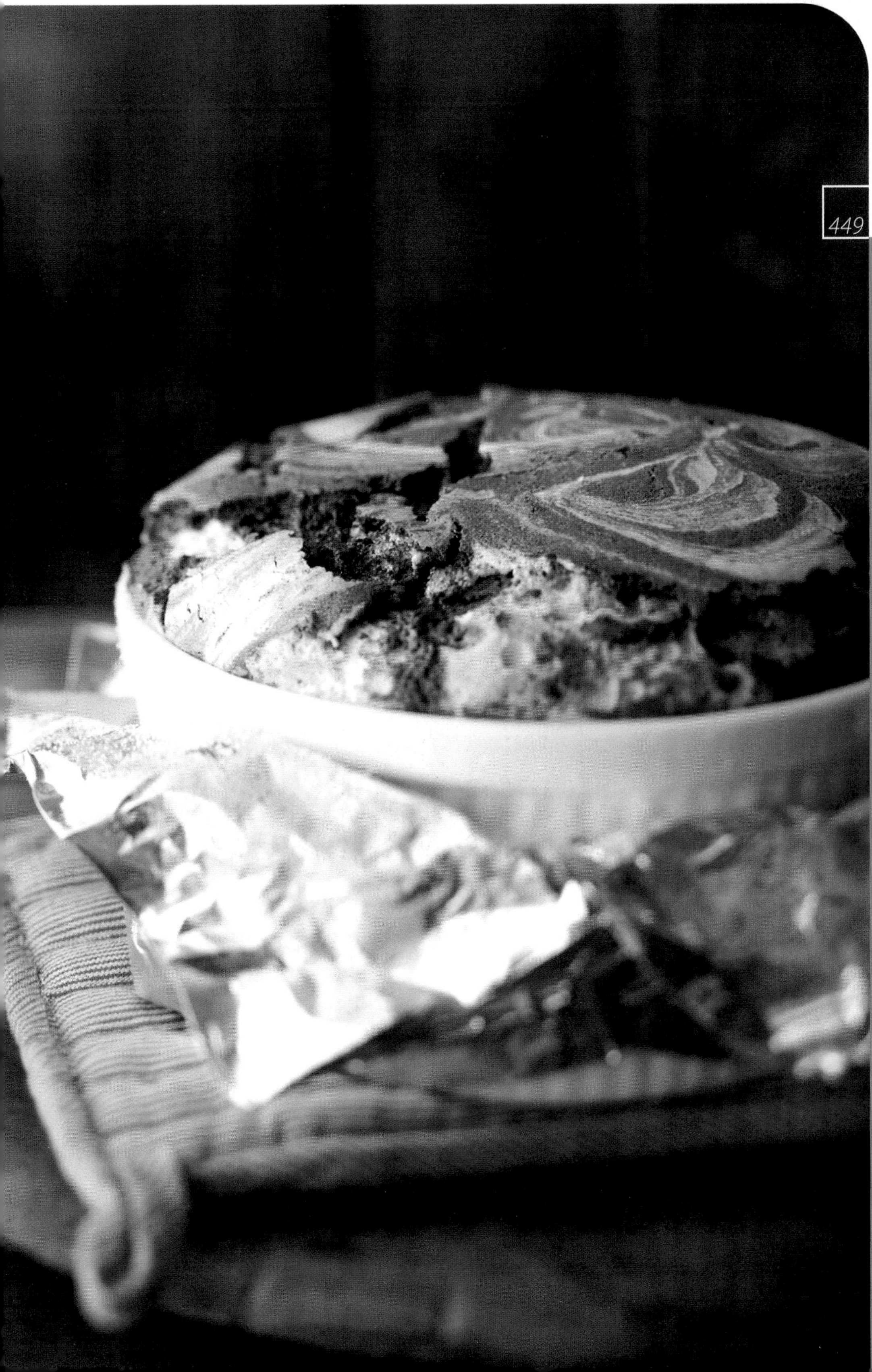

A creamy pumpkin filling crowned with a crunchy topping makes this a dessert to remember. Tote it to your next potluck.

pumpkin pie dessert

prep: 20 minutes chill: 2 hours bake: 50 minutes
oven: 350°F makes: 18 servings dish: 3-quart

1   29-ounce can
     pumpkin
1   cup sugar
1   teaspoon ground
     cinnamon
½   teaspoon salt
½   teaspoon ground
     nutmeg
½   teaspoon ground
     ginger
4   eggs, beaten
1   12-ounce can
     evaporated milk
1   package 2-layer-size
     yellow cake mix
1   cup chopped nuts
¾   cup butter or
     margarine, melted
     Frozen whipped
     dessert topping,
     thawed (optional)

1 Preheat oven to 350°F. Grease a 3-quart rectangular baking dish; set aside. In a large bowl combine pumpkin, sugar, cinnamon, salt, nutmeg, and ginger. Add eggs. Using a wooden spoon, beat lightly just until combined. Gradually stir in evaporated milk; mix well. Pour into prepared dish. Sprinkle dry cake mix evenly over pumpkin mixture; sprinkle evenly with nuts. Drizzle with melted butter.

2 Bake, uncovered, about 50 minutes or until edges are firm and top is golden brown. Cool in dish on a wire rack. Cover and chill for at least 2 hours before serving. If desired, serve with whipped dessert topping.

nutrition facts per serving: 328 cal., 17 g total fat (7 g sat. fat), 75 mg chol., 364 mg sodium, 41 g carb., 2 g dietary fiber, 5 g protein.

A toasted pumpkin seed and oatmeal topping adorns these individual desserts, which are reminiscent of pumpkin pie.

baked pumpkin pudding

prep: 20 minutes cool: 15 minutes bake: 40 minutes
oven: 350°F makes: 4 servings dish: 6-ounce dishes

Nonstick cooking
spray
1 cup canned pumpkin
½ cup milk
⅓ cup packed brown
sugar
2 egg whites, lightly
beaten
½ teaspoon pumpkin
pie spice
2 tablespoons quick-
cooking rolled oats
1 tablespoon toasted
pumpkin seeds or
coarsely chopped
pecans or pistachios
2 teaspoons packed
brown sugar
1 teaspoon butter,
softened
Toasted pumpkin
seeds (optional)

1 Preheat oven to 350°F. Lightly coat four 6-ounce ramekins or custard cups with cooking spray. Place ramekins in a 2-quart square baking dish. In a medium bowl stir together pumpkin, milk, ⅓ cup brown sugar, egg whites, and pumpkin pie spice. Divide pumpkin mixture among ramekins.

2 In a small bowl combine oats, the 1 tablespoon pumpkin seeds, 2 teaspoons brown sugar, and butter, stirring with a fork until crumbly. Sprinkle oat mixture evenly over pumpkin mixture.

3 Place baking dish on oven rack. Pour boiling water into the baking dish until water is 1 inch up sides of ramekins. Bake, uncovered, for 40 to 45 minutes or until a knife inserted near the center of each pudding comes out clean. Carefully remove ramekins from baking dish. Cool on a wire rack at least 15 minutes before serving. (Or, after cooling for up to 1 hour, cover and chill for up to 24 hours.) If desired, sprinkle with additional pumpkin seeds before serving.

nutrition facts per serving: 148 cal., 2 g total fat (10 g sat. fat), 3 mg chol., 59 mg sodium, 29 g carb., 2 g dietary fiber, 4 g protein.

16

party

dips &

Hot and bubbly dips, finger-lickin' wings, and succulent spiced shrimp! When it comes to casual party fare, the delectables here will top everyone's list of favorites. Make-ahead options invite you to spend less time in the kitchen and more time mingling.

bites

Your dream of serving ruebens to a large gathering is now possible, thanks to this flavorful dip. Pop it into the oven just before the party so guests can spread it warm on rye bread.

hot **reuben** dip

prep: 10 minutes **chill:** 24 hours **bake:** 25 minutes **oven:** 350°F
makes: 18 servings **dish:** 1½-quart

1 14- to 16-ounce can sauerkraut, rinsed and well drained
1½ cups shredded cheddar cheese (6 ounces)
1½ cups shredded Swiss cheese (6 ounces)
6 ounces corned beef, chopped (about 1 cup)
1 cup mayonnaise
Party rye bread, toasted baguette slices, and/or crackers

1 Preheat oven to 350°F. Pat sauerkraut dry with paper towels. In a large bowl combine sauerkraut, cheddar cheese and Swiss cheese, corned beef, and mayonnaise. Spread into a 1½-quart casserole or a 9-inch quiche dish.

2 Bake, uncovered, about 25 minutes or until heated through and bubbly. Serve with rye bread.

nutrition facts per serving: 190 cal., 17 g total fat (6 g sat. fat), 32 mg chol., 396 mg sodium, 2 g carb., 1 g dietary fiber, 7 g protein.

make-ahead directions: Prepare as directed through Step 1. Cover and chill for up to 24 hours. Bake in a 350°F oven for 25 minutes or until heated through and bubbly.

*A fresh tomato topping provides a cool
contrast to this chile-spiced corn dip.
To cut preparation time, use packaged
preshredded cheeses.*

baked santa fe dip

prep: 20 minutes **bake:** 25 minutes **oven:** 350°F
makes: 14 servings **dish:** quiche dish

1 8.75-ounce can whole
    kernel corn, drained
2 cups shredded
    cheddar cheese
    (8 ounces)
1 cup shredded
    Monterey Jack or
    mozzarella cheese
    (4 ounces)
1 4-ounce can diced
    green chiles,
    drained
½ cup light mayonnaise
2 teaspoons finely
    chopped canned
    chipotle chile
    pepper in adobo
    sauce*
¼ teaspoon garlic
    powder
½ cup chopped, seeded
    tomato (1 small)
¼ cup sliced
    scallions (2)
2 tablespoons snipped
    fresh cilantro
    Tortilla chips and/or
    vegetable dippers

1 Preheat oven to 350°F. In a large bowl stir together corn, cheddar cheese, Monterey Jack cheese, green chile peppers, mayonnaise, chipotle pepper, and garlic powder.

2 Spread mixture in an ungreased 9-inch quiche dish or pie plate. Bake, uncovered, about 25 minutes or until heated through.

3 Meanwhile, in a small bowl combine tomato, scallions, and cilantro. Sprinkle tomato mixture over baked cheese mixture. Serve with chips and/or vegetables.

nutrition facts per serving: 138 cal., 10 g total fat (6 g sat. fat), 24 mg chol., 274 mg sodium, 4 g carb., 6 g protein.

Fresh banana peppers are mild chiles that infuse this delightful dip with sweet and fruity flavos

artichoke and
banana pepper dip

prep: 25 minutes **bake:** 25 minutes **oven:** 350°F/400°F
makes: 22 servings **dish:** 1½-quart

3 9-ounce packages frozen artichoke hearts, cooked, drained, and coarsely chopped

2 cups finely shredded Parmigiano-Reggiano or Parmesan cheese (8 ounces)

1½ cups light mayonnaise

1 large red, yellow, or green sweet pepper, finely chopped

1 medium fresh banana chile pepper, sliced crosswise and seeded,* or ½ cup bottled banana peppers, drained

6 cloves garlic, minced

2 teaspoons ground cumin

1 recipe Pita Crisps

1 Preheat oven temperature to 400°F. In a large bowl combine artichokes, cheese, mayonnaise, sweet pepper, banana pepper, garlic, and cumin. Transfer mixture to an ungreased 1½-quart baking dish.

2 Bake, uncovered, for 25 to 30 minutes or until mixture is heated through and top is golden brown. Serve dip with Pita Crisps.

nutrition facts per serving: 101 cal., 8 g total fat (2 g sat. fat), 11 mg chol., 251 mg sodium, 5 g carb., 2 g dietary fiber, 4 g protein.

pita crisps: Preheat oven to 350°F. Split 3 pita bread rounds in half horizontally, separating each into two rounds. Cut rounds into 1-inch-wide strips. In a small bowl stir together 3 tablespoons olive oil, ½ teaspoon chili powder, and ¼ teaspoon garlic salt. Brush mixture lightly over rough surfaces of pita strips. Arrange strips, brushed sides up, in a single layer on baking sheets. Bake for 10 to 12 minutes or until crisp. Cool.

make-ahead directions: Prepare Pita Crisps as directed. Store in an airtight container at room temperature for up to 1 week.

*test kitchen tip: Because chile peppers contain oils that can burn your skin and eyes, avoid direct contact with them as much as possible. When working with chile peppers, wear rubber or plastic gloves. If your bare hands do touch the peppers, wash your hands and nails well with soap and warm water.

For a festive dip, sprinkle feta cheese and fresh snipped oregano on top.

greek party dip

prep: 25 minutes bake: 20 minutes oven: 350°F
makes: 7 cups dish: 1-quart

1 **pound ground lamb or bulk pork sausage**
²/₃ **cup chopped onion (2 small)**
4 **cloves garlic, minced**
2 **15-ounce cans tomato sauce**
1 **14.5-ounce can diced tomatoes, undrained**
1 **6-ounce can tomato paste**
¼ **cup pitted kalamata olives, chopped**
1 **tablespoon dried oregano, crushed**
1 **tablespoon dried basil, crushed**
2 **teaspoons sugar**
¼ **teaspoon crushed red pepper**
¼ **cup grated Parmesan cheese**
Toasted garlic bread slices and/or toasted foccacia bread slices

1 Preheat oven to 350°F. In a large skillet cook lamb, onion, and garlic over medium heat until meat is brown and onion is tender, using a wooden spoon to break up meat as it cooks. Drain off fat.

2 Return meat to skillet. Add tomato sauce, diced tomatoes, tomato paste, olives, oregano, basil, sugar, and crushed red pepper; mix well. Transfer to two ungreased 1-quart casseroles or au gratin dishes or one 2-quart casserole or au gratin dish. Sprinkle with Parmesan cheese. Bake, uncovered, for 20 to 25 minutes or until heated through. Serve with toasted garlic bread slices.

nutrition facts per ¼ cup: 70 cal., 4 g total fat (2 g sat. fat), 12 mg chol., 270 mg sodium, 5 g carb., 1 g dietary fiber, 4 g protein.

Unlike traditional spinach dips, which are built around sour cream, this lightened-up version gets its luscious tang and creaminess from yogurt.

spinach and roasted red pepper dip

prep: 20 minutes bake: 15 minutes oven: 350°F
makes: 2¼ cups dip dish: 9-inch pie plate

½ cup shredded part-skim mozzarella cheese (2 ounces)
½ cup plain low-fat or fat-free yogurt
½ cup mayonnaise
¼ cup grated Parmesan cheese
1 tablespoon all-purpose flour
1 teaspoon Dijon-style mustard
1 cup loosely packed fresh spinach leaves, coarsely chopped
¾ cup bottled roasted red sweet peppers, drained and chopped
¼ cup thinly sliced scallions (2)
Red and/or yellow sweet peppers, seeded and cut into strips; crackers; and/or flatbread

1 Preheat oven to 350°F. In a large bowl stir together mozzarella cheese, yogurt, mayonnaise, 2 tablespoons of the Parmesan cheese, the flour, and mustard. Stir in spinach, roasted sweet peppers, and 2 tablespoons of the scallions. Spread mixture evenly into an ungreased 1-quart ovenproof shallow dish or a 9-inch pie plate. Sprinkle with the remaining 2 tablespoons Parmesan cheese.

2 Bake, uncovered, for 15 to 20 minutes or until edges are bubbly and mixture is heated through. Sprinkle with the remaining 2 tablespoons scallions. Serve with sweet pepper strips, crackers, and/or flatbread.

nutrition facts per 2 tablespoons: 21 cal., 2 g total fat (0 g sat. fat), 3 mg chol., 47 mg sodium, 1 g carb., 1 g protein.

Pancetta gives an extra flavor boost to this party-time favorite, which also loads up on Parmesan cheese, sweet pepper, and parsley.

artichoke-leek dip

prep: 12 minutes **bake:** 20 minutes **oven:** 350°F
makes: 14 servings **dish:** 9-inch pie plate

1 medium leek, thinly sliced and quartered, or ⅓ cup sliced scallions
2 ounces chopped pancetta or bacon
2 teaspoons butter or cooking oil
1 14-ounce can artichoke hearts, drained and coarsely chopped
1 cup grated Parmesan cheese
1 7-ounce jar roasted red sweet peppers, drained and coarsely chopped
1 cup mayonnaise or light mayonnaise*
⅛ teaspoon ground black pepper
1 tablespoon snipped fresh Italian parsley
2 tablespoons grated Parmesan or Romano cheese
   Assorted crackers, flatbreads, and/or vegetable dippers

1 Preheat oven to 350°F. In a skillet, cook leek and pancetta in hot butter until leek is tender and pancetta begins to brown. Remove from heat. Stir in artichoke hearts, 1 cup Parmesan cheese, roasted sweet peppers, mayonnaise, and black pepper.

2 Transfer mixture to a 9-inch pie plate or ungreased 8-inch quiche dish, spreading evenly. Sprinkle with parsley and 2 tablespoons Parmesan cheese.

3 Bake, uncovered, about 15 minutes or until heated through. Serve with crackers, flatbreads, and/or vegetable dippers.

nutrition facts per serving: 40 cal., 4 g total fat (1 g sat. fat), 4 mg chol., 71 mg sodium, 1 g carb., 0 g dietary fiber, 1 g protein.

∗test kitchen tip: Do not use fat-free mayonnaise dressing or salad dressing. The dip will not set.

make-ahead directions: Prepare dip through Step 2. Cover and chill for up to 24 hours. Bake in a 350°F oven about 20 minutes or until heated through.

This super seven-layer dip is piled high with Mexican-style goodies and baked. You'll want to flag this recipe for your next game-day gathering or neighborhood block party.

tex-mex taco dip

prep: 30 minutes **bake:** 25 minutes **oven:** 325°F
makes: 24 servings **dish:** 3-quart

1½ pounds ground
    turkey breast
 1 fresh jalapeño chile
    pepper, seeded
    and finely chopped
    (optional)*
 1 1-ounce envelope
    reduced-sodium
    taco seasoning mix
 2 8-ounce packages
    cream cheese,
    softened
 2 16-ounce cans refried
    beans
 2 tablespoons lemon
    juice
 3 avocados, pitted,
    peeled, and mashed
 ½ cup sour cream
 ½ cup mayonnaise
 8 ounces shredded
    cheddar cheese
 2 cups shredded fresh
    spinach
 3 medium tomatoes,
    chopped
 ½ cup chopped scallions
    (4), (optional)
    Assorted vegetable
    dippers and/or
    baked tortilla chips

1 Preheat oven to 325°F. In a large skillet cook ground turkey and jalapeño pepper (if using), with half of the taco seasoning mix (about 2 tablespoons) until turkey is no longer pink; remove from heat.

2 Meanwhile, spread cream cheese into the bottom of an ungreased 3-quart rectangular baking dish. Spread cream cheese layer with refried beans. Stir the lemon juice into the mashed avocado and spread over refried bean layer. In a small bowl stir together sour cream, mayonnaise, and the remaining taco seasoning mix. Spread sour cream mixture over avocado layer. Top with ground turkey mixture. Sprinkle cheese over top.

3 Bake, uncovered, about 25 minutes or until heated through and cheese is evenly melted. Top with spinach, tomato, and scallions (if using). Serve with vegetable dippers and/or baked tortilla chips.

nutrition facts per serving: 243 cal., 17 g total fat (7 g sat. fat), 48 mg chol., 417 mg sodium, 10 g carb., 3 g dietary fiber, 13 g protein.

*test kitchen tip: Because chile peppers contain oils that can burn your skin and eyes, avoid direct contact with them as much as possible. When working with chile peppers, wear rubber or plastic gloves. If your bare hands do touch the peppers, wash your hands and nails well with soap and warm water.

Just a little super-spicy chipotle chile powder gives this dip a nice touch of heat. If you're feeling extra spicy, add a full teaspoon.

triple-smoked
salmon-pepper dip

prep: 20 minutes **bake:** 25 minutes **broil:** 10 minutes **stand:** 15 minutes
oven: 350°F **makes:** 3 cups dip **dish:** 1-quart

1 large green sweet pepper
1 8-ounce package reduced-fat cream cheese (Neufchâtel), softened
½ cup light sour cream
2 tablespoons fat-free milk
½ cup thinly sliced scallions (4 to 6)
2 cloves garlic, minced
½ teaspoon smoked paprika or paprika
½ to 1 teaspoon finely chopped canned chipotle chile pepper in adobo sauce
4 ounces hot-style smoked salmon, flaked, skin and bones removed
Toasted whole grain baguette-style French bread slices, carrot sticks, and/or cucumber slices

1 Line a baking sheet with foil. Cut green pepper into quarters, removing stem, seeds, and membranes. Place pepper quarters, skin sides up, on prepared baking sheet. Broil 4 to 5 inches from the heat for 10 to 15 minutes or until pepper skins are charred. Wrap pepper quarters in the foil; let stand 15 to 20 minutes or until cool enough to handle. Peel off skin and discard. Chop pepper.

2 Preheat oven to 350°F. In a large bowl beat cream cheese with an electric mixer on medium speed until smooth. Beat in sour cream and milk until smooth. Reserve ¼ cup of the scallions; stir the remaining scallions, the garlic, paprika, and chipotle pepper into cream cheese mixture. Gently fold in salmon and chopped green pepper. Spread in an ungreased 1-quart au gratin dish.

3 Bake, uncovered, about 25 minutes or until heated through, stirring once halfway through baking. Sprinkle with the remaining ¼ cup scallions. Serve warm with baguette slices, carrot sticks, and/or cucumber slices.

nutrition facts per ¼ cup: 81 cal., 6 g total fat (3 g sat. fat), 24 mg chol., 192 mg sodium, 3 g carb., 0 g dietary fiber, 4 g protein.

make-ahead directions: Prepare as directed through Step 2, except do not preheat oven. Cover and store dip and reserved scallions in the refrigerator for up to 24 hours. Bake in a 350° oven for 30 to 35 minutes or until dip is heated through, stirring once halfway through baking. Serve as directed in Step 3.

The licorice-like tones of fennel combine with blue cheese and bacon for one unbelievably good party dip.

baked **fennel–blue cheese** dip

prep: 35 minutes **bake:** 15 minutes **oven:** 400°F
makes: 4 cups dip **dish:** 16-ounce dishes

4 slices bacon
3 medium fennel bulbs*
2 cloves garlic, minced
1 8-ounce jar mayonnaise
1 8-ounce carton sour cream
1 4-ounce package crumbled blue cheese (1 cup)
20 whole black or pink peppercorns, crushed
2 tablespoons finely shredded Parmesan cheese
2 tablespoons fine dry bread crumbs
  Assorted vegetable dippers (Belgian endive leaves and/ or jicama sticks)

1 Preheat oven to 400°F. In a large skillet cook bacon over medium heat until crisp. Drain bacon on paper towels, reserving 1 tablespoon drippings in skillet. Crumble bacon; set aside.

2 Cut off and discard upper stalks of fennel. Remove any wilted outer layers and cut a thin slice from each fennel base. Cut fennel bulbs in half lengthwise; remove core. Cut crosswise into very thin slices.

3 Add fennel and garlic to reserved drippings. Cook over medium heat about 10 minutes or just until fennel is tender and starts to brown, stirring occasionally. Remove from heat. Add mayonnaise, sour cream, blue cheese, peppercorns, and bacon to fennel mixture; stir to combine.

4 Divide mixture between two ungreased 16-ounce soufflé dishes or au gratin dishes. Combine Parmesan cheese and bread crumbs; sprinkle over fennel mixture.

5 Bake, uncovered, about 15 minutes or just until mixture is heated through and tops are lightly browned (do not overbake). Serve dip with vegetable dippers.

nutrition facts per ¼ cup: 212 cal., 21 g total fat (7 g sat. fat), 24 mg chol., 287 mg sodium, 3 g carb., 1 g dietary fiber, 4 g protein.

This cheesy dip gets its kick from chorizo, a spicy Spanish pork sausage with a unique blend of spices, including chile, paprika, and garlic.

chile and chorizo
cheese dip

prep: 20 minutes **bake:** 10 minutes **oven:** 375°F
makes: 10 to 12 servings **dish:** 14-ounce dishes

8   ounces uncooked chorizo sausage
⅓   cup thinly sliced onion
1   4-ounce can diced green chiles, drained
¼   cup bottled roasted red sweet peppers, drained and sliced
4   cups shredded Monterey Jack cheese (1 pound)
    Tortilla chips or warm flour tortillas

1 Preheat oven to 375°F. In a 10-inch skillet cook sausage over medium heat until brown, using a wooden spoon to break up meat as it cooks. Remove sausage from skillet. Drain off fat. In the same skillet cook onion over medium heat until tender, stirring frequently. Stir in green chiles and roasted sweet peppers; heat through. Remove onion mixture from skillet.

2 Divide 3 cups of the cheese between two ungreased 14-ounce au gratin dishes; press gently to form an even layer. Divide cooked sausage, onion mixture, and the remaining 1 cup cheese between dishes.

3 Bake, uncovered, for 10 to 15 minutes or until cheese is melted. Serve with chips or spoon into tortillas and roll up.

nutrition facts per serving: 276 cal., 22 g total fat (12 g sat. fat), 60 mg chol., 552 mg sodium, 2 g carb., 0 g dietary fiber, 17 g protein.

Horseradish-chive Havarti cheese lets you add a windfall of flavors with just one ingredient. If you can't find it, see tip below for an easy substitution.

crab and horseradish havarti dip

prep: 15 minutes **bake:** 25 minutes **oven:** 350°F
makes: 3 cups dip **dish:** 1-quart

1 8-ounce package cream cheese, softened
1¼ cups shredded horseradish and chive Havarti cheese*
⅓ cup sour cream
¼ cup mayonnaise
6 ounces cooked lump crabmeat, flaked, or one 6-ounce can crabmeat, drained, flaked, and cartilage removed
1 cup shredded fresh baby spinach
   Breadsticks and/or other assorted breads

1 Preheat oven to 350°F. In a large bowl combine cream cheese, Havarti cheese, sour cream, and mayonnaise. Beat with an electric mixer on medium speed until well mixed. Fold in crabmeat and spinach.

2 Transfer mixture to an ungreased 1-quart soufflé dish or shallow baking dish. Bake about 25 minutes or until mixture is heated through. Serve dip with assorted breads.

nutrition facts per ¼ cup: 175 cal., 16 g total fat (6 g sat. fat), 47 mg chol., 296 mg sodium, 1 g carb., 0 g dietary fiber, 7 g protein.

＊test kitchen tip: If you can't find the horseradish and chive Havarti cheese, substitute 1¼ cups shredded Havarti cheese and add 1 tablespoon snipped fresh chives and 2 teaspoons prepared horseradish with the sour cream.

These chicken wings are sweetly glazed with pineapple juice, ketchup, and soy sauce—a perfect appetizer to take to potlucks.

sweet and sour chicken wings

prep: 20 minutes bake: 30 minutes oven: 350°F
makes: 12 to 15 pieces dish: 2-quart

1¼ pounds chicken wings
¼ cup all-purpose flour
¼ teaspoon garlic salt
¼ teaspoon lemon-pepper seasoning
4½ teaspoons cooking oil
⅓ cup sugar
¼ cup white wine vinegar or rice vinegar
2 tablespoons unsweetened pineapple juice
2 tablespoons ketchup
½ teaspoon soy sauce
Scallions (optional)

1 Preheat oven to 350°F. Cut off and discard tips of chicken wings. Cut wings at joints to form 12 to 15 pieces.

2 In a shallow dish combine flour, garlic salt, and lemon-pepper seasoning. Coat each chicken piece with the flour mixture.

3 Heat oil in a 10-inch skillet. Add coated chicken pieces to skillet. Cook, uncovered, until brown, turning occasionally. Remove chicken pieces from skillet and arrange in a 2-quart rectangular baking dish.

4 In a small saucepan whisk together sugar, vinegar, pineapple juice, ketchup, and soy sauce. Bring to boiling, stirring to dissolve sugar; pour over chicken. Bake, uncovered, about 30 minutes or until chicken is tender and no longer pink, turning pieces over after 15 minutes. If desired, garnish with scallions.

nutrition facts per piece: 153 cal., 9 g total fat (2 g sat. fat), 36 mg chol., 108 mg sodium, 9 g carb., 0 g dietary fiber, 9 g protein.

Tandoori refers to the superhot clay oven used to cook Indian breads and meats. You probably do not have a tandoori oven at home, but you can replicate the effect by cooking the chicken directly under the broiler.

tandoori chicken wings

prep: 45 minutes **marinate:** 4 hours **bake:** 25 minutes **broil:** 6 minutes

oven: 400°F **makes:** 16 servings **dish:** 3-quart

50 chicken drumettes*
    (about 5 pounds)
1   medium onion, cut
    into wedges
1   8-ounce can tomato
    sauce
1   6-ounce carton plain
    fat-free yogurt
1   tablespoon ground
    coriander
4   cloves garlic, coarsely
    chopped
2   teaspoons chopped
    fresh ginger
1½ teaspoons salt
1   teaspoon cumin seeds
1   teaspoon garam
    masala
½   to 1 teaspoon
    cayenne pepper
    (optional)
¼   to ½ teaspoon red
    food coloring
2   whole cloves
    Lemon wedges
    (optional)
    Thin wedges red
    onion (optional)

1 Place the chicken drumettes in a 3-quart rectangular baking dish; set aside.

2 For the tandoori masala, in a blender or food processor combine onion, tomato sauce, yogurt, coriander, garlic, ginger, salt, cumin seeds, garam masala, cayenne (if using), red food coloring, and whole cloves. Blend to a very smooth paste. (The color should be deep red.)

3 Pour the tandoori masala over the chicken drumettes; turn drumettes to coat. Cover and marinate in the refrigerator for 4 to 24 hours.

4 Preheat oven to 400°F. Drain chicken, discarding marinade. Arrange as many of the chicken drumettes on the unheated rack of a broiler pan as will fit in a single layer. Bake for 25 minutes. Turn oven to broil. Broil chicken 4 to 5 inches from heat for 6 to 8 minutes or until chicken is no longer pink and pieces just start to blacken, turning once halfway through broiling.

5 Transfer drumettes to a serving platter. Repeat baking and broiling of the remaining chicken drumettes. If desired, serve with lemon wedges and red onion wedges.

nutrition facts per serving: 119 cal., 4 g total fat (1 g sat. fat), 62 mg chol., 363 mg sodium, 3 g carb., 0 g dietary fiber, 16 g protein.

*test kitchen tip: If you cannot find chicken drumettes, use 25 chicken wings. Cut off and discard tips of chicken wings. Cut wings at joints to form 50 pieces.

Any cooking apple works in this oven-going appetizer. The baked apple mixture can also be served as a side dish with pork or chicken.

chunky **apple-sage** appetizers

prep: 25 minutes **bake:** 25 minutes **oven:** 400°F
makes: 16 servings **dish:** 1½-quart

3 medium apples (such as Pink Lady), peeled (if desired), cored, and chopped (about 3 cups)
¼ cup finely chopped red onion
2 tablespoons snipped fresh sage or 2 teaspoons dried sage, crushed, or 1 tablespoon snipped fresh thyme or 1 teaspoon dried thyme, crushed
2 tablespoons dried cranberries
1 tablespoon olive oil
1 tablespoon apple brandy (optional)
16 French bread slices, toasted
Shaved sharp white cheddar or regular cheddar cheese
Honey (optional)

1 Preheat oven to 400°F. In an ungreased 1½-quart casserole combine apples, onion, sage, and cranberries. Drizzle with oil; toss to combine. Bake, covered, for 25 to 30 minutes or until apples are softened, stirring once halfway through baking. Remove from oven. If desired, stir in apple brandy. Let cool slightly.

2 Serve baked apple mixture warm over French bread slices. Top with cheese and, if desired, drizzle with honey.

nutrition facts per serving: 150 cal., 4 g total fat (2 g sat. fat), 7 mg chol., 253 mg sodium, 24 g carb., 2 g dietary fiber, 6 g protein.

make-ahead directions: Prepare as directed in Step 1. Cover and refrigerate baked apple mixture for up to 6 hours. Reheat, if desired, or let stand at room temperature for 20 minutes serve as directed.

A trio of spices—curry powder, paprika, and nutmeg—adds intriguing flavors to the cream sauce. Serve the spicy bites with cocktail picks. Or present them at a special dinner, piled on top of cooked rice.

curried shrimp bites

prep: 20 minutes   **bake:** 15 minutes   **oven:** 400°F
makes: 8 servings   **dish:** 1-quart

1 pound fresh or
    frozen peeled and
    deveined cooked
    shrimp
1 tablespoon butter
2 teaspoons all-purpose
    flour
1 teaspoon curry
    powder
1/8 teaspoon paprika
1/4 cup half-and-half,
    light cream, or milk
2 teaspoons dry sherry
    (optional)
1 teaspoon grated fresh
    ginger
1/4 teaspoon
    Worcestershire
    sauce
1/8 teaspoon salt
    Chopped peanuts,
    sliced scallions,
    toasted coconut,
    and/or crushed red
    pepper (optional)

1 Thaw shrimp, if frozen. If desired, remove tails; set aside. Preheat oven to 400°F.

2 In a medium saucepan melt butter over medium heat. Stir in flour, curry powder, and paprika. Stir in half-and-half. Cook and stir until thickened. Stir in shrimp, sherry (if using), ginger, Worcestershire sauce, and salt. Transfer to an ungreased 1- to 1½-quart casserole.

3 Bake, uncovered, about 15 minutes or until heated through. Stir before serving. If desired, serve with peanuts, scallions, coconut, and/or crushed red pepper.

nutrition facts per serving: 82 cal., 3 g total fat (2 g sat. fat), 117 mg chol., 179 mg sodium, 1 g carb., 12 g protein.

metric information

The charts on this page provide a guide for converting measurements from the U.S. customary system, which is used throughout this book, to the metric system.

Product Differences

Most of the ingredients called for in the recipes in this book are available in most countries. However, some are known by different names. Here are some common American ingredients and their possible counterparts:

- Sugar (white) is granulated, fine granulated, or castor sugar.
- Powdered sugar is icing sugar.
- All-purpose flour is enriched, bleached, or unbleached white household flour. When self-rising flour is used in place of all-purpose flour in a recipe that calls for leavening, omit the leavening agent (baking soda or baking powder) and salt.
- Light corn syrup is golden syrup.
- Cornstarch is cornflour.
- Baking soda is bicarbonate of soda.
- Vanilla or vanilla extract is vanilla essence.
- Green, red, or yellow sweet peppers are capsicums or bell peppers.
- Golden raisins are sultanas.

Volume and Weight

The United States traditionally uses cup measures for liquid and solid ingredients. The chart below shows the approximate imperial and metric equivalents. If you are accustomed to weighing solid ingredients, the following approximate equivalents will be helpful.

- 1 cup butter, castor sugar, or rice = 8 ounces = ½ pound = 250 grams
- 1 cup flour = 4 ounces = ¼ pound = 125 grams
- 1 cup icing sugar = 5 ounces = 150 grams

Canadian and U.S. volume for a cup measure is 8 fluid ounces (237 ml), but the standard metric equivalent is 250 ml.

1 British imperial cup is 10 fluid ounces.

In Australia, 1 tablespoon equals 20 ml, and there are 4 teaspoons in the Australian tablespoon.

Spoon measures are used for smaller amounts of ingredients. Although the size of the tablespoon varies slightly in different countries, for practical purposes and for recipes in this book, a straight substitution is all that's necessary. Measurements made using cups or spoons always should be level unless stated otherwise.

Common Weight Range Replacements

Imperial / U.S.	Metric
½ ounce	15 g
1 ounce	25 g or 30 g
4 ounces (¼ pound)	115 g or 125 g
8 ounces (½ pound)	225 g or 250 g
16 ounces (1 pound)	450 g or 500 g
1¼ pounds	625 g
1½ pounds	750 g
2 pounds or 2¼ pounds	1,000 g or 1 Kg

Oven Temperature Equivalents

Fahrenheit Setting	Celsius Setting*	Gas Setting
300°F	150°C	Gas Mark 2 (very low)
325°F	160°C	Gas Mark 3 (low)
350°F	180°C	Gas Mark 4 (moderate)
375°F	190°C	Gas Mark 5 (moderate)
400°F	200°C	Gas Mark 6 (hot)
425°F	220°C	Gas Mark 7 (hot)
450°F	230°C	Gas Mark 8 (very hot)
475°F	240°C	Gas Mark 9 (very hot)
500°F	260°C	Gas Mark 10 (extremely hot)
Broil	Broil	Grill

Electric and gas ovens may be calibrated using Celsius. However, for an electric oven, increase Celsius setting 10 to 20 degrees when cooking above 160°C. For convection or forced air ovens (gas or electric) lower the temperature setting 25°F/10°C when cooking at all heat levels.

Baking Pan Sizes

Imperial / U.S.	Metric
9×1½-inch round cake pan	22- or 23×4-cm (1.5 L)
9×1½-inch pie plate	22- or 23×4-cm (1 L)
8×8×2-inch square cake pan	20×5-cm (2 L)
9×9×2-inch square cake pan	22- or 23×4.5-cm (2.5 L)
11×7×1½-inch baking pan	28×17×4-cm (2 L)
2-quart rectangular baking pan	30×19×4.5-cm (3 L)
13×9×2-inch baking pan	34×22×4.5-cm (3.5 L)
15×10×1-inch jelly roll pan	40×25×2-cm
9×5×3-inch loaf pan	23×13×8-cm (2 L)
2-quart casserole	2 L

U.S. / Standard Metric Equivalents

⅛ teaspoon = 0.5 ml

¼ teaspoon = 1 ml

½ teaspoon = 2 ml

1 teaspoon = 5 ml

1 tablespoon = 15 ml

2 tablespoons = 25 ml

¼ cup = 2 fluid ounces = 50 ml

⅓ cup = 3 fluid ounces = 75 ml

½ cup = 4 fluid ounces = 125 ml

⅔ cup = 5 fluid ounces = 150 ml

¾ cup = 6 fluid ounces = 175 ml

1 cup = 8 fluid ounces = 250 ml

2 cups = 1 pint = 500 ml

1 quart = 1 liter

emergency substitutions

If you don't have:	Substitute:
Bacon, 1 slice, crisp-cooked, crumbled	1 tablespoon cooked bacon pieces
Baking powder, 1 teaspoon	½ teaspoon cream of tartar plus ¼ teaspoon baking soda
Balsamic vinegar, 1 tablespoon	1 tablespoon cider vinegar or red wine vinegar plus ½ teaspoon sugar
Bread crumbs, fine dry, ¼ cup	¾ cup soft bread crumbs, or ¼ cup cracker crumbs, or ¼ cup cornflake crumbs
Broth, beef or chicken, 1 cup	1 teaspoon or 1 cube instant beef or chicken bouillon plus 1 cup hot water
Butter, 1 cup	1 cup shortening plus ¼ teaspoon salt, if desired
Buttermilk, 1 cup	1 tablespoon lemon juice or vinegar plus enough milk to make 1 cup (let stand 5 minutes before using), or 1 cup plain yogurt
Chocolate, semisweet, 1 ounce	3 tablespoons semisweet chocolate pieces, or 1 ounce unsweetened chocolate plus 1 tablespoon granulated sugar, or 1 tablespoon unsweetened cocoa powder plus 2 teaspoons sugar and 2 teaspoons shortening
Chocolate, sweet baking, 4 ounces	¼ cup unsweetened cocoa powder plus ⅓ cup granulated sugar and 3 tablespoons shortening
Chocolate, unsweetened, 1 ounce	3 tablespoons unsweetened cocoa powder plus 1 tablespoon cooking oil or shortening, melted
Cornstarch, 1 tablespoon (for thickening)	2 tablespoons all-purpose flour
Corn syrup (light), 1 cup	1 cup granulated sugar plus ¼ cup water
Egg, 1 whole	2 egg whites, or 2 egg yolks, or ¼ cup refrigerated or frozen egg product, thawed
Flour, cake, 1 cup	1 cup minus 2 tablespoons all-purpose flour
Flour, self-rising, 1 cup	1 cup all-purpose flour plus 1 teaspoon baking powder, ½ teaspoon salt, and ¼ teaspoon baking soda
Garlic, 1 clove	½ teaspoon bottled minced garlic, or ⅛ teaspoon garlic powder
Ginger, grated fresh, 1 teaspoon	¼ teaspoon ground ginger
Half-and-half or light cream, 1 cup	1 tablespoon melted butter or margarine plus enough whole milk to make 1 cup
Molasses, 1 cup	1 cup honey
Mustard, dry, 1 teaspoon	1 tablespoon prepared (in cooked mixtures)
Mustard, yellow, 1 teaspoon	½ teaspoon dry mustard plus 2 teaspoons vinegar
Onion, chopped, ½ cup	2 tablespoons dried minced onion, or ½ teaspoon onion powder
Sour cream, dairy, 1 cup	1 cup plain yogurt
Sugar, granulated, 1 cup	1 cup packed brown sugar, or 2 cups sifted powdered sugar
Sugar, brown, 1 cup packed	1 cup granulated sugar plus 2 tablespoons molasses
Tomato juice, 1 cup	½ cup tomato sauce plus ½ cup water
Tomato sauce, 2 cups	¾ cup tomato paste plus 1 cup water
Vanilla bean, 1 whole	2 teaspoons vanilla extract
Wine, red, 1 cup	1 cup beef or chicken broth in savory recipes; cranberry juice in desserts
Wine, white, 1 cup	1 cup chicken broth in savory recipes; apple juice or white grape juice in desserts
Yeast, active dry, 1 package	about 2¼ teaspoons active dry yeast
Seasonings	
Apple pie spice, 1 teaspoon	½ teaspoon ground cinnamon plus ¼ teaspoon ground nutmeg, ⅛ teaspoon ground allspice, and pinch ground cloves or ginger
Cajun seasoning, 1 tablespoon	½ teaspoon white pepper, ½ teaspoon garlic powder, ½ teaspoon onion powder, ½ teaspoon ground red pepper, ½ teaspoon paprika, and ½ teaspoon black pepper
Herbs, snipped fresh, 1 tablespoon	½ to 1 teaspoon dried herb, crushed, or ½ teaspoon ground herb
Poultry seasoning, 1 teaspoon	¾ teaspoon dried sage, crushed, plus ¼ teaspoon dried thyme or marjoram, crushed
Pumpkin pie spice, 1 teaspoon	½ teaspoon ground cinnamon plus ¼ teaspoon ground ginger, ¼ teaspoon ground allspice, and ⅛ teaspoon ground nutmeg

index